An American Primer

An American Primer

EDITED BY

DANIEL J. BOORSTIN

CHICAGO AND LONDON
THE UNIVERSITY OF CHICAGO PRESS

R
973

Library of Congress Catalog Card Number: 66–20576

THE UNIVERSITY OF CHICAGO PRESS, CHICAGO & LONDON

The University of Toronto Press, Toronto 5, Canada

© *1966 by The University of Chicago*

All rights reserved

Published 1966

Printed in the United States of America

Designed by John B. Goetz

RD
9 6

To All Rediscoverers
of the
New World

Copy 1

. . . the Eies of all people are vppon vs; soe that if wee shall deale falsely with our god in this worke wee haue vndertaken and soe cause him to withdrawe his present help from vs, wee shall be made a story and a by-word through the world. . . .

JOHN WINTHROP, 1630

I believe that man will not merely endure: he will prevail.

WILLIAM FAULKNER, 1950

Contents

CONTENTS

CONTENTS

xi

Introduction

DANIEL J. BOORSTIN

We call this an American Primer because it is a book of beginnings. It is a book of elements and, we hope, is elementary in the most sophisticated sense of the word. Like the New England Primer, one of the most popular books in the first century of settlement, it is a kind of American catechism—a catechism not of orthodoxy but of hopes and institutions. It introduces us to ourselves.

This is a book of Citizen's History. Our American past always speaks to us with two voices: the voice of the past, and the voice of the present. We are always asking two quite different questions. Historians reading the words of John Winthrop usually ask, "What did they mean to him?" Citizens ask, "What do they mean to us?" Historians are trained to seek the original meaning; all of us want to know the present meaning. These are two quite different quests which often get in each other's way. This book aims to bring the historian to the aid of the citizen, to vivify our sense of our past and remind us how we keep our traditions alive.

The historian plays a waiting game. He must be willing to work twenty years to give us a little more knowledge of the precise circumstances under which Grant and Lee met at Appomattox. He commits himself to a wager that in the race between the destructive powers of time and the reminiscent, reconstructive powers of man, somehow man is always gaining a little. Historian's history is the patient, endless effort to resurrect the dead past.

But the citizen cannot wait. The world will not let him be patient. Today he must act on the meaning of all the words uttered by the Winthrops and Franklins and Washingtons and Jeffersons. He must draw the moral from what they said—long before the historian is ready with an unambiguous, professionally satisfying account of what they really meant. The citizen must vote today, even though he might know more about the subject after another decade. The good historian warns against a too-simple moral, a too-clear answer to any question. The citizen's duty is to think and feel and act promptly. The historian who refuses to draw conclusions—until more evidence is in, or because we can never know—is fulfilling his vocation. The citizen who postpones (until historians have agreed on the true original meaning of the Monroe Doctrine) taking a position on his government's policies in Cuba or in the Dominican Republic is evading his duty. Therefore he must draw the best conclusions he can from the incomplete story and the inchoate tradition, and hope that the fuller, truer story will not disprove him.

Citizen's History, then, is but another name for the living tradition. The materials of Citizen's History are not mere relics. Unlike the fossils of geology or the artifacts of archeology, they are valuable actually because they were *not* petrified and so have *not* survived in their original unaltered shape. On the contrary, they have come to us because they were capable of a life of their own. Organisms, not things, they have responded to their changing environment. They have actually changed their environment in ever-changing fashion, and are likely to continue to do so. If words were mere things—like an Indian tomahawk, a Revolutionary musket, or the bed that George Washington slept in—they would not have this uncanny organic quality which makes them immortal forces.

Historians may lament the perversity which leads every generation to hear not what dead men wanted to say, but what the living want to hear. They may be shocked at the ventriloquism of the citizen who forces the past to speak his illusions about the present and his hopes for the future. And it is a duty of the historian to help us distinguish the true voice of the past from the echoes of ourselves. In this volume, our historians have tried to help us witness the alchemy by which a vital tradition transforms its past. In a nation which aims at self-government, Historian's History must be brought to enlighten Citizen's History. For, reality or illusion, Citizen's History rules the world.

It has become ever more difficult for us to see the irony, the adventure, and the drama in the living documents of our national past, precisely because they have become documentary equivalents of the Statue of Liberty—dignified, important, and inspiring, but somehow rigid and impersonal. This and other reasons have led me to enlist eighty-three historians to make a book of unfamiliar plan which may have some novel advantages, and may help refresh our past.

This book will, I hope, be personal. Personal in the sense that it speaks to the reader today, and that it speaks from the writer and the editor of each document. Along with standard items—the Declaration of Independence, the Constitution, and the Gettysburg Address—we also include many which are less familiar—the petition of the accused witch Mary Easty, Thomas A. Edison on the industrial research laboratory, Louis H. Sullivan on the skyscraper, and others. All these are the choice of the editor, with the advice and collaboration of the contributing editors. No item is here simply because it has always been included in anthologies of Americana. These are all here because they seem to us significant for the American present. These are not mere historical documents, but also *living* documents.

We hope that each item actually merits its place here; we know that others might have been added. We hope this book will be judged by what it has included, not by what it has omitted. While this is a long book, to make it even longer would have been easier. Although we have been selective, seeking only vivid messengers of still-living attitudes, beliefs, institutions, hopes, and prayers, we have aimed not to be arbitrary. American life is far more than merely our political life (what statesmen and politicians say or do) or what is sometimes called the "life of the mind" (what academic persons and professional intellectuals write and say).

The reader will find here samples of the rich complexity and contrariness of American life. He will hear Herbert Hoover cautioning against and Franklin Delano Roosevelt urging the vigorous and extensive uses of government; Louis D. Brandeis warning of the curse of bigness and John Wanamaker explaining its blessings; John Winthrop hoping for a firmer faith and Oliver Wendell Holmes, Jr., worrying over a too-firm faith; Henry Cabot Lodge pleading for national independence and Woodrow Wilson expounding global interdependence; Andrew Jackson extolling and Henry David Thoreau mistrusting the will of the majority. Here, the reader will find a hint of the American diapason, the concord of opposing notes which make our tradition. If this book were twenty times its present size it could not comprehend the full variety of our institutions. But even in these samples we can sense the vast range.

Here we have a hint, too, of the changefulness of our tradition. We find that words live and help make a tradition, not only by their vivid precision, but also by their iridescence, their ability to reflect the shifting new lights and new colors of each age. From the casual origins of many of these utterances we discover the ironic disproportion between the occasions which call words forth and the uses to which they are destined: between the imprisoning of Thoreau for one night for his failure to pay his poll-tax, and the political liberation of millions of American Negroes and hundreds of millions of Indian peasants; between the dispute of a single Boston shoemaker with his unionists, and the growth of a powerful American labor movement; between Frederick W. Taylor's personal preoccupation with how best to shovel coal and a national obsession with efficiency; between Albert Einstein's interest in theoretical physics, and the atomic Leviathan. We see also how hard it is to draw the line between the "use" and the "abuse" of the testaments of our history. Nearly everything reprinted here was called forth by unique personal, political, or social circumstances which can never be repeated. The Monroe Doctrine could never again have the precise meaning that it carried to President Monroe; George Washington's first inaugural address, Elizabeth Cady Stanton's speech on divorce, Louis H. Sullivan's comments on the skyscraper, none could ever again convey the precise meanings and ambiguities it once conveyed to its author's contemporaries.

A different editor has been selected for each item. He has been selected because he has been long familiar with the document and its subject; he is therefore qualified to interpret his subject with a rare intimacy. This has meant more than fourscore editors, and, inevitably, more than fourscore different ways of interpreting.

Glib talk about broad currents of history leads us to imagine that the crucial documents of our past were somehow delivered on an American Sinai, direct from God to the American people. But in this book we have emphasized the personal and the accidental. We have asked each editor to begin his chapter with a brief statement of when, where, how, and by whom the document was written. Whatever grand themes these momentous statements may illustrate—a "climate of opinion," a principle of political thought, a trait of national character, a long historical movement—each one was actually the work of a real person or persons. Sometimes these remain persons unknown. But we have tried in this book, so far as the evidence permits, to identify the actual human authors and the peculiar places, times, and circumstances of their work.

The core of each chapter is the living document. The editor for each chapter has selected the form in which the document is printed here. He has provided an authentic text, and, in his source note at the foot of the page where the document begins, he has explained any variations from the indicated source. Footnotes are those of the author, not of the chapter-editor. The titles here given to the documents are not always those under which they were first published (e.g., Thoreau's "Civil Disobedience" was originally titled "Resistance to Civil Government," Theodore Roosevelt's "New Nationalism" was originally simply "Speech at Osawatomie, Kansas"), but are chosen for ease and familiarity of identification.

Wherever feasible, the whole original document has been reprinted. In the few instances (e.g., Hamilton's "Report on Manufactures," Mann's "Twelfth Annual Report," Willkie's "One World," etc.) where the document is abridged, the abridgment has been made by the chapter-editor (all omissions are indicated), to provide us here with portions of the document which best serve the purposes of this volume.

The most interesting, most subtle, and most adventurous time in the life of a document is what I call its "Afterlife"—its life after the death of its author. Each contributor has concluded his chapter by a brief "Afterlife" essay, finally interpreting its significance for us today.

The afterlife of a document is vagrant, unpredictable, and often astonishing. The disproportion between the circumstances of the inspiration and the reach of the product is remarkable and sometimes bizarre. Words that have the inexplicable quality that makes them live on, become more and more transformed, enriched, and transmuted with the passage of time; they become more vital and more vivid the longer their authors have been dead. Some of this comes from the mere passage of time; the transmutation of the Declaration of Independence of 1776 (with its meaning to the men who fought the American Revolution) into the Declaration of Independence of 1876 (with its meaning to the men who had fought the Civil War) or the Declaration of Independence of 1966 (with its meaning to men who had fought two world wars) is as basic as the transmutation by which carbon-14 becomes carbon-12. Much of the history of our national testament consists in the ironies and the whimsies by which slogans cried up in one cause become shibboleths of quite other causes, causes which as often as not their original authors would have fought against. To read these remarkable "Afterlives" is to acquire a sobering humility about our power over our grandchildren, and to discover the extent and the limits of our ancestors' power over us. But it is also to realize our great power and our need, in every generation, to rediscover and to recreate our tradition.

The Mayflower Compact
1620

EDITED BY SAMUEL ELIOT MORISON

The Mayflower Compact, so called because it was drafted and signed on board the Mayflower as that ship approached Cape Cod on November 11, 1620, is justly regarded as a key document in American history. It proves the determination of the small group of English emigrants to live under a rule of law, based on the consent of the people, and to set up their own civil government. Also, it is the first (so far as we know) of hundreds of similar compacts or agreements made not only by other English colonists but, after 1775, by American citizens when they sought to "pitch new States, ez Old-World men pitch tents" beyond the pale of established government.

Special circumstances led to this compact. The Pilgrim Fathers, belonging to an English separatist congregation which had taken refuge in Leyden, decided to seek a new life in the English colonies. Owing to the liberal policy of the Virginia Company of London, they obtained from it a patent to a "particular plantation," giving them the right to locate where they chose within the vast domain of that Company, and to enjoy local self-government. They intended to locate near the northern boundary of the Company's territory, around the mouth of the Hudson River. Had they reached this objective they would have formed a civil compact after landing, as is proved by a farewell letter from their Leyden pastor, the Reverend John Robinson, who, assuming that they would form a "civil community," tells them they had better choose their officials with care.

But the Mayflower sailed so late in the year, and took so long on the voyage, that on November 10, 1620, when she encountered head winds and shoals south of Cape Cod, the leaders decided to double the Cape, anchor in what is now Provincetown Harbor, and thence "look out a place for habitation." This decision voided their patent, since they were now under the jurisdiction of the Northern Virginia Company, then being reorganized as the Council for New England. At the same time, some of the "strangers" who had been given passage on the Mayflower at the behest of the London merchants who were paying the expenses of this venture "let fall . . . that when they came ashore they would use their own liberty, for none had power to command them, the patent they had being for Virginia." William Bradford, the historian and for thirty-one years governor of Plymouth Colony, states that these threats of the "strangers" to do as they pleased ashore were one reason for the Compact's being hurriedly drafted and concluded before landing. The other reason he gives is even more significant: a "combination" (as he calls it) among themselves "might be as firm as any patent, and in some respects more sure." In other words, a compact freely entered into would be a stronger foundation than a company patent which might be revoked.

Church compacts, or covenants, as they were then called, were familiar to English Puritans and Scots Presbyterians. When a group of men and women decided to leave a church and set up a new one of their own, they drafted a covenant promising to live in love and charity with one another, to endeavor to lead the New Testament life, to support their church financially, and to obey the church elders whom they might elect. Every adult accepted as church member had to "own [accept or sign] the covenant." The Pilgrim Fathers, owing to their successive moves, had done this thrice. Thus it was natural for them to do likewise, for civil purposes, when locating outside any recognized jurisdiction. The forty-one signers of the Mayflower Compact included every head of a family, every adult bachelor—including those who had threatened trouble—and most of the hired menservants. The only males who did not sign were those under age, and two sailors who were obligated to stay but a year.

I N THE NAME of God Amen. We whose names are underwriten, the loyall subjects of our dread soveraigne Lord King James by the grace of God, of great Britaine, Franc, & Ireland king, defender of the faith, &c.

Haveing undertaken, for the glorie of God, and advancements of the Christian faith and honour of our king & countrie, a voyage to plant the first colonie in the Northerne parts of Virginia, doe by these presents solemnly & mutualy in the presence of God, and one of another, covenant & combine our selves togeather into a civill body politick; for our better ordering, & preservation & furtherance of the ends aforesaid; and by vertue hearof to enacte, constitute, and frame shuch just & equall lawes, ordinances, Acts, constitutions, & offices, from time to time, as shall be thought most meete & convenient for the generall good of the Colonie: unto which we promise all due submission and obedience.

In witnes whereof we have hereunder subscribed our names at Cap-Codd the •11• of November, in the year the raigne of our soveraigne Lord King James of England, France, & Ireland the eighteenth and of Scotland the fiftie fourth. An°: Dom. 1620.

John Carver	Edward Tilley	Degory Priest
William Bradford	John Tilley	Thomas Williams
Edward Winslow	Francis Cooke	Gilbert Winslow
William Brewster	Thomas Rogers	Edmund Margeson
Isaac Allerton	Thomas Tinker	Peter Brown
Myles Standish	John Rigdale	Richard Britterige
John Alden	Edward Fuller	George Soule
Samuel Fuller	John Turner	Richard Clarke
Christopher Martin	Francis Eaton	Richard Gardiner
William Mullins	James Chilton	John Allerton
William White	John Crakston	Thomas English
Richard Warren	John Billington	Edward Doty
John Howland	Moses Fletcher	Edward Leister
Stephen Hopkins	John Goodman	

The original paper or parchment on which the Compact was engrossed, and signed, has long since disappeared. The text was first printed in London in 1622 in a pamphlet generally known as *Mourt's Relation*, which contained extracts from Bradford's and Winslow's journals. Bradford copied the Compact into his history *Of Plymouth Plantation* at some time in the 1630's. It was next printed by the secretary of the colony, Nathaniel Morton, in *New Englands Memoriall* (1669), together with a list of the signers. Bradford's text is reprinted here, with the names of the signers from Morton's edition. The word "y°" of the original has been spelled out here as "the," since the "y" is really an abbreviated "th"

After the signing, relates Bradford, "They chose . . . Mr. John Carver (a man godly and well approved amongst them) their Governor for that year."

The extent of the Mayflower Compact's influence is debatable. It was certainly no constitution, or declaration of independence (note the references to the king), yet it was something more than a temporary expedient to keep trouble-makers in line. The twenty signers who survived the first six months ashore acted as "freemen" (voters) and as the governing body of the colony. In May, 1621, Governor Carver having died, they elected William Bradford their governor, and re-elected him no fewer than thirty times. The freemen admitted to the franchise, individually and sparingly, boys as they grew up, newcomers who proved cooperative, and hired servants who wished to remain in the colony after their terms of service expired. The freemen elected annually, from among their number, a governor, a secretary, and a few assistants. They also met at least once a year in a general court or assembly, which passed laws, acted as a supreme judicial court, and, after the colony had begun to spread out, set up a representative system. In 1636 the general court adopted a body of laws called the "general fundamentals," which included a bill of rights. But the Compact seems to have been at the bottom of everything; we have evidence from the records that it used to be read aloud when the assembly met.

William Hubbard, an early New England historian who knew the Pilgrim Fathers, confirms our view of the Compact in his Ecclesiastical History, written prior to 1682. The Compact, or "combination," as he calls it, was adopted because of "missing of the place" (i.e., the destination) intended and was meant to be temporary, pending the procurement of a royal charter. Hubbard adds, significantly, that the Plymouth people did not pretend to be governed exclusively by their own self-made laws, but also considered themselves bound by the common law of England. And it is evident from the Plymouth Colony records that they applied the common law in appropriate cases which were not covered by their own statutes.

The colony never did obtain a royal charter. The Warwick Patent, dated January 13, 1630, which it received from the Council for New England, besides defining the colony's boundaries, conferred the exclu-

---

and should be so read; and the interchangeable use of "u" and "v" has been modernized (in Bradford's day "v" was always used at the beginning of a word and "u" within).

sive right to govern on William Bradford, "his heires associates & assignes." But Governor Bradford "surrendered" his rights to "the whole Court, consisting of the Freemen . . . of New Plymouth," and government went on as before, based on the Compact. Obviously, the governor, even if he had secret yearnings to become another Lord Baltimore, would not have dared accept this responsibility after the colony for almost a decade had enjoyed government by consent of the freemen.

Now comes the question of the Compact's influence outside Plymouth. Lois K. Matthews cites about twenty civil compacts formed by English colonists in America, or by Americans going west after 1775. The first three were formed by secessionist movements from Massachusetts Bay: William Pynchon's Springfield Agreement of May 14, 1636, Roger Williams' Providence Covenant of August 20, 1636, and John Wheelwright's Exeter (New Hampshire) Covenant of 1639. Williams, who had sojourned at Plymouth, may well have read the original Compact; the language of the Providence Covenant is similar to that of the earlier document. And the Exeter Covenant states explicitly that the signers will apply not only their own laws, but also "such godly & christian laws as are established in the realme of England to our best knowledge."

Although the Providence and Exeter agreements may have been conscious imitations of the Mayflower Compact, it would be farfetched to claim Plymouth influence on the many later compacts cited by Mrs. Matthews, down to and including that of the San Francisco Committee of Vigilance of 1851. Much more likely they are other results of the circumstance that produced the Mayflower Compact—the propensity of English Protestants already accustomed to church covenants to use the same method of free association to create a temporary civil government in the wilderness. This was certainly the case with early compacts in the "Old West": e.g., the constitution for the Colony of Transylvania drawn up by a convention at Boonesborough in 1775; the "Articles of Agreement, or Compact of Government," the Cumberland County Compact of 1780; and the informal organization of the State of Franklin in 1785. It is highly improbable that the covenanters in any of these cases had heard of the Mayflower Compact; but, faced with a situation similar to that of the Pilgrim Fathers in 1620, they took parallel action to ensure a rule of law in a region which had none.

John Adams may possibly have had the Mayflower Compact in mind when he wrote, in the preamble to the Massachusetts Constitution of 1780, "The Body-Politic . . . is a social compact, by which the whole

5

people covenants with each Citizen, and each Citizen with the whole people, that all shall be governed by certain Laws for the Common good." But Adams' phraseology stems from John Locke's Second Treatise of Government (1690) and J. J. Rousseau's Contrat Social (1762), in which the theory is presented that all just government rests on a compact, implicit or explicit, between the people and their rulers. That idea was the basis of the Declaration of Independence: George III had broken the compact between himself and his American subjects, who consequently were justified in forming a new government of their own.

In any case, nobody applied the word "compact" to the Mayflower agreement until the works of Locke and Rousseau had become well known. Prior to 1793 the few writers who refer to the Mayflower document call it, variously, a "combination," an "association and agreement," or a "covenant." In 1764 appeared the first of many English translations of Rousseau, entitled The Social Compact; and the first American edition came out in 1784. The connection of the Mayflower document with Rousseau's theory was first noted by Alden Bradford, a young Harvard graduate who, writing in 1793 about his ancestor John Alden, said that he signed "the compact established immediately upon the arrival of the first settlers." Nobody since has called it anything else.

But it remained for John Quincy Adams to start the Mayflower Compact tradition. In an oration delivered at Plymouth in 1802 he declared that it was "perhaps the only instance, in human history, of that positive, original social compact, which speculative philosophers have imagined as the only legitimate source of government." This idea, that the Pilgrim Fathers had anticipated the compact theory 70 years before Locke and 140 years before Rousseau, was very flattering to Americans. Naturally it led to exaggeration. George Bancroft wrote, in his History of the United States (1837), "In the cabin of the Mayflower, humanity recovered its rights, and instituted government on the basis of 'equal laws' for 'the general good.'" And Winslow Warren, in a tercentennial address in 1920, asked the rhetorical question, "What other than a renewal of the spirit of earlier days sustained the men of the Revolution in their long contest and enabled them to embody in the Declaration of Independence and the Constitution of the United States the principles clearly shadowed forth in the Compact of 1620?"

Few today would subscribe to these fancies. But the fact remains that the Mayflower Compact is an early and very significant instance of the seventeenth-century Englishman's genius for self-government, and his determination to live under a rule of law, even "unto the uttermost part of the earth." It is the earliest known case in American history of people establishing a government for themselves by mutual agreement. Significant, also, is the opening invocation, indicating that these men believed Almighty God to be the author of all government. Moreover, their promise of "all due submission and obedience" to the laws they themselves would pass and the authorities they would elect indicates their belief that political liberty is fundamental to all liberty; that without it religion cannot flourish or social order be maintained.

John Winthrop
A Modell of Christian Charity
1630

EDITED BY LAWRENCE W. TOWNER

In the spring of 1630 eleven small cargo vessels, seven of them
haphazardly converted for carrying passengers, worked their perilous and
various ways three thousand miles across the Atlantic Ocean. On board
were some seven hundred men, women, and children, who were risking
their lives to establish a godly, Puritan community on Massachusetts'
shores. This was the Winthrop fleet, so called by historians after the
Moses of his people, Governor John Winthrop, Esq., lord of Groton
Manor, justice of the peace, and attorney in the royal Court of Wards.
Those he led were drawn from many ranks and stations of English life.
Sir Richard Saltonstall and the Lady Arbella Johnson, daughter of the
Earl of Lincoln, represented the upper classes. Lady Arbella's husband,
Isaac, held the rank of esquire along with John Winthrop. Robert Feake,
Josiah Plaistow, and William Pynchon were gentlemen; and nearly
twenty others could call themselves "Mister," including the Reverend
Mr. John Wilson, who was to become pastor of First Church, Boston.
The bulk of the passengers were artisans, tradesmen, and yeomen, with
their wives and children. Lowest in rank were a sprinkling of laborers and
servants, men and maids, and a few boys and girls of tender age who
belonged to the same class. The geographical origins of the emigrants
were as varied as their classes. They came from nineteen English
counties, from London, and from Holland. Not all were Puritans, even,
and those who were, were likely to run off in different geographical and

8

religious directions once land was reached. Strong people, capable of risking authority at home for conscience' sake and of daring the hazards of sea and a wild land for a new chance at life, they would not be easily shaped into a community or easily ruled. John Winthrop knew that great deeds would have to be done lest God's chosen people scatter widely and the holy experiment come to nothing.

As the Arbella, the flagship of the fleet, rose and fell on the Atlantic, John Winthrop composed his lay sermon "A Modell of Christian Charity," which he probably read to the assembled ship's company. It expresses his intention to unite his people behind a single purpose, the creation of a due form of government, ecclesiastical as well as civil, so that their community would be a model for the Christian world to emulate. Theirs was to be a "Citty vpon a Hill," as Winthrop called it in a paraphrase from Matthew 5:14.

The Governor had high hopes that the sacrifices to be demanded of those he led would be freely made in harmony with the precepts of Christian charity, or love. His sermon is a moving expression of that ideal. At the same time it is a recognition of the reality of the Puritans' situation. They were prepared to work with real people of all classes and with the human frailties common to us all. With pride, wrath, greed, sloth, and the other deadly sins of the medieval world, the Puritans were thoroughly familiar, and these they were ready to handle. If the spirit of Christ would not work from within, Winthrop was prepared to impose it from without. Otherwise the "Citty vpon a Hill" would become not a Modell for Christians everywhere, but a reproach to mankind. The alternatives to Life and Salvation were Death and Damnation, not just for the few who failed, but perhaps for all mankind.

The basis of the text here reproduced is that edited by Dr. Stewart Mitchell, late director of the Massachusetts Historical Society and editor of the *Winthrop Papers* (5 vols.; Boston, 1929———). His text (II, 282–95) has been compared with the contemporary manuscript in the possession of the New-York Historical Society, and minor alterations have been made accordingly. Dr. Mitchell's notes, especially his biblical references, have also been used freely.

A MODELL OF CHRISTIAN CHARITY.

Written
On Boarde the Arrabella,
On the Attlantick Ocean.
By the Honorable John Winthrop, Esq.

In His passage, (with the great Company of Religious people, of which Christian Tribes he was the Brave Leader and famous Governor;) from the Island of Great Brittaine, to New-England in the North America.   Anno 1630.

CHRISTIAN CHARITIE.

A Modell hereof

God Almightie in his most holy and wise providence hath soe disposed of the Condicion of mankinde, as in all times some must be rich some poore, some highe and eminent in power and dignitie; others meane and in subieccion.

The Reason hereof

1. REAS: First, to hold conformity with the rest of his workes, being delighted to shewe forthe the glory of his wisdome in the variety and differance of the Creatures and the glory of his power, in ordering all these differences for the preservacion and good of the whole, and the glory of his greatnes that as it is the glory of princes to haue many officers, soe this great King will haue many Stewards counting himselfe more honoured in dispenceing his guifts to man by man, then if hee did it by his owne immediate hand.

2. REAS: Secondly, That he might haue the more occasion to manifest the worke of his Spirit: first, vpon the wicked in moderateing and restraineing them: soe that the riche and mighty should not eate vpp the poore, nor the poore, and dispised rise vpp against theire superiours, and shake off theire yoake; 2ly in the regenerate in exerciseing his graces in them, as in the greate ones, theire loue mercy, gentlenes, temperance etc., in the poore and inferiour sorte, theire faithe patience, obedience etc:

3. REAS: Thirdly, That every man might haue need of other, and from hence they might be all knitt more nearly together in the Bond of brotherly affeccion; from hence it appeares plainely that noe man is made more honourable then another or more wealthy etc., out of any

perticuler and singuler respect to himselfe but for the glory of his Creator and the Common good of the Creature, Man; Therefore God still reserues the propperty of these guifts to himselfe as Ezek. 16:17. he there calls wealthe his gold and his silver etc. Prov. 3:9. he claimes theire seruice as his due[.] honour the Lord with thy riches etc. All men being thus (by divine providence) rancked into two sortes, riche and poore; vnder the first, are comprehended all such as are able to liue comfortably by theire owne meanes duely improued; and all others are poore according to the former distribution. There are two rules whereby wee are to walke one towards another: Justice and Mercy. These are allwayes distinguished in theire Act and in theire obiect, yet may they both concurre in the same Subiect in eache respect; as sometimes there may be an occasion of shewing mercy to a rich man, in some sudden danger of distresse, and allsoe doeing of meere Justice to a poor man in regard of some perticuler contract etc. There is likewise a double Lawe by which wee are regulated in our conversacion one towardes another: in both the former respects, the lawe of nature and the lawe of grace, or the morrall lawe or the lawe of the gospell, to omitt the rule of Justice as not propperly belonging to this purpose otherwise then it may fall into consideracion in some perticuler Cases; By the first of these lawes man as he was enabled soe withall [is] commaunded to loue his neighbour as himselfe[.] vpon this ground stands all the precepts of the morrall lawe, which concernes our dealings with men. To apply this to the works of mercy this lawe requires two things[,] first that every man afford his help to another in every want or distresse Secondly, That hee performe this out of the same affeccion, which makes him carefull of his owne good according to that of our Saviour Math. [7:12] Whatsoever ye would that men should doe to you. This was practised by Abraham and Lott in entertaineing the Angells and the old man of Gibea.

The Lawe of Grace or the Gospell hath some differance from the former as in these respectes first the lawe of nature was giuen to man in the estate of innocency; this of the gospell in the estate of regeneracy: 2ly, the former propounds one man to another, as the same fleshe and Image of god, this as a brother in Christ allsoe, and in the Communion of the same spirit and soe teacheth vs to put a difference betweene Christians and others. Doe good to all especially to the household of faith [Gal. 6:10]; vpon this ground the Israelites were to putt a differ-ence betweene the brethren of such as were strangers though not of the Canaanites. 3ly. The Lawe of nature could giue noe rules for dealeing with enemies for all are to be considered as freinds in the estate of innocency, but the Gospell commaunds loue to an enemy. proofe. If thine Enemie hunger feede him; Loue your Enemies doe good to them that hate you Math. 5:44.

This Lawe of the Gospell propoundes likewise a difference of seasons and occasions: there is a time when a christian must sell all and giue to the poore as they did in the Apostles times. There is a tyme allsoe when a christian (though they giue not all yet) must giue beyond theire abillity. as they of Macedonia Cor. 2:6. likewise community of perills calls for extraordinary liberallity and soe doth Community in some speciall seruice for the Churche. Lastly, when there is noe other meanes whereby our Christian brother may be releiued in this distresse wee must help him beyond our ability, rather then tempt God, in putting him vpon help by miraculous or extraordinary meanes.

This duty of mercy is exercised in the kindes, Giueing, lending, and forgiueing.

Quest: What rule shall a man observe in giueing in respect of the measure?

Ans: If the time and occasion be ordinary he is to giue out of his aboundance—let him lay aside as god hath blessed him. If the time and occasion be extraordinary he must be ruled by them; takeing this withall, that then a man cannot likely doe too much especially, if he may leaue himselfe and his family vnder probable meanes of comfortable subsistance.

Obiect[ion]. A man must lay vpp for posterity, the fathers lay vpp for posterity and children and he is worse then an Infidell that prouideth not for his owne [I Tim. 5:8].

Ans: For the first, it is plaine, that it being spoken by way of Comparison it must be meant of the ordinary and vsuall course of fathers and cannot extend to times and occasions extraordinary; for the other place the Apostle speakes against such as walked inordinately, and it is without question, that he is worse then an Infidell whoe throughe his owne Sloathe and voluptuousnes shall neglect to prouide for his family.

Obiect. The wise mans Eies are in his head (saith Salomon) [Eccles. 2:14] and foreseeth the plague, therefore wee must forecast and lay vpp against euill times when hee or his may stand in need of all he can gather.

Ans: This very Argument Salomon vseth to perswade to liberallity.

Eccle. [11:1] cast thy bread vpon the waters etc. for thou knowest not what euill may come vpon the land Luke 16. make you freinds of the riches of Iniquity; you will aske how this shall be; very well for first he that giues to the poore lends to the lord. and he will repay him euen in this life an hundred fold to him or his. The righteous is ever mercifull and lendeth and his seed enioyeth the blessing; and besides wee know what advantage it will be to vs in the day of account when many such Witnesses shall stand forthe for vs to witnesse the improuement of our Tallent. And I would knowe of those whoe pleade soe much for layeing vp for time to come, whether they hold that to be Gospell Math. 16:19. Lay not vpp for yourselues Treasures vpon Earth etc. if they acknowl-edge it what extent will they allowe it; if onely to those primitiue times lett them consider the reason wherevpon our Saviour groundes it, the first is that they are subiect to the moathe, the rust the Theife. Secondly, They will steale away the hearte, where the treasure is there will the heart be allsoe. The reasons are of like force at all times therefore the exhortacion must be generall and perpetuall which [applies] allwayes in respect of the loue and affeccion to riches and in regard of the things themselues when any speciall seruice for the churche or perticuler distresse of our brother doe call for the vse of them; otherwise it is not onely lawfull but necessary to lay vpp as Joseph did to haue ready vppon such occasions, as the Lord (whose stewards wee are of them) shall call for them from vs: Christ giues vs an Instance of the first, when hee sent his disciples for the Asse, and bidds them answer the owner thus, the Lord hath need of him [Matt. 21:2–3]; soe when the Tabernacle was to be builte his [he?] sends to his people to call for their silver and gold etc.: and yeildes them noe other reason but that it was for his worke, when Elisha comes to the widowe of Sareptah and findes her prepareing to make ready her pittance for herselfe and family, he bids her first provide for him, he challengeth first gods parte which shee must first giue before shee must serue her owne family, all these teache vs that the lord lookes that when hee is pleased to call for his right in any thing wee haue, our owne Interest wee haue must stand aside, till his turne be serued, for the other wee need looke noe further then to that of John 1. he whoe hath this worlds goodes and seeth his brother to neede, and shutts vpp his Compassion from him, how dwelleth the loue of god in him. which comes punctually to this Conclusion; if thy brother be in want and thou canst help him, thou needst not make doubt, what thou shouldst doe; if thou louest god thou must help him.

Quest: What rule must wee obserue in lending?

Ans: Thou must obserue whether thy brother hath present or probable, or possible meanes of repayeing thee, if ther be none of these, thou must giue him according to his necessity, rather then lend him as hee requires: if he hath present meanes of repayeing thee, thou art to looke at him, not as an Act of mercy, but by way of Commerce; wherein thou arte to walke by the rule of Justice, but, if his meanes of repayeing thee be onely probable or possible then is hee an obiect of thy mercy thou must lend him, though there be danger of looseing it Deut. 15:7. If any of thy brethren be poore etc. thou shalt lend him sufficient that men might not shift off this duty by the apparant hazzard, he tells them that though the Yeare of Jubile were at hand (when he must remitt it, if hee were not able to repay it before) yet he must lend him and that chearefully; it may not greiue thee to giue him (saith hee) and because some might obiect, why soe I should soone impoverishe my selfe and my family, he adds with all thy Worke etc. for our Saviour Math. 5:42. From him that would borrow of thee turne not away.

Quest: What rule must wee obserue in forgiueing?

Ans: Whether thou didst lend by way of Commerce or in mercy, if he haue noething to pay thee [thou] must forgiue him (except in cause where thou hast a surety or a lawfull pleadge) Deut. 15:2. Every seaventh yeare the Creditor was to quitt that which hee lent to his brother if hee were poore as appeares ver: 8[4]: saue when there shall be noe poore with thee. In all these and like Cases Christ was a generall rule Math. 7:22. Whatsoever ye would that men should doe to you doe yee the same to them allsoe.

Quest: What rule must wee obserue and walke by in cause of Community of perill?

Ans: The same as before, but with more enlargement towardes others and lesse respect towards our selues, and our owne right hence it was that in the primitiue Churche they sold all[,] had all things in Common, neither did any man say that that which he possessed was his owne [Acts 2:44–45; 4:32–35] likewise in theire returne out of the Captiuity, because the worke was greate for the restoreing of the church and the danger of enemies was Common to all Nehemiah exhortes the Jewes to liberallity and readines in remitting theire debtes to theire brethren, and disposeth liberally of his owne to such as wanted and stands not vpon his owne due, which hee might haue demaunded of them, thus did some of our forefathers in times of persecucion here in England, and soe did

14

many of the faithfull in other Churches whereof wee keepe an honourable remembrance of them, and it is to be obserued that both in
Scriptures and latter stories of the Churches that such as haue beene
most bountifull to the poore Saintes especially in these extraordinary
times and occasions god hath left them highly Commended to posterity,
as Zacheus, Cornelius, Dorcas[,] Bishop Hooper, the Cuttler of Brussells
and divers others[.] obserue againe that the scripture giues noe causion
to restraine any from being over liberall this way; but all men to the
liberall and cherefull practise hereof by the sweetest promises as to
instance one for many[.] Isaiah 58:6: Is not this the fast that I haue
chosen to loose the bonds of wickednes, to take off the heavy burdens to
lett the oppressed goe free and to breake every Yoake, to deale thy bread
to the hungry and to bring the poore that wander into thy house, when
thou seest the naked to cover them etc. then shall thy light breake forthe
as the morneing, and thy healthe shall growe speedily, thy righteousnes
shall goe before thee, and the glory of the lord shall embrace thee, then
thou shalt call and the lord shall Answer thee etc. 2:10 [Isa. 58:10]: If
thou power out thy soule to the hungry, then shall thy light spring out in
darknes, and the lord shall guide thee continually, and satisfie thy Soule
in draught, and make fatt thy bones; thou shalt be like a watered
Garden, and they shall be of thee that shall build the old wast places etc.
on the contrary most heavy cursses are layd vpon such as are straight-
ened towards the Lord and his people Judg. 5:[23] Cursse ye Meroshe
because the[y] came not to help the Lord etc. Pro. [21:13] Hee whoe
shutteth his eares from hearing the cry of the poore, he shall cry and
shall not be heard: Math. 25:[41–42] Goe ye curssed into everlasting fire
etc. I was hungry and ye fedd mee not. Cor. 2:9–16. [6.] he that soweth
spareingly shall reape spareingly.

Haueing allready sett forth the practise of mercy according to the rule
of gods lawe, it will be vsefull to lay open the groundes of it allsoe being
the other parte of the Commaundement and that is the affeccion from
which this exercise of mercy must arise, the Apostle tells vs that this loue
is the fullfilling of the lawe, not that it is enough to loue our brother and
soe noe further but in regard of the excellency of his partes giueing any
motion to the other as the Soule to the body and the power it hath to
sett all the faculties on worke in the outward exercise of this duty as
when wee bid one make the clocke strike he doth not lay hand on the
hammer which is the immediate instrument of the sound but setts on
worke the first mouer or maine wheele, knoweing that will certainely

15

produce the sound which hee intends; soe the way to drawe men to the workes of mercy is not by force of Argument from the goodnes or necessity of the worke, for though this course may enforce a rationall minde to some present Act of mercy as is frequent in experience, yet it cannot worke such a habit in a Soule as shall make it prompt vpon all occasions to produce the same effect but by frameing these affeccions of loue in the hearte which will as natiuely bring forthe the other, as any cause doth produce the effect.

The diffinition which the Scripture giues vs of loue is this Loue is the bond of perfection [Col. 3:14]. First, it is a bond, or ligament. 2ly, it makes the worke perfect. There is noe body but consistes of partes and that which knitts these partes together giues the body its perfeccion, because it makes eache parte soe contiguous to other as thereby they doe mutually participate with eache other, both in strengthe and infirmity in pleasure and paine, to instance in the most perfect of all bodies, Christ and his church make one body: the severall partes of this body considered aparte before they were vnited were as disproportionate and as much disordering as soe many contrary quallities or elements but when christ comes and by his spirit and loue knitts all these partes to him-selfe and each to other, it is become the most perfect and best propor-tioned body in the world Eph. 4:16. Christ by whome all the body being knitt together by every ioynt for the furniture thereof according to the effectuall power which is in the measure of every perfeccion of partes a glorious body without spott or wrinckle the ligaments hereof being Christ or his loue for Christ is loue 1 John 4:8. Soe this definition is right Loue is the bond of perfeccion.

From hence wee may frame these Conclusions.

1. first all true Christians are of one body in Christ 1. Cor. 12:12–13. 17. [27.] Ye are the body of Christ and members of [your?] parte.

2ly. The ligamentes of this body which knitt together are loue.

3ly. Noe body can be perfect which wants its propper ligamentes.

4ly. All the partes of this body being thus vnited are made soe contiguous in a speciall relacion as they must needes partake of each others strength and infirmity, ioy, and sorrowe, weale and woe. 1. Cor. 12:26. If one member suffers all suffer with it, if one be in honour, all reioyce with it.

5ly. This sensiblenes and Sympathy of each others Condicions will necessarily infuse into each parte a natiue desire and endeavour, to strengthen defend preserue and comfort the other.

To insist a little on this Conclusion being the product of all the former the truthe hereof will appeare both by precept and patterne i. John 3:10. yee ought to lay downe your liues for the brethren Gal. 6:2. beare ye one anothers burthens and soe fulfill the lawe of Christ.

For patterns wee haue that first of our Saviour whoe out of his good will in obedience to his father, becomeing a parte of this body, and being knitt with it in the bond of loue, found such a natiue sensiblenes of our infirmities and sorrowes as hee willingly yeilded himselfe to deathe to ease the infirmities of the rest of his body and soe heale theire sorrowes: from the like Sympathy of partes did the Apostles and many thousands of the Saintes lay downe theire liues for Christ againe, the like wee may see in the members of this body among themselues. 1. Rom. 9. Paule could haue beene contented to haue beene seperated from Christ that the Jewes might not be cutt off from the body: It is very obseruable which hee professeth of his affectionate part[ak]eing with every member: whoe is weake (saith hee) and I am not weake? whoe is offended and I burne not; and againe. 2 Cor. 7:13. therefore wee are comforted because yee were comforted. of Epaphroditus he speaketh Phil. 2:30. that he regarded not his owne life to [do] him seruice soe Phebe and others are called the seruantes of the Churche, now it is apparant that they serued not for wages or by Constrainte but out of loue, the like wee shall finde in the histories of the churche in all ages the sweete Sympathie of affeccions which was in the members of this body one towardes another, theire chearfullnes in serueing and suffering together how liberall they were without repineing harbourers without grudgeing and helpfull without reproacheing and all from hence they had feruent loue amongst them which onely make[s] the practise of mercy constant and easie.

The next consideracion is how this loue comes to be wrought; Adam in his first estate was a perfect modell of mankinde in all theire generacions, and in him this loue was perfected in regard of the habit, but Adam Rent in himselfe from his Creator, rent all his posterity allsoe one from another, whence it comes that every man is borne with this principle in him, to loue and seeke himselfe onely and thus a man continueth till Christ comes and takes possession of the soule, and infuseth another principle of loue to God and our brother, and this latter haueing continuall supply from Christ, as the head and roote by which hee is vnited get the predominency in the soule, soe by little and little expells the former 1 John 4:7. loue cometh of god and every one that loueth is borne of god, soe that this loue is the fruite of the new birthe, and none can haue it but the new Creature, now when this quallity is thus formed in the soules of men it workes like the Spirit vpon the drie bones Ezek. 37:[7] bone came to bone, it gathers together the scattered bones or perfect old man Adam and knitts them into one body againe in Christ whereby a man is become againe a liueing soule.

The third Consideracion is concerning the exercise of this loue, which is twofold, inward or outward, the outward hath beene handled in the former preface of this discourse, for vnfolding the other wee must take in our way that maxime of philosophy, Simile simili gaudet or like will to like; for as it is things which are carried with disafeccion to eache other, the ground of it is from a dissimilitude or [blank] ariseing from the contrary or different nature of the things themselues, soe the ground of loue is an apprehension of some resemblance in the things loued to that which affectes it, this is the cause why the Lord loues the Creature, soe farre as it hath any of his Image in it, he loues his elect because they are like himselfe, he beholds them in his beloued sonne; soe a mother loues her childe, because shee throughly conceiues a resemblance of herselfe in it. Thus it is betweene the members of Christ, each discernes by the worke of the spirit his owne Image and resemblance in another, and therefore cannot but loue him as he loues himselfe; Now when the soule which is of a sociable nature findes any thing like to it selfe, it is like Adam when Eue was brought to him, shee must haue it one with herselfe this is fleshe of my fleshe (saith shee) and bone of my bone shee conceiues a greate delighte in it, therefore shee desires nearenes and familiarity with it; shee hath a greate propensity to doe it good and receiues such content in it, as feareing the miscarriage of her beloued shee bestowes it in the inmost Closett of her heart, shee will not endure that it shall want any good which shee can giue it, if by occasion shee be withdrawne from the Company of it, shee is still lookeing towardes the place where shee left her beloued, if shee heare it groane shee is with it presently, if shee finde it sadd and disconsolate shee sighes and mournes with it, shee hath noe such ioy, as to see her beloued merry and thriueing, if shee see it wronged, shee cannot beare it without passion, shee setts noe boundes of her affeccions, nor hath any thought of reward, shee findes recompence enoughe in the exercise of her loue towardes it, wee may see this Acted to life in Jonathan and David.

Jonathan a valiant man endued with the spirit of Christ, soe soone as hee Discovers the same spirit in David had presently his hearte knitt to him by this linement of loue, soe that it is said he loued him as his owne soule, he takes soe great pleasure in him that hee stripps himselfe to adorne his beloued, his fathers kingdome was not soe precious to him as his beloued David; Dauid shall haue it with all his hearte, himselfe desires noe more but that hee may be neare to him to reioyce in his good hee chooseth to converse with him in the wildernesse even to the hazzard of his owne life, rather then with the greate Courtiers in his fathers Pallace; when hee sees danger towards him, hee spares neither care paines, nor perill to divert it, when Iniury was offered his beloued David, hee could not beare it, though from his owne father, and when they must parte for a Season onely, they thought theire heartes would haue broake for sorrowe, had not theire affeccions found vent by aboundance of Teares: other instances might be brought to shewe the nature of this affeccion as of Ruthe and Naomi and many others, but this truthe is cleared enough.

If any shall obiect that it is not possible that loue should be bred or vpheld without hope of requitall, it is graunted but that is not our cause, for this loue is allwayes vnder reward it never giues, but it allwayes receiues with advantage: first, in regard that among the members of the same body, loue and affection are reciprocall in a most equall and sweete kinde of Commerce. 2ly, in regard of the pleasure and content that the exercise of loue carries with it as wee may see in the naturall body the mouth is at all the paines to receiue, and mince the foode which serues for the nourishment of all the other partes of the body, yet it hath noe cause to complaine; for first, the other partes send backe by secret passages a due proporcion of the same nourishment in a better forme for the strengthening and comforteing the mouthe. 2ly the labour of the mouthe is accompanied with such pleasure and content as farre exceedes the paines it takes: soe is it in all the labour of loue, among christians, the partie loueing, reapes loue againe as was shewed before, which the soule covetts more then all the wealthe in the world. 2ly [3ly]. noething yeildes more pleasure and content to the soule then when it findes that which it may loue fervently, for to loue and liue beloued is the soules paradice, both heare and in heaven; In the State of Wedlock there be many comfortes to beare out the troubles of that Condicion; but let such as haue tryed the most, say if there be any sweetnes in that Condicion comparable to the exercise of mutuall loue.

From the former Consideracions ariseth these Conclusions.

1 First. This loue among Christians is a reall thing not Imaginarie.

2ly. This loue is as absolutely necessary to the being of the body of Christ, as the sinewes and other ligaments of a naturall body are to the being of that body.

3ly. This loue is a divine Spirituall nature free, actiue strong Couragious permanent vnder valueing all things beneathe its propper obiect, and of all the graces this makes vs nearer to resemble the virtues of our heavenly father.

4ly, It restes in the loue and wellfare of its beloued, for the full and certaine knowledge of these truthes concerning the nature vse, [and] excellency of this grace, that which the holy ghost hath left recorded 1. Cor. 13. may giue full satisfaccion which is needfull for every true member of this louely body of the Lord Jesus, to worke vpon theire heartes, by prayer meditacion continuall exercise at least of the speciall [blank] of this grace till Christ be formed in them and they in him all in eache other knitt together by this bond of loue.

It rests now to make some applicacion of this discourse by the present designe which gaue the occasion of writeing of it. Herein are 4 things to be propounded: first the persons, 2ly, the worke, 3ly, the end, 4ly the meanes.

1. For the persons, wee are a Company professing our selues fellow members of Christ, In which respect onely though wee were absent from eache other many miles, and had our imploymentes as farre distant, yet wee ought to account our selues knitt together by this bond of loue, and liue in the excercise of it, if wee would haue comforte of our being in Christ, this was notorious in the practise of the Christians in former times, as is testified of the Waldenses from the mouth of one of the adversaries Æneas Syluius, mutuo [blank] penè antequam norint, they vse to loue any of theire owne religion even before they were acquainted with them.

2ly. for the Worke wee haue in hand, it is by a mutuall consent through a speciall overruleing providence, and a more then an ordinary approbation of the Churches of Christ to seeke out a place of Cohabitation and Consorteshipp vnder a due forme of Goverment both ciuill and ecclesiasticall. In such cases as this the care of the publique must oversway all private respects, by which not onely conscience, but meare Ciuill pollicy doth binde vs; for it is a true rule that perticuler Estates cannott subsist in the ruine of the publique.

3ly. The end is to improue our liues to doe more seruice to the Lord the comforte and encrease of the body of christe whereof wee are members that our selues and posterity may be the better preserued from the Common corrupcions of this euill world to serue the Lord and worke out our Salvacion vnder the power and purity of his holy Ordinances.

4ly for the meanes whereby this must bee effected, they are 2fold, a Conformity with the worke and end wee aime at, these wee see are extraordinary, therefore wee must not content our selues with vsuall ordinary meanes whatsoever wee did or ought to haue done when wee liued in England, the same must wee doe and more allsoe where wee goe; That which the most in theire Churches maineteine as a truthe in profession onely, wee must bring into familiar and constant practise, as in this duty of loue wee must loue brotherly without dissimulation, wee must loue one another with a pure hearte feruently wee must beare one anothers burthens, wee must not looke onely on our owne things, but allsoe on the things of our brethren, neither must wee think that the lord will beare with such faileings at our hands as hee dothe from those among whome wee haue liued, and that for 3 Reasons.

1. In regard of the more neare bond of mariage, betweene him and vs, wherein he hath taken vs to be his after a most strickt and peculiar manner which will make him the more Jealous of our loue and obedience soe he tells the people of Israell, you onely haue I knowne of all the families of the Earthe therefore will I punishe you for your Transgressions.

2ly, because the lord will be sanctified in them that come neare him. Wee know that there were many that corrupted the seruice of the Lord some setting vpp Alters before his owne, others offering both strange fire and strange Sacrifices allsoe; yet there came noe fire from heaven, or other sudden Judgement vpon them as did vpon Nadab and Abihu [Lev. 10:1–2] whoe yet wee may thinke did not sinne presumptuously.

3ly When God giues a speciall Commission he lookes to haue it stricktly obserued in every Article, when hee gaue Saule a Commission to destroy Amaleck hee indented with him vpon certaine Articles and because hee failed in one of the least, and that vpon a faire pretence, it lost him the kingdome, which should haue beene his reward, if hee had obserued his Commission [I Sam. 15; 28:16–18]; Thus stands the cause betweene God and vs, wee are entered into Covenant with him for this worke, wee haue taken out a Commission, the Lord hath giuen vs leaue to drawe our owne Articles wee haue professed to enterprise these Accions vpon these and these ends, wee haue herevpon besought him of favour and blessing; Now if the Lord shall please to heare vs, and bring

21

vs in peace to the place wee desire, then hath hee ratified this Covenant and sealed our Commission, [and] will expect a strickt performance of the Articles contained in it, but if wee shall neglect the observacion of these Articles which are the ends wee haue propounded, and dissembling with our God, shall fall to embrace this present world and prosecute our carnall intencions, seekeing greate things for our selues and our posterity, the Lord will surely breake out in wrathe against vs be revenged of such a periured people and make vs knowe the price of the breache of such a Covenant.

Now the onely way to avoyde this shipwracke and to provide for our posterity is to followe the Counsell of Micah, to doe Justly, to loue mercy, to walke humbly with our God, for this end wee must be knitt together in this worke as one man, wee must entertaine each other in brotherly Affeccion, wee must be willing to abridge our selues of our superfluities, for the supply of others necessities, wee must vphold a familiar Commerce together in all meekenes, gentlenes, patience and liberallity, wee must delight in eache other, make others Condicions our owne reioyce together, mourne together, labour, and suffer together, allwayes haueing before our eyes our Commission and Community in the worke, our Community as members of the same body, soe shall wee keepe the vnitie of the spirit in the bond of peace, the Lord will be our God and delight to dwell among vs, as his owne people and will commaund a blessing vpon vs in all our wayes, soe that wee shall see much more of his wisdome power goodnes and truthe then formerly wee haue beene acquainted with, wee shall finde that the God of Israell is among vs, when tenn of vs shall be able to resist a thousand of our enemies, when hee shall make vs a prayse and glory, that men shall say of succeeding plantacions: the lord make it like that of New England; for wee must Consider that wee shall be as a Citty vpon a Hill, the Eies of all people are vppon vs; soe that if wee shall deale falsely with our god in this worke wee haue vndertaken and soe cause him to withdrawe his present help from vs, wee shall be made a story and a by-word through the world[,] wee shall open the mouthes of enemies to speake euill of the wayes of god and all professours for Gods sake; wee shall shame the faces of many of gods worthy seruants, and cause theire prayers to be turned into Cursses vpon vs till wee be consumed out of the good land whether wee are goeing; And to shutt vpp this Discourse with that exhortacion of Moses that faithfull seruant of the Lord in his last farewell to Israell Deut. 30: [15–19]. Beloued there is now sett before vs life, and good, deathe and euill in that wee are Commaunded this day to loue the Lord our God, and to loue one another to walke in his wayes and to keepe his Commaundements and his Ordinance, and his lawes, and the Articles of our Covenant with him that wee may liue and be multiplyed, and that the Lord our God may blesse vs in the land whether wee goe to possesse it: But if our heartes shall turne away soe that wee will not obey, but shall be seduced and worshipp [serue *cancelled*] other Gods our pleasures, and proffitts, and serue them; it is propounded vnto vs this day, wee shall surely perishe out of the good Land whether wee passe over this vast Sea to possesse it;

> Therefore lett vs choose life,
> that wee, and our Seede,
> may liue; by obeying his
> voyce, and cleaueing to him,
> for hee is our life, and
> our prosperity.

The fate of the original manuscript of Winthrop's sermon is unknown. After the Arbella dropped anchor at Salem on June 14, 1630, at the end of her voyage of two and one-half months, the sermon was probably circulated in manuscript form, perhaps in several copies. Not until the early nineteenth century did a copy—in a contemporary hand other than Winthrop's—reappear, when it was given to the New-York Historical Society by a descendant of the Governor. It has subsequently been published several times, the first edition being that of the Massachusetts Historical Society in its Collections in 1838. But long before that, back in the seventeenth century, there was at least one divine who argued that the sermon's vitality had already been largely dissipated.

Massachusetts failed as a Modell of Christian Charity at the same time that it achieved worldly success: the generations which followed Winthrop's concerned themselves less and less with the perfection of souls and the achievement of salvation, and what had begun as a community dominated by religious purpose rapidly became a society with a secular orientation. Only thirty-four years after the Arbella anchored and but fifteen after Winthrop's death, Roger Williams predicted in sorrow to John Winthrop, the younger: "Sir, when we that have been the eldest, and are rotting, (to-morrow or next day) a generation will act, I fear, far unlike the first Winthrops and their Models of Love: I fear that the common Trinity of the world, (Profit, Preferment, Pleasure) will here be the Tria omnia, as in all the world beside . . . that God Land will be (as now it is) as great a God with us English as God Gold was with the Spaniards. . . ."

By Williams' standards, Winthrop's message had ceased to be relevant. In reality, however, the sermon written on board the Arbella is almost as relevant to an understanding of America today as it is to an understanding of the Puritans of 1630. Implicit in the Puritans' point of view, and certainly in the "Modell of Christian Charity," despite its opening argument, is the concept of change. Society was no longer considered fixed and immutable as it had been in the Middle Ages. Economic, social, religious, and political institutions had changed in the past for the worse and might be changed in the present for the better. Man need not be a hostage to his past; he could free himself from it and construct a new order based, in this case, on the revealed word of God. This idea of change, still revolutionary in the seventeenth century and still seen then within the context of the Christian interpretation of history, has become commonplace in America of the twentieth. Some may curse that change as too fast, others as too slow, but all know it to be a part of American life. From the time of the Puritans, and more particularly, of the Revolution, we have believed that change need not be blind and purposeless, but, instead, directed and purposeful. The vast improvement in the lot of the American Negro over the past twenty years, a consequence of conscious thought and deliberate action, is but the latest remarkable demonstration of this fact.

This change and others like it in the twentieth century have been brought about in part because of a reawakened sense of community, an idea and an ideal made very explicit in Winthrop's "Modell." The Puritans had a strong sense of community, not only because of their precarious position on the edge of the wilderness, but also because it was a part of their cultural heritage. The idea of an intimately related community in which all parts were joined organically to the whole and suffered or prospered together was as natural to their way of thinking as was the use of the word "body" as a metaphor for the community. We may not use the same metaphor today, and we do not formulate the idea in religious terms as the Puritans did, but much of the social legislation enacted in the twentieth century under the two Roosevelts, Wilson, and Truman, and ratified by the Republicans under Eisenhower, is a practical, undoctrinaire expression of the sense of community that Winthrop wrote about. The graduated income tax, social security, public housing, unemployment compensation, the regulation of rates for public utilities are all evidence that we indeed consider ourselves our brother's keeper.

Under ordinary circumstances, the kind of community Winthrop described would have been rooted in a particular soil and linked together by ties of family, church, government, and ancient custom. By these standards, the Puritan community established in Massachusetts in 1630 was quite heterogeneous. Most of the settlers were English, and many were Puritan, but they all had been uprooted and they lacked the ordinary and expected common ties. This was a new community on new land with a new church not yet established, with a government of questionable legal force and without the customary forms. What Winthrop counted on to hold this body together was an extraordinary outpouring of Christian love. And it was the idea that they were a chosen people with a mission to perform that would call forth such an outpouring. That which was true of John Winthrop's America is even more true of ours. With every race, nationality, and culture represented among us, we are a far more various people than Winthrop ever could have imagined. We lack the common cultural roots, the single ancient homeland, to make a people of us. What unites America is devotion to an idea as worked out in the institutions and practical affairs of men.

Like the Puritan, the modern American also has a strong sense of being a part of a chosen people with a mission to perform. Our successful revolution provided the Revolutionary generation and its heirs with a set of dual goals, the extension of liberty within the country, according to its grand statement in the Declaration of Independence, and to other peoples and lands outside the American union. Democracy was our idea, and our mission was to spread it everywhere. Jefferson's Empire of Freedom, the nineteenth century's Manifest Destiny, the concept of the Civil War as a war to "test whether that nation or any nation so conceived and so dedicated can long endure," and our twentieth-century role in world affairs are all expressions, on different levels of understanding, of the sense that America is the stronghold of democracy, a "Citty vpon a Hill," which, if it should fail, would carry mankind with it down into the darkness of despotism or to destruction.

Mary Easty
Petition of an Accused Witch
1692

EDITED BY EDMUND S. MORGAN

In the nineteenth century, when the human race was moving rapidly toward perfection, through manifest destiny, survival of the fittest, and the gospel of wealth, American historians found the Salem witch trials a difficult topic. Everyone was proud of the progress that had carried America away from the superstition and injustice exhibited at Salem, but it was a little embarrassing that there had been so much progress to make. A man of the early nineteenth century could actually (as a child) have touched hands with someone who had (as a child) witnessed the hanging of the Salem witches. Though one might grow accustomed to the existence of apes among one's ancestors, it was unpleasant to contemplate the presence of witch-hunters almost within the family.

The twentieth century has learned more familiarity with the outrageous—and less contempt. As the witch trials have receded to a more comfortable distance in time, we have found ourselves approaching closer to them in spirit, in our new progress through total war and genocide toward holocaust. Anyone who reads today the record of the Salem witch trials will discover in them the devices of judicial murder familiar to our own age: secret torture, irregular procedures, inadmissible evidence, and false confessions.

Historians of early New England now see these phenomena as signs of the times, signs of a people with more problems than they knew how to handle. In 1692 Massachusetts was hard pressed. The charter that had given the colony virtual autonomy was gone; a new one subjected the holy Puritan experiment to unsympathetic English control; an expedition against Catholic Quebec had failed; bankruptcy was imminent; and subversive agents were evidently attempting to enlist youth in a covenant with hell. The devil appeared as a real threat to the seventeenth century, and in 1692 the devil seemed to be getting the upper hand in Massachusetts. It was no time to stand on ceremony, no time to follow ordinary or orderly procedures when dealing with an enemy who knew no scruples. So a special court tried the cases, following procedures that would not have been acceptable in normal times.

The result was the hanging of nineteen men and women and the pressing to death of one man who refused to plead either guilty or not guilty. Thousands of Europeans had died for witchcraft in the seventeenth century, but these twenty Americans stand out more painfully, like an Anne Frank among millions of Jews. Among the twenty, Mary Easty (or Eastick) is memorable, because she left behind a testament of courage and honesty.

It was because of her courage and because of her honesty that Mary Easty died. One purpose of punishment in a Puritan court was to demonstrate the community's disapproval of crime. Unless the criminal was punished, the community shared his guilt, and God would visit His judgment upon innocent and guilty alike, if not by fire and brimstone, then by drought, depression, and disease. But another purpose of punishment was repentance. God welcomed the penitent sinner, and so must his viceregents on earth, the governors of the state. If a man repented, he had already averted God's wrath, and there was no longer so much need for the state to punish him. Puritan courts were accordingly merciful to those who repented. But it was impossible to repent without having something to repent about, and persons accused of crime learned that it might be easier to admit guilt and repent than to demonstrate innocence.

In the witch trials the possibility of proving innocence scarcely existed. It was taken as evidence of guilt if hysterical teen-age girls testified that a disembodied image of the accused was pinching them. The only escape was to confess. And those who did so often sought to establish the sincerity of their confessions and to take attention from themselves by naming others as their confederates in crime. Mary Easty was accused by the afflicted girls as one whose image was tormenting them. They later changed their minds and denied it, only to accuse her again two days later. *The accusations were then confirmed by confessions of other accused witches, and Mary Easty was condemned to death.*

She might easily have escaped the punishment by admitting guilt and throwing herself on the mercy of the court. To have done so would have been to belie her conscience and jeopardize her soul. Mary Easty did not share our enlightenment about the nonexistence of witchcraft. She knew that Satan was abroad in the world and that the court which condemned her was doing its best to combat him. She wished her judges well. But she knew she was not guilty, and she did not dare lie to save her life. In the hope, however, of saving others from a death they did not deserve, and in order to assist the court in its conflict with Satan, she wrote a petition to her judges, directing their attention to the imperfection of their procedures. Since they had convicted her, and since she knew herself to be innocent, she knew, as they could not, that they must be wrong.

THE HUMBL petition of Mary Eastick unto his Excellencyes Sir Wm Phipps and to the honourd Judge and Bench now s[i]tting In Judiacature in Salem and the Reverend ministers humbly sheweth

That wheras your poor and humble Petition[er] being condemned to die Doe humbly begg of you to take it into your Judicious and pious considerations that your poor and humble petitioner knowing my own Innocencye Blised be the Lord for it and seeing plainly the wiles and subtility of my accusers by my selfe can not but Judg charitably of Others that are going the same way of my selfe if the Lord stepps not mightily in i was confined a whole month upon the same account that I am condemned now for and then cleared by the afflicked persons as some of your honours know and in two dayes time I was cryed out upon by them and have been confined and now am condemned to die   the Lord above knows my Innocencye then and likewise does now as att the great day will be known to men and Angells   I petition to your honours not for my own life for I know I must die and my appointed time is sett but

---

The original of the petition, from which it is here reprinted, is in the Essex County Archives, Essex County Courthouse, Salem, Massachusetts, in a set of documents labeled "Witchcraft, 1692," I, 126.

the Lord he knowes it is that if it be possible no more Innocent blood may be shed which undoubtidly cannot be Avoyd[e]d   In the way and course you goe in   I Question not but your honours does to the uttmost of your Powers in the discovery and detecting of witchcraft and witches and would not be gulty of Innocent blood for the world but by my own Innocencye I know you are in the wrong way   the Lord in his infinite mercye direct you in this great work if it be his blessed will that no more innocent blood be shed   I would humbly begg of you that your honours would be plesed to examine theis Aflicted persons strictly and keepe them apart some time and likewise to try some of these confesing wichis I being confident there is severall of them has belyed themselves and others as will appeare if not in this world I am sure in the world to come whither I am now agoing and I question not but youll see an alteration of thes things they say my selfe and others having made a League with the Divel we cannot confesse   I know and the Lord knowes as will thorlly appeare they belye me and so I Question not but they doe others   the Lord above who is the searcher of all hearts knowes that as I shall answer it att the Tribunall Seat that I know not the least thinge of witchcraft therfore I cannot I dare not belye my own soule   I beg your honers not to deny this my humble petition from a poor dying Innocent person and I Question not but the Lord will give a blesing to yor endevers

Five years after they killed Mary Easty, the people of Massachusetts recognized that she had been right and they had been wrong. It was time now for them to confess their sin before God and man. They had not ceased to believe in the power of Satan, and they did not suppose that all the witches had been innocent, but only "that such grounds were then laid down to proceed upon, which were too slender to evidence the crime they were brought to prove." Looking back, they remembered those days as a time when "we walked in the clouds, and could not see our way," a time when their own frantic zeal had trapped them into the very evil they strove to suppress.

The colony held a day of fasting on January 14, 1697, and in the churches men who had sat in judgment on the witches or testified against them examined their consciences. Samuel Sewall, one of the judges, stood with bowed head while the minister read aloud his wish to take "the Blame and shame" of it upon himself, lest God visit the whole land with wrath. "We ourselves," said some of the jurors, "were not capable to understand, nor able to withstand the mysterious delusions of the Powers of Darkness and Prince of the Air; but were for want of Knowledge in our selves, and better Information from others, prevailed with to take up with such Evidence against the Accused, as on further consideration, and better Information, we justly fear was insufficient for the touching the Lives of any, Deut. 17.6. whereby we fear we have been instrumental with others, tho Ignorantly and unwittingly, to bring upon ourselves and this People of the Lord, the Guilt of Innocent Blood."

Though it did not help the dead, it was a good thing for the living to do—as it would be a good thing for the state of Massachusetts to admit today that it did wrong in 1927 to two men who may or may not have been guilty but who received no more fair a trial than Mary Easty. It would also be good for future guardians of the public safety to heed in troublous times the words of Mary Easty and guard the rights of those who risk all because they cannot confess to what they did not do.

Gabriel Thomas
An Account of Pennsylvania
1698

EDITED BY DAVID M. POTTER

In the autumn of 1681, William Penn sent out a ship, the John and Sarah, from London with the first company of emigrants who were to settle his colony of Pennsylvania. Among this company was a twenty-one-year-old Welshman named Gabriel Thomas, a Quaker from the little town of Pontemoil in Monmouthshire. Thomas' parents and sisters also migrated to Pennsylvania, but the record does not show whether all of them went together on the John and Sarah, or whether the rest of the family followed him on a later voyage.

Thomas remained in Pennsylvania for about fifteen years. During these years, the colony flourished, and Philadelphia began the growth which was soon to make it the largest town in North America. Pennsylvania was the last of the colonial settlements except for Georgia, and the settlers knew how to avoid the mistakes of earlier colonists. Consequently, progress was steady and hardships were few. Penn advertised the attractions of his colony very widely and offered a measure of religious toleration that was not matched in the other colonies. As a result, immigrants, mostly of dissenting religions, poured in from Germany and Wales as well as from England, and the new colony became ethnically more diversified than any of the older ones.

About 1697, Thomas went back to London, and there, in 1698, he published a little book entitled An Historical and Geographical Account of the Province and Country of Pensilvania; and of West-New-Jersey in

America. . . . *This book was designed to inform and to encourage potential migrants to Penn's colonies.*

After this brief appearance in history, Thomas again disappears into obscurity. Apparently he returned to Pennsylvania, and later quarreled with Penn, who had not given him the kind of reward which he thought he deserved for writing a book which had "proved to the province's great advancement by causing great numbers of people to go over to those parts." He died in Philadelphia, perhaps somewhat embittered, in 1714.

T HIS City [Philadelphia] is Situated between Schoolkill-River and the great River Delaware, which derives its Name from Captain Delaware, who came there pretty early: Ships of Two or Three Hundred Tuns may come up to this City, by either of these two Rivers. Moreover, in this Province are Four Great Market-Towns, *viz,* Chester, the German Town, New-Castle, and Lewis-Town, which are mightily Enlarged in this latter Improvement. Between these Towns, the Water-Men constantly Ply their Wherries; likewise all those Towns have Fairs kept in them, besides there are several Country Villages, *viz.* Dublin, Harford [Haverford], Merioneth, and Radnor in Cumbry

---

The full title of Thomas' account was *An Historical and Geographical Account of the Province and Country of Pensilvania; and of West-New-Jersey in America. The Richness of the Soil, the Sweetness of the Situation, the Wholesomness of the Air, the Navigable Rivers, and others, the prodigious Encrease of Corn, the flourishing Condition of the City of Philadelphia, with the stately Buildings, and other Improvements there. The strange Creatures, as Birds, Beasts, Fishes, and Fowls, with the several sorts of Minerals, Purging Waters, and Stones, lately discovered. The Natives, Aboroqmes, their Language, Religion, Laws, and Customs; The first Planters, the Dutch, Sweeds, and English, with the number of its Inhabitants; As also a Touch upon George Keith's New Religion, in his second Change since he left the Quakers, with a Map of both Countries.* By Gabriel Thomas, who resided there about Fifteen Years. London, Printed for, and Sold by A. Baldwin, at the Oxon Arms in Warwick-Lane, 1698.

The text which is used here reproduces all of Thomas' tract except: a dedication to Penn; a preface; a long account of the physical appearance of Philadelphia and the layout of its streets; an account of the Indians; a criticism of some of the religious practices of a Quaker named George Keith; and a long, separate treatment of the West-Jersey province. The original text is followed exactly, with a few corrections and explanatory comments inserted in brackets, but the marginal glosses in the original are omitted.

[Cambria, a tract occupied by the Welsh settlers]; all which Towns, Villages and Rivers, took their Names from the several Countries whence the present Inhabitants came.

The Air here is very delicate, pleasant, and wholesom; the Heavens serene, rarely overcast, bearing mighty resemblance to the better part of France; after Rain they have commonly a very clear Sky, the Climate is something Colder in the depth of Winter and Hotter in the height of Summer; (the cause of which is its being a Main Land or Continent; the Days also are two Hours longer in the shortest Day in Winter, and shorter by two Hours in the longest Day of Summer) than here in England, which makes the Fruit so good, and the Earth so fertil.

The Corn-Harvest is ended before the middle of July, and most Years they have commonly between Twenty and Thirty Bushels of Wheat for every one they Sow. Their Ground is harrowed with Wooden Tyned Harrows, twice over in a place is sufficient; twice mending of their Plow-Irons in a Years time will serve. Their Horses commonly go without being shod; two Men may clear between Twenty and Thirty Acres of Land in one Year, fit for the Plough, in which Oxen are chiefly us'd, though Horses are not wanting, and of them Good and well shap'd. A Cart or a Wain may go through the middle of the Woods, between the Trees without getting any damage, and of such Land in a convenient place, the Purchase will cost between Ten and Fifteen Pounds for a Hundred Acres. Here is much Meadow Ground. Poor People both Men and Women, will get near three times more Wages for their Labour in this Country, than they can earn either in England or Wales.

What is Inhabited of this Country, is divided into Six Counties, though there is not the Twentieth Part of it yet Peopled by the Christians: It hath in it several Navigable Rivers for Shipping to come in, besides the Capital Delaware, wherein a Ship of Two Hundred Tuns may Sail Two Hundred Miles up. There are also several other small Rivers, in number hardly Credible; these, as the Brooks, have for the most part gravelly and hard Bottoms; and it is suppos'd that there are many other further up in the Country, which are not yet discover'd; the Names of the aforesaid Rivers, are, Hoorkill-River, alias Lewis River, which runs up to Lewis Town, the chiefest in Sussex County; Cedar-River, Muskmellon-River, all taking their Names from the great plenty of these things growing thereabouts; Mother-kill alias Dover-River, St. Jones's alias Cranbrook-River, where one John Curtice lives, who hath Three Hundred Head of Neat Beasts, besides great Numbers of Hogs,

Horses, and Sheep; Great Duck-River, Little Duck-River, Black-Bird-River, these also took their Original Names from the great Numbers of those Fowls which are found there in vast quantities; Apequinemy-River, where their Goods come to be Carted over to Mary-Land, St. George's-River, Christen-River, Brandy-Wine-River, Upland alias Chester-River, which runs by Chester-Town, being the Shire or County-Town; Schoolkill-River, Frankford-River, near which, Arthur Cook hath a most Stately Brick-House; and Nishamany-River, where Judge Growden hath a very Noble and Fine House, very pleasantly Situated, and likewise a Famous Orchard adjoyning to it, wherein are contain'd above a Thousand Apple Trees of various sorts; likewise there is the famous Derby-River, which comes down from the Cumbry by Derby-Town, wherein are several Mills, viz. Fulling-Mills, Corn-Mills, etc.

There is curious Building-Stone and Paving-Stone, also Tile-Stone, with which latter, Governor Penn covered his Great and Stately Pile, which he call'd Pennsbury-House, the Name it still retains. There is likewise Iron-Stone or Oar, (lately found) which far exceeds that in England, being Richer and less Drossy; some Preparations have been made to carry on an Iron-Work: There is also very good Lime-Stone in great plenty, and cheap, of great use in Buildings, and also in Manuring Land, (if there were occasion) but Nature has made that of it self sufficiently Fruitful; besides here are Load-Stones, Ising-Glass, and (that Wonder of Stones) the Salamander-Stone [asbestos], found near Brandy-Wine-River, having Cotton in Veins within it, which will not consume in the Fire; though held there a long time.

As to Minerals, or Metals, there is very good Copper, far exceeding ours in England, being much Finer, and of a more glorious Colour. Not two Mile from the Metropolis, are also Purging Mineral-Waters, that pass both by Siege and Urine, all out as good as Epsom; And I have reason to believe, there are good Coals also, for I observ'd, the Runs of Water have the same Colour as that which proceeds from the Coal-Mines in Wales.

Here is curious Diversion in Hunting, Fishing, and Fowling, especially upon that Great and Famous River Suskahanah, which runs down quite through the heart of the Country to Mary-Land, where it makes the Head of Chesepeck-Bay, in which place there are an Infinite Number of Sea and Land Fowl, of most sorts, viz. Swans, Ducks, Teal, (which two are the most Grateful and most Delicious in the World), Geese, Divers, Brands, Snipe, Curlew; as also Eagles, Turkies (of Forty or Fifty Pound

Weight) Pheasants, Partridges, Pidgeons, Heath-Birds, Black-Birds; and that Strange and Remarkable Fowl, call'd (in these Parts) the Mocking-Bird, that Imitates all sorts of Birds in their various Notes. And for Fish, there are prodigious quantities of most sorts, *viz.* Shadds, Cats-Heads, Sheeps-Heads, Herrings, Smelts, Roach, Eels, Perch. As also the large sort of Fish, as Whales (of which a great deal of Oyl is made), Salmon, Trout, Sturgeon, Rock, Oysters (some six Inches long), Crabs, Cockles (some as big as Stewing Oysters of which are made a Choice Soupe or Broth), Canok and Mussels, with many other sorts of Fish, which would be too tedious to insert.

There are several sorts of wild Beasts of great Profit, and good Food; *viz.* Panthers, Woolves, Fither, Deer, Beaver, Otter, Hares, Musk-Rats, Minks, Wild-Cats, Foxes, Rackoons, Rabits, and that strange Creature, the Possam, she having a false Belly to swallow her Yonng ones, by which means she preserveth them from danger, when any thing comes to disturb them. There are also Bears some[;] Wolves, are pretty well destroy'd by the Indians, for the sake of the Reward given them by the Christians for that Service. Here is also that Remarkable Creature the Flying-Squirrel, having a kind of Skinny Wings, almost like those of the Batt, though it hath the like Hair and Colour of the Common Squirrel, but is much less in Bodily Substance; I have (my self) seen it fly from one Tree to another in the Woods, but how long it can maintain its Flight is not yet exactly known.

There are in the Woods abundance of Red Deer (vulgarly called Stags) for I have bought of the Indians a whole Buck (both Skin and Carcass), for two Gills of Gunpowder. Excellent Food, most delicious, far exceeding that in Europe, in the Opinion of most that are Nice and Curious People. There are vast Numbers of other Wild Creatures, as Elks, Bufalos, &c., all which as well Beasts, Fowl, and Fish, are free and common to any Person who can shoot or take them, without any lett, hinderance or Opposition whatsover.

There are among other various sorts of Frogs, the Bull-Frog, which makes a roaring noise, hardly to be distinguished from that well known of the Beast, from whom it takes its Name: There is another sort of Frog that crawls up to the tops of Trees, there seeming to imitate the Notes of several Birds, with many other strange and various Creatures, which would take up too much room here to mention.

Next, I shall proceed to instance in the several sorts of Wild Fruits, as excellent Grapes, Red, Black, White, Muscadel, and Fox, which upon

frequent Experience have produc'd Choice Wine, being daily Cultivated by skilful Vinerons; they will in a short space of time, have very
good Liquor of their own, and some to supply their Neighbours, to their
great advantage; as these Wines are more pure, so much more wholsom;
the Brewing Trade of Sophisticating and Adulterating of Wines, as in
England, Holland (especially) and in some other places not being
known there yet, nor in all probability will it in many Years, through a
natural Probity so fixed and implanted in the Inhabitants, and (I hope)
like to continue. Wallnuts, Chesnuts, Filberts, Heckery-Nuts, Hartle-
berries, Mulberries, (white and black) Rasberries, Strawberries, Cram-
berries, Plumbs of several sorts, and many other Wild Fruits, in great
plenty, which are common and free for any to gather; to particularize
the Names of them all, would take up too much time; tire, not gratifie
the Reader, and be inconsistent with the intended Brevity of this little
Volume.

The common Planting Fruit-Trees, are Apples, which from a Kernel
(without Inoculating) will shoot up to be a large Tree, and produce very
delicious, large, and pleasant Fruit, of which much excellent Cyder is
made, in taste resembling that in England press'd from Pippins and
Pearmains, sold commonly for between Ten and Fifteen Shillings per
Barrel. Pears, Peaches, &c. of which they distil a Liquor much like the
taste of Rumm, or Brandy, which they Yearly make in great quantities:
There are Quinces, Cherries, Goosberries, Currants, Squashes, Pump-
kins, Water-Mellons, Muskmellons, and other Fruits in great Numbers,
which seldom fail of yielding great plenty. There are also many curious
and excellent Physical Wild Herbs, Roots, and Drugs of great Vertue,
and very sanative, as the Sassafras, and Sarsaparilla, so much us'd in
Diet-Drinks for the Cure of the Veneral Disease, which makes the
Indians by a right application of them, as able Doctors and Surgeons as
any in Europe, performing celebrated Cures therewith, and by the use of
some particular Plants only, find Remedy in all Swellings, Burnings,
Cuts, &c. There grows also in great plenty the Black Snake-Root, (fam'd
for its sometimes preserving, but often curing the Plague, being infused
only in Wine, Brandy or Rumm) Rattle-Snake-Root, Poke-Root, called
in England Jallop, with several other beneficial Herbs, Plants and Roots,
which Physicians have approved of, far exceeding in Nature and Vertue,
those of other Countries.

The Names of the Counties are as followeth; First, Philadelphia

County; Second, Bucks County; Third, Chester County; Fourth, New-Castle County; Fifth, Kent County; Sixth, Sussex County.

The chiefest and most commodious places for raising Tobacco, as also for Breeding and Improving all sorts of Cattle, are the Counties of Kent and New-Castle; the other[s] chiefly depend upon Raising and Improving English Grain, of which they have a prodigious Encrease, which I have particularly instanced in the beginning of this Book, both as to their Quality and Quantity: All those Counties also very much abound in all sorts of Cattle, both small and great, for the Use and Service of Man.

Their sorts of Grain are, Wheat, Rye, Pease, Oates, Barley, Buck-Wheat, Rice, Indian-Corn, Indian-Pease, and Beans, with great quantities of Hemp and Flax; as also several sorts of eating Roots, as Turnips, Potatoes, Carrats, Parsnips, &c., all which are produc'd Yearly in greater quantities than in England, those Roots being much larger, and altogether as sweet, if not more delicious; Cucumbers, Coshaws, Artichokes, with many others; most sorts of Saladings, besides what grows naturally Wild in the Country, and that in great plenty also, as Mustard, Rue, Sage, Mint, Tanzy, Wormwood, Penny-Royal and Purslain, and most of the Herbs and Roots found in the Gardens in England. There are several Husband-Men, who sow Yearly between Seventy and Eighty Acres of Wheat each, besides Barley, Oates, Rye, Pease, Beans, and other Grain.

They have commonly Two Harvests in the Year; First, of English Wheat, and next of Buck, (or French) Wheat. They have great Stocks both of Hogs and Horses, kept in the Woods, out of which, I saw a Hog kill'd, of about a Year old, which weigh'd Two Hundred weight; whose Flesh is much sweeter, and even more luscious than that in England, because they feed and fatten on the rich (though wild) Fruits, besides those fatned at home by Peaches, Cherries and Apples. Their Horses are very hardy, insomuch that being very hot with riding or otherwise, they are turn'd out into the Woods at the same Instant, and yet receive no harm; some Farmers have Forty, some Sixty, and from that Number to Two or Three Hundred Head of Cattle: Their Oxen usually weigh Two Hundred Pounds a Quarter. They are commonly fatter of Flesh, and yield more Tallow (by feeding only on Grass) than the Cattle in England. And for Sheep, they have considerable Numbers which are generally free from those infectious Diseases which are incident to those

Creatures in England, as the Rot, Scab, or Maggots; They commonly bring forth two Lambs at once, some twise in one Year, and the Wooll is very fine, and thick, and also very white.

Bees thrive and multiply exceedingly in those Parts, the Sweeds often get great store of them in the Woods, where they are free for any Body. Honey (and choice too) is sold in the Capital City for Five Pence per Pound. Wax is also plentiful, cheap, and a considerable Commerce. Tame Fowls, as Chickens, Hens, Geese, Ducks, Turkeys, &c., are large, and very plentiful all over this Countrey.

And now for their Lots and Lands in City and Countrey, in their great Advancement since they were first laid out, which was within the compass of about Twelve Years, that which might have been bought for Fifteen or Eighteen Shillings, is now sold for Fourscore Pounds in ready Silver; and some other Lots, that might have been then Purchased for Three Pounds, within the space of Two Years, were sold for a Hundred Pounds a piece, and likewise some Land that lies near the City, that Sixteen Years ago might have been Purchas'd for Six or Eight Pounds the Hundred Acres, cannot now be bought under One Hundred and Fifty, or Two Hundred Pounds.

Now the true Reason why this Fruitful Countrey and Florishing City advance so considerably in the Purchase of Lands both in the one and the other, is their great and extended Traffique and Commerce both by Sea and Land, *viz.* to New-York, New-England, Virginia, Mary-Land, Carolina, Jamaica, Barbadoes, Nevis, Monserat, Antego, St. Cristophers, Barmudoes, New-Found-Land, Maderas, Saltetudeous, and Old-England; besides several other places. Their Merchandize chiefly consists in Horses, Pipe-Staves, Pork and Beef Salted and Barrelled up, Bread, and Flower, all sorts of Grain, Pease, Beans, Skins, Furs, Tobacco, or Pot-Ashes, Wax, &c. which are Barter'd for Rumm, Sugar, Molasses, Silver, Negroes, Salt, Wine, Linen, Houshold-Goods, &c.

However there still remain Lots of Land both in the aforesaid City and Country, that any may Purchase almost as cheap as they could at the first Laying out or Parcelling of either City or Country; which is, (in the Judgment of most People) the likeliest to turn to account to those that lay their Money out upon it, and in a shorter time than the aforementioned Lots and Lands that are already improved, and for several Reasons. In the first place, the Countrey is now well inhabited by the Christians, who have great Stocks of all sorts of Cattle, that encrease extraordinarily, and upon that account they are oblig'd to go farther up into the Countrey, because there is the chiefest and best place for their Stocks, and for them that go back into the Countrey, they get the richest Land, for the best lies thereabouts.

Secondly, Farther into the Countrey is the Principal Place to Trade with the Indians for all sorts of Pelt, as Skins and Furs, and also Fat Venison, of whom People may Purchase cheaper by three Parts in four than they can at the City of Philadelphia.

Thirdly, Backwards in the Countrey lies the Mines where is Copper and Iron, besides other Metals, and Minerals, of which there is some Improvement made already in order to bring them, to greater Perfection; and that will be a means to erect more Inland Market-Towns, which exceedingly promote Traffick.

Fourthly, and lastly, Because the Countrey at the first laying out, was void of Inhabitants (except the Heathens, or very few Christians not worth naming) and not many People caring to abandon a quiet and easie (at least tolerable) Life in their Native Countrey (usually the most agreeable to all Mankind) to seek out a new hazardous, and careful one in a Foreign Wilderness or Desart Countrey, wholly destitute of Christian Inhabitants, and even to arrive at which, they must pass over a vast Ocean, expos'd to some Dangers, and not a few Inconveniencies: But now all those Cares, Fears and Hazards are vanished, for the Countrey is pretty well Peopled, and very much Improv'd, and will be more every Day, now the Dove is return'd with the Olive-branch of Peace in her Mouth.

I must needs say, even the present Encouragements are very great and inviting, for Poor People (both Men and Women) of all kinds, can here get three times the Wages for their Labour they can in England or Wales.

I shall instance in a few, which may serve; nay, and will hold in all the rest. The first was a Black-Smith (my next Neighbour), who himself and one Negro Man he had, got Fifty Shillings in one Day, by working up a Hundred Pound Weight of Iron, which at Six Pence per Pound (and that is the common Price in that Countrey) amounts to that Summ.

And for Carpenters, both House and Ship, Brick-layers, Masons, either of these Trades-Men, will get between Five and Six Shillings every Day constantly. As to Journey-Men Shooe-Makers, they have Two Shillings per Pair both for Men and Womens Shooes: And Journey-Men Taylors have Twelve Shillings per Week and their Diet. Sawyers get between Six and Seven Shillings the Hundred for Cutting of Pine-Boards. And for Weavers, they have Ten or Twelve Pence the Yard for Weaving of that which is little more than half a Yard in breadth. Wooll-Combers, have for combing Twelve Pence per Pound. Potters have Sixteen Pence for an Earthen Pot which may be bought in England for Four Pence. Tanners may buy their Hides green for Three Half Pence per Pound, and sell their Leather for Twelve Pence per Pound. And Curriers have Three Shillings and Four Pence per Hide for Dressing it; they buy their Oyl at Twenty Pence per Gallon. Brick-Makers have Twenty Shillings per Thousand for their Bricks at the Kiln. Felt-Makers will have for their Hats Seven Shillings a piece, such as may be bought in England for Two Shillings a piece; yet they buy their Wooll commonly for Twelve or Fifteen Pence per Pound. And as to the Glaziers, they will have Five Pence a Quarry [diamond-shaped pane] for their Glass. The Rule for the Coopers I have almost forgot; but this I can affirm of some who went from Bristol (as their Neighbours report), that could hardly get their Livelihoods there, are now reckon'd in Pensilvania, by a modest Computation to be worth some Hundreds (if not Thousands) of Pounds. The Bakers make as White Bread as any in London, and as for their Rule, it is the same in all Parts of the World that I have been in. The Butchers for killing a Beast, have Five Shillings and their Diet; and they may buy a good fat large Cow for Three Pounds, or thereabouts. The Brewers sell such Beer as is equal in Strength to that in London, half Ale and half Stout for Fifteen Shillings per Barrel; and their Beer hath a better Name, that is, is in more esteem than English Beer in Barbadoes, and is sold for a higher Price there. And for Silver-Smiths, they have between Half a Crown and Three Shillings an Ounce for working their Silver, and for Gold equivalent. Plasterers have commonly Eighteen Pence per Yard for Plastering. Last-Makers have Sixteen Shillings per dozen for their Lasts. And Heel-Makers have Two Shillings a dozen for their Heels. Wheel and Mill-Wrights, Joyners, Brasiers, Pewterers, Dyers, Fullers, Comb-Makers, Wyer-Drawers, Cage-Makers, Card-Makers, Painters, Cutlers, Rope-Makers, Carvers, Block-Makers, Turners, Button-Makers, Hair and Wood Sieve-Makers, Bodies-Makers, Gun-Smiths, Lock-Smiths, Nailers, File-Cuters, Skinners, Furriers, Glovers, Patten-Makers, Watch-Makers, Clock-Makers, Sadlers, Coller-Makers, Barbers, Printers, Book-Binders, and all other Trades-Men, their Gains and Wages are about the same proportion as the forementioned Trades in their Advancements, as to what they have in England.

Of Lawyers and Physicians I shall say nothing, because this Countrey is very Peaceable and Healt[h]y; long may it so continue and never have occasion for the Tongue of the one, nor the Pen of the other, both equally destructive to Mens Estates and Lives; besides forsooth, they, Hang-Man like, have a License to Murder and make Mischief. Labouring-Men have commonly here, between 14 and 15 Pounds a Year, and their Meat, Drink, Washing and Lodging; and by the Day their Wages is generally between Eighteen Pence and Half a Crown, and Diet also; But in Harvest they have usually between Three and Four Shillings each Day, and Diet. The Maid Servants Wages is commonly betwixt Six and Ten Pounds per Annum, with very good Accommodation. And for the Women who get their Livelihood by their own Industry, their Labour is very dear, for I can buy in London a Cheese-Cake for Two Pence, bigger than theirs at that price, when at the same time their Milk is as cheap as we can buy it in London, and their Flour cheaper by one half.

Corn and Flesh, and what else serves Man for Drink, Food and Rayment, is much cheaper here than in England, or elsewhere; but the chief reason why Wages of Servants of all sorts is much higher here than there, arises from the great Fertility and Produce of the Place; besides, if these large Stipends were refused them, they would quickly set up for themselves, for they can have Provision very cheap, and Land for a very small matter, or next to nothing in comparison of the Purchace of Lands in England; and the Farmers there, can better afford to give that great Wages than the Farmers in England can, for several Reasons very obvious.

As First, their Land costs them (as I said but just now) little or nothing in comparison, of which the Farmers commonly will get twice the encrease of Corn for every Bushel they sow, that the Farmers in England can from the richest Land they have.

In the Second place, they have constantly good price for their Corn, by reason of the great and quick vent [market] into Barbadoes and other Islands; through which means Silver is become more plentiful than here in England, considering the Number of People, and that causes a quick Trade for both Corn and Cattle; and that is the reason that Corn [wheat] differs now from the Price formerly, else it would be at half the Price it was at then; for a Brother of mine (to my own particular knowledge) sold within the compass of one Week, about One Hundred and Twenty fat Beasts, most of them good handsom large Oxen.

Thirdly, They pay no Tithes, and their Taxes are inconsiderable; the Place is free for all Persuasions, in a Sober and Civil way; for the Church of England and the Quakers bear equal Share in the Government. They live Friendly and Well together; there is no Persecution for Religion, nor ever like to be; 'tis this that knocks all Commerce on the Head, together with high Imposts, strict Laws, and cramping Orders. Before I end this Paragraph, I shall add another Reason why Womens Wages are so exorbitant; they are not yet very numerous, which makes them stand upon high Terms for their several Services, in Sempstering, Washing, Spinning, Knitting, Sewing, and in all the other parts of their Imployments; for they have for Spinning either Worsted or Linen, Two Shillings a Pound, and commonly for Knitting a very Course pair of Yarn Stockings, they have half a Crown a pair; moreover they are usually Marry'd before they are Twenty Years of Age, and when once in that Noose, are for the most part a little uneasie, and make their Husbands so too, till they procure them a Maid Servant to bear the burden of the Work, as also in some measure to wait on them too.

It is now time to return to the City of Brotherly-Love (for so much the Greek Word or Name Philadelphia imports) which though at present so obscure, that neither the Map-Makers, nor Geographers have taken the least notice of her, tho she far exceeds her Namesake of Lydia, (having above Two Thousand Noble Houses for her Five Hundred Ordinary) or Celisia, or Cælesyria; yet in a very short space of time she will, in all probability, make a fine Figure in the World, and be a most Celebrated Emporeum. Here is lately built a Noble Town-House or Guild-Hall, also a Handsom Market-House, and a convenient Prison. The Number of Christians both Old and Young Inhabiting in that Countrey, are by a Modest Computation, adjudged to amount to above Twenty Thousand.

The Laws of this Countrey, are the same with those in England; our Constitution being on the same Foot: Many Disputes and Differences are determined and composed by Arbitration; and all Causes are decided with great Care and Expedition, being concluded (generally) at furthest at the Second Court, unless they happen to be very Nice and Difficult Cases; under Forty Shillings any one Justice of the Peace has Power to

Try the Cause. Thieves of all sorts, are oblig'd to restore four fold after they have been Whipt and Imprison'd, according to the Nature of their Crime; and if they be not of Ability to restore four fold, they must be in Servitude till 'tis satisfied. They have Curious Wharfs, as also several large and fine Timber-Yards, both at Philadelphia, and New-Castle, especially at the Metropolis, before Robert Turner's Great and Famous House, where are built Ships of considerable Burthen; they Cart their Goods from that Wharf into the City of Philadelphia, under an Arch, over which part of the Street is built, which is called Chesnut-Street-Wharf, besides other Wharfs, as High-Street Wharf, Mulberry-Street Wharf, and Vine-S[t]reet Wharf, and all those are Common Wharfs; and likewise there are very pleasant Stairs, as Trus and Carpenter-Stairs, besides several others. There are above Thirty Carts belonging to that City, Four or Five Horses to each. There is likewise a very convenient Wharf called Carpenter's Wharf, which hath a fine necessary Crain belonging to it, with suitable Granaries, and Store-Houses. A Ship of Two Hundred Tun may load and unload by the side of it, and there are other Wharfs (with Magazines and Ware-Houses) which front the City all along the River, as also a Curious and Commodious Dock with a Draw-Bridge to it, for the convenient Reception of Vessels; where have been built some Ships of Two or Three Hundred Tuns each: They have very Stately Oaks to build Ships with, some of which are between Fifty and Sixty Foot long, and clear from Knots, being very straight and well Grain'd. In this famous City of Philadelphia there are several Rope-Makers, who have large and curious Rope-Walks especially one Joseph Wilcox. Also Three or Four Spacious Malt-Houses, as many large Brew-Houses, and many handsom Bake-Houses for Publick Use.

In the said City are several good Schools of Learning for Youth, in order to the Attainment of Arts and Sciences, as also Reading, Writing, &c. Here is to be had on any Day in the Week, Tarts, Pies, Cakes, &c. We have also several Cooks-Shops, both Roasting and Boyling, as in the City of London; Bread, Beer, Beef, and Pork, are sold at any time much cheaper than in England (which arises from their Plenty) our Wheat is very white and clear from Tares, making as good and white Bread as any in Europe. Happy Blessings, for which we owe the highest Gratitude to our Plentiful Provider, the great Creator of Heaven and Earth. The Water-Mills far exceed those in England, both for quickness and grinding good Meal, their being great choice of good Timber, and earlier

Corn than in the aforesaid Place, they are made by one Peter Deal, a Famous and Ingenious Workman, especially for inventing such like Machines.

All sorts of very good Paper are made in the German-Town; as also very fine German Linen, such as no Person of Quality need be asham'd to wear; and in several places they make very good Druggets, Crapes, Camblets, and Serges, besides other Woollen Cloathes, the Manufacture of all which daily improves: And in most parts of the Countrey there are many Curious and Spacious Buildings, which several of the Gentry have erected for their Country-Houses. As for the Fruit-Trees they Plant, they arrive at such Perfection, that they bear in a little more than half the time that they commonly do in England.

The Christian Children born here are generally well-favoured, and Beautiful to behold; I never knew any come into the World with the least blemish on any part of its Body, being in the general, observ'd to be better Natur'd, Milder, and more tender Hearted than those born in England.

There are very fine and delightful Gardens and Orchards, in most parts of this Countrey; but Edward Shippey (who lives near the Capital City) has an Orchard and Gardens adjoyning to his Great House that equalizes (if not exceeds) any I have ever seen, having a very famous and pleasant Summer-House erected in the middle of his extraordinary fine and large Garden abounding with Tulips, Pinks, Carnations, Roses, (of several sorts) Lilies, not to mention those that grow wild in the Fields.

Reader, what I have here written, is not a Fiction, Flam, Whim, or any sinister Design, either to impose upon the Ignorant, or Credulous, or to curry Favour with the Rich and Mighty, but in meer Pity and pure Compassion to the Numbers of Poor Labouring Men, Women, and Children in England, half starv'd, visible in their meagre looks, that are continually wandering up and down looking for Employment without finding any, who here need not lie idle a moment, nor want due Encouragement or Reward for their Work, much less Vagabond or Drone it about. Here are no Beggars to be seen (it is a Shame and Disgrace to the State that there are so many in England) nor indeed have any here the least Occasion or Temptation to take up that Scandalous Lazy Life.

Jealousie among Men is here very rare, and Barrenness among Women hardly to be heard of, nor are old Maids to be met with; for all commonly Marry before they are Twenty Years of Age, and seldom any young Married Woman but hath a Child in her Belly, or one upon her Lap.

What I have deliver'd concerning this Province, is indisputably true, I was an Eye-Witness to it all, for I went in the first Ship that was bound from England for that Countrey, since it received the Name of Pensilvania, which was in the Year 1681. The Ship's Name was the *John* and *Sarah* of London, Henry Smith Commander. I have declin'd giving any Account of several things which I have only heard others speak of, because I did not see them my self, for I never held that way infallible, to make Reports from Hear-say. I saw the first Cellar when it was digging for the use of our Governour Will. Penn.

Gabriel Thomas' Account of Pennsylvania has had no lasting fame, and did not mark a change in the course of history. But it represents a category of writings which played a unique and important role in American history. These were the tracts, broadsides, pamphlets, advertisements, letters, sermons, and other pieces which made up an immense body of what is called "promotional literature." Much of it was ephemeral, for it was prone to exaggerate the merits of particular places, to be unreliable in terms of fact, and to partake in general of the quality of advertising. But it is important because it reflected, as nothing else did, the motives and the hopes which drew immigrants first from their homes in Britain and Europe to the wilderness across the Atlantic, and later from settled and civilized communities in the older parts of America to the frontier regions which moved like a shifting battle line across North America during the eighteenth and nineteenth centuries. Other, more official, documents explained why the government wanted colonies to be founded, or why the financial backers of settlements believed that their projects would pay off. But nothing else has shown so clearly the aspirations of the American settlers. The authors of the promotional literature sensed what these men and women were seeking and hoping, what they would respond to, what they visualized as the "good life." The literature promised them a fulfillment of these dreams. It can be read today, therefore, either as an idealized description of realistic conditions, or as a supremely realistic definition of ideals that were never stated in philosophical or conceptual terms.

Thomas' is one of many thousands of items which testified, unconsciously, to what men wanted America to be, why they had faith in
America, and what they wanted to make it. The fact that this testimony
was unconscious makes it all the more reliable—it was a very direct
expression of what people wished, not too much complicated by any
sense of obligation to include also what they may have thought that they
ought to wish. Thus, it is striking that Thomas said very little about
abstract ideals. Although he was himself a Quaker (he left the Society of
Friends before his death), he gave little emphasis to the religious
freedom that existed in Pennsylvania. Although he was familiar with the
diversity of peoples (Swedes, Finns, Dutch, Germans, English, Welsh)
who made Pennsylvania America's first "melting pot," he did not
comment on the toleration that the various ethnic groups showed toward
each other. Instead, he bore down incessantly upon the economic
abundance which Pennsylvania offered—the fertility of its soil, the easy
availability of its land, the purity and navigability of its streams, the
profusion of its game and water-fowl and fish, the high yield of its crops,
the superiority of its wage-scales to those in England, the geniality of its
climate. This emphasis in Thomas is thoroughly characteristic of the
promotional writings in general, for as Howard Mumford Jones has
observed after a broad survey, "Perhaps the commonest element in the
promotion literature is the allure of economic plenitude."

The American emphasis on economic abundance has sometimes been
denounced as materialism, and, no doubt, in some of the forms it takes,
it has deserved this denunciation. But in the eighteenth-century world,
where men were stunted and deprived by poverty, the goal of abundance
for everyone seemed touched with real idealism. The perfect society
would be one where the age-old striving to escape want would be
mitigated, and where scarcity would not force men to fight with one
another over an insufficient supply of the necessities of life. As the bitter
struggle for existence was relaxed, the harsher, meaner qualities of human
nature would disappear, and men would approach nearer to perfection.
Even in their physiques they would be better. Women would bear more
children, and Thomas found that there was "seldom any young Married
Woman but hath a Child in her Belly or one upon her Lap." The
children would reflect this tendency toward perfection, and Thomas had
never known an infant born in Pennsylvania with "the least blemish on
any part of its Body." Even the temperament of the people—what we
may call their character—would be improved; the children born in
Pennsylvania, Thomas noted, were "in the general, observ'd to be better

Natur'd, Milder, and more tender Hearted than those born in England."

In a world where men could enjoy life in peace and amity, without having to fight one another for the means of subsistence, there seemed no great need for ideologies, since ideologies are weapons in social combat. In a world which was free of physical and social ills, there would be no need for such men as doctors and lawyers, whose business it is to deal with these ills: thus, Thomas hoped there would be no doctors and lawyers in Pennsylvania. His hope was doomed to frustration, and the term "Philadelphia lawyer" later became a byword for the most cunning and devious kind of legal practitioner.

The social ideal expressed in Gabriel Thomas' description of Pennsylvania has, like other ideals, failed of complete fulfillment. Even with the world's highest standard of living, Americans have not escaped the wounds and antagonisms of social conflict and ideological clash. American crime rates and social deviancy do not seem to bear out the hope that Americans would be better-natured or more tender-hearted than people with fewer blessings. American enterprise, in its recklessness, has done much to despoil nature of the riches which Thomas so lovingly described. If the dream has partially failed on the one side, it has also, to some extent, been perverted on the other—perverted into what we call boosterism. The optimism of the promotional literature, its tendency to look on the bright side, and to treat hopes for the future as if they were realities for the present—these qualities lent themselves to the impulse of every crossroads settlement to exaggerate its prospects, to inflate its claims, and to indulge in absurd pretensions. Thus there has been a touch of Gabriel Thomas in every Chamber of Commerce secretary who ever minimized the defects of some booming city or magnified the merits of some nondescript town.

But though the ideal represented by Thomas' Account may have been both frustrated and caricatured, it has historical significance simply because it has dominated the thought of several generations of Americans. The vision of social betterment through widespread economic abundance in a land of plenty has been one of the enduring concepts in the American mind. It has conditioned American attitudes and influenced American responses on many issues. For this reason and in this sense, Gabriel Thomas' little book of nearly three centuries ago, although poorly remembered, may still be entitled to a place among the living documents of American history.

Benjamin Franklin
Father Abraham's Speech,
or, The Way to Wealth
1757

EDITED BY LEONARD W. LABAREE

One of Benjamin Franklin's most successful ventures as a printer was the annual publication of an almanac he called Poor Richard. Beginning with the issue for 1733, he compiled twenty-six of the little pamphlets, ending with the one for 1758. Then, having gone to England as agent of the Pennsylvania Assembly, he turned over the responsibility for future issues to his partner David Hall. Poor Richard met heavy competition from other almanacs, especially in the early years, but it was so brightly entertaining that it soon became immensely popular; in time Franklin was selling about 10,000 copies every year in three editions, adapted respectively to the New England, middle, and southern colonies.

One of its most attractive features was the series of proverbs, maxims, and witty sayings with which Franklin "filled all the little Spaces that occurr'd between the Remarkable Days in the Calendar." Very few of these aphorisms were wholly original; he took nearly all from well-known anthologies of proverbial expressions. But in many instances Franklin rewrote them, shortening them and giving them more snap and point, and adapting them to an American public. They dealt with all sorts of matters: personal conduct, the foibles and weaknesses of human nature, the relations between the sexes, and man and society. Perhaps 10 or 15 per cent were aimed at encouraging industry, careful management, and thrift, as means toward financial success.

Before Franklin set sail for England in June, 1757, he apparently found time to prepare the calendar part of Poor Richard for 1758, including the space-filling proverbs, but he had not yet completed the preface that "Richard Saunders," mathematician and stargazer ("philomath") and ostensible compiler of the almanac, always addressed to the "Courteous Reader," nor had he put together the other "literary" materials that ordinarily filled at least a third of the pamphlet. These jobs he reserved to occupy part of his time during the five-week voyage to England.

As it turned out, the "preface" he wrote while at sea served both purposes. It was long enough to occupy not just the usual second page of the almanac but most of fourteen pages spread through the whole. In it "a plain clean old Man, with white Locks," called Father Abraham, delivered a speech to a crowd waiting to attend a "vendue" or public sale. Great Britain and her colonies were then involved in an expensive war with France, and, in answer to questions on how people could meet the "heavy Taxes" then in force, the old man selected about a hundred proverbs from the previous twenty-five Poor Richard almanacs dealing with industry, prudence, good management, and thrift, and strung them together in a connected discourse.

Franklin completed and dated his "preface" on July 7, 1757; when he landed in England twenty days later he sent it back by the first available ship. Upon receiving the manuscript David Hall set his printers to work and was able to advertise the new almanac as "just published" on October 6.

COURTEOUS READER,

I HAVE HEARD that nothing gives an Author so great Pleasure, as to find his Works respectfully quoted by other learned Authors. This Pleasure I have seldom enjoyed; for tho' I have been, if I may say it without Vanity, an *eminent Author* of Almanacks annually now a full Quarter of a Century, my Brother Authors in the same Way, for what Reason I know not, have ever been very sparing in their Applauses;

The text given here is that of the original pamphlet, the title page of which bore the following data: "*Poor Richard improved: Being an Almanack and Ephemeris . . . for the Year of our Lord 1758: . . .* By Richard Saunders, Philom. Philadelphia: Printed and Sold by B. Franklin, and D. Hall."

and no other Author has taken the least Notice of me, so that did not my Writings produce me some solid *Pudding*, the great Deficiency of *Praise* would have quite discouraged me.

I concluded at length, that the People were the best Judges of my Merit; for they buy my Works; and besides, in my Rambles, where I am not personally known, I have frequently heard one or other of my Adages repeated, with, *as Poor Richard says*, at the End on't; this gave me some Satisfaction, as it showed not only that my Instructions were regarded, but discovered likewise some Respect for my Authority; and I own, that to encourage the Practice of remembering and repeating those wise Sentences, I have sometimes *quoted myself* with great Gravity.

Judge then how much I must have been gratified by an Incident I am going to relate to you. I stopt my Horse lately where a great Number of People were collected at a Vendue of Merchant Goods. The Hour of Sale not being come, they were conversing on the Badness of the Times, and one of the Company call'd to a plain clean old Man, with white Locks, *Pray, Father Abraham, what think you of the Times? Won't these heavy Taxes quite ruin the Country? How shall we be ever able to pay them? What would you advise us to?*—Father Abraham stood up, and reply'd, If you'd have my Advice, I'll give it you in short, for a *Word to the Wise is enough*, and *many Words won't fill a Bushel*, as *Poor Richard says*. They join'd in desiring him to speak his Mind, and gathering round him, he proceeded as follows;

"Friends, says he, and Neighbours, the Taxes are indeed very heavy, and if those laid on by the Government were the only Ones we had to pay, we might more easily discharge them; but we have many others, and much more grievous to some of us. We are taxed twice as much by our *Idleness*, three times as much by our *Pride*, and four times as much by our *Folly*, and from these Taxes the Commissioners cannot ease or deliver us by allowing an Abatement. However let us hearken to good Advice, and something may be done for us; *God helps them that help themselves*, as Poor Richard says, in his Almanack of 1733.

It would be thought a hard Government that should tax its People one tenth Part of their *Time*, to be employed in its Service. But *Idleness* taxes many of us much more, if we reckon all that is spent in absolute *Sloth*, or doing of nothing, with that which is spent in idle Employments or Amusements, that amount to nothing. *Sloth*, by bringing on Diseases, absolutely shortens Life. *Sloth, like Rust, consumes faster than Labour wears, while the used Key is always bright*, as Poor Richard says.

50

But *dost thou love Life, then do not squander Time, for that's the Stuff Life is made of,* as Poor Richard says. How much more than is necessary do we spend in Sleep! forgetting that *The sleeping Fox catches no Poultry,* and that *there will be sleeping enough in the Grave,* as Poor Richard says. If Time be of all Things the most precious, *wasting Time* must be, as Poor Richard says, *the greatest Prodigality,* since, as he elsewhere tells us, *Lost Time is never found again;* and what we call *Time-enough, always proves little enough.* Let us then be up and be doing, and doing to the Purpose; so by Diligence shall we do more with less Perplexity. *Sloth makes all Things difficult, but Industry all easy,* as Poor Richard says; and *He that riseth late, must trot all Day, and shall scarce overtake his Business at Night.* While *Laziness travels so slowly, that Poverty soon overtakes him,* as we read in Poor Richard, who adds, *Drive thy Business, let not that drive thee;* and *Early to Bed, and early to rise, makes a Man healthy, wealthy and wise.*

So what signifies *wishing* and *hoping* for better Times. We may make these Times better if we bestir ourselves. *Industry need not wish,* as Poor Richard says, and *He that lives upon Hope will die fasting. There are no Gains, without Pains;* then *Help Hands, for I have no Lands,* or if I have, they are smartly taxed. And, as Poor Richard likewise observes, *He that hath a Trade hath an Estate,* and *He that hath a Calling hath an Office of Profit and Honour;* but then the *Trade* must be worked at, and the *Calling* well followed, or neither the *Estate,* nor the *Office,* will enable us to pay our Taxes. If we are industrious we shall never starve; for, as Poor Richard says, *At the working Man's House Hunger looks in, but dares not enter.* Nor will the Bailiff nor the Constable enter, for *Industry pays Debts, while Despair encreaseth them,* says Poor Richard. What though you have found no Treasure, nor has any rich Relation left you a Legacy, *Diligence is the Mother of Good luck,* as Poor Richard says, and *God gives all Things to Industry.* Then *plough deep, while Sluggards sleep, and you shall have Corn to sell and to keep,* says Poor Dick. Work while it is called To-day, for you know not how much you may be hindered To-morrow, which makes Poor Richard say, *One To-day is worth two To-morrows;* and farther, *Have you somewhat to do To-morrow, do it To-day.* If you were a Servant, would you not be ashamed that a good Master should catch you idle? Are you then your own Master, *be ashamed to catch yourself idle,* as Poor Dick says. When there is so much to be done for yourself, your Family, your Country, and your gracious King, be up by Peep of Day; *Let not the Sun look down and say, Inglorious here he lies.* Handle your Tools without Mittens; remember that *the Cat in Gloves catches no Mice,* as Poor Richard says. 'Tis true there is much to be done, and perhaps you are weak handed, but stick to it steadily, and you will see great Effects, for *constant Dropping wears away Stones,* and by *Diligence and Patience the Mouse ate in two the Cable;* and *little Strokes fell great Oaks,* as Poor Richard says in his Almanack, the Year I cannot just now remember.

Methinks I hear some of you say, *Must a Man afford himself no Leisure?* I will tell thee, my Friend, what Poor Richard says, *Employ thy Time well if thou meanest to gain Leisure;* and, *since thou art not sure of a Minute, throw not away an Hour.* Leisure, is Time for doing something useful; this Leisure the diligent Man will obtain, but the lazy Man never; so that, as Poor Richard says, a *Life of Leisure and a Life of Laziness are two Things.* Do you imagine that Sloth will afford you more Comfort than Labour? No, for as Poor Richard says, *Trouble springs from Idleness, and grievous Toil from needless Ease. Many without Labour, would live by their* WITS *only, but they break for want of Stock.* Whereas Industry gives Comfort, and Plenty, and Respect: *Fly Pleasures, and they'll follow you. The diligent Spinner has a large Shift,* and *now I have a Sheep and a Cow, every Body bids me Good morrow;* all which is well said by Poor Richard.

But with our Industry, we must likewise be *steady, settled* and *careful,* and oversee our own Affairs *with our own Eyes,* and not trust too much to others; for, as Poor Richard says,

I never saw an oft removed Tree,

Nor yet an oft removed Family,

That throve so well as those that settled be.

And again, *Three Removes is as bad as a Fire,* and again, *Keep thy Shop, and thy Shop will keep thee;* and again, *If you would have your Business done, go; If not, send.* And again,

He that by the Plough would thrive,

Himself must either hold or drive.

And again, *The Eye of a Master will do more Work than both his Hands;* and again, *Want of Care does us more Damage than Want of Knowledge;* and again, *Not to oversee Workmen, is to leave them your Purse open.* Trusting too much to others Care is the Ruin of many; for, as the Almanack says, *In the Affairs of this World, Men are saved, not by Faith, but by the Want of it;* but a Man's own Care is profitable; for, saith Poor Dick, *Learning is to the Studious,* and *Riches to the Careful,* as well as *Power to the Bold*, and *Heaven to the Virtuous*. And farther, *If you would have a faithful Servant, and one that you like, serve yourself*. And again, he adviseth to Circumspection and Care, even in the smallest Matters, because sometimes *a little Neglect may breed great Mischief*; adding, *For want of a Nail the Shoe was lost; for want of a Shoe the Horse was lost; and for want of a Horse the Rider was lost*, being overtaken and slain by the Enemy, all for want of Care about a Horse-shoe Nail.

So much for Industry, my Friends, and Attention to one's own Business; but to these we must add *Frugality*, if we would make our *Industry* more certainly successful. A Man may, if he knows not how to save as he gets, *keep his Nose all his Life to the Grindstone*, and die not worth a *Groat* at last. A *fat Kitchen makes a lean Will*, as Poor Richard says; and,

> *Many Estates are spent in the Getting,*
> *Since Women for Tea forsook Spinning and Knitting,*
> *And Men for Punch forsook Hewing and Splitting.*

If you would be wealthy, says he, in another Almanack, *think of Saving as well as of Getting: The Indies have not made Spain rich, because her Outgoes are greater than her Incomes*. Away then with your expensive Follies, and you will not have so much Cause to complain of hard Times, heavy Taxes, and chargeable Families; for, as Poor Dick says,

> *Women and Wine, Game and Deceit,*
> *Make the Wealth small, and the Wants great.*

And farther, *What maintains one Vice, would bring up two Children.* You may think perhaps, That a *little* Tea, or a *little* Punch now and then, Diet a *little* more costly, Clothes a *little* finer, and a *little* Entertainment now and then, can be no *great* Matter; but remember what Poor Richard says, *Many a Little makes a Mickle*; and farther, *Beware of little Expences; a small Leak will sink a great Ship*; and again, *Who Dainties love, shall Beggars prove*; and moreover, *Fools make Feasts, and wise Men eat them.*

Here you are all got together at this Vendue of *Fineries* and *Knicknacks*. You call them *Goods*, but if you do not take Care, they will prove *Evils* to some of you. You expect they will be sold *cheap*, and perhaps they may for less than they cost; but if you have no Occasion for them, they must be *dear* to you. Remember what Poor Richard says, *Buy what thou hast no Need of, and ere long thou shalt sell thy Necessaries*. And again, *At a great Pennyworth pause a while*: He means, that perhaps the Cheapness is *apparent* only, and not *real*; or the Bargain, by straitning thee in thy Business, may do thee more Harm than Good. For in another Place he says, *Many have been ruined by buying good Pennyworths*. Again, Poor Richard says, *'Tis foolish to lay out Money in a Purchase of Repentance*; and yet this Folly is practised every Day at Vendues, for want of minding the Almanack. *Wise Men*, as Poor Dick says, *learn by others Harms, Fools scarcely by their own*; but, *Felix quem faciunt aliena Pericula cautum*. Many a one, for the Sake of Finery on the Back, have gone with a hungry Belly, and half starved their Families; *Silks and Sattins, Scarlet and Velvets*, as Poor Richard says, *put out the Kitchen Fire*. These are not the *Necessaries* of Life; they can scarcely be called the *Conveniencies*, and yet only because they look pretty, how many *want* to *have* them. The *artificial* Wants of Mankind thus become more numerous than the *natural*; and, as Poor Dick says, *For one poor Person, there are an hundred* indigent. By these, and other Extravagancies, the Genteel are reduced to Poverty, and forced to borrow of those whom they formerly despised, but who through *Industry* and *Frugality* have maintained their Standing; in which Case it appears plainly, that a *Ploughman on his Legs is higher than a Gentleman on his Knees*, as Poor Richard says. Perhaps they have had a small Estate left them, which they knew not the Getting of; they think *'tis Day, and will never be Night*; that a little to be spent out of *so much*, is not worth minding; (*a Child and a Fool*, as Poor Richard says, *imagine Twenty Shillings and Twenty Years can never be spent*) but, *always taking out of the Meal-tub, and never putting in, soon comes to the Bottom*; then, as Poor Dick says, *When the Well's dry, they know the Worth of Water*. But this they might have known before, if they had taken his Advice; *If you would know the Value of Money, go and try to borrow some*; for, *he that goes a borrowing goes a sorrowing*; and indeed so does he that lends to such People, when he goes *to get it in again*. Poor Dick farther advises, and says,

Fond Pride of Dress, *is sure a very Curse*;
E'er Fancy *you consult, consult your Purse*.

And again, *Pride is as loud a Beggar as Want, and a great deal more saucy*. When you have bought one fine Thing you must buy ten more, that your Appearance may be all of a Piece; but Poor Dick says, *'Tis easier to suppress the first Desire, than to satisfy all that follow it*. And 'tis as truly Folly for the Poor to ape the Rich, as for the Frog to swell, in order to equal the Ox.

> *Great Estates may venture more,*
> *But little Boats should keep near Shore.*

'Tis however a Folly soon punished; for *Pride that dines on Vanity sups on Contempt,* as Poor Richard says. And in another Place, *Pride breakfasted with Plenty, dined with Poverty, and supped with Infamy.* And after all, of what Use is this *Pride of Appearance,* for which so much is risked, so much is suffered? It cannot promote Health, or ease Pain; it makes no Increase of Merit in the Person, it creates Envy, it hastens Misfortune.

> *What is a Butterfly? At best*
> *He's but a Caterpillar drest.*
> *The gaudy Fop's his Picture just,*

as Poor Richard says.

But what Madness must it be to *run in Debt* for these Superfluities! We are offered, by the Terms of this Vendue, *Six Months Credit;* and that perhaps has induced some of us to attend it, because we cannot spare the ready Money, and hope now to be fine without it. But, ah, think what you do when you run in Debt; *You give to another Power over your Liberty.* If you cannot pay at the Time, you will be ashamed to see your Creditor; you will be in Fear when you speak to him; you will make poor pitiful sneaking Excuses, and by Degrees come to lose your Veracity, and sink into base downright lying; for, as Poor Richard says, *The second Vice is Lying, the first is running in Debt.* And again, to the same Purpose, *Lying rides upon Debt's Back.* Whereas a freeborn Englishman ought not to be ashamed or afraid to see or speak to any Man living. But Poverty often deprives a Man of all Spirit and Virtue: *'Tis hard for an empty Bag to stand upright,* as Poor Richard truly says. What would you think of that Prince, or that Government, who should issue an Edict forbidding you to dress like a Gentleman or a Gentlewoman, on Pain of Imprisonment or Servitude? Would you not say, that you are free, have a Right to dress as you please, and that such an Edict would be a Breach of your Privileges, and such a Government tyrannical? And yet you are about to put yourself under that Tyranny when you run in Debt for such Dress! Your Creditor has Authority at his Pleasure to deprive you of your Liberty, by confining you in Gaol for Life, or to sell you for a Servant, if you should not be able to pay him! When you have got your Bargain, you may, perhaps, think little of Payment; but *Creditors,* Poor Richard tells us, *have better Memories than Debtors;* and in another Place says, *Creditors are a superstitious Sect, great*

Observers of set Days and Times. The Day comes round before you are aware, and the Demand is made before your are prepared to satisfy it. Or if you bear your Debt in Mind, the Term which at first seemed so long, will, as it lessens, appear extreamly short. *Time* will seem to have added Wings to his Heels as well as Shoulders. *Those have a short Lent,* saith Poor Richard, *who owe Money to be paid at Easter.* Then since, as he says, *The Borrower is a Slave to the Lender, and the Debtor to the Creditor,* disdain the Chain, preserve your Freedom; and maintain your Independency: Be *industrious* and *free*; be *frugal* and *free.* At present, perhaps, you may think yourself in thriving Circumstances, and that you can bear a little Extravagance without Injury; but,

For Age and Want, save while you may;
No Morning Sun lasts a whole Day,

as Poor Richard says. Gain may be temporary and uncertain, but ever while you live, Expence is constant and certain; and *'tis easier to build two Chimnies than to keep one in Fuel,* as Poor Richard says. So *rather go to Bed supperless than rise in Debt.*

Get what you can, and what you get hold;
'Tis the Stone that will turn all your Lead into Gold,

as Poor Richard says. And when you have got the Philosopher's Stone, sure you will no longer complain of bad Times, or the Difficulty of paying Taxes.

This Doctrine, my Friends, is *Reason* and *Wisdom*; but after all, do not depend too much upon your own *Industry,* and *Frugality,* and *Prudence,* though excellent Things, for they may all be blasted without the Blessing of Heaven; and therefore ask that Blessing humbly, and be not uncharitable to those that at present seem to want it, but comfort and help them. Remember Job suffered, and was afterwards prosperous.

And now to conclude, *Experience keeps a dear School, but Fools will learn in no other, and scarce in that;* for it is true, *we may give Advice, but we cannot give Conduct,* as Poor Richard says: However, remember this, *They that won't be counselled, can't be helped,* as Poor Richard says: And farther, That *if you will not hear Reason, she'll surely rap your Knuckles.*"

Thus the old Gentleman ended his Harangue. The People heard it, and approved the Doctrine, and immediately practised the contrary, just as if it had been a common Sermon; for the Vendue opened, and they began to buy extravagantly, notwithstanding all his Cautions, and their own Fear of Taxes. I found the good Man had thoroughly studied my Almanacks, and digested all I had dropt on those Topicks during the Course of Five-and-twenty Years. The frequent Mention he made of me must have tired any one else, but my Vanity was wonderfully delighted with it, though I was conscious that not a tenth Part of the Wisdom was my own which he ascribed to me, but rather the *Gleanings* I had made of the Sense of all Ages and Nations. However, I resolved to be the better for the Echo of it; and though I had at first determined to buy Stuff for a new Coat, I went away resolved to wear my old One a little longer. *Reader*, if thou wilt do the same, thy Profit will be as great as mine. I am, as ever, Thine to serve thee, RICHARD SAUNDERS. July 7, 1757.

Franklin's nephew, Benjamin Mecom, who had just started a new printing office in Boston, reproduced this extended preface, together with seven shorter "curious Pieces of Writing," as a twenty-four-page pamphlet, March 30, 1758; he reissued the preface alone in the autumn of 1760. Other printings in New London and New Haven followed soon after. In England the March, 1758, issue of the Grand Magazine of Universal Intelligence, which appeared a day or two after Mecom's first reprinting, also contained the piece, and it was reproduced almost at once in the London Chronicle. A Mrs. Ann Slack included it in 1770 in an anthology she called enticingly The Pleasing Instructor or Entertaining Moralist, and the next year the popular Gentleman's Magazine published it in the February issue, this time cut to about five-sixths of its original length. These earliest reprintings attached various titles to Franklin's preface, but in 1773 appeared the first of the hundreds of editions under the name by which it has been best known ever since: "The Way to Wealth." This happily chosen phrase was obviously taken from a passage in "Advice to a Young Tradesman," a Franklin composition of 1748: "In short, the Way to Wealth, if you desire it, is as plain as the Way to Market. It depends chiefly on two words, INDUSTRY and FRUGALITY." The new version was about the same length as that in Gentleman's Magazine, though not all the cuts and other changes were identical. From this time on printings in the British Isles and America rapidly

increased in number, sometimes using the full original form, more often the new, shorter version, including the new title.

Translations also began to appear, the first in Paris in 1773. Before the end of the century *Father Abraham's* speech was available also in Dutch, Gaelic, German, Italian, and Swedish. A French edition of 1777 (soon after Franklin had arrived in Paris on his diplomatic mission) gave the piece a new title, one destined to become as familiar in France, and in American naval history through the name of John Paul Jones's famous ship, as "The Way to Wealth" was becoming in England: La Science du Bonhomme Richard, ou moyen facile de payer les impôts. By 1800, at least 36 English-language reprints had been published in American towns and cities and 64 in the British Isles, and there had been 45 issues in other languages. It had appeared as a separate pamphlet, a chapbook, or a broadside to be hung up on the wall of a room, in anthologies, magazines, school readers, and other almanacs.

The popularity of the work continued. How many times it has been reprinted since 1800 nobody knows. Certainly the total runs into several hundred; perhaps it is as high as a thousand. Translations into ten additional languages are definitely known, including Catalan, Chinese, Greek, Hungarian, Japanese, Polish, and Russian. Perhaps many others would turn up in a systematic search of distant libraries. All in all, it seems probable that *Father Abraham's* speech has been reprinted more often than any other composition by an individual American, with the exception of that much shorter speech a very different Abraham once delivered at Gettysburg.

It was mentioned earlier that few of Poor Richard's sayings were strictly original with Franklin, yet because of the widespread and continued popularity of "The Way to Wealth" many of them have become part of the folklore only because Father Abraham repeated them. And, because Franklin chose to use in the compilation only those of his maxims which inculcated the somewhat materialistic "virtues" of hard work, diligence, careful management of one's affairs, and thrift, the public conception of his sense of values has been greatly distorted. He did believe, and many times he said so, that a young person wanting to get on in the world ought to plan carefully, work hard, and avoid extravagance and waste; but, as he also taught and as he showed in his own life, these practices ought not to be regarded as ends in themselves, but merely as means to a larger end, freedom and capacity to serve one's fellows. Witness the fact that after accumulating a modest competence, as wealth was measured in his day, he retired from active business as a printer at the age of forty-two to devote himself thereafter to science and public service at home and abroad. In a sense, too, in his compilation of sayings he was giving a highly secularized homily on the Puritan and Quaker "duty" of industriously pursuing one's calling.

It is not surprising, however, that he has been misunderstood, that he has been called the Apostle of Thrift, that, for example, the savings banks of the country have designated the week in January which includes his birthday as National Thrift Week. Nor is it surprising that various commentators have held views of "The Way to Wealth" which derive from their own attitudes toward the materialistic aspects of modern society. D. H. Lawrence complained that, having been brought up on "those Poor Richard tags," it had taken him "many years and countless smarts to get out of the barbed wire moral enclosure that Poor Richard rigged up." By contrast, a canny eighteenth-century Scot declared enthusiastically that Franklin's piece reflected "the quintessence of the wisdom accumulated in all the ages." However one may regard such opposing judgments as these, it is clear that "The Way to Wealth" has enriched the English language with many pithy sayings, and that the attitudes it reflects so entertainingly have played an important part, for better or for worse, in the development of the society in which we live.

Logan's Speech

1774

EDITED BY WILCOMB E. WASHBURN

In October of 1774, near the banks of the Scioto River in Ohio, the Mingo Indian leader Tachnechdorus, whom the whites called Logan, walked with General John Gibson, the Virginia emissary sent to arrange for peace with the Indians following their unsuccessful attempt to resist white settlement in the Ohio Valley. They approached a wooded spot close by the Indian camp, where Logan, "after shedding abundance of tears," spoke in his own language words that were to be projected far beyond that place and time. General Gibson, related by marriage to Logan, returned to the English camp and delivered the message, in translation, to Lord Dunmore, the royal governor of Virginia. Logan's speech was so striking and affecting that, according to Thomas Jefferson, "it became the theme of every conversation, in Williamsburgh particularly, and generally, indeed, wheresoever any of the officers resided or resorted." Jefferson learned it in Williamsburg at the time and recorded it in his pocket account book. The speech was published in the Virginia Gazette and in other periodicals in America and abroad.

In 1785 Jefferson privately printed in Paris several copies of his Notes on the State of Virginia, which he had composed a few years earlier. In this book, he attempted to refute the assertions of several European philosophers that, as he put it, there was "something in the soil, climate and other circumstances of America, which occasion animal nature to degenerate, not excepting even the man, native or adoptive, physical or moral." In rejecting the theory, Jefferson adduced Logan's speech as evidence of the high talents of the aborigines of the country.

60

In 1787 a regularly published, enlarged, and corrected edition of the Notes was brought out with Jefferson's approval. In 1797 a Maryland political opponent of Jefferson, Luther Martin, attacked him in the public press for accepting Logan's charge that Michael Cresap, Martin's father-in-law, was responsible for the murder of Logan's family. At the same time, Martin ridiculed Logan's speech as a fabrication. Jefferson, though declining to answer the attack in the newspapers, immediately wrote to General Gibson and others who were familiar with the affair, and obtained sworn depositions concerning it, which he published, in 1800, in an Appendix to the Notes. From the evidence gathered, Jefferson concluded that his first account had been essentially correct, though Logan's family may not have been among Cresap's victims, as Logan himself believed and as reported in the accounts upon which Jefferson relied at the time. Jefferson also secured additional evidence to support the authenticity of Logan's speech. In the light of his researches into the affair he prepared a revised account for later editions of the Notes on Virginia.

IN THE SPRING of the year 1774, a robbery was committed by some Indians on certain land adventurers on the River Ohio. The whites in that quarter, according to their custom, undertook to punish this outrage in a summary way. Captain Michael Cresap, and a certain Daniel Greathouse, leading on these parties, surprized, at different times, travelling and hunting parties of the Indians, having their women and children with them, and murdered many. Among these were unfortunately the family of Logan, a chief celebrated in peace and war, and long distinguished as the friend of the whites. This unworthy return provoked his vengeance. He accordingly signalized himself in the war which ensued. In the autumn of the same year a decisive battle was fought at the mouth of the Great Kanhaway, between the collected forces of the Shawanese, Mingoes and Delawares, and a detachment of the Virginia militia. The Indians were defeated and sued for peace. Logan, however, disdained to be seen among the suppliants. But lest the sincerity of a treaty should be distrusted, from which so distinguished a

The account of Logan and his speech is reprinted here from Jefferson's *Notes on Virginia* (New York, 1801).

chief absented himself, he sent, by a messenger [General Gibson], the following speech, to be delivered to lord Dunmore.

I appeal to any white man to say, if ever he entered Logan's cabin hungry, and he gave him not meat: if ever he came cold and naked, and he cloathed him not. During the course of the last long and bloody war Logan remained idle in his cabin, an advocate for peace. Such was my love for the whites, that my countrymen pointed as they passed, and said, 'Logan is the friend of white men.' I had even thought to have lived with you, but for the injuries of one man. Colonel Cresap, the last spring, in cold blood, and unprovoked, murdered all the relations of Logan, not even sparing my women and children. There runs not a drop of my blood in the veins of any living creature. This called on me for revenge. I have sought it: I have killed many: I have fully glutted my vengeance: for my country I rejoice at the beams of peace. But do not harbour a thought that mine is the joy of fear. Logan never felt fear. He will not turn on his heel to save his life. Who is there to mourn for Logan?—Not one.

The impact of Logan's speech, as previously noted, was immediate in Williamsburg and elsewhere. Jefferson's retelling of the story gave it a further impetus. His account was widely reprinted in school readers throughout the last half of the eighteenth century and the first half of the nineteenth century. When Logan's story appeared in the early editions of Dr. William Holmes McGuffey's Eclectic Fourth Reader: containing elegant extracts in prose and poetry, from the best American and English writers (Cincinnati, 1838), it started on a career that was to make it familiar to millions more American school children because of the incredible sales of the McGuffey Readers, estimated at more than 122,000,000 between 1836 and 1920. The story appeared also in the Fifth Reader prepared by Alexander H. McGuffey, a younger brother of Dr. McGuffey. Although the speech was published in various editions of the Readers throughout the nineteenth century and into the twentieth, its use was heaviest in the pre–Civil War period.

Logan and his speech were remembered in other ways. On July 28, 1841, at an assemblage of pioneers and citizens of the Scioto Valley, meeting at Westfall, in Pickaway County, the Logan Historical Society was formed to "perpetuate those principles for which Logan suffered the sneers of his red brethren, by the erection of a monument to his memory, and by the careful collection, safe keeping, and lasting preservation, for the use of posterity, [of] the many scattered but interesting fragments of the history of the early settlements of the western country, . . ." Logan's speech, as reported by Jefferson, was to be "fully engraved in gilt letters on said monument," and the hope was expressed of finding the remains of the Indian statesman. Other monuments were erected at his presumed birthplace in Auburn, New York, and under an elm near Circleville, Ohio, where local tradition assumed his speech to have been made.

Throughout the nineteenth century, friends of Cresap and enemies of Jefferson, following the lead of Luther Martin, sought to impeach the veracity of Jefferson and of his Indian subject. Typical of such critics was John J. Jacob, who, in A Biographical Sketch of the Life of the Late Captain Michael Cresap (Cumberland, Maryland, 1826, reprinted in Cincinnati, 1866), insisted that "your Logan speech, your fine specimen of Indian oratory, is a lie, a counterfeit, and never in fact had any existence as a real Indian speech!" In 1903, M. Louise Stevenson, in an uncritical filiopietistic defense of Cresap, concluded that "it is high time that this 'conversation' should be eliminated from the school books. . . ." And, in fact, it is rare to find, in the school books of the twentieth century, the celebrated speech of Logan. Indeed, such was the force of the attack on the speech that even the detail, implicit in the accounts of both Jefferson and General Gibson, the translator, that Logan delivered his message in his native tongue was forgotten or challenged.

The language of the translation, with its overtones of biblical power and directness, made a strong impression on a people whose principal literary inheritance was the Bible. It is only in the present age, in which biblical rhetoric is lost amidst the blaring of "commercials," the elephantine obscurity of "governmentese," and the saccharine hypocrisy of social chit-chat, that Logan's prose is beginning to seem archaic, if it is remembered at all.

But though the words may be forgotten, Logan's message remains imprinted in the minds of white Americans. Logan's history is, in microcosm, the history of the Indian-white relationship. Its outline follows the conventional pattern: (1) initial befriending of whites by the Indians; (2) personal outrage against the Indians by frontier ruffians; (3) seeking of violent revenge by the Indians, since other avenues were closed to them; (4) a formal retaliatory military expedition from the

63

interior to "put down" the "Indian uprising"; and (5) the defeat of the Indians followed by their loss of land and spirit.

Logan's story is the story of the American Indian from Jamestown and Plymouth Rock forward. It symbolizes the death of one society as the Declaration of Independence marks the creation of a new one. It is a tragedy because, given human behavior, it was inevitable, though, given human ideals, it was unnecessary. The American may not have a material past of castles and monuments, but he has a psychological past of wrongs committed and not expiated. The recency of those wrongs gives our emotional past greater strength, as the lack of ruins gives our material past less significance. As mythos, Logan's story has become part of the American experience—not as a fable, but as a poetic rendering of a historic process. That historic process has incorporated Logan's past into America's past and given a national answer to Logan's private plaint: "Who is there to mourn for Logan?"

Thomas Jefferson
The Declaration of Independence
1776

EDITED BY HENRY STEELE COMMAGER

It was in March of 1775 that Patrick Henry made his famous appeal to the Virginia Convention to endorse those resolutions from Fairfax County "that the Colony be immediately put into a posture of defense." "Gentlemen may cry Peace, Peace"—so William Wirt later reported it—"but there is no peace. The war is actually begun. The next gale that sweeps from the north will bring to our ears the clash of resounding arms! Our brethren are already in the field! Why stand we here idle?"

The next gale did bring the news of Lexington and Concord, yet there was still to be Ticonderoga and the invasion of Canada, Bunker Hill and the siege of Boston, there was still to be the Declaration of the Causes and Necessity of Taking Up Arms, the Olive Branch petition, the Royal Proclamation of Rebellion, before Americans generally were ready to consider independence. Not until the winter and spring of 1776 did the intransigence of George III, the failure of peace overtures to materialize, the ever-increasing scope of military operations, and the influence of Thomas Paine's revolutionary pamphlet Common Sense combine to bring about a swift change in American opinion.

Finally, during May and June, the continuing deliberations and debates of the Continental Congress over the issue of independence for the American colonies reached a high point. On June 7, Richard Henry Lee, "the Cicero of America," introduced three resolutions calling for independence, foreign alliances, and confederation. After spirited debate, the Congress voted to postpone a decision for three weeks, and on June 11 appointed a committee to "prepare a declaration" of independence. The members of this committee were Thomas Jefferson, Dr. Franklin, John Adams, Roger Sherman—all strong advocates of independence— and Robert Livingston of New York, a moderate.

Thomas Jefferson had come up to the Continental Congress the previous year, bringing with him, as John Adams recalled, "a reputation for literature, science, and a happy talent of composition. "His writings," Adams added, were "remarkable for the peculiar felicity of expression." In the Congress he had contributed the answer to Lord North's proposal for reconciliation, and a substantial part of the Declaration of the Causes and Necessity of Taking Up Arms. Back to Virginia in late December, he had not returned to Philadelphia until May 14, 1776, just in time for the great debates on independence.

Then the committee appointed to draw up a declaration of independence asked him to draft the document. John Adams, to be sure, remembered it differently. There was a subcommittee of two—Jefferson and himself—and it was he who persuaded Jefferson to take on the task of providing the first draft, with the improbable argument that "you can write ten times better than I can." Jefferson himself recalled nothing of a subcommittee, but only that the committee "unanimously" asked him to prepare a draft. While there is no precisely contemporary account of the writing of the Declaration, we can reconstruct it with some accuracy, chiefly from Jefferson's recollections, written shortly after the event. We know that Jefferson wrote the Declaration in some two weeks, for it was worked over by the committee and submitted to the Congress on June 28. We know that he wrote it at a desk in a second-floor parlor of the house of a young German bricklayer named Graff. We have his word for it that in the writing he "turned neither to book nor pamphlet" but that "all its authority rests . . . on the harmonizing sentiments of the day, whether expressed in conversation, in letters, printed essays, or in the elementary books of public right, as Aristotle, Cicero, Locke, Sidney, etc." We know too, though Jefferson himself fails to mention the matter, that the body of the Declaration—the statement of that "long train of abuses and usurpations" which evinced "a design to reduce them under absolute despotism"—was taken over from the parallel list of grievances which he had written into his draft Constitution for Virginia only a few weeks earlier. And we may confidently accept Jefferson's statement made, to be sure, almost fifty years later, that the object of the Declaration was "an appeal to the tribunal of the world," that in the Declaration he undertook "to place before mankind the common sense of the subject, in terms so plain and firm as to command their assent," and that "neither aiming at originality of principle or sentiment . . . it was intended to be an expression of the American mind, and to give to that expression the proper tone and spirit called for by the occasion."

We have every reason to believe that the committee, or some of its members, met frequently to discuss what was to go into the proposed declaration, and we know that Jefferson submitted it, privately, to both Dr. Franklin and John Adams. Franklin, it appears, made five changes, and Adams two, largely verbal. Jefferson himself revised his first draft, doubtless in the light of criticisms and suggestions from Franklin and Adams, and made no less than sixteen changes. In addition he added three paragraphs to his original draft, one of which—that which referred to "calling legislative bodies at places unusual, etc."—was pretty clearly suggested by Adams. On June 28 Jefferson's draft was finished, and submitted to the Congress.

After herculean efforts by the radical delegates to intimidate the intransigents and convert the moderates, on July 2 the Congress, approving Lee's resolution, voted "unanimously" for independence, with the New York delegates abstaining. With Lee's resolution out of the way, the Congress turned at once to a consideration of Jefferson's draft of a declaration of independence, and discussed and debated it on the afternoon of July 2, on July 3, and, apparently, on much of July 4 as well. We have no record of these debates, except those by Jefferson himself, which are fragmentary and almost desultory. In the course of the discussion the Congress made fairly substantial changes in the document, mostly in striking out Jefferson's highly emotional denunciation of slavery and the slave trade, and some sharp animadversions on George III.

Writing some time later—we do not know precisely when—Jefferson asserted that "on the evening of [the fourth of July] . . . the declaration was reported by the commee., agreed to by the house, and signed by every member present except Mr. Dickinson." Whether this was a lapse of memory, or whether there may have been two signings, we do not know with certainty. The evidence, however, is strongly against a signing on July 4. On that day the Congress ordered that the Declaration be "authenticated and printed." On July 19 it further resolved that the Declaration "be fairly engrossed on parchment" and that the same, "when engrossed, be signed by every member of Congress." Not until

67

August 2 do we read that "the declaration of independence being engrossed and compared at the table was signed by the members." At least one additional name was added as late as November. And not for almost six months were the names of the signers published. On January 18, 1777, an authenticated copy of the Declaration, with the names of members of the Congress subscribing to the same, was sent to each of the United States.

W HEN in the Course of human events, it becomes necessary for one people to dissolve the political bands which have connected them with another, and to assume among the powers of the earth, the separate and equal station to which the Laws of Nature and of Nature's God entitle them, a decent respect to the opinions of mankind requires that they should declare the causes which impel them to the separation. We hold these truths to be self-evident, that all men are created equal, that they are endowed by their Creator with certain unalienable Rights, that among these are Life, Liberty and the pursuit of Happiness. That to secure these rights, Governments are instituted among Men, deriving their just powers from the consent of the governed, That whenever any Form of Government becomes destructive of these ends it is the Right of the People to alter or to abolish it, and to institute new Government, laying its foundation on such principles and organizing its powers in such form, as to them shall seem most likely to effect their Safety and Happiness. Prudence, indeed, will dictate that Governments long established should not be changed for light and transient causes; and accordingly all experience hath shewn, that mankind are more disposed to suffer, while evils are sufferable, than to right themselves by abolishing the forms to which they are accustomed. But when a long train of abuses and usurpations, pursuing invariably the same Object evinces a design to reduce them under absolute Despotism, it is their right, it is their duty, to throw off such Government, and to provide new Guards for their future security. Such

The text is reprinted here from *The Papers of Thomas Jefferson,* edited by Julian P. Boyd (Princeton: Princeton University Press, 1950————). This is the text of the parchment copy of the Declaration (now in the National Archives) which was signed on August 2, 1776. It is generally accepted as the most authentic of various copies.

has been the patient sufferance of these Colonies; and such is now the necessity which constrains them to alter their former Systems of Government. The history of the present King of Great Britain is a history of repeated injuries and usurpations, all having in direct object the establishment of an absolute Tyranny over these States. To prove this, let Facts be submitted to a candid world. He has refused his Assent to Laws, the most wholesome and necessary for the public good. He has forbidden his Governors to pass Laws of immediate and pressing importance, unless suspended in their operation till his Assent should be obtained; and when so suspended, he has utterly neglected to attend to them. He has refused to pass other Laws for the accommodation of large districts of people, unless those people would relinquish the right of Representation in the Legislature, a right inestimable to them and formidable to tyrants only. He has called together legislative bodies at places unusual, uncomfortable, and distant from the depository of their public Records, for the sole purpose of fatiguing them into compliance with his measures. He has dissolved Representative Houses repeatedly, for opposing with manly firmness his invasions on the rights of the people. He has refused for a long time, after such dissolutions, to cause others to be elected; whereby the Legislative powers, incapable of Annihilation, have returned to the People at large for their exercise; the State remaining in the mean time exposed to all the dangers of invasion from without, and convulsions within. He has endeavoured to prevent the population of these States; for that purpose obstructing the Laws for Naturalization of Foreigners; refusing to pass others to encourage their migrations hither, and raising the conditions of new Appropriations of Lands. He has obstructed the Administration of Justice, by refusing his Assent to Laws for establishing Judiciary powers. He has made Judges dependent on his Will alone, for the tenure of their offices, and the amount and payment of their salaries. He has erected a multitude of New Offices, and sent hither swarms of Officers to harrass our people, and eat out their substance. He has kept among us, in times of peace, standing Armies without the Consent of our legislatures. He has affected to render the Military independent of and superior to the Civil power. He has combined with others to subject us to a jurisdiction foreign to our constitution, and unacknowledged by our laws; giving his Assent to their Acts of pretended Legislation: For Quartering large bodies of armed troops among us: For protecting them, by a mock Trial, from punishment for any Murders which they should commit on the Inhabitants of these States: For cutting off our Trade with all parts of the world: For imposing Taxes on us without our Consent: For depriving us in many cases of the benefits of Trial by Jury: For transporting us beyond Seas to be tried for pretended offences: For abolishing the free System of English Laws in a neighbouring Province, establishing therein an Arbitrary government, and enlarging its Boundaries so as to render it at once an example and fit instrument for introducing the same absolute rule into these Colonies: For taking away our Charters, abolishing our most valuable Laws, and altering fundamentally the Forms of our Governments: For suspending our own Legislatures, and declaring themselves invested with power to legislate for us in all cases whatsoever. He has abdicated Government here, by declaring us out of his Protection and waging War against us. He has plundered our seas, ravaged our Coasts, burnt our towns, and destroyed the Lives of our people. He is at this time transporting large Armies of foreign Mercenaries to compleat the works of death, desolation and tyranny, already begun with circumstances of Cruelty & perfidy scarcely paralleled in the most barbarous ages, and totally unworthy the Head of a civilized nation. He has constrained our fellow Citizens taken Captive on the high Seas to bear Arms against their Country, to become the executioners of their friends and Brethren, or to fall themselves by their Hands. He has excited domestic insurrections amongst us, and has endeavoured to bring on the inhabitants of our frontiers, the merciless Indian Savages, whose known rule of warfare, is an undistinguished destruction of all ages, sexes and conditions. In every stage of these Oppressions We have Petitioned for Redress in the most humble terms: Our repeated Petitions have been answered only by repeated injury. A Prince, whose character is thus marked by every act which may define a Tyrant, is unfit to be the ruler of a free people. Nor have We been wanting in attentions to our Brittish brethren. We have warned them from time to time of attempts by their legislature to extend an unwarrantable jurisdiction over us. We have reminded them of the circumstances of our emigration and settlement here. We have appealed to their native justice and magnanimity, and we have conjured them by the ties of our common kindred to disavow these usurpations, which, would inevitably interrupt our connections and correspondence. They too have been deaf to the voice of justice and of consanguinity. We must, therefore, acquiesce in the necessity, which denounces our Separation, and hold them, as we hold the rest of mankind, Enemies in War, in Peace Friends.

We, therefore, the Representatives of the united States of America, in General Congress, Assembled, appealing to the Supreme Judge of the world for the rectitude of our intentions, do, in the Name, and by Authority of the good People of these Colonies, solemnly publish and declare, That these United Colonies are, and of Right ought to be Free and Independent States; that they are Absolved from all Allegiance to the British Crown, and that all political connection between them and the State of Great Britain, is and ought to be totally dissolved; and that as Free and Independent States, they have full Power to levy War, conclude Peace, contract Alliances, establish Commerce, and to do all other Acts and Things which Independent States may of right do. And for the support of this Declaration, with a firm reliance on the protection of divine Providence, we mutually pledge to each other our Lives, our Fortunes and our sacred Honor.

John Hancock

Button Gwinnett	Thos. Nelson jr.	Richd. Stockton
Lyman Hall	Francis Lightfoot Lee	Jno Witherspoon
Geo Walton.	Carter Braxton	Fras. Hopkinson
Wm. Hooper	Robt. Morris	John Hart
Joseph Hewes,	Benjamin Rush	Abra Clark
John Penn	Benja. Franklin	Josiah Bartlett
Edward Rutledge.	John Morton	Wm: Whipple
Thos. Heyward Junr.	Geo Clymer	Saml. Adams
Thomas Lynch Junr.	Jas. Smith.	John Adams
Arthur Middleton	Geo. Taylor	Robt. Treat Paine
Samuel Chase	James Wilson	Elbridge Gerry
Wm. Paca	Geo. Ross	Step. Hopkins
Thos. Stone	Cæsar Rodney	William Ellery
Charles Carroll of	Geo Read	Roger Sherman
Carrollton	Tho M:Kean	Saml. Huntington
George Wythe	Wm. Floyd	Wm. Williams
Richard Henry Lee	Phil. Livingston	Oliver Wolcott
Th: Jefferson	Frans. Lewis	Matthew Thornton
Benja. Harrison	Lewis Morris	

To members of the Continental Congress, and to most of their contemporaries, it was the "facts submitted to a candid world" that were important about the Declaration of Independence. Here, after all, was

71

the argument on which the signers proposed to rest their case; here was the evidence that George III, and Parliament—though that body was not mentioned in the Declaration—did indeed propose "the establishment of an absolute Tyranny over these States." But with the passing of years these "facts," once so sensational and so persuasive, have lost their luster and their pride of place, and become dim and elusive. Interest has shifted to the preamble, to the statement of political philosophy with which Jefferson introduced his list of grievances. Nothing in the original Resolution of June 11 required Jefferson and his committee to formulate a statement of political principles as a preamble to the actual declaration of independence. It was because members of that committee—notably Jefferson and Franklin and Adams—were children of the Enlightenment and adopted naturally the vocabulary of political philosophy, that we have what has proved the most memorable and influential part of the Declaration.

What we have in the condensed, lucid, and eloquent preamble is nothing less than a comprehensive philosophy of politics. The principles of this philosophy are almost too familiar for repetition: And Jefferson does not undertake to prove the validity of these principles. The truths which he here announces are "self-evident," such as all men of good sense and good will would inevitably endorse. That is why it was quite safe to display a "decent respect to the opinions of mankind."

Here, in summary form, are the principles:

First, that all men are created equal.

Second, that they are endowed with "unalienable" rights.

Third, that these rights include "life, liberty, and the pursuit of happiness."

Fourth, that it was to "secure" these rights that governments were instituted among men.

Fifth, that such governments "derive" (perhaps the most crucial word in the Declaration) their powers—their "just" powers—from the consent of the governed.

Sixth, that, when government becomes destructive of these ends men may "alter or abolish" it.

Seventh, that they have a right to "institute" new governments designed to "effect their safety and happiness."

We need not inquire here into the sources of this philosophy; that mine has been sufficiently quarried. Certainly it was not original with

Jefferson, nor with the revolutionary generation, but was, as Jefferson himself admitted, deeply rooted in the past. Further, as Jefferson also observed, borrowing, perhaps unconsciously, from Tom Paine, the ideas of the Declaration were "the common sense" of the matter.

Americans did not originate or invent these principles, but they did something more: they institutionalized them. As John Adams wrote, "they realized the doctrines of the wisest writers." The concept of natural and inalienable rights was as old as philosophy itself and, in the hands of a James Otis or a Samuel Adams, had proved immensely useful in the debate with the Mother Country over the question whether the "original" rights of the colonists could be forfeited, or "alienated" by ignorance or neglect. Now Americans, for the first time in history, translated this concept of natural rights into constitutional guarantees. Philosophers had long asserted that all power is limited, that no government could exercise unlimited power—indeed, according to the Reverend Jonathan Mayhew, God himself was "limited by law . . . and the everlasting tables of right reason." The Americans, however, were the first to set up governments which were, in fact, limited—limited by written constitutions, bills of rights, separation of powers, checks and balances, and, in time, judicial review. Philosophers had said, or imagined, that men originally made government by compact, or contract. The Americans contrived the fundamental mechanism whereby men did, in fact, come together (even in a state of nature) and set up government by compact—the constitutional convention. This famous institution not only provided the mechanism whereby government could "derive" its powers from the "consent of the governed," but also, for the first time in history, it legalized revolution.

The implementation of other parts of the Preamble was more difficult, if for no other reason than that the words themselves elude definition. What did Jefferson, what did members of the Congress mean by such phrases as "created equal" and "pursuit of happiness"? This is not only a difficult question; it is an unfair question. "No language," as Madison was later to remark, "is so copious as to supply words and phrases for every complex idea, or so correct as not to include many equivocally denoting different ideas." He was speaking of the Constitution and it is relevant to keep in mind that Justices of the Supreme Court have differed for a century and a half on the meaning of such words as "due process of law," "interstate commerce," an "establishment of religion," and "the executive power." There is no reason to suppose that we can know, with certainty, what Jefferson and his colleagues meant by "happiness" or "equality."

"Pursuit of happiness"—a familiar enough phrase in that eighteenth century which was everywhere obsessed with happiness—probably embraced not only the right to, and the search for, but also the attainment of happiness. Many American state constitutions guarantee not only the pursuit of happiness but its attainment as well. "Created equal" is a more difficult phrase. It is absurd to suppose that Jefferson was not aware that Negro slaves and, for that matter, indentured servants, did not enjoy equality with their masters; absurd to suppose that he was insensitive to the palpable inequalities in natural talents and fortunes among individuals in his own society. What Jefferson probably meant was what he said— that men were created equal, created by Nature, created by God. Such inequalities as flourished were a product not of Nature or of God but of man, of society, of government, of good or bad fortune. It should be remembered that Jefferson's original draft of the Declaration read that "all men are created equal and independent, that from that equal creation they derive rights inherent and inalienable"; and that it contained, too, a violent attack upon Negro slavery. And it should not be forgotten that Jefferson's campaign to overthrow primogeniture and entail and the Established Church, his crusade for education, and his contributions to a more democratic order in the West were all designed to ameliorate the inequalities which had been created by the political and social order.

As with so much of the Declaration, the words "created equal" proved to have a life of their own. Indeed what "created equal" came to mean is a good deal more important than what it may have meant at the time it was so casually accepted by members of the Continental Congress: its significance is not descriptive but prophetic. That ultimate meaning was best stated by Lincoln in his Springfield speech of 1857. The Founding Fathers, said Lincoln,

meant to set up a standard maxim for free society which should be familiar to all, and revered by all; constantly looked to, constantly labored for, and even though never perfectly attained, constantly approximated, and thereby constantly spreading and deepening its influence and augmenting the happiness and value of life to all people of all colors everywhere. . . . Its authors meant it to be—as, thank God, it is now proving itself—a stumbling-block to all those who in after times might seek to turn a free people back into the hateful paths of despotism. They knew the proneness of prosperity to breed tyrants, and they meant when such should reappear in this fair land and commence their vocation, they should find left for them at least one hard nut to crack.

Certainly it is true that the concept of equality, first announced as a general principle in the Declaration, worked like a ferment in American society. Each successive generation, none more guiltily than our own, has felt called upon to square the reality with the principle. The concept of equality was applied to the political processes, and helped to strike down limitations on suffrage and office-holding for men, and eventually for women, too. It was applied to social institutions and practices and challenged every manifestation of class and privilege; and if it did not prevent such manifestations, it ameliorated them. It was applied to the economy and helped create an economic order where material well-being came to be assumed both as a foundation to equality, and as a right. It was applied to religion and made impossible not only a religious establishment, but the association of any one church with social or political power; violations of this principle, as in Congregational Connecticut or Mormon Utah, proved only temporary. It was applied to education, and eventually required an equal opportunity for education to all who were fortunate enough to be white, and in our time to all, white or black.

Nor was the influence of the Declaration confined to America. Along with such documents as the Virginia Bill of Rights, Common Sense, and the Virginia Statute of Religious Liberty, it inspired radicals in England and rebels in Ireland and excited the enthusiasm of the philosophes who were precursors to the French Revolution and of leaders of that Revolution like Mirabeau, Lafayette, Condorcet, and Brissot. It was translated into German, and Italian, and gave comfort to the liberals in some of the states of Germany and Italy, while Henrik Steffens recalled the enthusiasm with which it was greeted by his family in Denmark. It fired the spirit of the ardent Miranda, and of other leaders of the South American crusade for freedom and independence. It entered, eventually, into the mainstream of history—especially revolutionary history—on every continent.

Benjamin Franklin
Address to the Federal Convention
1787

EDITED BY RALPH L. KETCHAM

Near the end of the troubled year 1786, George Washington wrote that he hoped "the federal government, may be considered with calm and deliberate attention. . . . Let prejudices, unreasonable jealousies, and local interests, yield. . . . Let us look to our national character, and to things beyond the present moment. No morn ever dawned more favorably than ours did; and no day was ever more clouded than the present. Wisdom and good examples are necessary at this time to rescue the political machine from the impending storm." A few months later, after it was certain that the Federal Convention, to meet in May, 1787, would have a large and distinguished membership, James Madison further cautioned that ". . . no very sanguine expectations can well be indulged. The probable diversity of opinions and prejudices . . . renders the issue totally uncertain. The existing embarrassments and mortal diseases of the Confederacy form the only ground of hope, that a spirit of concession on all sides may be produced by the general chaos, or at least partitions of the Union, which offers itself as the alternative." At the threshold of its national organization, the leaders of the new United States knew that brilliant theories of government, heartfelt concern for the public welfare, and delegates of prestige and power would not be enough; a disposition to compromise was essential.

Fortunately, a world-famous conciliator had been elected to the Convention. Benjamin Franklin, already the patron saint of prudence and practicality, had agreed to head the Pennsylvania delegation. At eighty-two he was more than twenty years older than any other delegate. Over half the rest were under forty. He told his sister that he "attended the Business of [the Convention] 5 Hours in every Day from the Beginning, which is something more than four Months . . . my Health continues; some tell me I look better, and they suppose the daily Exercise of going and returning from the Statehouse has done me good." As President of Pennsylvania he entertained the delegates with tea and lively conversation under a large mulberry tree in the courtyard of his new house near Independence Hall.

Though the Convention quickly but respectfully rejected Franklin's pet ideas—a unicameral legislature, unsalaried officials, and a plural executive—the delegates were grateful for his presence and somehow expected he would make a crucial contribution. Since he was too infirm to remain long on his feet, his few formal speeches were read by James Wilson; otherwise he took only an occasional and often ineffectual part in the debates. Successfully, he opposed absolute executive veto, approved impeachment of officeholders, opposed federal property qualifications for voters, and urged liberal naturalization laws. Unsuccessfully, he disapproved any Senate voice in money bills, urged that the President be ineligible for re-election, and sought explicit power for federal canal-building. Twice during the hot summer (one delegate recorded thirty-three "hot" and three "warm" days, and only twenty-four "cool" and four "cold" days), however, he made important conciliatory moves.

On June 28, after a long harangue by Luther Martin, Franklin moved that "henceforth Prayers imploring the assistance of Heaven and its blessings on our Deliberations, be held in this assembly every morning," observing that without God's aid "we shall succeed in this Building no better than the Builders of Babel; we shall be divided by our little, partial Interests. . . ." Though rejected because the members were unlikely to agree on the mode of prayer, the motion lifted the attention of the members above the acrimonies of debate, emphasized the need for compassion and humility, and marked the beginning of the move toward "the Great Compromise." Shortly thereafter, Franklin made the key motion that the states be represented equally in the Senate, and the people be represented equally in the House.

His legendary charm and readiness with an appropriate story prepared the way for the acceptance of this motion. In recommending some accommodation between the large and small states, he remarked that

77

"When a broad table is to be made, and the edges of the plank do not fit, the artist takes a little from both and makes a good joint." At another time, during a hot, frustrating stretch in July when Washington reported that "the counsels . . . are now if possible in a worse train than ever. . . . I almost despair of seeing a favorable issue to the proceedings," Franklin dramatized the need for compromise by showing to a group having tea in his garden a phial containing a two-headed snake. The elder scientist-statesman observed that the reptile, if its heads took opposite sides of a stalk on the way to a stream, might die of thirst unless the difference were accommodated. Franklin might have added, from Poor Richard's Almanac, "the wise and the brave dares own he was wrong." When the members approved a final draft of the Constitution, scarcely daring to believe the extent of their success, it was proposed that Franklin address the Convention asking all the delegates, despite misgivings, to sign the document. At an evening meeting Franklin presented a draft of his proposed remarks and final strategy was settled. The next morning, September 17, 1787, the day set for the final signing of the Constitution, Franklin rose and asked the Convention's attention while Wilson read Franklin's words.

MR. PRESIDENT

I CONFESS that I do not entirely approve of this Constitution at present, but Sir, I am not sure I shall never approve it: For having lived long, I have experienced many Instances of being oblig'd, by better Information or fuller Consideration, to change Opinions even on important Subjects, which I once thought right, but found to be otherwise. It is therefore that the older I grow the more apt I am to doubt my own Judgment, and to pay more Respect to the Judgment of others. Most Men indeed as well as most Sects in Religion, think themselves in Possession of all Truth, and that wherever others differ from them it is so far Error. Steele, a Protestant in a Dedication tells the Pope, that the only Difference between our two Churches in their Opinions of the Certainty of their Doctrine, is, the Romish Church is infallible, and the Church of England is never in the Wrong. But tho' many private Persons think almost as highly of their own

---

Franklin's address is transcribed here from the original, which is in the Cornell University Library.

Copy 1

Infallibility, as of that of their Sect, few express it so naturally as a certain French Lady, who in a little Dispute with her Sister, said, I don't know how it happens, Sister, but I meet with no body but myself that's *always* in the right. *Il n'y a que moi qui a toujours raison.*

In these Sentiments, Sir, I agree to this Constitution, with all its Faults, if they are such; because I think a General Government necessary for us, and there is no *Form* of Government but what may be a Blessing to the People if well administred; and I believe farther that this is likely to be well administred for a Course of Years, and can only end in Despotism as other Forms have done before it, when the People shall become so corrupted as to need Despotic Government, being incapable of any other. I doubt too whether any other Convention we can obtain, may be able to make a better Constitution: For when you assemble a Number of Men to have the Advantage of their joint Wisdom, you inevitably assemble with those Men all their Prejudices, their Passions, their Errors of Opinion, their local Interests, and their selfish Views. From such an Assembly can a perfect Production be expected? It therefore astonishes me, Sir, to find this System approaching so near to Perfection as it does; and I think it will astonish our Enemies, who are waiting with Confidence to hear that our Councils are confounded, like those of the Builders of Babel, and that our States are on the Point of Separation, only to meet hereafter for the Purpose of cutting one anothers Throats. Thus I consent, Sir, to this Constitution because I expect no better, and because I am not sure that it is not the best. The Opinions I have had of its Errors, I sacrifice to the Public Good. I have never whisper'd a Syllable of them abroad. Within these Walls they were born, and here they shall die. If every one of us in returning to our Constituents were to report the Objections he has had to it, and use his Influence to gain Partizans in support of them, we might prevent its being generally received, and thereby lose all the salutary Effects and great Advantages resulting naturally in our favour among foreign Nations, as well as among ourselves, from our real or apparent Unanimity. Much of the Strength and Efficiency of any Government, in procuring and securing Happiness to the People depends on Opinion, on the general Opinion of the Goodness of that Government as well as of the Wisdom and Integrity of its Governors. I hope therefore that for our own Sakes, as a Part of the People, and for the sake of our Posterity, we shall act heartily and unanimously in recommending this Constitution, wherever our Influence may extend, and turn our future Thoughts and Endeavours to the Means of having it well administred.

On the whole, Sir, I cannot help expressing a Wish, that every Member of the Convention, who may still have Objections to it, would with me on this Occasion doubt a little of his own Infallibility, and to make *manifest* our *Unanimity,* put his Name to this Instrument.

After his address had been read Franklin moved, as Gouverneur Morris had planned, that the Convention vote to approve the Constitution by the "unanimous consent of the states present," a form adopted to allow delegates who refused a personal approval, to sign their names. After some debate, the Convention, voting by states, adopted Franklin's motion unanimously, but three delegates present nevertheless withheld their signatures.

Though the Convention proceedings were secret, the nature of Franklin's speech and the respect everywhere accorded him made the early disclosure of his remarks certain. On October 11, 1787, William Lewis, an ardent Philadelphia federalist, sent a paraphrase of the speech to Thomas Jefferson in Paris, probably intending that through him it would be shown to Franklin's friends there. Later that month Nathaniel Gorham, a Massachusetts delegate, asked for a copy to print in Boston newspapers since it was "exceedingly well calculated to correct positive attachment which men are apt to have for their own ideas. . . . [It] inculcates . . . a temper . . . which prevents war and bloodshed. You can have no idea of the weight and influence it would have in N England and I verily believe throughout America." Franklin readily sent "a Copy of that little Speech," observing that though he had "hitherto refused to permit its Publication, . . . your Judgment that it may do good weighs much more with me than my own Scruples." On December 3 the speech, minus some of the most candid remarks about disagreements within the Constitutional Convention, began appearing in newspapers in Boston, where it had "a wonderful effect" on the hotly contested election of delegates to the state convention. Gorham wrote that "it has been read and applauded by almost everybody—it has been much in use in Town Meetings to inculcate moderation and a due respect to the opinions of others, and is said . . . to contain those sentiments which only can procure the establishment of a Government in Peace—some of your old Friends in Boston say that by this Speech they can see you . . . as the same Man you was forty years ago."

Antifederalists attacked "the puerile speech" and its author: ". . . it is beneath the dignity of a statesman to consent to a constitution he confessedly dislikes. . . . The doubting Doctor, who has been remarkable for skepticism from fourteen to four score, [should have doubts about the new Constitution]. It is not surprising, that when the body is debilitated, and the mind worn out . . . the enfeebled sage should wish to rid himself the trouble of thinking deeply on the fatal consequences of the assumed powers and bold designs of the system makers in Philadelphia . . . [his speech contains] confusion and doubt, inconsistencies and absurdities." A Franklin defender replied that the person "whose little mind poured forth the unqualified torrent of abuse on the GREAT Franklin . . . is advised to attempt an enlargement (if possible) of his little faculties, which, if effected, he may be able to discern the wisdom of the doctor's address."

New York newspapers reprinted the speech on December 10 and 11, and it appeared in Connecticut during the next two days, helping to elect federalist delegates in both states. Franklin approved publication of the full speech in The American Museum (Philadelphia) in December, 1787. John Armstrong of Carlisle, Pennsylvania, wrote Franklin on Christmas Day that "Your last speech in the federal Convention will be in our paper tomorrow." In heavily antifederal western Pennsylvania, Armstrong hoped it would have "some good effect" in persuading the people to accept the new Constitution. To defend Franklin against Luther Martin's slanders, Daniel Carroll read the speech before the Maryland House of Delegates. Madison sent copies of it to George Washington for his use and information. In South Carolina, Charles Pinckney noted that had Franklin's final advice been heeded, abusive charges about the Constitutional Convention could have been avoided. In the critical months when the Constitution was under review, Franklin's speech was reprinted at least fifty times, much more often than the Federalist Papers, and probably was the most influential contribution to the ratification debates.

In delivering his final speech, Franklin was the right man saying the right thing at the right time. In 1787 he was widely reckoned the wisest man in America. As Poor Richard he had dispensed folklore for a generation. As the conqueror of lightning he seemed in league with the

Heavens. As plain Ben Franklin at the Court of Versailles he had persuaded the proudest monarch in Europe to furnish vital help to a band of republican rebels. All through the summer of 1787 he had listened patiently and spoken calmly as the Constitution had been hammered into shape. That he discerned the key to the Convention's success and at the same time sensed the spirit necessary to vitalize the new Constitution surprised no one. James Madison was a more astute political theorist, James Wilson was more learned in the law, and Alexander Hamilton planned more brilliantly for national greatness, but Franklin taught them all the art of conciliation needed to make the Constitution work.

In placing the principle of compromise at the center of the new government, Franklin marked out a feature of American public life indispensable from that day to this. Without day-to-day compromises no nation would have survived for Jefferson, Jackson, Lincoln, and Wilson to inspire with redefined ideals and purposes. Faithful to the mood of Franklin's final speech, Henry Clay, the Great Compromiser, held the Union together on three notable occasions and in innumerable smaller ways as well. From the Supreme Court bench Oliver Wendell Holmes revived a spirit of toleration and humility in a nearly petrified Constitution. Speaker Sam Rayburn's peerless stature as a constructive congressional leader was due largely to his patient adherence to the art of accomplishing the possible by accepting generously and good-naturedly what he could of the dogmas and whims of his colleagues. Franklin's final speech is well known to students of American politics and it has had occasional direct use in pleas for later desperately needed accommodations; the New Republic, for example, printed it in 1919 as part of an appeal for the League of Nations. Pre-eminently, however, it is a landmark in the development of Anglo-American willingness to make a principled concession of principles to give full scope to what a modern philosopher of compromise, T. V. Smith, has called "the unearned increment created by human accord."

The Constitution of the
United States of America
1787

The Preamble

EDITED BY CLARENCE L. VER STEEG

The Preamble to the Constitution of the United States consists of two parts: the first part defines the source of authority from which the constitutional instrument is derived; the second defines the objects for which the Constitution and the government based upon it are formed. The theoretical constitutional relationship expressed by the Preamble remains unchanged today, but the meaning invested in the phrases employed has changed dramatically.

Although repetitive use has softened its revolutionary connotation, the assertion "We the people . . . do ordain and establish this Constitution" set a decidedly radical tone to the ordered blueprint of constitutional government. The Articles of Confederation, adopted in 1781, had been introduced by the explicit statement that the authority of that document was derived from the sovereign states. The Preamble to the Constitution makes clear from the outset that a wholly different constitutional framework, what we have since called the federal system, was being established, in which the people in their sovereign capacity delegated certain powers to the national government and other powers to the states.

Considered in its eighteenth-century context, "people" meant the responsible electorate; thus the basis of authority for the Constitution in a literal sense was a selective group rather than all the people. More precisely, in fact, "people" implied the layer upon layer of oligarchical ruling groups rooted in town and county which rose like a pyramid to an apex of state and interstate connections. Only as democratization occurred did the theoretical and literal definition of "people" more closely correspond.

The second part of the Preamble, which designates the objectives of the Constitution—to form a more perfect union, to insure domestic tranquillity, to provide for the common defense, to promote the general welfare, and to secure the blessings of liberty—reflects, in its contemporary context, the anxieties of the 1780's. The Articles of Confederation, it was feared, had not measured up to the exigencies of the union; thus, "a more perfect union" was desirable. The specter of Shays' Rebellion, as well as other domestic disturbances, awakened latent fears that "domestic tranquillity" would end, that disorder would degenerate into chaos, that chaos would lead to tyranny, and that tyranny would bring a loss of liberty for all men. Historians recognize that these fears were greatly exaggerated and even unwarranted, as many men realized at the time, but the objectives outlined in the Preamble derived at least a part of their definition from these fears. Fortunately, the nobility of expression in the Preamble allowed its familiar phrases to be invested with new and more profound meaning as the American experiment in government unfolded. In this way the "objectives" as stated in the Preamble became principles.

In the Philadelphia convention on August 6, 1787, the first draft of the Constitution was reported by the Committee of Detail (also called the Committee of Five), Nathaniel Gorham, Oliver Ellsworth, Edmund Randolph, John Rutledge, and James Wilson. The Preamble in this draft embraced the intent of the final version, but lacked grace, felicity, and precision. "We, the people of the states of [the names of the various states] do ordain, declare, and establish, the following Constitution for the government of ourselves and our posterity." This draft of the Preamble was followed by Article I, "The style of this government shall be 'The United States of America.'" No change was made in this draft until the Federal Convention neared the end of its work. A five-member Committee of Revision was elected on September 8 "to revise the style." William Samuel Johnson, Alexander Hamilton, Gouverneur Morris, James Madison, and Rufus King were named, with Johnson designated as chairman. The committee entrusted the principal task of rewriting the document to Gouverneur Morris, and one of his specific contributions was the revision of the Preamble into its final form.

84

WE THE People of the United States, in Order to form a more perfect Union, establish Justice, insure domestic Tranquillity, provide for the common defence, promote the general Welfare, and secure the Blessings of Liberty to ourselves and our Posterity, do ordain and establish this Constitution for the United States of America.

The meaning of the Preamble was debated in the state ratifying conventions of Massachusetts, New York, Pennsylvania, and North Carolina, but the issues involved in the debate were best represented in the Virginia convention. The flaming patriot and founder, Patrick Henry, challenged the right of the delegates to the Federal Convention to introduce the Constitution on the basis of "We, the people." "What right had they to say, We, the people? . . ." he demanded. "Who authorized them to speak the language of, We the people, instead of, We the states? . . . The people gave them no power to use their name. That they exceeded their power is perfectly clear."

Governor Randolph and Edmund Pendleton answered Henry. "Who," Pendleton asked, "but the people can delegate powers? Who but the people have a right to form a government? . . . If the objection be, that the Union ought to be not of the people, but of the state governments, then I think the choice of the former very happy and proper. What have the state governments to do with it? Were they to determine, the people would not, in that case, be the judges upon what terms it was adopted."

This exchange skirted the essential issue, and it remained for Henry ("Light-Horse Harry") Lee, a veteran soldier of the Revolution, to pronounce the truth of the matter. "This expression [We the people] was introduced into that paper [the Constitution] with great propriety. This system is submitted to the people for their consideration, because on them it is to operate, if adopted. It is not binding on the people until it becomes their act." Judge Iredell in the North Carolina Convention

The Preamble and the other parts of the Constitution are quoted in this volume from the "literal print" of the document, as reproduced in *The Constitution of the United States of America: Analysis and Interpretation* (Washington, D.C.: U.S. Government Printing Office, 1964). The original manuscript is in the National Archives, Washington, D.C.

agreed with this interpretation. "We, the People, was not to be applied to the members [of the Federal Convention] themselves, but was to be the style of the Constitution, when it should be ratified in their respective states."

This construction became the touchstone for judicial decision, once the Constitution was ratified by the appropriate number of state conventions. In M'Culloch v. Maryland, 1819, Chief Justice Marshall declared:

From these Conventions the constitution derives its whole authority. The government proceeds directly from the people; is "ordained and established" in the name of the people; and is declared to be ordained "in order to form a more perfect union, establish justice, insure domestic tranquillity, and secure the blessings of liberty to themselves and to their posterity." The assent of the States, in their sovereign capacity, is implied in calling a Convention, and thus submitting that instrument to the people. But the people were at perfect liberty to accept or reject it; and their act was final. . . . The government of the Union, then . . . is emphatically and truly a government of the people. In form and in substance it emanates from them, its powers are granted by them, and are to be exercised directly on them, and for their benefit.

In effect, the Preamble serves as the artery which transmits life to the Constitution by infusing it with authority in somewhat the same fashion as Article VI, Section 2, specifies precisely how that authority is to operate.

The theme enunciated in the Preamble pervades almost every convolution of the national mind—from President Lincoln's Gettysburg Address to the shrill of the political hack, from Whittier's "The Poor Voter on Election Day" to the rote recitation of classroom exercises in government, from the Insular Cases (especially Downes v. Bidwell, 182 U.S. 244 [1901]) of judicial import to the oversimplified superpatriotism of the newspaper tabloids, from the serious education of the immigrant-citizen who wishes to learn his responsibilities, to the complaint of the deported mobster who believes his rights are being denied.

In fact, after more than a century of experience with the Constitution, the theme of the Preamble was invoked so frequently as to become perfunctory. In An Economic Interpretation of the Constitution (1913), Charles A. Beard reminded his readers that the Constitution was not created by "the whole people." He painstakingly reviewed the contemporary economic interests which, in his judgment, challenged the "juristic" view of the origins and nature of the Constitution and the misleading use of "We the people . . . do ordain and establish this

Constitution . . ." Beard's book was invaluable in rescuing the Preamble and, indeed, the Constitution as a whole, from the antiseptic milieu that had enveloped it. But Beard, while bringing a renewed sense of reality and earthiness back into the twentieth-century discussion, failed to recognize that the theoretical statement of the relationship to the people as the source of constitutional authority was life-giving rather than lifeless, simply because the framers had the perception to allow the definition of "people" to change.

Abandonment of property requirements for voting, emancipation of slaves, the Fourteenth Amendment, the enfranchisement of women, and civil-rights legislation of 1964–65 broadened the definition of "people" who do (present tense), not did, "ordain and establish this Constitution. . . ." In accordance with the Preamble, therefore, the people as currently conceived continually animate anew the Constitution and the objects of government it enunciates. This is true even though the theoretical equality implied by the source of authority is not fulfilled in its exercise, because of special interests which are reflected in the unequal financial power and social organization of those who live under the Constitution, a fact clearly recognized by the framers. Unfortunately, the source of constitutional authority is too frequently confused with the empirical operation of the government under that authority.

Article I

EDITED BY C. HERMAN PRITCHETT

Article I of the Constitution established the national legislature and defined the legislative powers of the new government. In creating the Congress of the United States, the framers of the Constitution had a model which it was their conscious purpose not to follow—the Congress then existing under the Articles of Confederation. That body had grudgingly authorized the Constitutional Convention to meet for the "sole and express purpose of revising the Articles of Confederation."

Congress under the Articles was a single house representing the thirteen states, each of which had one vote. A two-thirds vote was required for the adoption of important measures, and amendments to the Articles required unanimous consent. There was no separation of executive from legislative powers; Congress appointed such committees and civil officers as seemed necessary to carry on executive work. Congress could not levy taxes; it could only make requisitions on the states for its fiscal needs. Nor could Congress regulate interstate commerce, with the result that the states freely retaliated against each other's trade.

When the Convention met in Philadelphia in May, 1787, its members agreed that a stronger governmental structure was required. Two competing plans were presented. The Virginia Plan proposed to scrap the Articles and create a strong national government. The New Jersey Plan, supported by the smaller states, would have maintained a confederation while giving it more adequate powers. The New Jersey Plan was defeated within the first few weeks of the Convention, and from that point on the framers accepted the obligation to design a new national government with the power to collect its own taxes, control commerce among the states, make its own laws and enforce them in its own courts.

88

The legislature under the new Constitution, unlike Congress under the Articles, had to share governmental power with the executive and the judiciary. Montesquieu's work on the separation of powers was known in America at that time and was occasionally quoted at the Convention, but it was probably not very influential with the delegates. The allocation of powers to three separate branches, and the division of authority so that each could impose some limits on the actions of the other two, were adopted not to fit any theoretical models but to handle the very practical problems the Convention faced.

In determining that Congress would be composed of two houses, the Convention was following the example of England and almost all of the states. The delegates generally agreed from the beginning that the members of the House of Representatives would be elected directly by the people, and that the number allotted to each state would be proportionate to its population. Much more difficult was the composition and basis of selection of the Senate. The general sentiment was for election of senators by the state legislatures. The Virginia Plan called for Senate representation to be based on population, just as in the House.

This issue was the rock on which the Convention almost foundered. The small states, which under the Articles, and in the Convention itself, had equal voting strength with the large states, would not agree to any plan which did not guarantee their status in some way. The discussions and arguments were long and bitter. Compromises were proposed by the large states, such as that Senate representation be on the basis of state wealth, or that the states be divided into three population classes, with one, two, and three senators respectively. But on July 16 equal representation of the states in the Senate was adopted by a five-to-four vote, with Massachusetts divided and New York not voting. Madison records that the next morning the large states held an indignation meeting to discuss what could be done, but that "the time was wasted in vague conversation." And so the decision stood.

At first the Convention sought to avoid spelling out the powers of Congress, proposing instead that it have the right "to legislate in all cases to which the separate States are incompetent," or "in all cases for the general interests of the Union." But several delegates objected, asking for a more "exact enumeration" of powers. Ultimately the Convention agreed, and spelled out in detail in Section 8 of Article I a long list of powers, the absence of which in the Confederation had made the movement for a new Constitution necessary.

While the general emphasis of the Convention was on assuring that Congress had sufficient authority, conflicting sectional interests led the delegates to insist on certain prohibitions on national power. The slave interest was the one which most feared discriminatory action by the new government. A majority of the Convention was opposed to "this infernal trafic," as George Mason called it, but North Carolina, South Carolina, and Georgia would have refused to join the Union without some guarantee of the status of slavery. Consequently a compromise was adopted in Section 9, guaranteeing no interference with the importation of slaves until 1808. The prohibition placed on the power of Congress to levy direct taxes, unless they were apportioned among the states according to population, also represented the efforts of slavery supporters to assure that internal taxes applying solely to slaves could not be adopted.

The relation of congressional powers to those of the states was considered in several contexts. The original Virginia Plan proposed that Congress have the power "to negative all laws passed by the several States, contravening in the opinion of the National Legislature the articles of Union." This idea of congressional veto of state laws was not popular and was dropped, being replaced by the supremacy clause of Article VI. However, there were certain areas in which the delegates so strongly opposed state action that, in Section 10, they banned legislation in forthright language. The sharpest antagonism was toward state paper money and debtor relief laws, which were among the subjects specifically prohibited to the states.

Article I is by far the longest of the seven articles composing the original Constitution. In fact, it amounts in length to more than half of the entire document. It incorporates most of the basic decisions made by the Convention, decisions which primarily determined the nature and character of the new government. In inventive genius it may not quite compare with Article II, which created the Presidency. But it established a representative, responsible, and workable legislature; it successfully blended the principles of a national and a federal system; and it implemented the conclusion that domestic tranquillity, the common defense, and the general welfare could not be achieved except through a government endowed with adequate powers.

Section. 1. All legislative Powers herein granted shall be vested in a Congress of the United States, which shall consist of a Senate and House of Representatives.

Section. 2. The House of Representatives shall be composed of Members chosen every second Year by the People of the several States, and the Electors in each State shall have the Qualifications requisite for Electors of the most numerous Branch of the State Legislature.

No Person shall be a Representative who shall not have attained to the age of twenty five Years, and been seven Years a Citizen of the United States, and who shall not, when elected, be an Inhabitant of that State in which he shall be chosen.

Representatives and direct Taxes shall be apportioned among the several States which may be included within this Union, according to their respective Numbers, which shall be determined by adding to the whole Number of free Persons, including those bound to Service for a Term of Years, and excluding Indians not taxed, three fifths of all other Persons. The actual Enumeration shall be made within three Years after the first Meeting of the Congress of the United States, and within every subsequent Term of ten Years, in such Manner as they shall by Law direct. The Number of Representatives shall not exceed one for every thirty Thousand, but each State shall have at Least one Representative; and until such enumeration shall be made, the State of New Hampshire shall be entitled to chuse three, Massachusetts eight, Rhode-Island and Providence Plantations one, Connecticut five, New-York six, New Jersey four, Pennsylvania eight, Delaware one, Maryland six, Virginia ten, North Carolina five, South Carolina five, and Georgia three.

When vacancies happen in the Representation from any State, the Executive Authority thereof shall issue Writs of Election to fill such Vacancies.

The House of Representatives shall chuse their Speaker and other Officers; and shall have the sole Power of Impeachment.

Section. 3. The Senate of the United States shall be composed of two Senators from each State, chosen by the Legislature thereof, for six Years; and each Senator shall have one Vote.

Immediately after they shall be assembled in Consequence of the first Election, they shall be divided as equally as may be into three Classes. The Seats of the Senators of the first Class shall be vacated at the

Expiration of the second Year, of the second Class at the Expiration of the fourth Year, and of the third Class at the Expiration of the sixth Year, so that one third may be chosen every second Year; and if Vacancies happen by Resignation, or otherwise, during the Recess of the Legislature of any State, the Executive thereof may make temporary Appointments until the next Meeting of the Legislature, which shall then fill such Vacancies.

No Person shall be a Senator who shall not have attained to the Age of thirty Years, and been nine Years a Citizen of the United States, and who shall not, when elected, be an Inhabitant of that State for which he shall be chosen.

The Vice President of the United States shall be President of the Senate, but shall have no Vote, unless they be equally divided.

The Senate shall chuse their other Officers, and also a President pro tempore, in the Absence of the Vice President, or when he shall exercise the Office of President of the United States.

The Senate shall have the sole Power to try all Impeachments. When sitting for that Purpose, they shall be on Oath or Affirmation. When the President of the United States is tried the Chief Justice shall preside: And no Person shall be convicted without the Concurrence of two thirds of the Members present.

Judgment in Cases of Impeachment shall not extend further than to removal from Office, and disqualification to hold and enjoy any Office of honor, Trust or Profit under the United States: but the Party convicted shall nevertheless be liable and subject to Indictment, Trial, Judgment and Punishment, according to Law.

Section. 4. The Times, Places and Manner of holding Elections for Senators and Representatives, shall be prescribed in each State by the Legislature thereof; but the Congress may at any time by Law make or alter such Regulations, except as to the Places of chusing Senators.

The Congress shall assemble at least once in every Year, and such Meeting shall be on the first Monday in December, unless they shall by Law appoint a different Day.

Section. 5. Each House shall be the Judge of the Elections, Returns and Qualifications of its own Members, and a Majority of each shall constitute a Quorum to do Business; but a smaller Number may adjourn from day to day, and may be authorized to compel the Attendance of absent Members, in such Manner, and under such Penalties as each House may provide.

Each House may determine the Rules of its Proceedings, punish its Members for disorderly Behaviour, and, with the Concurrence of two thirds, expel a Member.

Each House shall keep a Journal of its Proceedings, and from time to time publish the same, excepting such Parts as may in their Judgment require Secrecy; and the Yeas and Nays of the Members of either House on any question shall, at the Desire of one fifth of those Present, be entered on the Journal.

Neither House, during the Session of Congress, shall, without the Consent of the other, adjourn for more than three days, nor to any other Place than that in which the two Houses shall be sitting.

Section. 6. The Senators and Representatives shall receive a Compensation for their Services, to be ascertained by Law, and paid out of the Treasury of the United States. They shall in all Cases, except Treason, Felony and Breach of the Peace, be privileged from Arrest during their attendance at the Session of their respective Houses, and in going to and returning from the same; and for any Speech or Debate in either House, they shall not be questioned in any other Place.

No Senator or Representative shall, during the Time for which he was elected, be appointed to any civil Office under the Authority of the United States, which shall have been created, or the Emoluments whereof shall have been encreased during such time; and no Person holding any Office under the United States, shall be a Member of either House during his Continuance in Office.

Section. 7. All Bills for raising Revenue shall originate in the House of Representatives; but the Senate may propose or concur with amendments as on other Bills.

Every Bill which shall have passed the House of Representatives and the Senate, shall, before it become a Law, be presented to the President of the United States; If he approve he shall sign it, but if not he shall return it, with his Objections to that House in which it shall have originated, who shall enter the Objections at large on their Journal, and proceed to reconsider it. If after such Reconsideration two thirds of that

House shall agree to pass the Bill, it shall be sent, together with the Objections, to the other House, by which it shall likewise be reconsidered, and if approved by two thirds of that House, it shall become a Law. But in all such Cases the Votes of both Houses shall be determined by yeas and Nays, and the Names of the Persons voting for and against the Bill shall be entered on the Journal of each House respectively. If any Bill shall not be returned by the President within ten Days (Sunday excepted) after it shall have been presented to him, the Same shall be a Law, in like Manner as if he had signed it, unless the Congress by their Adjournment prevent its Return, in which Case it shall not be a Law.

Every Order, Resolution, or Vote to which the Concurrence of the Senate and House of Representatives may be necessary (except on a question of Adjournment) shall be presented to the President of the United States; and before the Same shall take Effect, shall be approved by him, or being disapproved by him, shall be repassed by two thirds of the Senate and House of Representatives, according to the Rules and Limitations prescribed in the Case of a Bill.

Section. 8. The Congress shall have Power To lay and collect Taxes, Duties, Imposts and Excises, to pay the Debts and provide for the common Defence and general Welfare of the United States; but all Duties, Imposts and Excises shall be uniform throughout the United States;

To borrow Money on the credit of the United States;

To regulate Commerce with foreign Nations, and among the several States, and with the Indian Tribes;

To establish an uniform Rule of Naturalization, and uniform Laws on the subject of Bankruptcies throughout the United States;

To coin Money, regulate the Value thereof, and of foreign Coin, and fix the Standard of Weights and Measures;

To provide for the Punishment of counterfeiting the Securities and current Coin of the United States;

To establish Post Offices and post Roads;

To promote the Progress of Science and useful Arts, by securing for limited Times to Authors and Inventors the exclusive Right to their respective Writings and Discoveries;

To constitute Tribunals inferior to the supreme Court;

To define and punish Piracies and Felonies committed on the high Seas, and Offences against the Law of Nations;

To declare War, grant Letters of Marque and Reprisal, and make Rules concerning Captures on Land and Water;

To raise and support Armies, but no Appropriation of Money to that Use shall be for a longer Term than two Years;

To provide and maintain a Navy;

To make Rules for the Government and Regulation of the land and naval Forces;

To provide for calling forth the Militia to execute the Laws of the Union, suppress Insurrections and repel Invasions;

To provide for organizing, arming, and disciplining, the Militia, and for governing such Part of them as may be employed in the Service of the United States, reserving to the States respectively, the Appointment of the Officers, and the Authority of training the Militia according to the discipline prescribed by Congress;

To exercise exclusive Legislation in all Cases whatsoever, over such District (not exceeding ten Miles square) as may, by Cession of Particular States, and the Acceptance of Congress, become the Seat of the Government of the United States, and to exercise like Authority over all Places purchased by the Consent of the Legislature of the State in which the Same shall be, for the Erection of Forts, Magazines, Arsenals, dock-Yards, and other needful Buildings;—And

To make all Laws which shall be necessary and proper for carrying into Execution the foregoing Powers, and all other Powers vested by this Constitution in the Government of the United States, or in any Department or Officer thereof.

Section. 9. The Migration or Importation of such Persons as any of the States now existing shall think proper to admit, shall not be prohibited by the Congress prior to the Year one thousand eight hundred and eight, but a Tax or duty may be imposed on such Importation, not exceeding ten dollars for each Person.

The Privilege of the Writ of Habeas Corpus shall not be suspended, unless when in Cases of Rebellion or Invasion the public Safety may require it.

No Bill of Attainder or ex post facto Law shall be passed.

No Capitation, or other direct, Tax shall be laid, unless in Proportion to the Census of Enumeration herein before directed to be taken.

No Tax or Duty shall be laid on Articles exported from any State.

No Preference shall be given by any Regulation of Commerce or

Revenue to the Ports of one State over those of another; nor shall Vessels bound to, or from, one State, be obliged to enter, clear or pay Duties in another.

No Money shall be drawn from the Treasury, but in Consequence of Appropriations made by Law; and a regular Statement and Account of the Receipts and Expenditures of all public Money shall be published from time to time.

No Title of Nobility shall be granted by the United States: And no Person holding any Office of Profit or Trust under them, shall, without the Consent of the Congress, accept of any present, Emolument, Office, or Title, of any kind whatever, from any King, Prince or foreign State.

Section. 10. No State shall enter into any Treaty, Alliance, or Confederation; grant Letters of Marque and Reprisal; coin Money; emit Bills of Credit; make any Thing but gold and silver Coin a Tender in Payment of Debts; pass any Bill of Attainder, ex post facto Law, or Law impairing the Obligation of Contracts, or grant any Title of Nobility.

No State shall, without the Consent of the Congress, lay any Imposts or Duties on Imports or Exports, except what may be absolutely necessary for executing it's inspection Laws: and the net Produce of all Duties and Imposts, laid by any State on Imports or Exports, shall be for the Use of the Treasury of the United States; and all such Laws shall be subject to the Revision and Controul of the Congress.

No State shall, without the Consent of Congress, lay any Duty of Tonnage, keep Troops, or Ships of War in time of Peace, enter into any Agreement or Compact with another State, or with a foreign Power, or engage in War, unless actually invaded, or in such imminent Danger as will not admit of delay.

As far as the organization and structure of Congress is concerned Article I of the Constitution did its job well. Little has been required in the way of amendment. The principal change was that effected by the Seventeenth Amendment, adopted in 1913, which provided for the election of senators by popular vote instead of by the state legislatures.

A major issue in regard to the House of Representatives has been its size and the districting problem. The number of seats, originally 65, was increased by Congress after each decennial census until a figure of 435 was reached in 1911. That number was then fixed as the permanent size of the House, on the ground that any further increase would make the body unwieldy. These 435 seats are reapportioned among the states according to population after each census, with the aid of complicated mathematical formulas.

Having been informed of its quota of seats in the House, each state is then responsible for dividing its territory into the appropriate number of electoral districts. Fair principles of representation require that these districts be roughly equal in population, but in fact they have often been quite unequal, either because the state legislatures refused to redraw the boundaries when there had been population changes or because boundaries were redrawn with deliberate discriminatory intent. In Colegrove v. Green, 328 U.S. 549 (1946), the Supreme Court refused to compel the remedying of gross inequalities in Illinois congressional districts, on the ground that this was a "political" question in which courts should not interfere. However, in Baker v. Carr, 369 U.S. 186 (1962), the Court reversed itself to the extent of opening the way for judicial review of legislative apportionments. Then in Wesberry v. Sanders, 376 U.S. 1 (1964), the Court held that the Constitution had the "plain objective of making equal representation for equal numbers of people the fundamental goal for the House of Representatives." Consequently congressional districts were required to be made roughly equal in population, and the long-standing overrepresentation of rural areas in the House was ended.

With respect to participation in elections, Article I, Section 2, provided that persons in each state having "the qualifications requisite for electors of the most numerous branch" of that state's legislature would be eligible to vote in federal elections. Under this arrangement the states determine which of their citizens have the privilege of the franchise. However, once a state has decided who is eligible to vote, then Section 2 steps in to guarantee their right to vote for federal officials.

The freedom of a state to determine its electorate has subsequently been limited by four of the Amendments to the Constitution. The "equal protection" clause of the Fourteenth Amendment has been interpreted to forbid discriminatory practices by state election officials. The Fifteenth Amendment forbids denial of the franchise because of race or color, and the Nineteenth guarantees the vote to women. The Twenty-fourth Amendment, adopted in 1964, forbids the states to use the poll tax as a voting requirement in federal elections. These constitutional standards are not self-enforcing, however, and federal action has been required to remedy the long-standing denial of the franchise to Negroes in southern states. The Civil Rights Acts of 1957 and 1960 marked the beginning of congressional interest in this problem, but it was not until the Voting Rights Act of 1965 that Congress effectively intervened to compel the grant of the franchise to Negroes in certain recalcitrant areas. The Act, which suspended voting qualification laws such as literacy tests in states where these tests had been used to bar Negroes from voting, and provided for the appointment of federal voting registrars where local registrars had refused to register Negroes, was upheld by the Supreme Court in South Carolina v. Katzenbach, 86 S. Ct. 803 (1966).

Although Article I vests "all legislative powers herein granted" in Congress, it also makes the President a necessary participant in the lawmaking process. All legislation must be submitted to the President for his signature before it becomes effective. Initially Presidents vetoed proposed legislation only when they believed it to be unconstitutional. Andrew Jackson was the first President to veto bills simply because he regarded them as objectionable. Vetoes are seldom overridden by Congress, since to do so requires a two-thirds majority in both houses. Franklin Roosevelt vetoed 631 bills, and only 9 were repassed over his veto.

The congressional power of impeachment has proved to be too cumbersome to be of much importance. While the threat to impeach the President is sometimes heard during periods of political turmoil, the attempt was actually made only once. In the aftermath of the Civil War, the Radical Republicans in Congress, motivated by vindictive partisanship, sought to impeach Andrew Johnson, but the Senate failed by a margin of one vote to convict him. The defeat of that effort has discouraged subsequent use of impeachment as a weapon for political purposes. Apart from Andrew Johnson's case, impeachment actions have been brought against nine federal judges, four of whom were convicted, and one Cabinet member.

Problems of interpreting the powers granted to Congress by Article I arose very early in American history. At the end of the long list of powers granted in Section 8, Congress is authorized "to make all laws which shall be necessary and proper for carrying into execution the foregoing powers. . . ." The relationship of this clause to the enumerated powers preceding it became very quickly the subject of controversy between Federalists and Jeffersonians, between broad and strict constructionists. The issue was joined over Hamilton's plan for a national bank, as accepted by the First Congress. There was no authorization in the Constitution for Congress to create a bank, so President Washington invited Hamilton and Jefferson to submit their respective views on whether he should sign the bill.

Jefferson denied that Congress could create a bank. He emphasized the "necessary" in the necessary and proper clause. Since all the enumerated powers could be carried out without a bank, it was not necessary and consequently not authorized. Hamilton, on the other hand, argued that the powers granted to Congress included the right to employ "all the means requisite and fairly applicable to the attainment of the ends of such power," unless they were specifically forbidden or immoral or contrary to the "essential ends of political society." Washington signed the bill.

In 1819 Chief Justice John Marshall gave the definitive statement of the Hamiltonian theory in the great case of M'Culloch v. Maryland, 4 Wheat. 316. Again congressional authority to incorporate a bank—the Second Bank of the United States—was at issue. Marshall found implied congressional authority to establish a bank in the expressly granted powers to collect taxes, to borrow money, to regulate commerce, to declare and conduct a war; for "it may with great reason be contended, that a government, entrusted with such ample powers, on the due exercise of which the happiness and prosperity of the nation so vitally depends, must also be entrusted with ample means for their execution." The Jeffersonian interpretation, he said, would "almost annihilate" the right of Congress to select the means for carrying out its purposes.

Among the enumerated powers in Section 8, the authority "to regulate commerce with foreign nations, and among the several states . . ." has been perhaps the most significant and certainly the most litigated. The language is in terms of a positive grant of power to Congress, but in fact its purpose was also to take away from the states this power which they had so seriously abused under the Articles of Confederation. As it turned out, Congress was slow to utilize its authority over commerce, and for the first century of national existence the primary problem in interpreting the commerce clause was to decide how much regulatory power remained with the states.

In the famous case of Gibbons v. Ogden, 9 Wheat. 1 (1824), John

Marshall held that New York State could not grant a monopoly of steamboat transportation on waters within the state. In the course of his opinion Marshall laid down principles which have largely dominated all subsequent thinking about the commerce clause. One of his important pronouncements was that congressional power over commerce "may very well be restricted to that commerce which concerns more states than one." Eventually this suggestion was developed into the distinction between "interstate" and "intrastate" commerce.

Interstate commerce is typically defined as commerce which crosses a state line, and over such commerce Congress has complete control insofar as it wishes to exercise it—not only to protect and promote, but also to restrict or even to prohibit. Congress has thus been able to use the commerce power as a kind of national police power to proceed against such evils as lottery tickets, impure food and drugs, and the white-slave traffic.

Congressional power has never depended entirely on the test of crossing a state line, however. Marshall also recognized that commercial transactions taking place entirely within a state might have such an effect on commerce among the states as to justify or require their regulation. The Court has employed the "effect" doctrine in numerous decisions to justify congressional regulation, but in 1935 and 1936 it struck down certain New Deal recovery statutes which relied on this claim. This proved to be only a temporary aberration, however, for in NLRB v. Jones & Laughlin Corp., 301 U.S. 1 (1937), the Court returned to what it called a "practical conception" of interstate commerce and upheld the constitutionality of the Wagner Act. This decision stated such a broad basis for the commerce power that few serious questions about the constitutional scope of congressional authority over commerce have subsequently arisen. In the words of Justice Cardozo, the commerce power is "as broad as the need that evokes it."

The grant of taxing power to Congress in Section 8 has proved adequate for federal needs and has created few problems. The ban in Section 2 on direct taxes unless apportioned by population did cause trouble, however. A federal income tax adopted by Congress in 1894 was held by the Supreme Court to be a direct tax, and since it was not apportioned by population it was unconstitutional. This decision, for which there was little justification, delayed the inauguration of income taxation until 1913, when the Sixteenth Amendment was adopted.

Similarly the spending authority of Section 8 leaves Congress substantially free from limitations. The principal tests have occurred in connection with federal grant-in-aid legislation under which Congress makes federal funds available to the states for financing programs which Congress wishes to promote. An effort to attack the constitutionality of such federal spending under the Maternity Act of 1921 was frustrated by the Supreme Court in Massachusetts v. Mellon, 262 U.S. 447 (1923), on the ground that no federal taxpayer had legal standing to bring such a suit. The only exception to this rule that the appropriating power is judicially unreviewable occurred in United States v. Butler, 297 U.S. 1 (1936), where the joining of a taxing and spending program in the same agricultural program made it possible for the Supreme Court to consider the purpose of the spending and to hold it unconstitutional.

Congress has constitutionally unlimited power to borrow money. There is no specific authority to issue paper money, and the "greenbacks" by which the Civil War was financed were at first held unconstitutional in 1870 by a four-to-three vote of the Supreme Court. However, after two vacancies on the Court had been filled by President Grant, the Court reconsidered and overruled the earlier decision by a vote of five to four.

The power of Congress to conduct investigations is not mentioned in Article I. It is an implied power, supplementary to the specifically assigned functions to legislate, to appropriate, to pass on the elections and returns of members, and so on. It is an extremely broad power, because the need of Congress for information is broad, but it is not entirely free from constitutional limitations. In McGrain v. Daugherty, 273 U.S. 135 (1927), the Supreme Court, while upholding the inquiry Congress had made into the Teapot Dome scandals, did point out that Congress had no "general" power to inquire into private affairs and compel disclosures, and that a witness might rightfully refuse to answer where the bounds of congressional power were exceeded, or the questions were not pertinent to the matter under inquiry. In Watkins v. United States, 354 U.S. 178 (1957), the Court said that investigatory power was limited by the First Amendment and upheld the refusal of a witness to testify before the House Un-American Activities Committee, but this position was substantially abandoned in 1959, when the Court reverted to the policy earlier urged by Justice Jackson: "I should . . . leave the responsibility for the behavior of its committees squarely on the shoulders of Congress."

The American Congress has had its successes and its failures. The Senate, with its special responsibility in the ratifying of treaties and the confirmation of executive and judicial appointments, has certainly been the most influential and distinguished second house in the history of representative institutions. For the most part the failures of Congress have not resulted from provisions of Article I, but from practices adopted voluntarily by the two houses—the seniority rule on committees, archaic rules of procedure, abuse of unlimited debate in the Senate. Congress has performed least well when, either because of weakness in the executive or the ambition of its own leaders, it has sought to run the government. Congress is an institution adapted to discussion, not to action. Its task is appraisal and judgment, not leadership. Article I created a sound legislative structure, but each generation has to supply the wisdom and understanding to make it work.

Article II

EDITED BY ARTHUR SCHLESINGER, JR.

Article II of the Constitution—the article dealing with the executive power—emerged, like the rest of the document, from the debates at Philadelphia in 1787. Its initial source was the so-called Virginia Plan, drafted in large part by James Madison and presented to the Federal Convention by Edmund Randolph. Randolph's seventh resolution proposed a "National Executive" to be "chosen by the National Legislature" for a fixed term and to be ineligible a second time. The executive, "besides a general authority to execute the National laws, . . . ought to enjoy the Executive rights vested in Congress by the Confederation."

This language immediately raised a number of questions: Should the executive consist of one person or of several persons? Who should be eligible for it? How long should its term be? Should it indeed be chosen by the national legislature? Should it indeed be ineligible for a second term? What were these "Executive rights"? Should it share these rights with some form of executive council? Should it, by itself or in association with the council, have the authority to negative acts of the national legislature? What should happen in case of death or disability? Should it be liable to impeachment?

On June 1, 1787, three days after Randolph submitted his plan, the Committee of the Whole began its consideration of these matters. It was evident from the start that a deeper question lay beneath the particular issues—the question whether the proposed executive should be, as Roger Sherman of Connecticut believed, "nothing more than an institution for carrying the will of the Legislature into effect," or, as Gouverneur Morris of Pennsylvania argued, "the guardian of the people, even of the lower classes, agst Legislative tyranny." Those who wished to subordinate the executive to the legislature tended to favor a plural executive, chosen by the legislature, ineligible for reappointment, hedged in by an executive council, endowed with specific and limited powers, and subject to impeachment. Those who wished to secure the independence and authority of the executive tended to favor a single executive, chosen by the people, indefinitely re-eligible, unhampered by an executive council, endowed with general powers, and free from the threat of impeachment.

Thus, on the first day of debate over Randolph's seventh resolution, James Wilson of Pennsylvania advocated a single magistrate "as giving most energy, dispatch and responsibility to the office," while Randolph denounced "unity in the Executive magistracy" as "the foetus of monarchy" and called for an executive of three, to be drawn from different parts of the country. The Convention itself soon decided on a single executive. The question of who should choose this single executive gave more trouble. Roger Sherman, supporting the approach in the Virginia Plan, contended for his "appointment by the Legislature, and for making him absolutely dependent on that body, as it was the will of that which was to be executed." Gouverneur Morris responded that the executive "will be the mere creature of the Legisl: if appointed & impeachable by that body. He ought to be elected by the people at large." The Convention seemed to favor the thesis of the Virginia Plan and endorsed the idea of legislative choice at least five times in the course of the debates. In similar manner the argument between dependence and authority in the executive determined the reaction of the delegates to questions of length of term, re-eligibility, veto power, and the rest.

On July 24 the Convention appointed a Committee of Detail to embody the recommendations of the Committee of the Whole in a comprehensive draft of the new Constitution. The Committee of Detail reported back on August 6. Article X of its draft began: "The Executive Power of the United States shall be vested in a single person." The article went on to provide that this person should be chosen by the national legislature for one term of seven years; he could not serve a second time. He was to be charged with executing the laws. He could appoint officers in all cases not otherwise provided for by the Constitution (but Article IX gave the Senate power to appoint ambassadors and Supreme Court justices). He would be commander-in-chief of the armed forces. He had the power to receive foreign ambassadors (but Article IX gave the Senate power to make treaties). He could convene and adjourn the legislature. He was subject to impeachment; and, in case of removal, disability, or death, the President of the Senate was to exercise his powers and duties. In addition, Article VI gave the executive the power to veto acts of the legislature (and the legislature the power to override his veto by a two-thirds vote).

The advocates of a strong executive had made progress; but several provisions, notably those giving Congress authority to elect the executive, make treaties, and appoint high officials, still made for the clear subordination of the executive to the legislative. The Convention discussed these and other questions for another five weeks and then, on September 8, appointed a Committee on Style to write a final draft. Gouverneur Morris, chairman of this committee, was probably the main author of the text submitted to the Convention on September 12, and he undoubtedly took full advantage of the opportunity to strengthen the presidential prerogative.

Article II of the final draft began with an unequivocal affirmation of presidential autonomy and authority: "The executive power shall be vested in a president of the United States of America." This represented a notable expansion of the language in the earlier draft. In other respects too the new text differed from the proposals of the Committee of Detail. Most important of all, it took the election of the President away from the national legislature and assigned it to electors designated in whatever manner each state legislature might direct; the executive, said Madison, a little sweepingly, "is now to be elected by the people." The new draft also shortened the presidential term to four years and removed the ban to indefinite re-eligibility. It transferred to the President the authority to make treaties, though with the advice and consent of the Senate. It transferred to him authority to appoint all government officials, including ambassadors and Supreme Court justices, though again with the Senate's advice and consent. In case of removal, disability, or death, his powers and duties would now devolve on the Vice-President; Congress was authorized to make provision by law for succession beyond the Vice-President. And it added a definition of the conditions of presidential eligibility.

These changes provoked surprisingly little debate, partly because the delegates were eager to wrap the document up and go home, partly because, as Pierce Butler of South Carolina wrote a friend, "many of the members cast their eyes toward General Washington as President; and shaped their ideas of the Powers to be given to a President, by their opinions of his Virtue." In any case the Convention adopted the

Constitution, including Article II, on September 15, the document was ratified in another year, and the world's first modern experiment in democratic government began.

Section. 1. The executive Power shall be vested in a President of the United States of America. He shall hold his Office during the term of four Years, and, together with the Vice President, chosen for the same Term, be elected, as follows

Each State shall appoint, in such Manner as the Legislature thereof may direct, a number of Electors, equal to the whole Number of Senators and Representatives to which the State may be entitled in the Congress: but no Senator or Representative, or Person holding an Office of Trust or Profit under the United States, shall be appointed an Elector.

The Electors shall meet in their respective States, and vote by Ballot for two Persons, of whom one at least shall not be an Inhabitant of the same State with themselves. And they shall make a List of all the Persons voted for, and of the Number of Votes for each; which List they shall sign and certify, and transmit sealed to the Seat of the Government of the United States, directed to the President of the Senate. The President of the Senate shall, in the Presence of the Senate and House of Representatives, open all the Certificates, and the Votes shall then be counted. The Person having the greatest Number of Votes shall be the President, if such Number be a Majority of the whole Number of Electors appointed; and if there be more than one who have such Majority, and have an equal Number of Votes, then the House of Representatives shall immediately chuse by Ballot one of them for President; and if no Person have a Majority, then from the five highest on the List the said House shall in like Manner chuse the President. But in chusing the President, the Votes shall be taken by States, the Representation from each State having one Vote; a quorum for this Purpose shall consist of a Member or Members from two thirds of the States, and a Majority of all the States shall be necessary to a Choice. In every Case, after the Choice of the President, the Person having the greatest Number of Votes of the Electors shall be the Vice President.

But if there should remain two or more who have equal Votes, the Senate shall chuse from them by Ballot the Vice President.

The Congress may determine the Time of chusing the Electors, and the Day on which they shall give their Votes; which Day shall be the same throughout the United States.

No Person except a natural born Citizen, or a Citizen of the United States, at the time of the Adoption of this Constitution, shall be eligible to the Office of President; neither shall any person be eligible to that Office who shall not have attained to the Age of thirty five Years, and been fourteen Years a Resident within the United States.

In Case of the Removal of the President from Office, or of his Death, Resignation, or Inability to discharge the Powers and Duties of the said Office, the Same shall devolve on the Vice President, and the Congress may by Law provide for the Case of Removal, Death, Resignation or Inability, both of the President and Vice President, declaring what Officer shall then act as President, and such Officer shall act accordingly, until the Disability be removed, or a President shall be elected.

The President shall, at stated Times, receive for his Services, a Compensation, which shall neither be encreased nor diminished during the Period for which he shall have been elected, and he shall not receive within that Period any other Emolument from the United States, or any of them.

Before he enter on the Execution of his Office, he shall take the following Oath or Affirmation:—"I do solemnly swear (or affirm) that I will faithfully execute the Office of President of the United States, and will to the best of my Ability, preserve, protect and defend the Constitution of the United States."

Section. 2. The President shall be Commander in Chief of the Army and Navy of the United States, and of the Militia of the several States, when called into the actual Service of the United States; he may require the Opinion, in writing, of the principal Officer in each of the executive Departments, upon any Subject relating to the Duties of their respective Offices, and he shall have Power to grant Reprieves and Pardons for Offenses against the United States, except in Cases of Impeachment.

He shall have Power, by and with the Advice and Consent of the Senate, to make Treaties, provided two thirds of the Senators present concur; and he shall nominate, and by and with the Advice and Consent of the Senate, shall appoint Ambassadors, other public Ministers and Consuls, Judges of the supreme Court, and all other Officers of the United States, whose Appointments are not herein otherwise provided for, and which shall be established by Law: but the Congress may by Law vest the Appointment of such inferior Officers, as they think proper, in the President alone, in the Courts of Law, or in the Heads of Departments.

The President shall have Power to fill up all Vacancies that may happen during the Recess of the Senate, by granting Commissions which shall expire at the End of their next Session.

Section. 3. He shall from time to time give to the Congress Information of the State of the Union, and recommend to their Consideration such Measures as he shall judge necessary and expedient; he may, on extraordinary Occasions, convene both Houses, or either of them, and in Case of Disagreement between them, with Respect to the Time of Adjournment, he may adjourn them to such Time as he shall think proper; he shall receive Ambassadors and other public Ministers; he shall take Care that the Laws be faithfully executed, and shall Commission all the Officers of the United States.

Section. 4. The President, Vice President and all Civil Officers of the United States, shall be removed from Office on Impeachment for, and Conviction of, Treason, Bribery, or other high Crimes and Misdemeanors.

Though Article II established the basic framework within which the executive power would operate, it did not seek to solve all the problems of scope and application. The drafters knew they were writing a document not just for their own generation, but for many generations to come. With their masterly instinct for ambiguity, they bequeathed a series of vital questions to the future. Thus the language of the Constitution did not end the debate over whether the executive should be weak or strong. It only settled the context in which subsequent phases of that debate would take place.

From the start, Article II was subject to minimum and maximum interpretations. Thomas Paine and those who understood democracy as meaning the supremacy of the legislative power contended for a passive President serving as the executive officer of the Congress. They became advocates of a "strict" construction of the Constitution. Alexander Hamilton, on the other hand, wrote in The Federalist, No. 70, "Energy in the executive is a leading character in the definition of good government." As Secretary of the Treasury under George Washington, he became the champion of executive initiative and a "broad" construction of the Constitution. The debate has gone on ever since—and history, as it has subjected the institution of the Presidency to strain and challenge, has had to speak where the Constitution was silent.

It fell to George Washington, the first President under the Constitution, to begin the process of filling out the blank spaces in Article II. While not an activist President in the modern sense, Washington was a strong executive who effectively vindicated the dignity and independence of the presidential office. John Adams followed in his footsteps, if with less success. The next great test of the Presidency came with the election of the third President, Thomas Jefferson, who was nominally a strict constructionist. But Jefferson's decision to go ahead with the Louisiana Purchase—a decision for which he could find no warrant in the Constitution—showed how national need could enlarge the presidential authority, even when the President himself might be disposed against it.

The Jefferson Administration also saw the replacement of paragraph 3 of Article II, Section 1, by the Twelfth Amendment. The drafters of the Constitution had supposed that the members of the electoral college would make their own decisions about President and Vice-President; they had not anticipated the rise of political parties. By 1796 these assumptions were plainly wrong. The election of 1800, resulting in a tie between Jefferson and Aaron Burr in the electoral college, emphasized the urgency of reform. The Twelfth Amendment required electors to vote separately for President and Vice-President and thereby accommodated the method of choice to the party system.

The first man to realize the Hamiltonian conception of the Presidency was Andrew Jackson, who took his oath half a century after the ratification of the Constitution. Jackson revolutionized the presidential office and may be said to have invented the modern Presidency. He saw himself as the tribune of the people, defending the people's rights against whatever body might threaten them—the executive bureaucracy, the Congress, the judiciary, state governments which set themselves against *the national authority.* In this spirit, Jackson subdued the Cabinet and the executive branch; he expanded presidential powers of initiation and control in Congress (he vetoed more bills, for example, than all his predecessors put together and secured the presidential right to veto clearly constitutional measures); he set his own interpretation of the Constitution beside that of the Supreme Court; and he made it impossible for sovereign states to nullify federal legislation.

One effect of the Jacksonian revolution was to transform the conception of the strong President, which Gouverneur Morris and Alexander Hamilton had seen as the instrument of the elite, into an instrument of the people. Another was to revive in full vigor the old debate about the powers of the President. Jackson's opponents, led by the great senators of the time, Henry Clay and Daniel Webster, denounced Jackson as a tyrant and strove to reassert the legislative prerogative. They formed the Whig Party, dedicated to the thesis of a strong Congress and a weak President. And, though James K. Polk a decade later sustained the Hamilton-Jackson view of the President, a succession of weak Presidents before the Civil War renewed hopes of congressional supremacy.

The next great expansion of presidential authority came during the Civil War, when Abraham Lincoln, claiming to act in response to "a popular demand and a public necessity," invoked the new idea of "the war power of the government" to justify acts undertaken by no previous President. But the years after the Civil War were another time of revulsion against executive activism. The Presidency was in decline; and Woodrow Wilson, writing about the American political system in this period, entitled his book Congressional Government. During this period, too, Congress used the authority granted by Section II to pass the Presidential Succession Act of 1886, providing that, if both the President and Vice-President were eliminated, the Secretary of State would succeed to the Presidency, and so on down through the Cabinet.

But new developments brought the reign of Congress to an end. For one thing, the emergence of a national economy created domestic problems requiring national policies and national solutions. For another, the emergence of the United States as a world power created foreign problems requiring national leadership to defend the national interest. These developments, seizing public attention at the turn of the century, imposed new demands on the national government and thus on the Presidency. With the accession of Theodore Roosevelt in 1901 came an exuberant rebirth of the Hamilton-Jackson (or, as Roosevelt called it, the

Jackson-Lincoln) thesis of the Presidency. "I declined," Roosevelt wrote in his Autobiography, "to adopt the view that what was imperatively necessary for the Nation could not be done by the President unless he could find some specific authorization to do it. My belief was that it was not only his right but his duty to do anything that the needs of the Nation demanded unless such action was forbidden by the Constitution or by the laws." This view was opposed by Roosevelt's successor, William Howard Taft, who advanced what Roosevelt called the Buchanan-Taft thesis in these words: "The true view of the Executive function is, as I conceive it, that the President can exercise no power which cannot be fairly and reasonably traced to some specific grant of power or justly implied and included within such express grant as proper and necessary to its exercise. Such specific grant must be either in the Federal Constitution or in an act of Congress. . . . There is no undefined residuum of power which he can exercise because it seems to him to be in the public interest." The debate has continued throughout this century, with Wilson, Franklin Roosevelt, Truman, Kennedy, and Johnson supporting the Jackson-Lincoln thesis and Harding, Coolidge, Hoover, and Eisenhower in the Buchanan-Taft camp.

While the "strong" Presidents of the century, acting under the spur of war, depression, and social need, proceeded to unfold potentialities inherent in the Constitution—Congress, the Supreme Court, and the nation through the amending process have modified various aspects of Article II, some modifications strengthening, others limiting, the executive power. Thus not only did Congress, especially in the 1930's, multiply the functions of government; but the Government Reorganization Act of 1939 offered the Presidency new means of personal control through the establishment of the Executive Office of the President, in which are now gathered such powerful presidential agencies as the Bureau of the Budget, the National Security Council, and the Council of Economic Advisers. On the other hand, the Presidential Succession Act of 1947 revised the act of 1886 by having the succession devolve from the Vice-President to the Speaker of the House and the President pro tempore of the Senate rather than, at first instance, to the cabinet. The Supreme Court in the Curtiss-Wright case of 1936 (299 U.S. 304) confirmed the President's right to exercise very wide powers in foreign policy; in the Steel Seizure case of 1952 (343 U.S. 579), however, it struck a blow at the conception of the implied powers of the Presidency. The Twentieth Amendment (1933) provided for the speedier installation of a newly elected President and Congress, thereby reducing the "lame duck" presence in the government. Then the Twenty-second Amendment (1951) gave the two-term tradition constitutional status.

American history thus by no means records an uninterrupted enlargement of the powers granted the President under Article II. Nearly every strong President has provoked a reaction in favor of the limitation of executive powers, even if the reaction has never quite cut these powers back to their earlier level. Moreover, every branch of the government in recent years has enlarged its own powers as against the Presidency. The Congress, as a result of the increasing dependence of foreign policy on appropriations, has more control over the conduct of foreign affairs than ever before in American history. The Supreme Court has shown a new and aggressive activism. Even the executive bureaucracy has developed an independence and obduracy which enable it on occasion to ignore or sabotage presidential policy. With all these qualifications, however, the course of American history and the tempo of world change appear to have created an increasing demand for vigorous presidential leadership if the system is not to bog down in a morass of checks-and-balances. Over the long haul, the role of the President has increased steadily in American history. As Woodrow Wilson wrote of the responsibilities of the President, "The Constitution bids him speak and times of stress and change more and more thrust upon him the attitude of originator of policies."

Article III

EDITED BY DAVID FELLMAN

Those who drafted the American Constitution at the Philadelphia Convention of 1787 did not write upon a clean slate or act upon merely abstract excogitation. Their stock of knowledge was drawn from many sources, notably the precedents of English constitutional history and common-law principles, the colonial political and legal experience, the existing state constitutions, and the Articles of Confederation, the grave inadequacies of which had led to the convoking of the Convention in 1787. The over-all purpose of the authors of the Constitution was to lay the foundations for a federal union strong enough to promote and protect the national interests of the American people. The third article of the Constitution, which authorized the creation of national courts operating independently of state power, and endowed with ample jurisdiction, was an essential part of the plan to create a truly adequate national authority.

Under the Articles of Confederation, the central government had some judicial power, but not very much. Congress was authorized to appoint ad hoc courts which could make "final and conclusive" decisions in disputes between two or more states. It also was empowered to appoint courts for the trial of piracies and felonies on the high seas, but it simply designated the state courts for this purpose. In addition, Congress was authorized to establish an appeals court for prize cases, and this it promptly did. The three-judge Court of Appeals in Cases of Captures was, during the short life of the Articles of Confederation, the only appellate tribunal with jurisdiction over the whole country. All other judicial power was exercised, during the Confederation period, by the state courts.

The delegates to the Constitutional Convention had serious disagreements which led to justly celebrated compromises, but with regard to the judicial branch of the proposed national government there was substantial agreement from the start. The delegates recognized that the lack of an effective judiciary had been a central weakness of the Confederation government. Thus, very early in its proceedings, on June 4, the Convention adopted, by unanimous vote, a resolution "that a national Judiciary be established," and then added a provision that it should consist of one "supreme tribunal" and a number of "inferior tribunals." During the course of the Convention's deliberations there was no controversy as to the jurisdiction of the federal courts. There was some disagreement over the method of selecting federal judges, but the main disagreement was concerned with the desirability of having inferior federal courts. Many delegates preferred to leave all judicial business in the hands of the state courts, subject to appeal to a federal supreme court where questions of federal law were concerned. Thus the New Jersey Plan, which reflected the localistic inclinations of some of the small states, provided only for a "supreme Tribunal" with appellate powers over state courts in cases involving legal issues of a federal character. The solution was a compromise, engineered by Madison and Wilson, which merely authorized, but did not require, Congress to create inferior courts. The very first Congress, in the seminal Judiciary Act of 1789, created the United States district courts to serve as the trial courts of the national government, and we have had inferior federal tribunals ever since. Finally, a proposal was made, repeatedly, to unite the Supreme Court with the executive in a council of revision which would exercise a veto power over legislation, but it was voted down four times on the ground of incompatibility with the principle of the separation of powers.

There was relatively little debate about Article III in the Convention. The Convention agreed with the general language of the Randolph or Virginia Plan, and the specifications were worked out partly on the floor, but largely by the Committee of Detail and later the Committee on Style. The five members of the Committee of Detail—especially James Wilson, who was probably its most effective member—favored a strong judiciary. Similarly, the five members of the Committee on Style were all in favor of a strong judiciary, and Gouverneur Morris, who was mainly responsible for the final language of the document, once said that in drafting Article III he had gone as far as he could go.

The ninth Randolph Resolution proposed that the federal judicial power should extend to "all piracies and felonies on the high seas; captures from an enemy; cases in which foreigners, or citizens of other States, applying to such jurisdictions, may be interested; or which respect the collection of the national revenue; impeachments of any national officers; and questions which may involve the national peace and harmony." With the exception of the clause relating to impeachments, the jurisdictional provisions of Article III followed the line taken by the Virginia Plan, a line which was also taken, with minor differences, by the New Jersey Plan.

The federal judicial power was structured to enable the new national government to enforce its own laws, which were to be binding directly upon the individual, in its own courts, and which were to be construed in a uniform way throughout the country. Thus national supremacy and uniformity were two of the main objectives of the jurisdictional clauses of Article III. In addition, the federal judiciary was given great responsibilities for umpiring the inevitable controversies between states and between citizens of different states. Accordingly, the Supreme Court was given original jurisdiction over suits between states, and the judicial power of the United States was made applicable to suits between citizens of different states. In order to protect the vital interests of the national government, and especially its fiscal needs, the judicial power was extended to all cases in which the United States is a party. Since a central purpose of the new Constitution was to give the national government full control over foreign affairs, to the exclusion of the states, the federal judicial power was extended to admiralty and maritime cases, piracies and felonies on the high seas, and cases involving ambassadors, public ministers, treaties, foreign states, and foreign citizens.

Maritime commerce was much more important, relatively, in the eighteenth century than it is today, and the authors of the Constitution had no doubt that it would be most unwise to permit jurisdiction over such commerce to remain in the state courts. "The most bigoted idolizers of State authority," Hamilton wrote in No. 80 of The Federalist, "have not thus far shewn a disposition to deny the national judiciary the cognizance of maritime causes. These so generally depend on the law of nations, and so commonly affect the rights of foreigners, that they fall within the considerations which are relative to the public peace." Furthermore, the Convention delegates must have had fresh in their memories the famous circular letter which the Secretary of Foreign

Affairs had drafted, and which the Confederation Congress had sent to the states on April 13, 1787, as a result of the protests of the British government against American violations of the peace treaty of 1783. The states were asked to take steps to abrogate all laws which were contrary to the treaty obligations of the Confederation. The letter pleaded that "the faith of treaties remain inviolate," and pointed out that when a treaty has been constitutionally entered into, "it immediately becomes binding on the whole nation, and superadded to the laws of the land, without the intervention of State legislatures." In addition, the Congress urged the state courts to declare all legislation in conflict with treaty provisions a nullity. This experience was clearly reflected in the jurisdictional clauses of Article III.

The federal judicial power extends, under Article III, to two types of cases. First, there are the cases where jurisdiction proceeds from the fact that they involve questions arising under the Constitution, or statutes or treaties made under its authority, or questions of admiralty or maritime law. These are known as the "federal question" cases. The other class of cases includes those which come within the jurisdiction of the federal courts because of the nature of the parties involved. These include cases in which the United States is itself a party, cases involving ambassadors and other public ministers, controversies between two or more states, or between a state and citizens of another state, or between citizens of different states.

The jurisdictional clauses of Article III were intended, first and foremost, to help establish an effective national government which could maintain the supremacy of federal law, protect the interests of the national government, and umpire the federal system. In addition, they were designed to give the central government effective control over international affairs. Finally, they extended federal protection to property and trade, and thus enlisted the support of the business and propertied community. The federal question and diversity of citizenship jurisdictions were designed to protect property and trade from unfriendly state legislation, and to give traders access to federal courts which would be independent of local political influence.

The last three paragraphs of Article III expressed a concern with the protection of basic civil liberties. The ancient right of trial by jury in the vicinage was guaranteed in criminal cases. The elements of the heinous crime of treason were spelled out precisely, as a protection against use of *the charge of treason for mere political ends. Finally, through the prohibition of bills of attainder, Congress was forbidden to try men for crimes legislatively.*

Section. 1. The judicial Power of the United States, shall be vested in one supreme Court, and in such inferior Courts as the Congress may from time to time ordain and establish. The Judges, both of the supreme and inferior Courts, shall hold their Offices during good Behaviour, and shall, at stated Times, receive for their Services, a Compensation, which shall not be diminished during their Continuance in Office.

Section. 2. The judicial Power shall extend to all Cases, in Law and Equity, arising under this Constitution, the Laws of the United States, and Treaties made, or which shall be made, under their Authority;—to all Cases affecting Ambassadors, other public Ministers and Consuls;—to all Cases of admiralty and maritime Jurisdiction;—to Controversies to which the United States shall be a Party;—to Controversies between two or more States;—between a State and Citizens of another State;—between Citizens of different States;—between Citizens of the same State claiming Lands under Grants of different States, and between a State, or the Citizens thereof, and foreign States, Citizens or Subjects.

In all Cases affecting Ambassadors, other public Ministers and Consuls, and those in which a State shall be Party, the supreme Court shall have original Jurisdiction. In all the other Cases before mentioned, the supreme Court shall have appellate Jurisdiction, both as to Law and Fact, with such Exceptions, and under such Regulations as the Congress shall make.

The Trial of all Crimes, except in Cases of Impeachment, shall be by Jury; and such Trial shall be held in the State where the said Crimes shall have been committed; but when not committed within any State, the Trial shall be at such Place or Places as the Congress may by Law have directed.

Section. 3. Treason against the United States, shall consist only in levying War against them, or in adhering to their Enemies, giving them

Aid and Comfort. No Person shall be convicted of Treason unless on the Testimony of two Witnesses to the same overt Act, or on Confession in open Court.

The Congress shall have Power to declare the Punishment of Treason, but no Attainder of Treason shall work Corruption of Blood, or Forfeiture except during the Life of the Person attainted.

While our national system of government is based on the principle of the separation of powers, there are in fact many important points of contact between the three great branches of government. All federal judges are appointed by the President, subject to confirmation by the Senate. The Senate, sitting as a court of impeachment, may remove federal judges from office, after trial on charges brought by the House of Representatives. All federal courts are created by acts of Congress, and Congress determines how many judges shall serve in these courts, and how much salary they shall be paid. In addition, Congress may abolish courts and judgeships, except that it cannot constitutionally abolish the Supreme Court. Finally, Congress defines by statute the jurisdiction of all federal courts, with the exception of the limited original jurisdiction of the Supreme Court, which is spelled out in Article III. At the same time, the federal judges enjoy a great deal of independence, since they hold office for "good behavior," and can be removed only by impeachment. They do not live in fear that political retribution may unseat them if their decisions prove unpopular.

The courts have much to do with Congress and the President because the judges are called upon to construe the meaning of statutes and of executive ordinances, and to help enforce them. Above all, the courts have the authority to declare acts of Congress or of the President to be unenforceable on the ground that they violate the Constitution. This is known as the power of judicial review. Of all the powers of the federal courts, it is the most distinctive, the most crucial, and the most controversial.

Since Article III does not say, in so many words, that the courts possess the power of judicial review, the legitimacy of the exercise of this authority has always been a subject of debate. That judicial review is a natural outgrowth of a written constitution has always been the position of the Supreme Court. In 1803, in the celebrated case of Marbury v. Madison, 1 Cranch 137, Chief Justice John Marshall, speaking for the Court, held that since it is the province of a court to declare the law, and since the written Constitution is both law and the supreme law of the land, it follows that when a statute is in conflict with a provision of the Constitution, the latter must prevail over the former. This assertion of the power of judicial review was consistent with practice in the state courts, and had been regarded by most of the authors of Article III to be a normal aspect of judicial power. Accordingly, Hamilton declared, in No. 78 of The Federalist:

The interpretation of the laws is the proper and peculiar province of the courts. A Constitution is in fact, and must be, regarded as a fundamental law. It therefore belongs to them to ascertain its meaning as well as the meaning of any particular act proceeding from the legislative body. If there should happen to be an irreconcileable variance between the two, that which has the superior obligation and validity ought of course to be preferred; or in other words, the constitution ought to be preferred to the statute, the intention of the people to the intention of their agents.

The Supreme Court's power of judicial review also extends to state legislation. There were members of the Constitutional Convention who were strongly in favor of a congressional veto over state statutes. Thus on August 23, Charles Pinckney moved to give the Congress the power "to negative all laws passed by the several States interfering, in the opinion of the Legislature, with the general interests and harmony of the Union. . . . " A lively debate ensued, during which the motion was opposed on the ground that in any event, as Sherman argued, the laws of the federal government would be paramount and supreme. On the other hand, the Pinckney motion was supported with the contention that, as Wilson maintained, "the firmness of Judges is not of itself sufficient." The Pinckney motion was finally defeated by a vote of 5 to 6. Accordingly, the Convention settled for a federal judicial rather than a legislative veto of unconstitutional state legislation. In fact, this was one of the great compromises of the Convention.

As the agency which interprets the Constitution authoritatively and with finality, the Supreme Court has been, in the words of Lord Bryce, "the living voice of the Constitution," and indeed, "the conscience of the people, who have resolved to restrain themselves from hasty or unjust action by placing their representatives under the restriction of a permanent law." While judicial review is an important aspect of American

119

government, and a source of great power, the Supreme Court has exercised this power over the years with considerable restraint. It should always be assumed, the Court maintains, that when a legislative body enacted a given statute, it did not intend to violate the Constitution; thus the burden of proof is on those who attack the validity of the statute, and all doubts should be resolved in favor of upholding the statute. Furthermore, if a statute can reasonably be read in more than one way, the Court prefers so to construe the statute as to lead to a conclusion which will sustain its validity. The Court has always taken the position that it will not exercise its great powers except in actual cases or controversies in which adverse parties are concerned with valuable legal rights; it will not give advisory opinions, therefore, and will not hear a suit unless the parties to it have proper standing to sue. The parties must have used up all other possible remedies, and must present substantial legal problems for decision. The Court regards some constitutional questions as political in character, and therefore nonjusticiable. The Court also declines to rule on the motives of legislators, or the wisdom of their legislation.

Whether the Supreme Court observes its own rules of self-restraint is often a matter of lively debate. There have been periods of great judicial activism, when the Court has used its judicial review powers rather freely, and then there have been other periods of relative quiescence. The Supreme Court was very active, for example, in the Reconstruction period, and invalidated a large body of federal legislation through a process of strict construction of the Civil War Amendments to the Constitution. There was another flurry of activity in the 1890's, which led, above all, to judicial nullification of the first modern federal income tax. In the 1920's and during the first four years of the New Deal in the 1930's, the Court was dominated by a majority which found ways of invalidating a great amount of reform legislation, especially in the field of economic regulation. More recently, during the 1950's and 1960's, the Court has been concerned primarily with questions regarding civil rights and civil liberties. The 1954 decision outlawing racial segregation in the public schools, and the 1962 decision which asserted jurisdiction over the problem of the reapportionment of legislative bodies, have in recent years stirred up immense interest and great controversy.

Throughout the course of American history, the Supreme Court has performed the vital functions of defining the limits of state and national power. The Court, however, is itself an agency of the national government, and while there have been some exceptions, as a general rule the tendency of the Court has been to take a national point of view. Thus, it has generally construed the commerce power of the federal government broadly, and has given its sanction to a growing body of national legislation in the field of interstate commerce. At the same time, the Court has tried to accommodate the local needs of the states in the commerce field by upholding a large body of police legislation enacted to protect the health, safety, and welfare of the public in areas where Congress has taken no action and where uniform national rules do not seem to be essential. In the past quarter of a century, however, the Court has been preoccupied with spelling out the meaning of civil rights and civil liberties, especially in regard to freedom of religion, liberty of speech, press, and association, the right to vote, the fair-procedure rights of defendants in criminal cases, and freedom from racial discrimination. So far as state action is concerned this has involved a broad and generous construction of the "due process" and "equal protection" clauses of the Fourteenth Amendment. The steady growth of the concept of due process of law may well be regarded as the central theme of modern constitutional law in the jurisprudence of the United States Supreme Court.

Article IV

EDITED BY J. A. C. GRANT

In the drafting of Article IV of the Constitution, Section 1 and the first two clauses of Section 2 of Article IV were copied from the similar provisions in the Articles of Confederation. Of these, only the second sentence of Section 1 was subjected to debate either in the Philadelphia Convention or in the state ratifying conventions. This sentence had been added on the motion of Gouverneur Morris, and although a committee recommended restricting congressional authority to the effect of judgments, the broader language ultimately adopted was restored by a vote of 6 to 3. The third clause of Section 2 was modeled after Article 6 of the Northwest Ordinance of July 13, 1787. The northern delegates first protested that there is "no more propriety in the public seizing and surrendering a slave or servant, than a horse," but in the end insisted only upon omitting such words as "slave" and "legally held."

Whereas the Articles of Confederation had required that (except in the case of Canada) nine states would have to agree to the admission of a new state, it was generally agreed at Philadelphia that this power should be given to the national legislature. However, Gouverneur Morris proposed that "the rule of representation ought to be so fixed as to secure to the Atlantic States a prevalence in the National Councils," and John Rutledge and Pierce Butler hoped that the same end could be accomplished through basing representation on taxes or property rather than population. Elbridge Gerry proposed that the total number of representatives in the lower house from the new states should never exceed the total from the original states. Apparently only James Madison, George Mason, Charles C. Pinckney, Edmund Randolph, Roger Sherman, and James Wilson spoke in favor of admitting new states on a plane of equality, but their views prevailed in the Committee of Detail. It proposed, "If the admission be consented to, the new States shall be admitted on the same terms with the original States." Following further debate this sentence was deleted by a vote of 9 to 2, a spokesman for the majority explaining that it "did not wish to bind down the Legislature to admit Western States on the terms here stated."

The Committee of Detail's draft also required the consent of a state's legislature before the state could be divided. This version prevailed, but only after strenuous opposition from many delegates who felt that Congress should be free to admit Maine, Vermont, and the western territories of Georgia, of North Carolina, and of Virginia to statehood without consulting the states from which the new states would be carved. This provision was one of those relied upon by Luther Martin for recommending that Maryland should not ratify the Constitution. He insisted that "republican government" was suited only to a small and compact territory and could not prevail unless the larger and less compact states were divided.

The passage of the Northwest Ordinance pointed up the need for an express provision in the Constitution for the power of Congress to govern and dispose of western and other lands and property belonging to the nation. The first phrase of clause 2 of Section 3 was thus accepted almost automatically. But the rest of the clause was hammered out in the course of debate. The language finally adopted was that proposed on August 30 by Gouverneur Morris, whose fine hand is to be seen so often in this Article. It was assumed that contested claims would be settled by negotiation or by suit in the federal Supreme Court.

Item 11 in the plan submitted to the Convention on May 29, 1787, by Edmund Randolph provided that "a Republican Government and the territory of each State . . . ought to be guaranteed by the United States to each State." Six weeks later Article 5 of the Northwest Ordinance provided that "the constitution and government" of each of the new states to be erected beyond the Ohio "shall be republican." James Madison expressed doubts as to the accuracy of "republican" to describe a government where slavery existed, but the Convention accepted it for lack of a better word to distinguish popular government from aristocracy and monarchy. Our records of the debates yield no other meaning of the word.

While everyone seemed anxious to guarantee to each state a republican form of government, that was as far as unanimity went. Gouverneur Morris was "very unwilling that such laws as exist in Rhode Island should be guaranteed." William Houston "was afraid of perpetuating the existing Constitution of the States," some of which—especially that of his own state, Georgia—he considered very defective. Consequently the additional guarantee of "its existing laws," although approved on June 11, was abandoned, making it clear that each state was to remain free to alter either its constitution or its laws by peaceful means.

Although all the Convention delegates readily agreed to a national guarantee against foreign invasion, the provision concerning the power of the United States government to protect against domestic violence was secured only after long debate. Luther Martin's motion to permit Congress to divide a state without the consent of its legislature was defeated by a 6 to 5 vote. That led many, including John Dickinson, to stress "the impropriety of requiring the small States to secure the large ones in their extensive claims of territory." Martin himself, in pleading with Maryland not to ratify the Constitution, could foresee his state "called upon to assist, with her wealth and her blood, in subduing the inhabitants of Franklin, Kentucky, Vermont, and the provinces of Maine and Sagadohock" when in all justice they should be independent states. Dickinson's disappointment was shorter lived. He actually led an unsuccessful effort to authorize national intervention to suppress domestic violence without any request from the state. He was successful in a less ambitious move, securing insertion of the phrase, "or of the Executive (when the Legislature cannot be convened)." But nothing that he or others said seems to justify the charge made later by the opponents of the Constitution, in the Virginia ratifying convention, that the language used in Section 4 gives exclusive jurisdiction to the nation to use the state's militia to put down domestic violence. This was left, and was intended to be left, as a primary obligation of the state itself.

Section. 1. Full Faith and Credit shall be given in each State to the public Acts, Records, and judicial Proceedings of every other State. And the Congress may by general Laws prescribe the Manner in which such Acts, Records and Proceedings shall be proved, and the Effect thereof.

Section. 2. The Citizens of each State shall be entitled to all Privileges and Immunities of Citizens in the several States.

A Person charged in any State with Treason, Felony, or other Crime, who shall flee from Justice, and be found in another State, shall on Demand of the executive Authority of the State from which he fled, be delivered up, to be removed to the State having Jurisdiction of the Crime.

No Person held to Service or Labour in one State, under the Laws thereof, escaping into another, shall, in Consequence of any Law or Regulation therein, be discharged from such Service or Labour, but shall be delivered up on Claim of the Party to whom such Service or Labour may be due.

Section. 3. New States may be admitted by the Congress into this Union; but no new State shall be formed or erected within the Jurisdiction of any other State; nor any State be formed by the Junction of two or more States, or Parts of States, without the Consent of the Legislatures of the States concerned as well as of the Congress.

The Congress shall have Power to dispose of and make all needful Rules and Regulations respecting the Territory or other Property belonging to the United States; and nothing in this Constitution shall be so construed as to Prejudice any Claims of the United States, or of any particular State.

Section. 4. The United States shall guarantee to every State in this Union a Republican Form of Government, and shall protect each of them against Invasion; and on Application of the Legislature, or of the Executive (when the Legislature cannot be convened) against domestic Violence.

Congressional legislation under the "full faith and credit" clause has provided that properly authenticated legislative acts and judicial rulings "have the same full faith and credit in every court within the United States and its Territories and Possessions as they have by law in the courts of such State, Territory or Possession." It was logical of Congress to go beyond the sweep of Article IV and include all American jurisdictions under a single set of rules. The extension to legislative acts was not added until 1948, but the courts had applied the same doctrines under the accepted principles of private international law. In fact, the only

important effect of the clause and its implementing statute was to nationalize the basic principles of private international law.

Without such a clause we would be a league of states instead of a nation. Undoubtedly some states would have clung to the common-law doctrine that a money judgment is only presumptively valid, so that the merits of the original controversy could always be reopened when enforcement is sought in another state. The Supreme Court, in Mills v. Duryee, 7 Cranch 481 (1813), rejected this rule for the sounder one that such a judgment is conclusive of the merits. Although many disagree with the rules the Supreme Court has adopted on such contentious subjects as migratory divorces or the exterritorial application of workmen's compensation acts, there can be little question that the benefit of a single set of rules interpreted by a single court of last resort is far superior to any result possible under a system of fifty-one courts of last resort.

Congress has left the development of the "full faith and credit" clause largely to the courts. There is much that Congress could do that courts cannot do. It could, for example, provide more expeditious means for enforcing foreign judgments or the service of process. Doubtless it could provide standards to determine jurisdiction over divorce and the allied problems of alimony, child support, and the like. Indeed, even the legislative possibilities envisioned by the framers have scarcely been approached.

Section 2 opens with the "comity" clause. This is self-executing, and as construed by the Supreme Court merely forbids one state to discriminate against the citizens of other states in favor of its own. But it does not require that nonresidents be permitted to share the "public patrimony" of a state. Thus game fishing or hunting by outsiders may be restricted or even forbidden; but "commercial shrimping in the marginal sea, like other common callings, is within the purview" of the guarantee (Toomer v. Witsell, 334 U.S. 385, 403 [1948]). One does not carry his status as a doctor, as a dentist, or even as an insurance broker with him to another state, but must meet the standards set by the state concerned, including where appropriate a prescribed period of residence (La Tourette v. McMaster, 248 U.S. 465 [1919]). Nor does the clause protect corporations (Paul v. Virginia, 8 Wall. 168 [1869]), which must rely upon the commerce clause and the Fourteenth Amendment when they seek recognition beyond the confines of their state of incorporation.

The second clause of Section 2 provides for interstate rendition. Although Congress long has required governors to cause fugitives to be

126

arrested and delivered up upon demand, the Supreme Court has construed this to be merely declaratory, unenforceable by court action (Kentucky v. Dennison, 24 How. 66 [1861]). The recent reapportionment decisions and particularly statements in Baker v. Carr, 369 U.S. 186, 210 (1962), indicate that Congress can strengthen this act if it chooses. It also has made fleeing from one state to another to evade prosecution for felony a federal crime. Accepted principles of international law dictate that an offender may be tried only "for the offence with which he is charged in the proceedings for his extradition, until a reasonable time and opportunity have been given him, after his release or trial upon such charge, to return to the country from whose asylum he had been forcibly taken" (United States v. Rauscher, 119 U.S. 407, 430 [1886]). As no such limitation has been found in Article IV, a fugitive extradited from another state may be tried for an offense other than that for which he was surrendered (Lascelles v. Georgia, 148 U.S. 537 [1893]).

The third clause of Section 2 was the basis for passage of the Fugitive Slave Acts of 1793; the Thirteenth Amendment, of course, rendered it obsolete in 1865.

The power of Congress to admit new states has now made us more than a mere continental union. Maine, Vermont, and the western territories of Georgia, of North Carolina, and of Virginia received the independent status so earnestly desired by many delegates to the Philadelphia Convention without the bloodshed or other difficulties envisaged by some. The first clause of Section 3 has proved to be one of the most successful provisions in the Constitution, in part because it has not been construed or applied as those who wrote it intended. Whereas Vermont (1791) and Kentucky (1792) were simply admitted as states, Tennessee (1796) was welcomed "on an equal footing with the original states in all respects whatsoever." Although such a statement is found either in the Enabling Act or the Act of Admission of every state subsequently admitted, Congress soon departed from it by imposing restrictions intended to be binding upon the new state forever. Examples are Louisiana (1812), forbidden to curb religious liberty, to deny jury trial in criminal cases, or to charge tolls for the use of its navigable waters; Nevada (1864), forbidden to authorize slavery or to curb religious freedom; Nebraska (1867), denied the right to use a racial test for voters; Utah (1896), required to grant religious toleration and to forbid polygamy. The Supreme Court held the restrictions against Louisiana

unenforceable in Permoli v. Municipality No. 1, 3 How. 589 (1845), and
has never departed from the views there expressed. The most frequently
quoted ruling sustained Oklahoma in its disregard of the attempt of
Congress to prevent it from establishing a permanent state capital until
the state was more developed (Coyle v. Smith, 221 U.S. 559 [1911]).
Thus state equality, rather than congressional discretion, has become the
command of the living Constitution.

The second clause of Section 3 has been used by Congress to lease
federally owned lands as well as to dispose of them by gift, sale, or under
homestead acts. The decision of the Supreme Court in Ashwander v.
T.V.A., 297 U.S. 288 (1936), relied on it, together with the war power
and control over navigation, to sustain a vast electric power and area
development program. It has been cited to justify both the establishment
of territorial governments and direct congressional control over the
territories, although the Supreme Court conceded that "the right to
govern may be the inevitable consequence of the right to acquire
territory" (American Insurance Co. v. Canter, 1 Pet. 511, 543 [1828]).

It is "the United States" that under Section 4 "shall guarantee to every
State in this Union a republican form of government" and protect it
against invasion or domestic violence. These are the only instances where
the government by its corporate name is given a duty. Literally the
obligation would seem to rest upon all departments of the government,
but obviously the courts must have only a minor role so far as invasion or
insurrection are concerned. Although the only meaning that can be
gathered from the Convention debates is that a republican government is
a popular rather than an aristocratic or monarchical one, the majority
opinion in Calder v. Bull, 3 Dall. 386, 387–88 (1798), intimated that it is
one in which the government respects "the purposes for which men enter
into society." Thus construed, it could have become the equivalent of a
full bill of rights binding upon all branches of the state governments,
giving the courts authority to void even statutes considered by them to
violate basic principles of right and justice. But this early promise failed
to develop. Instead, the Supreme Court soon withdrew completely from
the field, treating all questions of "republican government" as political
ones where the decisions of Congress or the executive are final. The only
exception is Minor v. Happersett, 21 Wall. 162 (1875), holding (prior to
the Nineteenth Amendment) that the suffrage may be denied to
women.

Congress used the clause to justify the Reconstruction Acts following

128

the Civil War. At that time Charles Sumner referred to it as "a sleeping giant in the Constitution." It may yet become significant, although the expanded meaning given to the Fourteenth Amendment militates against this.

The final clause of Article IV requires a request from the legislature or the executive of a state before the nation may protect it from domestic violence. The vastly expanded scope of federal activity, coupled with the In Re Debs, 158 U.S. 564, 582 (1895), doctrine that "the entire strength of the nation" may be used "to enforce in any part of the land the full and free exercise of all national powers and the security of all rights entrusted by the Constitution to its care" have virtually removed this limitation. It is rare indeed that violence on a scale that is of interest to the nation can fail to meet this test. John Dickinson has finally had his way.

Article V and the Amending Process
EDITED BY PHILIP B. KURLAND

However natural it may now seem for the Constitution to provide for its own amendment, we should remember Holmes's warning against confusing the familiar with the necessary. There are other, more recent, national constitutions that make no such provision. The nature of the political compromises that resulted from the 1787 Convention was reason enough for those present not to tolerate a ready method of undoing what they had done. Article V, like most of the important provisions of the Constitution, must be attributed more to the prevailing spirit of compromise that dominated the Convention than to dedication to principle.

Although the original Virginia Plan provided for a method of amendment, the first essential question resolved by the Convention was whether any method of amendment should be provided. Despite strong opposition from men such as Charles Pinckney of South Carolina, the Convention soon agreed in principle to the desirability of specifying a mode for amendment, with Mason, Randolph, and Madison of Virginia, Gouverneur Morris of Pennsylvania, Elbridge Gerry of Massachusetts, and Hamilton of New York leading the Convention toward accepting the necessity of such a provision.

The Virginia Plan not only specified an amendment process but provided also that the national legislature be excluded from participation in that process. And it was on the question of the proper role of Congress that the second major conflict was fought. When first reported by the Committee of Detail, the provision called for amendment by a convention to be called—apparently as a ministerial action—by the national legislature on application of the legislatures of two-thirds of the states. Although this plan was first approved, the issue was again raised on Gerry's motion for reconsideration, seconded by Hamilton, and supported by Madison. On reconsideration, Sherman of Connecticut sought to have the power given to the national legislature to propose amendments to the states for their approval. Wilson of Pennsylvania suggested that the approval of two-thirds of the states should be sufficient, and when this proposal was lost he was able to secure consent to a requirement of three-fourths of the states. At this point Madison offered what was in effect a substitute for the Committee of Detail's amended recommendation. It read, as the final draft was to read, in terms of alternative methods. Two-thirds of each house of Congress or two-thirds of the state legislatures could propose amendments. The amendments were to be ratified when approved either by three-fourths of the state legislatures or by conventions in three-fourths of the states. This compromise eventually overcame the second difficulty. By providing for alternative methods of procedure, the Madison proposal also made possible the compromise between those who would, from fear of the reticence of the national legislature to correct its own abuses, utilize the convention as the means of initiating change, and those who, like Mason, wanted the national legislature to be the sole sponsor of amendments.

This compromise did not, however, end the disputes over the content of the amendment article. Rutledge of South Carolina insisted that approval could not be forthcoming if the provisions relating to slavery theretofore approved were to be subject to amendment. Again compromise carried the day and it was decided that these sections of the Constitution were not to be subject to amendment prior to 1808. Having learned that state interests could be protected against amendment, at least for some period of time, Sherman moved that the Constitution should not be subject to amendment to limit the internal authority of the states nor to deprive any of them of their equal representation in the Senate. A different form of compromise was the result of this effort. Sherman lost in his effort to secure the states against interference with the exercise of their police power, but he won a guaranty that the right of equal representation in the Senate should not be changed. The latter protection, it quickly became apparent, was absolutely necessary to assure approval by the small states that had backed the New Jersey Plan, and it was written into the Constitution without a single objection.

Article V, which resulted from these deliberations, must be attributed largely to Madison, with the obvious active participation of Hamilton.

☆

The Congress, whenever two thirds of both Houses shall deem it necessary, shall propose Amendments to this Constitution, or, on the Application of the Legislatures of two thirds of the several States, shall call a Convention for proposing Amendments, which, in either Case, shall be valid to all Intents and Purposes, as Part of this Constitution, when ratified by the Legislatures of three fourths of the several States, or by Conventions in three fourths thereof, as the one or the other Mode of Ratification may be proposed by the Congress; Provided that no Amendment which may be made prior to the Year One thousand eight hundred and eight shall in any Manner affect the first and fourth Clauses in the Ninth Section of the first Article; and that no State, without its Consent, shall be deprived of it's equal Suffrage in the Senate.

Although the Constitution has been the subject of twenty-four different amendments, resort has never once been made to a national convention to initiate the process. And only once, in the case of the Twenty-first Amendment, was the state-convention process utilized for purposes of ratifying an amendment.

For the most part, the amendments have been minor rather than major rearrangements of the constitutional plan. The first ten amendments, the Bill of Rights, came so hard on the heels of the original document that they must be treated, for almost all purposes, as part of it. The only truly basic changes came in the Civil War amendments, the Thirteenth, Fourteenth, and Fifteenth. Although intended primarily for the benefit of the Negroes, who ultimately were the beneficiaries, the amendments have proved to be the essential vehicles for the transfer of power from the states to the national government and, within the national government, to the Supreme Court, which has since exercised a veto power over the actions of the state legislatures, executives, and judiciaries. This evolution, together with the authority of judicial review, secured earlier by the Court, has made the amendment process all but superfluous. The Court has been aptly referred to as a continuing constitutional convention, updating the meaning of the Constitution as new times and new situations demand that new meanings be given to the words of the document itself. Whether for this reason or another, there can be little doubt of the truth of Felix Frankfurter's observation that there has been throughout our history an "absence of any widespread or sustained demand for a general revision of the Constitution."

On the other hand, it should be noted that some of the amendments have been attributable solely to the need to correct a Supreme Court construction of the Constitution. Thus, the Eleventh Amendment was promulgated to overrule the case of Chisholm v. Georgia, 2 Dall. 419 (1793), in which the Court held that sovereign immunity was not available as a defense to a suit by a citizen of one state against another state. The necessity for the Civil War amendments derived in no small measure from the awful case of Dred Scott v. Sanford, 19 How. 393 (1857). The Sixteenth Amendment, authorizing the income tax, was a direct consequence of the Court's highly dubious decisions in Pollock v. Farmers' Loan and Trust Co., 157 U.S. 429 (1895), 158 U.S. 601 (1895).

The other major category of amendments includes those relating to the mechanics of the national government itself. These are due, first, to the need to eliminate ambiguities that became apparent through experience and, second, to the tendency toward extension of the franchise, a movement notable in all democratic countries during the nineteenth and twentieth centuries. In the first group fall the Twelfth Amendment, made necessary by the tied vote for Jefferson and Burr in the 1800 election; the Twentieth Amendment, a response to the increased efficiency of communications and transportation that made it possible to provide for the succession of the newly elected government at a date much closer to the election, as well as to the need to eliminate the ambiguities about filling a presidential vacancy; the Twenty-second Amendment, which adopted George Washington's notion that two terms were enough for any man to occupy the Presidency, an unwritten constitutional tradition broken by Franklin Delano Roosevelt's election to the office for four successive terms. In the second category, the amendments that enhance popular sovereignty, fall the Seventeenth, providing for popular election of senators; the Nineteenth, providing for women's suffrage; the Twenty-third, giving a voice to citizens of the District of Columbia in the election of the President; and the Twenty-fourth, eliminating the poll tax as a requirement for voting in national elections.

The only two other amendments are concrete evidence of the undesirability of promulgating a minority's notions of morality as part of the nation's fundamental law. The Eighteenth Amendment, the Prohibition Amendment, was a ban on commerce in intoxicating liquors. The horrible results of the "noble experiment" that led an entire nation into a lawlessness from which it has never recovered caused the repeal of the Eighteenth Amendment by the Twenty-first Amendment.

Perhaps the primary importance of Article V may be found in the in terrorem effect of an ultimate appeal to the people for the correction of the abuses of their government. But it is not a weapon ready for use and its cumbersome method is both its virtue and its vice.

The first ten amendments and the Civil War amendments (XIII–XV) are reproduced in the following sections of this volume. The text of the others appears here.

AMENDMENT [XI.]

The Judicial power of the United States shall not be construed to extend to any suit in law or equity, commenced or prosecuted against one of the United States by Citizens of another State, or by Citizens or Subjects of any Foreign State.

AMENDMENT [XII.]

The Electors shall meet in their respective states and vote by ballot for President and Vice-President, one of whom, at least, shall not be an inhabitant of the same state with themselves; they shall name in their ballots the person voted for as President, and in distinct ballots the person voted for as Vice-President, and they shall make distinct lists of all persons voted for as President, and of all persons voted for as Vice-President, and of the number of votes for each, which lists they shall sign and certify, and transmit sealed to the seat of the government of the United States, directed to the President of the Senate;—The President of the Senate shall, in the presence of the Senate and House of Representatives, open all the certificates and the votes shall then be counted;—The person having the greatest number of votes for President, shall be the President, if such number be a majority of the whole number of Electors appointed; and if no person have such majority, then from the persons having the highest numbers not exceeding three on the list of those voted for as President, the House of Representatives shall choose immediately, by ballot, the President. But in choosing the President, the votes shall be taken by states, the representation from each state having one vote; a quorum for this purpose shall consist of a member or members from two-thirds of the states, and a majority of all the states shall be necessary to a choice. And if the House of Representatives shall not choose a President whenever the right of choice shall devolve upon them, before the fourth day of March next following, then the Vice-President shall act as President, as in the case of the death or other constitutional disability of the President—The person having the greatest number of votes as Vice-President, shall be the Vice-President, if such number be a majority of the whole number of Electors appointed, and if no person have a majority, then from the two highest numbers on the list, the Senate shall choose the Vice-President; a quorum for the purpose shall consist of two-thirds of the whole number of Senators, and a majority of the whole number shall be necessary to a choice. But no person constitutionally ineligible to the office of President shall be eligible to that of Vice-President of the United States.

Amendment XVI.

The Congress shall have power to lay and collect taxes on incomes, from whatever source derived, without apportionment among the several States, and without regard to any census or enumeration.

Amendment [XVII.]

The Senate of the United States shall be composed of two Senators from each State, elected by the people thereof, for six years; and each Senator shall have one vote. The electors in each State shall have the qualifications requisite for electors of the most numerous branch of the State legislatures.

When vacancies happen in the representation of any State in the Senate, the executive authority of such State shall issue writs of election to fill such vacancies: *Provided*, That the legislature of any State may empower the executive thereof to make temporary appointments until the people fill the vacancies by election as the legislature may direct.

This amendment shall not be so construed as to affect the election or term of any Senator chosen before it becomes valid as part of the Constitution.

AMENDMENT [XVIII.]

SECTION 1. After one year from the ratification of this article the manufacture, sale, or transportation of intoxicating liquors within, the importation thereof into, or the exportation thereof from the United States and all territory subject to the jurisdiction thereof for beverage purposes is hereby prohibited.

SEC. 2. The Congress and the several States shall have concurrent power to enforce this article by appropriate legislation.

SEC. 3. This article shall be inoperative unless it shall have been ratified as an amendment to the Constitution by the legislatures of the several States, as provided in the Constitution, within seven years from the date of the submission hereof to the States by the Congress.

AMENDMENT [XIX.]

The right of citizens of the United States to vote shall not be denied or abridged by the United States or by any State on account of sex.

Congress shall have power to enforce this article by appropriate legislation.

AMENDMENT [XX.]

SECTION 1. The terms of the President and Vice President shall end at noon on the 20th day of January, and the terms of Senators and Representatives at noon on the 3d day of January, of the years in which such terms would have ended if this article had not been ratified; and the terms of their successors shall then begin.

SEC. 2. The Congress shall assemble at least once in every year, and such meeting shall begin at noon on the 3d day of January, unless they shall by law appoint a different day.

SEC. 3. If, at the time fixed for the beginning of the term of the President, the President elect shall have died, the Vice President elect shall become President. If a President shall not have been chosen before the time fixed for the beginning of his term, or if the President elect shall have failed to qualify, then the Vice President elect shall act as

President until a President shall have qualified; and the Congress may by law provide for the case wherein neither a President elect nor a Vice President elect shall have qualified, declaring who shall then act as President, or the manner in which one who is to act shall be selected, and such person shall act accordingly until a President or Vice President shall have qualified.

SEC. 4. The Congress may by law provide for the case of the death of any of the persons from whom the House of Representatives may choose a President whenever the right of choice shall have devolved upon them, and for the case of the death of any of the persons from whom the Senate may choose a Vice President whenever the right of choice shall have devolved upon them.

SEC. 5. Sections 1 and 2 shall take effect on the 15th day of October following the ratification of this article.

SEC. 6. This article shall be inoperative unless it shall have been ratified as an amendment to the Constitution by the legislatures of three-fourths of the several States within seven years from the date of its submission.

AMENDMENT [XXI.]

SECTION 1. The eighteenth article of amendment to the Constitution of the United States is hereby repealed.

SEC. 2. The transportation or importation into any State, Territory or possession of the United States for delivery or use therein of intoxicating liquors, in violation of the laws thereof, is hereby prohibited.

SEC. 3. This article shall be inoperative unless it shall have been ratified as an amendment to the Constitution by conventions in the several States, as provided in the Constitution, within seven years from the date of the submission hereof to the States by the Congress.

AMENDMENT [XXII.]

SECTION 1. No person shall be elected to the office of the President more than twice, and no person who has held the office of President, or acted as President, for more than two years of a term to which some other person was elected President shall be elected to the office of the President more than once. But this Article shall not apply to any person holding the office of President when this Article was proposed by the

Congress, and shall not prevent any person who may be holding the office of President, or acting as President, during the term within which this Article becomes operative from holding the office of President or acting as President during the remainder of such term.

SEC. 2. This Article shall be inoperative unless it shall have been ratified as an amendment to the Constitution by the legislatures of three-fourths of the several States within seven years from the date of its submission to the States by the Congress.

AMENDMENT [XXIII.]

SECTION 1. The District constituting the seat of Government of the United States shall appoint in such manner as the Congress may direct:

A number of electors of President and Vice President equal to the whole number of Senators and Representatives in Congress to which the District would be entitled if it were a State, but in no event more than the least populous State; they shall be in addition to those appointed by the States, but they shall be considered, for the purposes of the election of President and Vice President, to be electors appointed by a State; and they shall meet in the District and perform such duties as provided by the twelfth article of amendment.

Sec. 2. The Congress shall have power to enforce this article by appropriate legislation.

AMENDMENT [XXIV.]

SECTION 1. The right of citizens of the United States to vote in any primary or other election for President or Vice President, for electors for President or Vice President, or for Senator or Representative in Congress, shall not be denied or abridged by the United States or any State by reason of failure to pay any poll tax or other tax.

SECTION 2. The Congress shall have power to enforce this article by appropriate legislation.

Articles VI and VII

EDITED BY ALFRED H. KELLY

By far the most significant provision in Article VI of the United States Constitution is the "supremacy" clause. This guarantees the ascendancy of all three forms of federal law (Constitution, treaties, and congressional enactments) over state law, and charges the state courts with enforcing that guarantee.

The supremacy clause had its origins in the failure of the Articles of Confederation, the charter of union which the United States put into effect in 1781, to solve the problem of federal-state relations. The problem was that of establishing some principle for dividing sovereignty effectively between the national government and the states, and of establishing some mechanism to assure the smooth and effective coordination of the two spheres in actual operation. The Articles of Confederation had delegated to the Confederation Congress certain specific sovereign functions—notably foreign relations, war, treaties, Indian affairs, coinage, and the post office—while at the same time reserving the great residue of sovereign powers, those not specifically delegated to Congress, to the several states. The principle involved in this division of powers anticipated directly that resorted to in the Constitution of 1787.

Unfortunately, however, the Articles had failed almost completely to make this system effective or workable. First, they left Congress without the means to execute its own functions properly. There was neither any federal court system for implementing the enforcement of Confederation law nor any federal revenue system for taxing individuals directly. Instead, in both instances, Congress was obliged to use the states as its agents to implement its will. This system in actual practice worked very badly, mainly because the states almost invariably subordinated national policy and law to their own legal systems. Thus in most instances where

139

Confederation law came into conflict with that of a state in cases before the state courts, state judges chose to enforce the pertinent provisions of their own constitutions and laws and to ignore appropriate provisions of national law. The system of state agency was ineffective for the collection of federal revenues. The states were chronically deficient in the payment of their respective levies, a situation which soon brought about a condition of national bankruptcy.

The obvious defects in this system of state-agency early led to demands for the reform of the Articles. In 1780, even before the Articles had taken final effect, Hamilton wrote that Congress ought at once to assert "complete sovereignty" over the states in its sphere of authority. A year later, James Madison, then a member of Congress from Virginia, proposed a constitutional amendment authorizing Congress to use force to compel the states to fulfill their obligations to the Union. This idea that Congress ought somehow be empowered to coerce derelict states recurred repeatedly during the Confederation era, a "Grand Committee" of Congress suggesting it once more in 1786. More significant, however, was another suggestion Madison made several times, that Congress be provided with a veto of all state laws contravening the federal constitutional system, an idea he obviously had borrowed from the right of review and possible disallowance formerly exercised by the Crown with respect to colonial legislation.

The Constitutional Convention which met in Philadelphia between May and September, 1787, was for the most part firmly in the control of a group of vigorous young nationalists who were strongly resolved to establish a supreme national government effectively equipped to implement its own sovereignty. At the outset of proceedings, one of their leaders, Gouverneur Morris of Pennsylvania, introduced a resolution declaring that "no union of states merely federal" would suffice, but "that a national government ought to be established, consisting of supreme Legislative, Executive, and Judiciary." Here was terse expression of the nationalists' intent: to abandon state agency and to create in its place a "national government," i.e., one operating directly upon individuals through its own agents, and to guarantee the supremacy of its laws over the states through some effective mechanism.

This last problem, that of providing some device to implement national supremacy, gave the delegates great difficulty. The Virginia Plan, mainly the work of James Madison, which became the basis for the

Convention's labors, provided for a national government operating directly upon individuals through its own courts and its own personnel. This was a large part of the solution of the problem. But there remained a serious difficulty: how to guarantee the effective supremacy of national over state law where the two systems of sovereignty came into conflict. The Virginia Plan offered three possible solutions to this problem: first, that Congress be empowered to coerce states acting in violation of the federal Constitution; second, that Congress be empowered to disallow state laws conflicting with the federal Constitution and laws; and, third, that state officers be required to take an oath of loyalty to the national government.

After some debate, however, the delegates abandoned both coercion and disallowance as involving "wrong principles." Madison himself pointed out that coercion assumed that the states would still function as agents of the national government, a system the delegates now proposed to abandon. The national government, in short, now would impose coercion upon individuals, not upon the states as such. The Convention's lawyers also objected to congressional disallowance, which they considered to involve a judicial rather than a legislative type of function. Over Madison's bitter protest, the delegates voted to give up the idea.

The Convention's final solution was found in a hitherto obscure clause in the New Jersey Plan, a proposal introduced by a states'-rights faction in late June in an effort to check the nationalists' demands. In itself, the New Jersey Plan was little more than a revision of the Articles of Confederation. However, it contained a highly significant "supremacy clause" declaring the Constitution, acts of Congress, and treaties to be the supreme law of the respective states and binding the judges in the state courts to their enforcement as such.

Following the abandonment of congressional disallowance in late July, Luther Martin of Maryland, himself a strong states'-rights advocate, moved to incorporate the New Jersey Plan's "supremacy clause" in the new Constitution. Without opposition or debate, the delegates accepted this proposal. Later the Convention made one small but extremely important change in language: it substituted the phrase "supreme law of the land" for "supreme law of the respective states."

The provision that state officers should subscribe to an oath to support the Constitution, now modified by the Convention to include federal officials as well, was carried over into the Constitution unchallenged from

141

the Virginia Plan. However, at the suggestion of Charles Pinckney of South Carolina, a further clause was attached to ban the imposition of any religious qualifications in any such oath for federal officials. This prohibition, adopted virtually without debate, obviously reflected the prevailing rationalistic Enlightenment spirit to which most of the delegates adhered. The clause was spiritual cousin to the Virginia Statute on Religious Liberty of 1785 and to the prohibition on religious establishments presently to be written into the First Amendment.

The clause in Article VI guaranteeing the Confederation debt was a product of very late deliberation in the Convention. As originally proposed by a "Committee of Eleven" in late August, the provision would have obliged Congress not only to "fulfill the engagements which have been entered into by the United States" but also "to discharge the debts of the United States as well as the debts incurred by the States" in the late war. Several delegates, notably George Mason of Virginia and Elbridge Gerry of Massachusetts, attacked this provision as calculated to "compel payment" of federal and state funds to "blood-sucking speculators" who had bought up such securities cheaply against the possibility of redemption. As a result, Edmund Randolph of Virginia, on August 25, introduced a provision that "all debts contracted, and engagements entered into, by and under the authority of Congress, shall be valid against the United States under this Constitution, as under the Confederation." This clause, which eliminated any mention of state debts and which was regarded as considerably more ambiguous in its import generally, satisfied the opponents of "speculative stock-jobbers," and the Convention thereupon adopted it.

Article VII, with its provision for ratification of the Constitution by state conventions, was also a product of the prevailing nationalistic spirit among the delegates. The Morris resolution of May had very plainly implied the outright abandonment of the Articles rather than their amendment. As the Convention drew to a close, the delegates agreed quite generally that it would be "folly" to submit the work to the hazard of the Articles' requirement of unanimous ratification by the several state legislatures. Accordingly, the Convention in late August voted first to "recommend to Congress" that the proposed Constitution be submitted to conventions in the several states. At the last moment, however, the delegates dropped the idea of a mere "recommendation" and decided instead to provide in the Constitution itself that their work be submitted directly to state conventions, and that ratification by any nine would be *sufficient for adoption. This provision not only virtually bypassed the Confederation Congress; what was more important, it also symbolized the Convention's entire abandonment of the Articles of Confederation and the Convention's insistence upon the idea that it was endowed with original organic powers.*

Article. VI.

All Debts contracted and Engagements entered into, before the Adoption of this Constitution, shall be as valid against the United States under this Constitution, as under the Confederation.

This Constitution, and the Laws of the United States which shall be made in Pursuance thereof; and all Treaties made, or which shall be made, under the Authority of the United States, shall be the supreme Law of the Land; and the Judges in every State shall be bound thereby, any Thing in the Constitution or Laws of any State to the Contrary notwithstanding.

The Senators and Representatives before mentioned, and the Members of the several State Legislatures, and all executive and judicial Officers, both of the United States and of the several States, shall be bound by Oath or Affirmation, to support this Constitution; but no religious Test shall ever be required as a Qualification to any Office or public Trust under the United States.

Article. VII.

The Ratification of the Conventions of nine States, shall be sufficient for the Establishment of this Constitution between the States so ratifying the Same.

done in Convention by the Unanimous Consent of the States present the Seventeenth Day of September in the Year of our Lord one thousand seven hundred and Eighty seven and of the Independence of the United States of America the Twelfth In witness whereof We have hereunto subscribed our Names,

G.° Washington—Presid.ᵗ
and deputy from Virginia

New Hampshire	{	JOHN LANGDON
		NICHOLAS GILMAN

Massachusetts	{	NATHANIEL GORHAM
		RUFUS KING

Connecticut	{	W.ᵐ SAM.¹ JOHNSON
		ROGER SHERMAN

New York . . .   ALEXANDER HAMILTON

New Jersey	{	WIL: LIVINGSTON
		DAVID BREARLEY.
		W.ᵐ PATERSON.
		JONA: DAYTON

Pensylvania	{	B FRANKLIN
		THOMAS MIFFLIN
		ROBT MORRIS
		GEO. CLYMER
		THO.ˢ FITZSIMONS
		JARED INGERSOLL
		JAMES WILSON
		GOUV MORRIS

Delaware	{	GEO: READ
		GUNNING BEDFORD jun
		JOHN DICKINSON
		RICHARD BASSETT
		JACO: BROOM

Maryland	{	JAMES MCHENRY
		DAN OF Sᵗ THO.ˢ JENIFER
		DANˡ CARROLL

Virginia	{	JOHN BLAIR—
		JAMES MADISON Jr.

North Carolina	{	W.ᵐ BLOUNT
		RICH.ᵈ DOBBS SPRAIGHT
		HU WILLIAMSON

South Carolina	{	J. RUTLEDGE
		CHARLES COTESWORTH PINCKNEY
		CHARLES PINCKNEY
		PIERCE BUTLER

Georgia	{	WILLIAM FEW
		ABR BALDWIN

144

In Convention Monday, September 17th 1787.
Present
The States of
New Hampshire, Massachusetts, Connecticut, Mr. Hamilton from New York, New Jersey, Pennsylvania, Delaware, Maryland, Virginia, North Carolina, South Carolina and Georgia.

Resolved,

That the preceeding Constitution be laid before the United States in Congress assembled, and that it is the Opinion of this Convention, that it should afterwards be submitted to a Convention of Delegates, chosen in each State by the People thereof, under the Recommendation of its Legislature, for their Assent and Ratification; and that each Convention assenting to, and ratifying the Same, should give Notice thereof to the United States in Congress assembled. Resolved, That it is the Opinion of this Convention, that as soon as the Conventions of nine States shall have ratified this Constitution, the United States in Congress assembled should fix a Day on which Electors should be appointed by the States which shall have ratified the same, and a Day on which the Electors should assemble to vote for the President, and the Time and Place for commencing Proceedings under this Constitution. That after such Publication the Electors should be appointed, and the Senators and Representatives elected: That the Electors should meet on the Day fixed for the Election of the President, and should transmit their Votes certified, signed, sealed and directed, as the Constitution requires, to the Secretary of the United States in Congress assembled, that the Senators and Representatives should convene at the Time and Place assigned; that the Senators should appoint a President of the Senate, for the sole Purpose of receiving, opening and counting the Votes for President; and, that after he shall be chosen, the Congress, together with the President, should, without Delay, proceed to execute this Constitution.

By the Unanimous Order of the Convention

G.° WASHINGTON—Presid.ᵗ

W. JACKSON Secretary.

☆

The supremacy clause in Article VI was destined ultimately to become the very foundation of the American constitutional system. On the surface, the clause appeared to be innocuous enough. It affirmed the supremacy of the Constitution and federal law over all state law. But it entrusted the guardianship of that system of supremacy to agents of the several states, the judges of the state courts. Superficially considered, therefore, as the disappointed young nationalists maintained, state-federal relations under the new Constitution might be considered even now to be at the mercy of the several states, as had been the case under the Articles of Confederation.

Hamilton, Madison, and other staunch nationalists, however, soon detected a possible means for converting the comparatively weak supremacy clause into an adequate guarantee of federal sovereignty. If decisions in the state courts in cases involving the Constitution and laws of the United States were made subject to appeal to the federal judiciary, the entire import of the clause would be altered. An agent of the national government, the Supreme Court of the United States, now ultimately would be charged with maintaining the Constitution's guarantee of national supremacy. The Court would accomplish this simply by enforcing the primacy of federal law over state law in the federal courts, and presumably by taking on appeal and reversing those cases arising in the state courts where the latter had failed to recognize federal supremacy. Thus the Supreme Court would possess a veto over state laws "contravening the Articles of Union"—essentially the solution Madison had advocated in the Philadelphia Convention, except that he had sought to lodge the "veto" with Congress.

The new Constitution did not specifically grant the right of appeal from state to federal courts on constitutional questions. But it was possible to construe that right reasonably enough by a very plausible legal argument. And the nationalists soon realized that the right of appeal had to be established beyond question, were the new government to have its sovereignty protected effectively.

The First Congress under the Constitution, an assemblage firmly in the control of Madison and other nationalists, presently incorporated the right of appeal in the statute since known as the Judiciary Act of 1789. This law set up the federal court system, pursuant to authority granted to Congress in Article III of the Constitution. In Section 25 of the Act, Congress in effect provided that, whenever federal and state law came into conflict in a case arising in a state court and the state court ruled in favor of the application of the state law, there would exist an automatic right of appeal to the appropriate federal court. Since the Supreme Court of the United States, both by the Constitution and by the Judiciary Act itself, was the final court of appeals in federal cases, Article 25 thus in effect lodged the ultimate power to decide conflicts between national and state sovereignty in that Court—an agency of the national government.

The system of national supremacy incorporated in Article VI and the Judiciary Act of 1789 soon found a powerful champion in Chief Justice John Marshall, who presided over the Supreme Court of the United States between 1801 and 1835. In a series of great decisions beginning in 1810, Marshall repeatedly invoked the supremacy clause and Section 25 of the Judiciary Act of 1789 to strike down state laws contravening the Constitution and the laws of the United States. Again and again he pointed out that the Constitution had established a national government whose sphere of sovereignty was admittedly limited but which, by the terms of Article VI, was supreme in its own sphere and that all state laws to the contrary must fail as unconstitutional.

Marshall's most dramatic defense of Article VI and Section 25 of the Judiciary Act came in Cohens v. Virginia, 6 Wheat. 264, a case decided in 1821 on appeal from the supreme court of Virginia. The Cohens, father and son, had been convicted in the Virginia courts of selling lottery tickets and so violating the state's laws against gambling. In their defense, the Cohens had relied heavily upon a congressional act, adopted during the War of 1812 as a desperate financial expedient, authorizing the sale of lottery tickets in the District of Columbia. But the Virginia supreme court, on appeal, had swept the federal statute aside to uphold the state law. And when the Cohens then appealed to the United States Supreme Court, attorneys for Virginia, pursuant to a doctrine then popular in that state, had attacked Section 25 as unconstitutional, denying outright that any constitutional right of appeal from state to federal courts existed at all.

Marshall's opinion in which the Court concurred unanimously, rested very heavily upon Article VI and the doctrine of national supremacy. The Constitution, he pointed out, declared itself the supreme law of the land and bound state judges to observe it as such. Further, the Constitution created a sovereign government which "though limited as to its objects is supreme with respect to its objects." As a supreme government, he continued, the United States could "legitimately control all individuals or governments within the American territory." It followed that state laws, "so far as they are repugnant to the Constitution and laws of the United States, are absolutely void." It was, he said, a mere "corollary" from the foregoing that the federal courts possessed "a power to revise the judgment rendered in them by state tribunals." (Ironically, Marshall found that Virginia's gambling statute, properly construed, did not conflict with the federal lottery law in question, the latter being confined in application to the District of Columbia.)

Many years were to pass, however, before the right of the Supreme Court to function as the ultimate interpreter of the Constitution and expositor of national supremacy won general acceptance. In the Virginia and Kentucky Resolutions adopted by the legislatures of those states in 1798, Thomas Jefferson and Madison himself (the latter temporarily converted to the states'-rights cause) challenged directly the right of the federal courts to exercise final authority over the constitutional system and insisted instead that the final power to judge constitutional questions was properly lodged in the legislatures of the several states. Further, they argued somewhat vaguely, the states properly could "interpose" their sovereignty against a "usurpation" of power by the federal courts or by Congress.

A generation later John C. Calhoun of South Carolina took over this vague doctrine of interposition and elaborated and refined it into a complete doctrine of state sovereignty, which, had it won acceptance, would have rendered meaningless the supremacy clause in Article VI. According to Calhoun, the states antedated the federal Union. Since their sovereignty, he insisted, could not properly be divided or abrogated, it followed that the states were completely sovereign. The federal government, by the same token, was a mere agent of the sovereign states without sovereignty of its own. The Constitution, Calhoun asserted, despite the language in Article VI, was neither law nor supreme; it was, instead, a mere treaty between sovereign states. Final power to interpret the federal constitutional system properly was lodged not in the federal courts but in "Organic Conventions" in the several states, and a state through such a convention lawfully could "nullify" any federal law contravening the Constitution. Should the other states, by a three-fourths vote of their own like organic conventions, refuse to concur in the state's act of nullification, the nullifying state had one final remedy— as an absolutely sovereign entity, it could withdraw from the Union.

In the tariff crisis of 1832, South Carolina actually invoked Calhoun's scheme, only to have nullification break down when put to the test of actual practice. Yet the doctrine of state sovereignty, completely contradictory to Marshall's interpretation of the supremacy clause, became "orthodox" political doctrine with southern sectionalists in the next generation, and the basis upon which rested the southern doctrine of the right of secession, invoked by the South in the crisis of 1860–61.

In a constitutional sense, the Civil War was a great conflict between two constitutional doctrines, that of John Marshall and that of John Calhoun. By 1861, Lincoln and the great majority of northerners had adopted the Hamilton-Marshall doctrine of national sovereignty and national supremacy, based upon the supremacy clause, as the orthodox view of the Union. Union victory in 1865 effectively established the final efficacy of Article VI and national constitutional supremacy as prevailing American constitutional doctrine. The impact of the supremacy clause upon the American constitutional system has not been challenged effectively since that time.

Thus the "shadow-doctrine" of interposition, raised by certain southern lawyers and politicians after 1954 in an effort to obfuscate the Supreme Court's judicial veto of state segregation laws, is hardly to be taken as serious constitutional doctrine. In November, 1960, Federal Judge Skelly Wright, denouncing Louisiana's attempt to defy federal judicial authority by invoking the ghostly doctrine of Madison and Jefferson, ridiculed "interposition" as "a preposterous perversion, disavowed by the Constitution of the United States" and "an illegal defiance of federal authority." Significantly, Judge Wright's decision shortly was upheld by the Supreme Court itself.

The oath provision in Article VI has had an uneventful history, only occasionally rising to the surface of political or judicial controversy. In 1866, Congress made the oath the basis for the provision in Section 3 of the Fourteenth Amendment which barred from federal and state office all former officeholders, state and federal, who in that capacity had taken the required oath to support the Constitution of the United States, and who thereafter participated in rebellion against the United States. Congress later removed this disability, in a series of amnesty acts passed between 1872 and 1898 by two-thirds vote, as the Fourteenth Amendment empowered it to do.

In the twentieth century, the oath clause has only occasionally been the object of judicial attention. In Cooper v. Aaron, however, a case decided in 1958, the Supreme Court handed down a stern rebuke to state officials who in disregard of their oath had defied and evaded desegregation orders of the federal judiciary. No state official, the Court warned, "can war on the Constitution without violating his oath to support it, . . . else . . . the Constitution becomes a solemn mockery."

The provision in Article VI guaranteeing the Confederation debt soon became the center of considerable political controversy. In 1790, Alexander Hamilton, now Secretary of the Treasury in the Washington Administration, submitted a comprehensive financial plan to Congress for the new government. One part of the plan called for funding the Confederation debt by paying off the former government's securities at face value to present holders, in bonds of the new government.

This proposal at once reawakened the controversy over rewarding "blood-sucking speculators" which had broken out three years earlier on the floor of the Constitutional Convention. Madison, now a member of the House of Representatives, attacked Hamilton's plan, suggesting instead that Confederation bond-holders be paid merely their purchase price, the difference between that sum and face value to be awarded to original purchasers. Hamilton objected in turn that Madison's scheme not only was impractical but also that it would endanger the credit of the new government. This argument carried the day, and Congress by law provided for redemption at par, in new bonds, to present holders.

Article VII, which provided that the new Constitution was to be submitted to conventions in the several states, and was to take effect when nine states had ratified the document, set the stage for a struggle over adoption of the Constitution that lasted ten months, from September, 1787, to July, 1788. Technically, the provisions of Article VII were "unconstitutional," since they violated the clause in the Article of Confederation requiring that all amendments to the Articles be submitted to the states by Congress for ratification by legislative action, the unanimous concurrence of all the states being necessary for adoption.

Yet the Convention's "unconstitutional" mode of submitting its work aroused remarkably little controversy. The Confederation Congress itself in effect acceded to the provision ten days after the Philadelphia Convention adjourned, when it submitted the new Constitution to the states for consideration. The legislatures in every state except one presently issued a call for ratifying conventions. Rhode Island alone, which had refused to send delegates to the Philadelphia Convention, now refused to call a state convention to consider ratification.

The argument over ratification soon divided the country along intense if temporary partisan lines. The supporters of the new Constitution, known as Federalists, were for the most part drawn from the coastal region, from urban centers, and from the propertied, mercantile, and professional classes and the more prosperous commercial farmers, all of whom stood to gain substantially from a stable and effective national government. By contrast, the opponents of the Constitution, known as anti-Federalists, were drawn generally from the small farmers of the interior upland plain. Federalist argument stressed the necessity for establishing an adequate and financially sound national government, and warned of the chaos which would ensue were the Constitution rejected. Anti-Federalists attacked the Constitution's lack of a bill of rights, the threat it posed to the sovereignty of the states, the "dictatorial" powers of taxation the new government would possess, and its remoteness from the people.

The Constitution, with its provision for state equality in the Senate, was thought to be favorable to the less populous states, and several small states—Delaware, New Jersey, Georgia, Connecticut, and Maryland—ratified the Constitution between December and April, by large majorities. The Federalists, strong in Pennsylvania and South Carolina, also easily swept these states into the fold. In Massachusetts, Virginia, New York, and New Hampshire, however, there were bitter ratification struggles, and adoption came only by the narrowest of margins. New York's ratification in July, by a vote of 30 to 27, made eleven states for the Union. North Carolina and Rhode Island failed to ratify until 1789 and 1790, respectively, after the government under the Constitution was in actual operation.

The Federalists carried the day mainly because in widespread national debate they had much the better argument. The Federalist essays in New York, the work of Madison, Hamilton, and John Jay, and like arguments elsewhere, won over numerous doubtful supporters. Pro-Federalist political management was also excellent, much opposition being dispelled by the promise that a bill of rights would be adopted once the Constitution was ratified. In addition, several of the state conventions, in all of which the delegates were chosen from the same districts as those in the corresponding legislatures, were somewhat "gerrymandered" in favor of pro-Federalist tidewater regions. Yet the fact remains that the Constitution was ratified by a process more democratic than that available anywhere else in the world at that time, while the new Constitution was itself flexible enough to become the charter for a modern constitutional democracy.

The Bill of Rights: Amendments I–X

EDITED BY MILTON R. KONVITZ

The Constitution as it was approved by the Convention on September 17, 1787, contained provisions of some important liberties. There was a prohibition against suspension of the privilege of the writ of habeas corpus. There was a prohibition on the enactment of ex post facto laws and bills of attainder. There was a guarantee of trial by jury for criminal offenses. And there was a prohibition against a religious test as a qualification for public office.

These could by no means be thought of as petty liberties, but there were many persons who thought that the Constitution did not go far enough. A few delegates had left the Convention with the determination to oppose ratification by their states; and Thomas Jefferson wrote to James Madison, three months after the Convention had ended its work, that while there were many things about the proposed Constitution that pleased him, first among the things he did not like was "the omission of a bill of rights, providing clearly, and without the aid of sophism, for freedom of religion, freedom of the press, . . . and trials by jury in all matters of fact triable by the laws of the land. . . ."

At the Convention hardly a word was said in favor of a bill of rights. George Mason's proposal of such a bill came late and almost as an afterthought. This was not because the delegates were against fundamental rights and liberties, but because they agreed with James Wilson that since the federal government was to have only powers explicitly granted by the Constitution, the new government could never misuse powers not given to it—powers reserved to the states or the people. On the level of political theory, Wilson was right; but Mason, Jefferson, and others had the political instinct not to let so important a matter rest on mere inference. A bill of rights, Jefferson told Madison, "is what the people are entitled to against every government on earth, . . . and what no just government should refuse. . . ."

In 1787 the only governments on earth that were limited by bills of rights were those of the six states that had adopted such bills following the precedent set by Virginia's Declaration of Rights (1776), drawn up by Mason. The states that did not adopt separate bills of rights incorporated fundamental guarantees into their state constitutions or relied on their colonial charters.

The colonists had insisted, against England, that they should enjoy all the fundamental rights of Englishmen. They claimed to be beneficiaries of Magna Carta (1215), and of the laws of England that made provision for the writ of habeas corpus; for trial by jury; for the right of an accused to have aid of counsel; for the right to avoid self-incrimination; for liberties that flowed out of the Petition of Right (1628) and the Bill of Rights (1689), including a prohibition on cruel and unusual punishments, the right to bear arms, the right of petition for relief of grievances, and a prohibition on excessive bail. They knew that the press-licensing acts had come to an end in 1695. They knew of the successful attacks on general warrants by John Wilkes. They were familiar with the commendable but unsuccessful struggle of the Levellers to get a written bill of rights.

They had behind them notable colonial charters, like that of Rhode Island (1663), which, in its broad statement of religious liberty, reflected the work of Roger Williams; the Massachusetts Body of Liberties (1641), mainly the work of Nathaniel Ward, which had been enacted by the General Court; the Maryland Toleration Act (1649); the West Jersey Concessions or Agreements (1676–77), in large part the work of William Penn. They had the Pennsylvania Charter of Privileges (1701), signed by Penn and accepted by the colony's assembly, which spoke of a people's "greatest Enjoyment of civil Liberties" and against abridgment "of the Freedom of their Consciences," and of God as "the only Lord of Conscience." They had the Declaration and Resolves of the Continental Congress (1774), which referred to certain acts of Parliament affecting the colonies as "impolitic, unjust, and cruel, as well as unconstitutional, and most dangerous and destructive of American rights," and of the right of colonists to "life, liberty, and property," which "they have never ceded to any sovereign power whatever. . . ." They also had as a model Jefferson's Bill for Establishing Religious Freedom, adopted by Virginia in 1786, which provided for absolute religious liberty and equality; and the Northwest Ordinance of 1787, which promised religious liberty, trial by jury, and other basic freedoms to those who would colonize the Ohio country.

They knew, too, John Locke's Second Treatise of Civil Government (1689), which was one of the foundations of the Declaration of Independence (1776); and thus doctrine could be added to legal precedents, and the latter could be translated into and elevated to natural rights. In their turn, natural rights could be translated into civil liberties. And the main point of the argument by Jefferson and Mason for a bill of rights was that civil liberties should be made into constitutional rights.

When the Convention was over, Mason left with the determination to carry his fight for a bill of rights to his state, Virginia, where the proposed Constitution would come up for ratification, and Elbridge Gerry decided to do the same in Massachusetts. The latter was the first state to ratify, but the Convention in that state adopted recommendations for amendments. Virginia ratified, but with a vote of only 89 to 79; and a committee was chosen to report on amendments to be brought to the first Congress. New York ratified, but with a bill of rights attached. Rhode Island and North Carolina waited with their ratifications.

Thus, when the First Congress convened, it was clear to Madison, who had been elected to the House of Representatives, that practicalities were to overrule theoretical considerations and that he must sponsor constitutional amendments. His own preference was to amend the Constitution by putting into it at various points where they would seem to fit eight provisions, five of which concerned fundamental freedoms. The debate started on June 8, 1789. On July 21 Madison's amendments were referred to a Committee of Ten. On August 13 the committee reported, recommending fourteen amendments. These underwent some changes and were approved by the House of Representatives on August 24; and the House decided that the amendments were to be appended as a supplement to the Constitution rather than distributed throughout the document.

These amendments were then introduced in the Senate. There were some differences between the Senate and the House of Representatives, which were adjusted by a joint committee. The House had adopted seventeen amendments; but when on September 25 the Senate acted approvingly on the final draft recommended by the House, the amendments had been reduced to twelve. The first two (relating to apportionment of Representatives and compensation of members of Congress) failed of ratification by the states; the other ten were ratified in the form in which they had been submitted, and they were added to the Constitution as our Bill of Rights when Virginia, on December 15, 1791, became the eleventh state to ratify.

The Bill of Rights had been before Congress for only three and a half months. Perhaps no more than a total of seven or eight session days had been spent by Congress considering and debating the proposed amendments. The brevity of this process was possible because the Bill of Rights was the culmination of human experience with despotic governments. One hears in its phrases—"establishment of religion," "freedom of speech, or of the press," "a redress of grievances," "twice put in jeopardy of life or limb," "a witness against himself," "cruel and unusual punishment"—Wordsworth's "still, sad music of humanity." There is plenty of doctrine in the Bill of Rights, but it is no doctrinaire document; for it is rooted in the experience, no less than in the faith, of the people who wanted it.

Amendment [I.]

Congress shall make no law respecting an establishment of religion, or prohibiting the free exercise thereof; or abridging the freedom of speech, or of the press; or the right of the people peaceably to assemble, and to petition the Government for a redress of grievances.

Amendment [II.]

A well regulated Militia, being necessary to the security of a free State, the right of the people to keep and bear Arms, shall not be infringed.

Amendment [III.]

No Soldier shall, in time of peace be quartered in any house, without the consent of the Owner, nor in time of war, but in a manner to be prescribed by law.

Amendment [IV.]

The right of the people to be secure in their persons, houses, papers, and effects, against unreasonable searches and seizures, shall not be violated, and no Warrants shall issue, but upon probable cause, supported by Oath or affirmation, and particularly describing the place to be searched, and the persons or things to be seized.

AMENDMENT [V.]

No person shall be held to answer for a capital, or otherwise infamous crime, unless on a presentment or indictment of a Grand Jury, except in cases arising in the land or naval forces, or in the Militia, when in actual service in time of War or public danger; nor shall any person be subject for the same offence to be twice put in jeopardy of life or limb; nor shall be compelled in any criminal case to be a witness against himself, nor be deprived of life, liberty, or property, without due process of law; nor shall private property be taken for public use, without just compensation.

AMENDMENT [VI.]

In all criminal prosecutions, the accused shall enjoy the right to a speedy and public trial, by an impartial jury of the State and district wherein the crime shall have been committed, which district shall have been previously ascertained by law, and to be informed of the nature and cause of the accusation; to be confronted with the witnesses against him; to have compulsory process for obtaining witnesses in his favor, and to have the Assistance of Counsel for his defence.

AMENDMENT [VII.]

In Suits at common law, where the value in controversy shall exceed twenty dollars, the right of trial by jury shall be preserved, and no fact tried by a jury, shall be otherwise re-examined in any Court of the United States, than according to the rules of the common law.

AMENDMENT [VIII.]

Excessive bail shall not be required, nor excessive fines imposed, nor cruel and unusual punishments inflicted.

AMENDMENT [IX.]

The enumeration in the Constitution, of certain rights, shall not be construed to deny or disparage others retained by the people.

Amendment [X.]

The powers not delegated to the United States by the Constitution, nor prohibited by it to the States, are reserved to the States respectively, or to the people.

As recently as 1943 it was possible for an authority on constitutional law to state that the record "discloses not a single case, in a century and a half, where the Supreme Court has protected freedom of speech, press, assembly, or petition against congressional attack." There are, he said, "very few instances where the Congress has threatened the integrity of the constitutional system or the guarantee of the Bill of Rights." These statements were substantially correct when made, but they soon thereafter became "dated."

As to the subjection of state acts to judgment under the Bill of Rights: In a case that came before the Supreme Court in 1833 it was contended that a state had violated the Fifth Amendment by taking private property for public use without just compensation. The Court, in an opinion by Chief Justice Marshall, held that the Bill of Rights imposes no restriction on the states. The adoption of the Fourteenth Amendment in 1868 gave rise to the argument that some or all of the guarantees of the Bill of Rights may now be enforced against the states under the provision that no state shall deprive any person of his liberty without due process of law. But in 1907 Justice Holmes stated for the Court: "We leave undecided the question whether there is to be found in the 14th Amendment a prohibition similar to that in the 1st." Only Justice Harlan, dissenting, contended that freedom of speech and the press, being an essential part of every man's liberty, was protected by the "due process" clause of the Fourteenth Amendment against abridgment by state action. In 1925, however, in Gitlow v. New York, 268 U.S. 652, the Court for the first time assumed that freedom of speech and the press "are among the fundamental personal rights and 'liberties' protected by the due process clause of the Fourteenth Amendment from impairment by the states." In 1940 the Court included religious freedom in the concept of "liberty" as the term is used in the "due process" clause.

Are all the guarantees of the Bill of Rights incorporated into this concept of "liberty," and thus protected against infringement by the states? There are conflicting schools of thought in the Supreme Court with respect to this matter. In 1937 Justice Cardozo, in Palko v. Connecticut, 302 U.S. 319, distinguished fundamental liberties from those of inferior significance, and said that the Bill of Rights includes both types. The former are "implicit in the concept of ordered liberty." Were they sacrificed, "neither liberty nor justice would exist." These include, he said, the freedoms of the First Amendment, and "the right of one accused of crime to the benefit of counsel." On the other hand, he said, the requirement of trial by jury and the provision that no person may be compelled in any criminal case to be a witness against himself are not of "the very essence of a scheme of ordered liberty." This "selective process" has been followed by the Court. But a minority, led by Justice Black, have contended that the original purpose of the Fourteenth Amendment was to extend the complete protection of the Bill of Rights against infringement by the states.

The "selective process" has not, however, proved to be a substantial obstacle standing in the way of a broadening of the concept of "liberty." Thus the Court has held, for example, that the guarantee of the Eighth Amendment against cruel punishment is a limit on the states; that the substance of the procedural requirements of the Sixth Amendment applies to the states insofar as these requirements provide for "fundamental rights." Thus the Bill of Rights, on one theory or another, has served as a standard for the states with almost the same degree of constitutional compulsion as that felt by the federal government. The Court progressively has assumed the burden of supervision over the administration of criminal justice, testing procedures by the guarantees of the Bill of Rights as requiring fundamentals of justice, fairness, and equality.

There has also been a broadening in the reach of the First Amendment freedoms. For instance, in 1907 the Court, in an opinion written by Justice Holmes, held that the purpose of the guarantee of freedom of the press was only to prevent all restraints previous to publication but not to prevent subsequent punishment—which was freedom of the press as it was understood by Blackstone. The First Amendment, it was assumed, was no bar against prohibiting or punishing acts that "may be deemed contrary to public welfare." Freedom of the press is no longer defined in Blackstonian terms, nor are the First Amendment freedoms limited by the sweep of "public welfare."

But it must be acknowledged that the Court is searching continually for rational ways of formulating the reach and the limits of these freedoms. In Schenck v. United States, 249 U.S. 47 (1919) Justice Holmes, for the Court, said that it may be "that the prohibition of laws abridging the freedom of speech is not confined to previous restraints," and then went on to say that the question in every case is "whether the words used are used in such circumstances and are of such a nature as to create a clear and present danger that they will bring about the substantive evils that Congress has a right to prevent. It is a question of proximity and degree." This "clear and present danger" test competed with the common law test of "public welfare" and the "dangerous tendency" of speech to bring about evil results (such as a breach of the peace). It was not until 1940 that the Court clearly adopted the "clear and present danger" test and reversed convictions. But the subsequent career of the test or doctrine has been extremely checkered. In Dennis v. United States, 341 U.S. 494 (1951) a majority of the Court made it clear that not all speech is constitutionally protected; that there are other social values to which the value of speech must at times give way; that the clear and present danger test is not a rigid rule; that the test means: "In each case [courts] must ask whether the gravity of the 'evil,' discounted by its improbability, justifies such invasion of free speech as is necessary to avoid the danger."

The Court has often found itself moderating between the extreme claim of Justice Black that the guarantees of the Bill of Rights are "absolutes" which allow no opposing considerations, and the extreme claim of Justice Frankfurter that the Court must exercise judicial self-restraint and must not convert any one interest or value into a dogma, but must always weigh competing interests in the light of many and complex factors.

The tensions within the Court have come out most clearly in cases involving acts of Congress dealing with Communism and involving the investigations of congressional committees into Communist and "front" organizations. There has been much more agreement on the breadth and depth of the religion clauses of the First Amendment, which have been interpreted in well-nigh absolute terms; and the Court has tended to give maximum protection to the claims of freedom in literature and the arts.

Madison in 1788 argued that the political truths declared in a solemn manner in a bill of rights would acquire "the character of fundamental maxims of free Government, and as they become incorporated with the national sentiment, counteract the impulses of interest and passion." It

159

can scarcely be questioned that the guarantees of the Bill of Rights have become fundamental maxims of American government; nor can it be questioned that they have served as a check on interest and passion. Thus the Bill of Rights has helped mold the American nation as well as its political institutions. In any case, it has interacted with the people and its governments in an amazingly organic way, so that it has become inextricably intertwined with the American character and with the ideals of an open, free, pluralistic society.

Other nations, all over the world, have copied its form and words, but have not always succeeded in giving it meaning in the lives, thoughts, and aspirations of their peoples. But even the enemies of freedom pay homage to the virtues of the Bill of Rights by copying its guarantees, even if only as "parchment barriers," as Madison would say, against the exercise of power.

The Civil War Amendments: XIII–XV

EDITED BY FRANCIS A. ALLEN

The American Civil War was, among other things, a struggle between competing ideas of constitutionalism and the rights of man. When the epic conflict ended with victory of the Union forces on the battlefield, it was inevitable that there would be efforts to consolidate the military victory by giving expression in our fundamental law to certain principles and propositions until then in dispute. Between 1865 and 1870 three amendments were added to the Constitution which have ever since profoundly influenced our public law and policy.

The first problem demanding attention was the abolition of Negro slavery. The institution of slavery in the border states, as well as in the states in rebellion, created serious dilemmas for President Lincoln and Congress in the conduct of the war. The final proclamation of emancipation, issued by President Lincoln on January 1, 1863, left many fundamental issues unresolved. Even before the final proclamation was issued, President Lincoln had asked Congress to approve a constitutional amendment providing compensation to every state that abolished slavery before the beginning of the twentieth century. "In giving freedom to the slaves," he wrote, "we assure freedom to the free—honorable alike in what we give and what we preserve. We shall nobly serve or meanly lose the last best hope of earth." In the months following the final proclamation, Congress was offered various proposals for constitutional amendment. What was to become the Thirteenth Amendment passed the Senate on April 8, 1864, but the proposal received less than the requisite two-thirds vote in the House of Representatives. Only after the re-election of President Lincoln in November, 1864, did the amendment carry the House. The vote was 119 to 56—a margin so narrow that a shift of only three votes would have altered the result. The Thirteenth

Amendment was declared adopted by Secretary of State Seward on December 6, 1865. Included among the ratifying states were eight of the former Confederacy.

At the end of the military hostilities, Congress and the nation were confronted by the myriad problems involved in restoring the southern states to the Union, giving protection to the rights of the recently emancipated Negro population, and establishing new patterns of political power. Issues so fundamental were thought by many to require further alterations in the fundamental law; and a great variety of proposals for constitutional amendment were advanced within a year of Appomattox. The purposes and motivation of those active in the drafting of the Fourteenth Amendment were many and complex. Because of the importance of the Fourteenth Amendment in our developing constitutional law, the adoption of the amendment has been closely studied by modern scholars. Although the main outlines are clear, many important matters remain in doubt and controversy. One of the important factors leading to the adoption of the Fourteenth Amendment was congressional reaction to the "black codes" adopted by southern state legislatures at the close of the war—laws severely restrictive of the civil rights of the emancipated slaves. As demonstrated by the Freedman's Bureau Act and the Civil Rights Law of 1866, many members of Congress felt that, unless vigorously defended by federal law, the rights of the Negro which the Thirteenth Amendment was intended to establish would prove illusory. The Civil Rights Law is particularly important, for it sought both to protect Negroes from discrimination in the enjoyment of certain basic rights, such as the right to acquire property, and to effect a legislative repeal of the famous Dred Scott decision which had denied the capacity of the Negro to become a citizen of the United States. Although the Act was vital to the program of the Radical group in Congress and was passed by a two-thirds vote of both Houses to override President Johnson's veto, many members, even among the Radicals, doubted its constitutional validity. One of the purposes of the first section of the Fourteenth Amendment was, accordingly, to establish the constitutional validity of the Civil Rights Law of 1866 and to guard against the consequences of its possible repeal by some subsequent Congress.

The text of the Fourteenth Amendment evolved slowly in the congressional joint committee on Reconstruction. The third and fourth sections relate to issues of immediate concern growing out of the Civil War and possess little but historical interest today. The second section

162

represents an effort to protect rights of Negro suffrage, an effort soon perceived to be inadequate. The first and the fifth sections, however, remain among the most vital provisions of our public law. The Fourteenth Amendment was approved by Congress on June 13, 1866. Formal pronouncement of its ratification was made by Secretary Seward on July 28, 1868. Among the states counted as ratifying were two, Ohio and New Jersey, that had first adopted resolutions of ratification but later sought to withdraw consent and six southern states that were required to ratify the Fourteenth Amendment as a condition of their restoration in the Union.

The draftsmen of the Fourteenth Amendment sought to protect Negro rights of suffrage in Section 2, which, in effect, requires curtailment of congressional representation of any state in proportion to the number of persons disenfranchised in the state on grounds of race. Representative Thaddeus Stevens of Pennsylvania, a Radical leader, expressed the view that these provisions were the most important in the Fourteenth Amendment. Section 2 failed to achieve its purpose, however; and very soon proposals were advanced for constitutional amendment to provide more direct and effective protection of the Negro's right to vote. Various considerations underlay these proposals. To some it appeared that the civil rights of the Negro could be achieved only when he was accorded the right of full participation in the political life of the community. The proposals were also consistent with a general movement for expanded suffrage, which constituted one important aspect of nineteenth-century liberalism. Finally, it appears clear that some northern congressional leaders feared the rise of white political power in the South as a threat to their own political dominance in Congress and to the interests they represented. The Fifteenth Amendment was approved by Congress on February 26, 1869. Formal announcement of its ratification was made on May 30, 1870.

AMENDMENT XIII.

SECTION 1. Neither slavery nor involuntary servitude, except as a punishment for crime whereof the party shall have been duly convicted, shall exist within the United States, or any place subject to their jurisdiction.

SECTION 2. Congress shall have power to enforce this article by appropriate legislation.

AMENDMENT XIV.

SECTION 1. All persons born or naturalized in the United States and subject to the jurisdiction thereof, are citizens of the United States and of the State wherein they reside. No State shall make or enforce any law which shall abridge the privileges or immunities of citizens of the United States; or shall any State deprive any person of life, liberty, or property, without due process of law; nor deny to any person within its jurisdiction the equal protection of the laws.

SECTION 2. Representatives shall be apportioned among the several States according to their respective numbers, counting the whole number of persons in each State, excluding Indians not taxed. But when the right to vote at any election for the choice of electors for President and Vice President of the United States, Representatives in Congress, the Executive and Judicial officers of a State, or the members of the Legislature thereof, is denied to any of the male inhabitants of such State, being twenty-one years of age, and citizens of the United States, or in any way abridged, except for participation in rebellion, or other crime, the basis of representation therein shall be reduced in the proportion which the number of such male citizens shall bear to the whole number of male citizens twenty-one years of age in such State.

SECTION 3. No person shall be a Senator or Representative in Congress, or elector of President and Vice President, or hold any office, civil or military, under the United States, or under any State, who, having previously taken an oath, as a member of Congress, or as an officer of the United States, or as a member of any State legislature, or as an executive or judicial officer of any State, to support the Constitution of the United States, shall have engaged in insurrection or rebellion against the same, or given aid or comfort to the enemies thereof. But Congress may by a vote of two-thirds of each House, remove such disability.

SECTION 4. The validity of the public debt of the United States, authorized by law, including debts incurred for payment of pensions and bounties for services in suppressing insurrection or rebellion, shall not be questioned. But neither the United States nor any State shall assume or pay any debt or obligation incurred in aid of insurrection or rebellion against the United States, or any claim for the loss or emancipation of any slave; but all such debts, obligations and claims shall be held illegal and void.

SECTION 5. The Congress shall have power to enforce, by appropriate legislation, the provisions of this article.

AMENDMENT XV.

SECTION 1. The right of citizens of the United States to vote shall not be denied or abridged by the United States or by any State on account of race, color, or previous condition of servitude.

SECTION 2. The Congress shall have power to enforce this article by appropriate legislation.

The Fourteenth Amendment is, without doubt, the most important addition made to the text of the Constitution since the adoption of the Bill of Rights in 1790. Of the five sections of the amendment, the first has proved to be of prime significance. Included in the language of Section 1 are the great protean phrases, "due process of law" and "equal protection of the laws." The draftsmen of the amendment provided no specific meanings for these grand generalizations. This is not to say that the language was wholly devoid of historical content. The powers of Congress are limited in the Fifth Amendment by a "due process" clause; and many state constitutions contained similar provisions that had frequently been interpreted by state courts. Moreover, "due process" suggests the traditions of Magna Carta and "the law of the land." "Equal protection," too, although less redolent of the past, invokes certain historical connotations.

Yet the great moral imperatives of due process and equal protection could not be confined to their historical understandings when applied to the emerging issues of modern American life. There is evidence that those who drafted Section 1 intended that the meanings of these phrases should evolve and expand with the passage of time and changes of circumstance. This, in any event, is what occurred. As a result, the history of Fourteenth Amendment interpretation reveals in sharp and accurate focus the principal public issues with which generations of Americans have been preoccupied in the past three-quarters of a century.

Two great issues, one political and the other primarily economic, dominate the first half-century of Fourteenth Amendment interpretation. Neither is directly or necessarily concerned with the rights of racial minorities. The first issue was: What changes did the Civil War and the postwar amendments effect in the fundamental structure of American federalism? At least some of the congressional proponents of constitutional change desired basic and far-reaching alterations and assumed that significant aggrandizement of federal power had been achieved by adoption of the postwar amendments. From the first, however, the Supreme Court made clear that the amendments had not replaced the essential features of the American system. The most important teaching of the Slaughter-House Cases, 16 Wall. 36, decided in 1873 when nationalist feeling was still high in Congress, is that the postwar amendments did not effect a revolution in the American form of government. Ten years later Justice Bradley maintained that the Fourteenth Amendment does not grant Congress power "to establish a code of municipal law." In the years that followed, a practical redistribution of authority between state and federal governments occurred, and the Fourteenth Amendment sometimes contributed to this development. Broader interpretations of the powers of Congress under Section 5 of the amendment may one day significantly accelerate these tendencies. For the most part, however, the new importance of federal power has evolved in response to conditions of the modern world that are largely independent of the Fourteenth Amendment and its interpretation.

The second great issue confronted by the nineteenth-century Court involved the scope of the regulatory powers of the states over the burgeoning economic activity of the nation. The response was at first tentative and restrained. Thus in the Slaughter-House Cases, Justice Miller, speaking of the "due process" clause, observes: "We doubt very much whether any action of a state not directed by way of discrimination against the Negroes . . . will ever be held to come within the purview of this provision." Only a short time later the Court's decision in Munn v. Illinois, 94 U.S. 113 (1876), recognized broad state legislative authority over the rates of public utilities. But beginning in the eighties a much more restrictive view of state authority was expressed, and in the four decades that followed much state legislation fell afoul of the Court's interpretation of the "due process" clause. Among the casualties were state laws seeking to regulate rates, prices, minimum wages of workers, maximum hours of labor, and other terms of employment. These decisions expressed the judicial view then dominant that the full promise of American life could be realized only through the release of creative energies in the economic sphere, largely unimpeded by governmental restraint, and that the attainment of civil and political liberty in all aspects depended upon the defense of freedom of economic enterprise. At no time were these assumptions fully shared by all segments of American public opinion; and after the turn of the century criticism of the Court's role in these cases became more vocal and more organized.

It was not until the decade of the thirties that the Court fundamentally revised its views as to the permissible scope of state regulatory power. A majority of the Court has never wholly forsworn its authority to test the validity of state economic regulation against the requirements of due process, but today state legislation is not to be invalidated when supportable on any rational basis. The validity of state economic regulation is, therefore, no longer a central problem of Fourteenth Amendment interpretation.

The twentieth century brought to the nation new issues and new concerns, many of which found expression in judicial interpretations of "due process" and "equal protection." The years beginning with World War I may be regarded as a period of crisis for individual liberty, not only in the United States, but throughout the Western world. These concerns have been faithfully reflected in the work of the Supreme Court. Virtually all the constitutional law relating to the freedoms of expression, of association, and of religion, has been announced in the years since World War I. In 1925 the Court recognized that the imperatives of the First Amendment were part of the concept of "liberty" protected by the Fourteenth Amendment against invasion by the states, and many modern "due process" cases present such issues as the establishment of religion and freedom of speech. One of the most important questions of modern constitutional law has been whether the Fourteenth Amendment "incorporates" the provisions of the first nine amendments, traditionally understood to apply only to Congress and the federal government, and makes them applicable to the states. Efforts to interpret the "privileges and immunities" clause of the Fourteenth Amendment to achieve that end were frustrated by the Court in early cases arising under the amendment. No majority of the modern court has gone the entire distance of recognizing the full applicability of the Bill of Rights to the states. But a series of recent decisions dealing with particular rights has recognized that in most essential matters the states are subject to restraints comparable to those that limit the powers of the federal government.

Included in the modern judicial preoccupation with problems of civil liberty are the Fourteenth Amendment cases involving issues of fair procedure in state criminal proceedings. In the first half-century of the amendment's life, the Court had numerous occasions to consider the application of the "due process" clause to state criminal procedure. In virtually all these cases, the state procedures were upheld and a broad area of local self-determination was recognized. With the important decision of Powell v. Alabama, 287 U.S. 45 (1932), however, a new era of "due process" interpretation began. The Powell case recognized that the appointment of counsel for the impoverished accused was, in the circumstances presented, an indispensable part of the fair hearing which the state court was required to provide. Since that time the Court has spoken to an impressive range of questions involving, not only the right to counsel, but coerced confessions, unreasonable search and arrest practices, and many other aspects of the criminal trial and police activity. The consequence has been the formulation of an extensive body of constitutional doctrine within the span of a single generation.

The rights and interests of the recently emancipated slaves were obviously matters of primary concern to the proponents of the Civil War amendments. This concern is manifest in the explicit language of the Thirteenth and Fifteenth Amendments. The Fourteenth Amendment undoubtedly encompassed other objectives; but here, too, the problems of race were central. In general, the judicial interpretation of "involuntary servitude" in the Thirteenth Amendment has been kept within rather narrow bounds. Efforts to find in that amendment legal protections for a broad range of civil rights, such as the right of access to public accommodations, were firmly rejected by a majority of the Court in cases arising in the early postwar period. The Fifteenth Amendment has received numerous applications, but social conditions and, until recently, the absence of valid and effective implementing legislation have frustrated full realization of the rights of Negro suffrage.

Despite the purposes of its framers and the circumstances out of which it evolved, the Fourteenth Amendment made surprisingly small contributions to the civil rights of the Negro population in the half-century following its adoption. Judicial holdings that the amendment's protections applied only to "state action," and not to the action of private persons, required invalidation of much protective legislation enacted by Congress in the postwar period. By the end of the century the Court found legally enforceable segregation of the races consistent with the requirements of equal protection of the laws, so long as "separate but equal" accommodations were provided. Not until the fourth decade of the twentieth century did stirrings of conscience in the American public and a new determination of Negro groups force substantial judicial consideration of racial discrimination as a Fourteenth Amendment problem. A series of decisions of the highest importance were handed down. The institution of the "white primary" in southern states was held to be in violation of the Constitution. Criminal convictions infected by racial discrimination were reversed. In Shelley v. Kraemer, 334 U.S. 1 (1948), enforcement of restrictive covenants barring Negroes from ownership and occupancy of dwellings was found to offend the "equal protection" clause. Beginning in the 1930's the Court entertained a succession of cases involving racial segregation in public education, culminating in the landmark decision of Brown v. Board of Education, 347 U.S. 483 (1954). There the Court confronted the "separate but equal" doctrine, established more than a half-century before, and laid it to rest. The Brown case represents only the beginning of the Fourteenth Amendment's serious involvement in the issue of admitting minority groups to full participation in American life. Once again the great generalizations of the Fourteenth Amendment—"due process" and "equal protection"—have identified and illuminated the central issues of the time.

George Washington
First Inaugural Address
1789

EDITED BY CLINTON ROSSITER

The First Inaugural Address was delivered by George Washington in the Senate Chamber of Federal Hall in New York City on April 30, 1789. Despite the historic importance of the occasion, and also of the words that graced it, we have almost no reliable evidence about the genesis of this first of all inaugural addresses. It must have been written sometime around March 1, 1789, by which date Washington could doubt no longer that he had been elected unanimously to the Presidency, and could therefore not beg off this last momentous duty to his country; and the place of writing, or at least of polishing, must have been Mount Vernon, from which he did not set forth for New York until April 16. Knowing what we do of his writing habits both as warrior and as statesman, we may take it for granted that he turned to a trusted friend for help in drafting the address. Never a man from whom words flowed in easy abundance, always a man of genuine modesty about his own intellectual capacities, he had given the American art of "ghost-writing" its first major trial in the course of the Revolution. Well satisfied with the results, he continued to rely heavily on the literary skills of his colleagues until the end of his career.

This is not at all to say that Washington made himself the prisoner of the clever pens of clever men, or that, to be specific, the First Inaugural should be credited to another man. To the contrary, so explicit were the written and oral directions, so clearly understood the principles and prejudices, so piercing the critical eye, and so commanding the presence of this "first character of the world" that not even his most persuasive friends could make him say things he had not wanted to say in the first place. Like Andrew Jackson and Franklin D. Roosevelt he sought the help of men who were better with words than he could ever be, yet also like them he saw to it that the words of his great state papers were, in the most meaningful sense, his very own.

The man to whom Washington most probably turned in this instance was James Madison, who in 1789 was every bit as close to him as Alexander Hamilton had been a few years before and was to be forever after. Armed with a lengthy rough draft of Washington's ideas and guided by several face-to-face talks before the fireplace at Mt. Vernon, Madison seems to have spent his last few days in Virginia—from which he set forth March 2 to take his seat in the First Congress—putting these ideas in a form that would dignify the first official utterance of the first President of the first republic to arise in the New World as a challenge to the Old. That Washington was well satisfied with Madison's labors is plain from a letter of May 5, 1789, in which he invited his friend "to finish . . . the good work" he had begun by drafting a brief reply to the response of the House of Representatives.

Washington's purposes are clear on the face of this noble address. To remind his fellow citizens that the event of his accession to power was not of his own choosing, to beg their representatives not to embarrass him with "pecuniary compensation" for doing his duty, to invoke the blessings of Heaven, to jab a quick punch or two at "local attachments" and "party animosities," to celebrate morality as the foundation of liberty, and to put this experiment in free government in full historical perspective—these were the messages he had wanted to deliver, and these, thanks to Madison's loyal assistance and his own awareness of the gravity of the occasion, were delivered with the best of all possible effects. While the caustic senator from Pennsylvania, William Maclay, complained that Washington was "agitated and embarrassed more than ever he was by the leveled cannon or pointed musket," one suspects that his bearing was attuned perfectly to the demands of a fateful moment. The sense of the gathering that listened to these words was perhaps more accurately expressed by Fisher Ames, the most eloquent member of the First Congress, who confessed frankly that he had "sat entranced" in the face of this "allegory in which virtue was personified."

☆

FELLOW CITIZENS OF THE SENATE AND OF THE
HOUSE OF REPRESENTATIVES

AMONG the vicissitudes incident to life, no event could have filled me with greater anxieties than that of which the notification was transmitted by your order, and received on the fourteenth day of the present month:—On the one hand, I was summoned by my Country, whose voice I can never hear but with veneration and love, from a retreat which I had chosen with the fondest predilection, and, in my flattering hopes, with an immutable decision, as the asylum of my declining years: a retreat which was rendered every day more necessary as well as more dear to me, by the addition of habit to inclination, and of frequent interruptions in my health to the gradual waste committed on it by time.—On the other hand, the magnitude and difficulty of the trust to which the voice of my Country called me, being sufficient to awaken in the wisest and most experienced of her citizens, a distrustful scrutiny into his qualifications, could not but overwhelm with dispondence, one, who, inheriting inferior endowments from nature and unpractised in the duties of civil administraton, ought to be peculiarly conscious of his own deficiencies.—In this conflict of emotions, all I dare aver, is, that it has been my faithful study to collect my duty from a just appreciation of every circumstance, by which it might be affected.—All I dare hope, is, that, if in executing this task I have been too much swayed by a grateful remembrance of former instances, or by an affectionate sensibility to this transcendent proof, of the confidence of my fellow-citizens; and have thence too little consulted my incapacity as well as disinclination for the weighty and untried cares before me; my *error* will be palliated by the motives which misled me, and its consequences be judged by my Country, with some share of the partiality in which they originated.—

Such being the impressions under which I have, in obedience to the public summons, repaired to the present station; it would be peculiarly improper to omit in this first official Act, my fervent supplications to that Almighty Being who rules over the Universe,—who presides in the Councils of Nations,—and whose providential aids can supply every human defect, that his benediction may consecrate to the liberties and

---

The reading copy of this address in Washington's handwriting is preserved in the files of the United States Senate in the National Archives; it has been reproduced as National Archives Facsimile No. 22 (Washington, 1952), under the title *Washington's Inaugural Address of 1789*. The document is reprinted here in its original form, including a few misspelled words.

happiness of the People of the United States, a Government instituted by themselves for these essential purposes: and may enable every instrument employed in its administration to execute with success, the functions allotted to his charge.—In tendering this homage to the Great Author of every public and private good, I assure myself that it expresses your sentiments not less than my own;—nor those of my fellow-citizens at large, less than either.—No People can be bound to acknowledge and adore the invisible hand, which conducts the affairs of men more than the People of the United States.—Every step, by which they have advanced to the character of an independent nation, seems to have been distinguished by some token of providential agency.—And in the important revolution just accomplished in the system of their United Government; the tranquil deliberations and voluntary consent of so many distinct communities, from which the event has resulted, cannot be compared with the means by which most Governments have been established, without some return of pious gratitude along with an humble anticipation of the future blessings which the past seem to presage.—These reflections, arising out of the present crisis, have forced themselves too strongly on my mind to be suppressed.—You will join with me I trust in thinking, that there are none under the influence of which, the proceedings of a new and free Government can more auspiciously commence.—

By the article establishing the Executive Department, it is made the duty of the President "to recommend to your consideration, such measures as he shall judge necessary and expedient."—The circumstances under which I now meet you, will acquit me from entering into that subject, farther than to refer to the Great Constitutional Charter under which you are assembled; and which, in defining your powers, designates the objects to which your attention is to be given.—It will be more consistent with those circumstances, and far more congenial with the feelings which actuate me, to substitute, in place of a recommendation of particular measures, the tribute that is due to the talents, the rectitude, and the patriotism which adorn the characters selected to devise and adopt them.—In these honorable qualifications, I behold the surest pledges, that as on one side, no local prejudices, or attachments; no seperate views, nor party animosities, will misdirect the comprehensive and equal eye which ought to watch over this great assemblage of communities and interests: so, on another, that the foundations of our National policy will be laid in the pure and immutable principles of private morality; and the pre-eminence of free Government, be exemplified by all the attributes which can win the affections of its Citizens, and command the respect of the world.—I dwell on this prospect with every satisfaction which an ardent love for my Country can inspire: since there is no truth more thoroughly established, than that there exists in the economy and course of nature, an indissoluble union between virtue and happiness,—between duty and advantage,—between the genuine maxims of an honest and magnanimous policy, and the solid rewards of public prosperity and felicity:—Since we ought to be no less persuaded that the propitious smiles of Heaven, can never be expected on a nation that disregards the eternal rules of order and right, which Heaven itself has ordained:—And since the preservation of the sacred fire of liberty, and the destiny of the Republican model of Government, are justly considered as *deeply*, perhaps as *finally* staked, on the experiment entrusted to the hands of the American people.—

Besides the ordinary objects submitted to your care, it will remain with your judgment to decide, how far an exercise of the occasional power delegated by the Fifth article of the Constitution is rendered expedient at the present juncture by the nature of objections which have been urged against the system, or by the degree of inquietude which has given birth to them.—Instead of undertaking particular recommendations on this subject, in which I could be guided by no lights derived from official opportunities, I shall again give way to my entire confidence in your discernment and pursuit of the public good:—For I assure myself that whilst you carefully avoid every alteration which might endanger the benefits of an United and effective Government, or which ought to await the future lessons of experience; a reverence for the characteristic rights of freemen, and a regard for the public harmony, will sufficiently influence your deliberations on the question how far the former can be more impregnably fortified, or the latter be safely and advantageously promoted.—

To the preceeding observations I have one to add, which will be most properly addressed to the House of Representatives.—It concerns myself, and will therefore be as brief as possible.—When I was first honoured with a call into the service of my Country, then on the eve of an arduous struggle for its liberties, the light in which I contemplated my duty required that I should renounce every pecuniary compensation. —From this resolution I have in no instance departed.—And being still under the impressions which produced it, I must decline as inapplicable to myself, any share in the personal emoluments, which may be indispensably included in a permanent provision for the Executive Department; and must accordingly pray that the pecuniary estimates for the Station in which I am placed, may, during my continuance in it, be limited to such actual expenditures as the public good may be thought to require.—

Having thus imparted to you my sentiments, as they have been awakened by the occasion which brings us together,—I shall take my present leave;—but not without resorting once more to the benign parent of the human race, in humble supplication that since he has been pleased to favour the American people, with opportunities for deliberating in perfect tranquility, and dispositions for deciding with unparellelled unanimity on a form of Government, for the security of their Union, and the advancement of their happiness, so this divine blessing may be equally *conspicuous* in the enlarged views, the temperate consultations,—and the wise measures on which the success of this Government must depend.—

The afterlife of this touching little sermon on personal duty and national glory has been marked by none of the excitement that has attended the progress of the Farewell Address through the pages of history. Yet if Washington's First Inaugural is no match for Jefferson's as an exposition of a mighty political faith, for Lincoln's as an appeal to "the better angels of our nature," or for Franklin D. Roosevelt's as a summons to greatness in a time of hesitation, it has an importance for Americans that is bound to grow with the passage of the years of our never-ending experiment in constitutional democracy.

In the first place, it was an audible if disciplined cry from the heart of George Washington, and those who go in search of an understanding of the urges and aspirations of "this great man" (as even Maclay felt compelled to salute him) can do no better than to begin with the critical inventory of his own "endowments" in the opening sentences, the assertions of the existence of a force or standard called "the public good" sprinkled all through the address, and the stoutly rationalist insistence upon calling God anything except God—"Almighty Being," "Great Author," "invisible hand," "benign parent of the human race."

Second, the address set an example that has been converted by time and memory into one of our few great national rituals. Just what person or what reading or what intuition put it in Washington's mind to deliver an inaugural address can never be known for certain, but that he must have pondered this step carefully cannot be doubted. Throughout his eight years in the Presidency Washington was conscious almost to the point of anxiety that, as he wrote to Madison in his note of May 5, 1789, "the first of every thing, in our situation will serve to establish a Precedent," indeed a precedent that might guide men for centuries to come. This is one instance in which history has vindicated his judgment without reservation.

Finally, in a time in which it has suddenly become important for America to have a "national purpose," that is to say, a destiny more exalted than our own freedom and well-being, it is useful to recall that the first clear public acknowledgment of the suspicion that we had been granted such a destiny is to be found in the words in which Washington accepted the fateful, formless burdens of the Presidency. As Lincoln's quiet remarks at Gettysburg were the most refined expression of the old and unspoiled idea of the American Mission, so Washington's quiet remarks in New York were the most challenging. It made the Mission a living presence in American politics; it gave dignity and legitimacy to even the most savage contests for power in the next three generations. Of all the words of inspiration that Washington spoke in his career as public man, none were more influential, because none were more expressive of the American character, than this awesome reminder that into our hands had been committed the decisive trial of strength with the age-old enemies of free government—ignorance, cruelty, pride, poverty, disorder, irrational behavior. If it had said nothing else, the First Inaugural Address would be a document to cherish because it asks us, as it asked the men of 1789, to remember that "the preservation of the sacred fire of liberty, and the destiny of the Republican model of Government, are justly considered as deeply, perhaps as finally staked, on the experiment entrusted to the hands of the American people."

Alexander Hamilton
Report on Manufactures
1791

EDITED BY THOMAS C. COCHRAN

Submitted by Alexander Hamilton, as Secretary of the Treasury, to the
House of Representatives on December 5, 1791, the Report on Manufactures
was the last of his famous messages to Congress. Since the
population of the country was then predominantly agricultural and
economic theories condemning industry were popular, the problem of
writing a convincing report in favor of stimulating manufactures was a
delicate one. Hamilton had delayed presentation of this message for
nearly two years, both for the collection of data and for the discussion of
successive drafts with various experts. He was able to draw upon the ideas
of several advocates of manufacturing. One of these was William Barton,
secretary of the Pennsylvania Society for the Encouragement of Manufactures
and the Useful Arts, who in 1786 had published a paper on the
benefits of manufacturing to agriculture; another was President Washington,
who, before coming to the government, had been developing a
plan for making Alexandria, Virginia, a textile-manufacturing center.
More immediately, Hamilton had the aid of Tenche Coxe, who became
Assistant to the Secretary of the Treasury in May, 1790. Coxe was the
foremost economic thinker of the Pennsylvania Society, a man conversant
with both theoretical literature and American facts. Since one draft
of the lengthy Report exists in Coxe's handwriting, he must have cooperated
extensively in its preparation; in particular, he probably supplied
many of the facts and figures. Thus, while the final Report represents

177

Hamilton's mature and carefully reasoned ideas, it is also a comprehensive statement of an important school of American thought that placed a pragmatic policy for the development of the nation ahead of any abstract economic principles.

THE SECRETARY of the Treasury, in obedience to the order of the House of Representatives, of the 15th day of January, 1790, has applied his attention at as early a period as his other duties would permit, to the subject of Manufactures, and particularly to the means of promoting such as will tend to render the United States independent on foreign nations, for military and other essential supplies; and he thereupon respectfully submits the following report. . . .

The expediency of encouraging manufactures in the United States, which was not long since deemed very questionable, appears at this time to be pretty generally admitted. . . .

There still are, nevertheless, respectable patrons of opinions unfriendly to the encouragement of manufactures. . . . It has been maintained, that agriculture is not only the most productive, but the only productive species of industry. The reality of this suggestion, in either respect, has, however, not been verified by any accurate detail of facts and calculations; and the general arguments which are adduced to prove it, are rather subtile and paradoxical, than solid or convincing. . . .

One of the arguments made use of in support of the idea, may be pronounced both quaint and superficial. It amounts to this: That, in the production of the soil, nature co-operates with man; and that the effect of their joint labor must be greater than that of the labor of man alone.

This, however, is far from being a necessary inference. It is very conceivable, that the labor of man alone, laid out upon a work requiring great skill and art to bring it to perfection, may be more productive, in

The *Report* is reprinted here, in abridged form, from *The Works of Alexander Hamilton*, edited by John C. Hamilton (New York: Charles S. Francis & Company, 1850–51), Vol. III. There are three drafts of the *Report* in the Hamilton Papers in the Library of Congress. Another draft, in Tenche Coxe's handwriting, is in the Tenche Coxe Papers in the collection of the Historical Society of Pennsylvania, Philadelphia. The parts of the *Report* reproduced here make up somewhat less than a third of the total manuscript, in which many of the arguments are expanded in great detail.

value, than the labor of nature and man combined, when directed towards more simple operations and objects; and when it is recollected to what an extent the agency of nature, in the application of the mechanical powers, is made auxiliary to the prosecution of manufactures, the suggestion which has been noticed loses even the appearance of plausibility. . . .

Another, and that which seems to be the principal argument offered for the superior productiveness of agricultural labor, turns upon the allegation, that labor employed on manufactures, yields nothing equivalent to the rent of land; or to that net surplus, as it is called, which accrues to the proprietor of the soil.

But this distinction, important as it has been deemed, appears rather verbal than substantial.

It is easily discernible, that what, in the first instance, is divided into two parts, under the denominations of the ordinary profit of the stock of the farmer and rent to the landlord, is, in the second instance, united under the general appellation of the ordinary profit on the stock of the undertaker; and that this formal or verbal distribution constitutes the whole difference in the two cases. . . .

To affirm that the labor of the manufacturer is unproductive, because he consumes as much of the produce of the land as he adds value to the raw material which he manufactures, is not better founded, than it would be to affirm that the labor of the farmer, which furnishes materials to the manufacturer, is unproductive, because he consumes an equal value of manufactured articles. Each furnishes a certain portion of the produce of his labor to the other, and each destroys a correspondent portion of the produce of the labor of the other. In the mean time, the maintenance of two citizens, instead of one, is going on; the State has two members instead of one; and they, together, consume twice the value of what is produced from the land. . . .

It is now proper to proceed a step further, and to enumerate the principal circumstances from which it may be inferred that manufacturing establishments not only occasion a positive augmentation of the produce and revenue of the society, but that they contribute essentially to rendering them greater than they could possibly be, without such establishments. These circumstances are:

1. The division of labor.
2. An extension of the use of machinery.

3. Additional employment to classes of the community not ordinarily engaged in business.
4. The promoting of emigration from foreign countries.
5. The furnishing greater scope for the diversity of talents and dispositions, which discriminate men from each other.
6. The affording a more ample and various field for enterprise.
7. The creating, in some instances, a new, and securing, in all, a more certain and steady demand for the surplus produce of the soil.

Each of these circumstances has a considerable influence upon the total mass of industrious effort in a community; together, they add to it a degree of energy and effect, which are not easily conceived. . . .

Though it should be true that, in settled countries, the diversification of industry is conducive to an increase in the productive powers of labor, and to an augmentation of revenue and capital; yet it is scarcely conceivable that there can be any thing of so solid and permanent advantage to an uncultivated and unpeopled country, as to convert its wastes into cultivated and inhabited districts. If the revenue, in the mean time, should be less, the capital, in the event, must be greater.

To these observations, the following appears to be a satisfactory answer:

If the system of perfect liberty to industry and commerce were the prevailing system of nations, the arguments which dissuade a country, in the predicament of the United States, from the zealous pursuit of manufactures, would doubtless have great force. It will not be affirmed that they might not be permitted, with few exceptions, to serve as a rule of national conduct. In such a state of things, each country would have the full benefit of its peculiar advantages to compensate for its deficiencies or disadvantages. If one nation were in a condition to supply manufactured articles, on better terms than another, that other might find an abundant indemnification in a superior capacity to furnish the produce of the soil. And a free exchange, mutually beneficial, of the commodities which each was able to supply, on the best terms, might be carried on between them, supporting, in full vigor, the industry of each. . . .

But the system which has been mentioned, is far from characterizing the general policy of nations. The prevalent one has been regulated by an opposite spirit. The consequence of it is, that the United States are, to a certain extent, in the situation of a country precluded from foreign commerce. They can, indeed, without difficulty, obtain from abroad the manufactured supplies of which they are in want; but they experience numerous and very injurious impediments to the emission and vent of their own commodities. . . .

In such a position of things, the United States cannot exchange with Europe on equal terms; and the want of reciprocity would render them the victim of a system which should induce them to confine their views to agriculture, and refrain from manufactures. A constant and increasing necessity, on their part, for the commodities of Europe, and only a partial and occasional demand for their own, in return, could not but expose them to a state of impoverishment, compared with the opulence to which their political and natural advantages authorize them to aspire. . . .

The remaining objections to a particular encouragement of manufactures in the United States, now require to be examined.

One of these turns on the proposition, that industry, if left to itself, will naturally find its way to the most useful and profitable employment. Whence it is inferred, that manufactures, without the aid of government, will grow up as soon and as fast as the natural state of things and the interest of the community may require. . . .

Experience teaches, that men are often so much governed by what they are accustomed to see and practise, that the simplest and most obvious improvements, in the most ordinary occupations, are adopted with hesitation, reluctance, and by slow gradations. The spontaneous transition to new pursuits, in a community long habituated to different ones, may be expected to be attended with proportionably greater difficulty. . . .

The apprehension of failing in new attempts, is, perhaps, a more serious impediment. There are dispositions apt to be attracted by the mere novelty of an undertaking; but these are not always those best calculated to give it success. To this it is of importance that the confidence of cautious, sagacious capitalists, both citizens and foreigners, should be excited. And to inspire this description of persons with confidence, it is essential that they should be made to see in any project which is new—and for that reason alone, if for no other, precarious—the prospect of such a degree of countenance and support from government, as may be capable of overcoming the obstacles inseparable from first experiments.

The superiority antecedently enjoyed by nations who have preoccupied and perfected a branch of industry, constitutes a more formidable obstacle than either of those which have been mentioned, to the introduction of the same branch into a country in which it did not before exist. . . .

But the greatest obstacle of all to the successful prosecution of a new branch of industry in a country in which it was before unknown, consists, as far as the instances apply, in the bounties, premiums, and other aids, which are granted in a variety of cases, by the nations in which the establishments to be imitated are previously introduced. . . . Hence the undertakers of a new manufacture have to contend, not only with the natural disadvantages of a new undertaking, but with the gratuities and remunerations which other governments bestow. To be enabled to contend with success, it is evident that the interference and aid of their own governments are indispensable. . . .

The objections to the pursuit of manufactures in the United States, which next present themselves to discussion, represent an impracticability of success, arising from three causes: scarcity of hands, dearness of labor, want of capital. . . .

With regard to scarcity of hands, the fact itself must be applied with no small qualification to certain parts of the United States. There are large districts which may be considered as pretty fully peopled; and which, notwithstanding a continual drain for distant settlements, are thickly interspersed with flourishing and increasing towns. . . .

But there are circumstances . . . that materially diminish, every where, the effect of a scarcity of hands. These circumstances are, the great use which can be made of women and children, on which point a very pregnant and instructive fact has been mentioned—the vast extension given by late improvements to the employment of machines— which, substituting the agency of fire and water, has prodigiously lessened the necessity for manual labor; the employment of persons ordinarily engaged in other occupations, during the seasons or hours of leisure, which, besides giving occasion to the exertion of a greater quantity of labor, by the same number of persons, and thereby increasing the general stock of labor, as has been elsewhere remarked, may also be taken into the calculation, as a resource for obviating the scarcity of hands; lastly, the attraction of foreign emigrants. . . . It is not unworthy of remark, that the objection to the success of manufactures, deduced from the scarcity of hands, is alike applicable to trade and navigation, and yet these are perceived to flourish, without any sensible impediment from that cause.

As to the dearness of labor (another of the obstacles alleged), this has relation principally to two circumstances: one, that which has just been discussed, or the scarcity of hands; the other, the greatness of profits. . . . It is also evident, that the effect of the degree of disparity, which does truly exist, is diminished in proportion to the use which can be made of machinery. . . .

To procure all such machines as are known in any part of Europe, can only require a proper provision and due pains. The knowledge of several of the most important of them is already possessed. The preparation of them here is, in most cases, practicable on nearly equal terms. As far as they depend on water, some superiority of advantages may be claimed, from the uncommon variety and greater cheapness of situations adapted to millseats, with which different parts of the United States abound. . . .

The supposed want of capital for the prosecution of manufactures in the United States, is the most indefinite of the objections. . . .

It is very difficult to pronounce any thing precise concerning the real extent of the moneyed capital of a country, and still more, concerning the proportion it bears to the objects that invite the employment of capital. It is not less difficult to pronounce, how far the effect of any given quantity of money, as capital, or in other words, as a medium for circulating the industry and property of a nation, may be increased by the very circumstance of the additional motion which is given to it, by new objects of employment. . . .

The introduction of banks, as has been shown on another occasion, has a powerful tendency to extend the active capital of a country. Experience of the utility of these institutions, is multiplying them in the United States. It is probable that they will be established wherever they can exist with advantage; and wherever they can be supported, if administered with prudence, they will add new energies to all pecuniary operations. . . .

It is a well known fact that there are parts of Europe which have more capital than profitable domestic objects of employment. Hence, among other proofs, the large loans continually furnished to foreign States. And it is equally certain, that the capital of other parts may find more profitable employment in the United States than at home. . . .

It is not impossible, that there may be persons disposed to look, with a jealous eye, on the introduction of foreign capital, as if it were an instrument to deprive our own citizens of the profits of our own industry; but, perhaps, there never could be a more unreasonable jealousy. Instead of being viewed as a rival, it ought to be considered as a most valuable auxiliary, conducing to put in motion a greater quantity of productive labor, and a greater portion of useful enterprise, than could exist without it. It is at least evident, that, in a country situated like the United States, with an infinite fund of resources yet to be unfolded, every farthing of foreign capital which is laid out in internal meliorations, and in industrious establishments, of a permanent nature, is a precious acquisition.

And, whatever be the objects which originally attract foreign capital, when once introduced, it may be directed towards any purpose of beneficial exertion which is desired. And to detain it among us, there can be no expedient so effectual, as to enlarge the sphere within which it may be usefully employed: though introduced merely with views to speculations in the funds, it may afterwards be rendered subservient to the interests of agriculture, commerce, and manufactures. . . .

But, while there are circumstances sufficiently strong to authorize a considerable degree of reliance on the aid of foreign capital, towards the attainment of the object in view, it is satisfactory to have good grounds of assurance, that there are domestic resources, of themselves adequate to it. It happens that there is a species of capital, actually existing in the United States, which relieves from all inquietude, on the score of want of capital. This is the funded debt. . . . Public funds answer the purpose of capital, from the estimation in which they are usually held by moneyed men; and, consequently, from the ease and dispatch with which they can be turned into money. . . . This operation of public funds as capital, is too obvious to be denied; but it is objected to the idea of their operating as an augmentation of the capital of the community, that they serve to occasion the destruction of some other capital, to an equal amount. . . .

Hitherto, the reasoning has proceeded on a concession of the position, that there is a destruction of some other capital, to the extent of the annuity appropriated to the payment of the interest, and the redemption of the principal of the debt; but in this too much has been conceded. There is, at most, a temporary transfer of some other capital, to the amount of the annuity, from those who pay, to the creditor, who receives; which he again restores to the circulation, to resume the offices of a capital. This he does either immediately, by employing the money in some branch of industry, or mediately, by lending it to some other person, who does so employ it, or by spending it on his own maintenance. . . . When the payments of interest are periodical and quick, and made by the instrumentality of banks, the diversion or suspension of capital may almost be denominated momentary. . . .

In the question under discussion, it is important to distinguish between an absolute increase of capital, or an accession of real wealth, and an artificial increase of capital, as an engine of business, or as an instrument of industry and commerce. In the first sense, a funded debt has no pretensions to being deemed an increase of capital; in the last, it has pretensions which are not easy to be controverted. Of a similar nature is bank credit; and in an inferior degree, every species of private credit.

But, though a funded debt is not, in the first instance, an absolute increase of capital, or an augmentation of real wealth; yet, by serving as a new power in the operations of industry, it has, within certain bounds, a tendency to increase the real wealth of a community, in like manner, as money, borrowed by a thrifty farmer, to be laid out in the improvement of his farm, may, in the end, add to his stock of real riches. . . .

There remains to be noticed an objection to the encouragement of manufactures, of a nature different from those which question the probability of success. This is derived from its supposed tendency to give a monopoly of advantages to particular classes, at the expense of the rest of the community, who, it is affirmed, would be able to procure the requisite supplies of manufactured articles on better terms from foreigners than from our own citizens; and who, it is alleged, are reduced to the necessity of paying an enhanced price for whatever they want, by every measure which obstructs the free competition of foreign commodities. . . .

But, though it were true that the immediate and certain effect of regulations controlling the competition of foreign with domestic fabrics, was an increase of price, it is universally true that the contrary is the ultimate effect with every successful manufacture. When a domestic manufacture has attained to perfection, has engaged in the prosecution of it a competent number of persons, it invariably becomes cheaper. Being free from the heavy charges which attend the importation of foreign commodities, it can be afforded, and accordingly seldom ever fails to be sold, cheaper, in process of time, than was the foreign article for which it is a substitute. The internal competition which takes place, soon does away every thing like monopoly, and by degrees reduces the price of the article to the minimum of a reasonable profit on the capital employed. This accords with the reason of the thing, and with experience. . . .

The objections which are commonly made to the expediency of encouraging, and to the probability of succeeding in manufacturing pursuits, in the United States, having now been discussed, the considerations, which have appeared in the course of the discussion, recommending that species of industry to the patronage of the Government, will be materially strengthened by a few general, and some particular topics, which have been naturally reserved for subsequent notice.

There seems to be a moral certainty that the trade of a country, which is both manufacturing and agricultural, will be more lucrative and prosperous than that of a country which is merely agricultural. . . . There is always a higher probability of a favorable balance of trade, in regard to countries in which manufactures, founded on the basis of a thriving agriculture, flourish, than in regard to those which are confined wholly, or almost wholly, to agriculture. . . .

Not only the wealth, but the independence and security of a country, appear to be materially connected with the prosperity of manufactures. Every nation, with a view to those great objects, ought to endeavor to possess within itself, all the essentials of a national supply. These comprise the means of subsistence, habitation, clothing, and defence. . . .

The want of a navy, to protect our external commerce, as long as it shall continue, must render it a peculiarly precarious reliance for the supply of essential articles, and must serve to strengthen prodigiously the arguments in favor of manufactures. . . .

Our distance from Europe, the great fountain of manufactured supply, subjects us, in the existing state of things, to inconvenience and loss in two ways.

The bulkiness of those commodities, which are the chief productions of the soil, necessarily imposes very heavy charges on their transportation to distant markets. . . . The charges on manufactured supplies, brought from Europe, are greatly enhanced by the same circumstances of distance. . . .

The equality and moderation of individual property, and the growing settlements of new districts, occasion, in this country, an unusual demand for coarse manufactures; the charges of which being greater in proportion to their bulk, augment the disadvantage which has just been described. . . .

These disadvantages press, with no small weight, on the landed interests of the country. In seasons of peace, they cause a serious deduction from the intrinsic value of the products of the soil. In the time of a war, which should either involve ourselves, or another nation possessing a considerable share of our carrying trade, the charges on the transportation of our commodities, bulky as most of them are, could hardly fail to prove a grievous burthen to the farmer, while obliged to depend, in so great a degree as he now does, upon foreign markets, for the vent of the surplus of his labor. . . .

Particular encouragements of particular manufactures may be of a nature to sacrifice the interest of landholders to those of manufacturers; but it is nevertheless a maxim, well established by experience, and generally acknowledged, where there has been sufficient experience, that the aggregate prosperity of manufactures and the aggregate prosperity of agriculture are intimately connected. . . .

If, then, it satisfactorily appears, that it is the interest of the United States, generally, to encourage manufactures, it merits particular attention, that there are circumstances which render the present a critical moment for entering, with zeal, upon the important business. The effort cannot fail to be materially seconded by a considerable and increasing influx of money, in consequence of foreign speculations in the funds, and by the disorders which exist in different parts of Europe. . . .

The disturbed state of Europe inclining its citizens to emigration, the requisite workmen will be more easily acquired than at another time; and the effect of multiplying the opportunities of employment to those who emigrate, may be an increase of the number and extent of valuable acquisitions to the population, arts, and industry, of the country. . . .

In order to [form] a better judgment of the means proper to be resorted to by the United States, it will be of use to advert to those which have been employed with success in other countries. The principal of these are:

Protecting duties—or duties on those foreign articles which are the rivals of the domestic ones intended to be encouraged. . . .

The propriety of this species of encouragement need not be dwelt upon, as it is not only a clear result from the numerous topics which have been suggested, but is sanctioned by the laws of the United States, in a variety of instances; it has the additional recommendation of being a source of revenue. . . .

Pecuniary bounties.

This has been found one of the most efficacious means of encouraging manufactures, and is, in some views, the best. . . .

It is a species of encouragement more positive and direct than any other, and, for that very reason, has a more immediate tendency to stimulate and uphold new enterprises, increasing the chances of profit, and diminishing the risks of loss, in the first attempts.

It avoids the inconvenience of a temporary augmentation of price, which is incident to some other modes; or it produces it to a less degree, either by making no addition to the charges on the rival foreign article, as in the case of protecting duties, or by making a smaller addition. . . . Bounties have not, like high protecting duties, a tendency to produce scarcity. . . . Bounties are, sometimes, not only the best, but the only proper expedient for uniting the encouragement of a new object of agriculture with that of a new object of manufacture. . . .

It cannot escape notice, that a duty upon the importation of an article can no otherwise aid the domestic production of it, than by giving the latter greater advantages in the home market. It can have no influence upon the advantageous sale of the article produced in foreign markets— no tendency, therefore, to promote its exportation.

The true way to conciliate these two interests is to lay a duty on foreign manufactures of the material, the growth of which is desired to be encouraged, and to apply the produce of that duty, by way of bounty, either upon the production of the material itself, or upon its manufacture at home, or upon both. . . .

Except the simple and ordinary kinds of household manufacture, or those for which there are very commanding local advantages, pecuniary bounties are, in most cases, indispensable to the introduction of a new branch. . . .

Premiums.

Premiums serve to reward some particular excellence or superiority, some extraordinary exertion or skill, and are dispensed only in a small number of cases. But their effect is to stimulate general effort; contrived so as to be both honorary and lucrative, they address themselves to different passions—touching the chords, as well of emulation as of interest. They are, accordingly, a very economical mean of exciting the enterprise of a whole community. . . .

The encouragement of new inventions and discoveries at home, and of the introduction into the United States of such as may have been made in other countries; particularly, those which relate to machinery.

This is among the most useful and unexceptionable of the aids which can be given to manufactures. The usual means of that encouragement are pecuniary rewards, and, for a time, exclusive privileges. The first must be employed, according to the occasion, and the utility of the invention or discovery. For the last, so far as respects "authors and inventors," provision has been made by law. . . .

Judicious regulations for the inspection of manufactured commodities.

This is not among the least important of the means by which the prosperity of manufactures may be promoted. It is, indeed, in many cases, one of the most essential. Contributing to prevent frauds upon consumers at home, and exporters to foreign countries; to improve the quality, and preserve the character of the national manufactures; it cannot fail to aid the expeditious and advantageous sale of them, and to serve as a guard against successful competition from other quarters. . . .

The facilitating of the transportation of commodities. . . .

There is, perhaps, scarcely any thing, which has been better calculated to assist the manufactures of Great Britain, than the melioration of the public roads of that kingdom, and the great progress which has been of late made in opening canals. Of the former, the United States stand much in need; for the latter, they present uncommon facilities. . . .

There is little room to hope, that the progress of manufactures will so equally keep pace with the progress of population, as to prevent even a gradual augmentation of the product of the duties on imported articles. . . .

. . . This surplus will serve—

First. To constitute a fund for paying the bounties which shall have been decreed.

Second. To constitute a fund for the operations of a board to be established, for promoting arts, agriculture, manufactures, and commerce. Of this institution, different intimations have been given in the

189

course of this report. An outline of a plan for it shall now be submitted.

Let a certain annual sum be set apart, and placed under the management of commissioners, not less than three, to consist of certain officers of the Government and their successors in office.

Let these commissioners be empowered to apply the fund confided to them, to defray the expenses of the emigration of artists, and manufacturers in particular branches of extraordinary importance; to induce the prosecution and introduction of useful discoveries, inventions, and improvements, by proportionate rewards, judiciously held out and applied; to encourage by premiums, both honorable and lucrative, the exertions of individuals and of classes, in relation to the several objects they are charged with promoting; and to afford such other aids to those objects as may be generally designated by law. . . .

There is reason to believe that the progress of particular manufactures has been much retarded by the want of skilful workmen. And it often happens, that the capitals employed are not equal to the purposes of bringing from abroad workmen of a superior kind. Here, in cases worthy of it, the auxiliary agency of the Government would, in all probability, be useful. There are also valuable workmen in every branch, who are prevented from emigrating, solely, by the want of means. Occasional aids to such persons, properly administered, might be a source of valuable acquisitions to the country. . . .

The great use which may be made of a fund of this nature, to procure and import foreign improvements, is particularly obvious. Among these, the articles of machines would form a most important item. . . .

In countries where there is great private wealth, much may be effected by the voluntary contributions of patriotic individuals; but in a community situated like that of the United States, the public purse must supply the deficiency of private resource. In what can it be so useful, as in promoting and improving the efforts of industry?

All which is humbly submitted.

ALEXANDER HAMILTON
Secretary of the Treasury.

The analyses in Hamilton's Report were so thorough and the arguments on subjects such as the tariff so cogent that over the next century they were paraphrased in editorials and political speeches whenever these

topics became public issues. Mathew Carey, for example, the great champion of protective tariff between the War of 1812 and the Civil War, added little to the basic arguments of the Report. The same could be said of post–Civil War protectionists such as William ("Pig-Iron") Kelley, William McKinley, or Nelson Dingley. Mid-twentieth-century students of economic development find Hamilton's explanation of the factors that hamper the initiation of industrial enterprise enlightened and penetrating.

On the other hand, to remember that Hamilton represented the extreme political right, and that Jefferson on the liberal left fought these proposals under the banner of laissez faire, gives perspective on the ebb and flow of ideas in politics. The arguments of the Report were those currently thought suitable by many business leaders in a country where capital and labor were scarce and management weak and inexperienced. A century later, with labor and capital ample and management confident and powerful, business leaders were turning against Hamilton's view of the use of the national state. Only his ideas on protective tariff had a strong conservative following.

Early in the twentieth century the Report's advocacy of the paternalistic state was embraced by Theodore Roosevelt, Herbert Croly, George F. Perkins, and other moderate progressives. But, whereas Hamilton and his school would have used the state chiefly to advance economic development, these progressives would have used it also to bring about social justice.

Still later the approach inherent in the Report was mirrored in such laws as the National Industrial Recovery and the Full Employment Acts. New Deal economists also agreed with the Report that there was no immediate danger in an increasing debt owed to the citizens of the nation. Thus, by mid-twentieth century, Hamilton, as a political figure, was in an anomalous position. While the Democrats, as in President Johnson's Great Society, supported Hamilton's economic views of the use of the state, they shunned his name because of his conservative politics. The Republicans, on the other hand, revered him as a political ancestor but were tacitly in opposition to most of his economic ideas.

George Washington
Farewell Address
1796

EDITED BY RICHARD B. MORRIS

Long in formulation, President Washington's great state paper took the shape of a political testament. Promulgated at the end of his second term in the Presidency, it embodied his momentous decision not to stand for a third term, a decision which for long was accepted as an unwritten law of the Constitution. As a matter of fact Washington had considered retiring at the end of his first term. Back in February, 1792, he had asked James Madison to prepare a draft of an address concerning his contemplated retirement. Madison complied, sending him a "Form for an Address." Washington put it aside for the time being.

When he definitely decided to retire at the end of his second term, Washington made a draft of his own, embodying some material from Madison's earlier draft, but introducing numerous new elements. These included his concern with the divisiveness of the evolving party alignments, a defense of his own integrity, and some cautions about America's foreign policy. The last had been prompted by the bitterness of the debates in the Senate over Jay's Treaty, and by the attempt of the House of Representatives to assert a role in the making of treaties. After consulting Madison again, Washington sent on to Madison's chief antagonist, Alexander Hamilton, a brief introduction, Madison's draft, and the President's own lengthy addition. Hamilton prepared two new drafts, faithfully following Washington's scheme of organization and the President's main ideas, but rephrasing these in a masterly way. At

192

Washington's request, Hamilton discussed his drafts with John Jay, but we have no documentation on the changes Hamilton may have incorporated as a result of Jay's suggestions.

Despite a considerable amount of collaboration, the final state paper was still very much Washington's own. The President even rephrased Hamilton's revision in some cases, often making the text less wordy. For example, Hamilton's "Original Draft" asks:

Why should we forego the advantages of so felicitous a situation? Why quit our own ground to stand upon foreign ground?

Washington changed that to read:

Why forego the advantages of so peculiar a situation? Why quit our own to stand upon foreign ground?

Hamilton:

Permanent alliances, intimate connection with any part of the foreign world is to be avoided; so far, (I mean) as we are now at liberty to do it.

Washington:

It is our true policy to steer clear of permanent alliances with any portion of the foreign world, so far, I mean, as we are now at liberty to do it.

Washington showed himself to be a more cautious, and perhaps less full-blown, isolationist than Hamilton. Thus, Hamilton's "Original Draft":

Taking care always to keep ourselves by suitable establishments in a respectably defensive position, we may safely trust to occasional alliances for extraordinary war emergencies.

Washington changed the sentence to read:

Taking care always to keep ourselves by suitable establishments on a respectable defensive posture, we may safely trust to temporary alliances for extraordinary emergencies.

By substituting "temporary" for "occasional" Washington introduced a subtle but important change of concept.

Washington wrote John Jay early in May, 1796, disclosing his definite intention to retire, but he yielded to Hamilton's urging to hold off his public announcement. Hamilton advised him to time the announcement for two months before the meeting of the presidential electors, but Washington did not wait quite that long. Three months before the electors convened he submitted his Farewell Address to the Cabinet, and, four days later, on September 19, 1796, he gave it to the people in the columns of the Philadelphia Daily American Advertiser. It was never delivered orally.

FRIENDS AND FELLOW-CITIZENS:

THE PERIOD for a new election of a citizen to administer the Executive Government of the United States being not far distant, and the time actually arrived when your thoughts must be employed in designating the person who is to be clothed with that important trust, it appears to me proper, especially as it may conduce to a more distinct expression of the public voice, that I should now apprise you of the resolution I have formed to decline being considered among the number of those out of whom a choice is to be made.

I beg you at the same time to do me the justice to be assured that this resolution has not been taken without a strict regard to all the considerations appertaining to the relation which binds a dutiful citizen to his country; and that in withdrawing the tender of service, which silence in my situation might imply, I am influenced by no diminution of zeal for your future interest, no deficiency of grateful respect for your past kindness, but am supported by a full conviction that the step is compatible with both.

The acceptance of and continuance hitherto in the office to which your suffrages have twice called me have been a uniform sacrifice of inclination to the opinion of duty and to a deference for what appeared to be your desire. I constantly hoped that it would have been much earlier in my power, consistently with motives which I was not at liberty to disregard, to return to that retirement from which I had been reluctantly drawn. The strength of my inclination to do this previous to the last election had even led to the preparation of an address to declare it to you; but mature reflection on the then perplexed and critical posture of our affairs with foreign nations and the unanimous advice of persons entitled to my confidence impelled me to abandon the idea. I rejoice that the state of your concerns, external as well as internal, no longer renders the pursuit of inclination incompatible with the senti-

The address is reprinted here as it originally appeared in the Philadelphia *Daily American Advertiser* of September 19, 1796.

ment of duty or propriety, and am persuaded, whatever partiality may be retained for my services, that in the present circumstances of our country you will not disapprove my determination to retire.

The impressions with which I first undertook the arduous trust were explained on the proper occasion. In the discharge of this trust I will only say that I have, with good intentions, contributed toward the organization and administration of the Government the best exertions of which a very fallible judgment was capable. Not unconscious in the outset of the inferiority of my qualifications, experience in my own eyes, perhaps still more in the eyes of others, has strengthened the motives to diffidence of myself; and every day the increasing weight of years admonishes me more and more that the shade of retirement is as necessary to me as it will be welcome. Satisfied that if any circumstances have given peculiar value to my services they were temporary, I have the consolation to believe that, while choice and prudence invite me to quit the political scene, patriotism does not forbid it.

In looking forward to the moment which is intended to terminate the career of my political life my feelings do not permit me to suspend the deep acknowledgment of that debt of gratitude which I owe to my beloved country for the many honors it has conferred upon me; still more for the steadfast confidence with which it has supported me, and for the opportunities I have thence enjoyed of manifesting my inviolable attachment by services faithful and persevering, though in usefulness unequal to my zeal. If benefits have resulted to our country from these services, let it always be remembered to your praise and as an instructive example in our annals that under circumstances in which the passions, agitated in every direction, were liable to mislead; amidst appearances sometimes dubious; vicissitudes of fortune often discouraging; in situations in which not unfrequently want of success has countenanced the spirit of criticism, the constancy of your support was the essential prop of the efforts and a guaranty of the plans by which they were effected. Profoundly penetrated with this idea, I shall carry it with me to my grave as a strong incitement to unceasing vows that Heaven may continue to you the choicest tokens of its beneficence; that your union and brotherly affection may be perpetual; that the free Constitution which is the work of your hands may be sacredly maintained; that its administration in every department may be stamped with wisdom and virtue; that, in fine, the happiness of the people of these States, under the auspices of liberty, may be made complete by so careful a preservation and so prudent a use of this blessing as will acquire to them the glory of recommending it to the applause, the affection, and adoption of every nation which is yet a stranger to it.

Here, perhaps, I ought to stop. But a solicitude for your welfare which can not end but with my life, and the apprehension of danger natural to that solicitude, urge me on an occasion like the present to offer to your solemn contemplation and to recommend to your frequent review some sentiments which are the result of much reflection, of no inconsiderable observation, and which appear to me all important to the permanency of your felicity as a people. These will be offered to you with the more freedom as you can only see in them the disinterested warnings of a parting friend, who can possibly have no personal motive to bias his counsel. Nor can I forget as an encouragement to it your indulgent reception of my sentiments on a former and not dissimilar occasion.

Interwoven as is the love of liberty with every ligament of your hearts, no recommendation of mine is necessary to fortify or confirm the attachment.

The unity of government which constitutes you one people is also now dear to you. It is justly so, for it is a main pillar in the edifice of your real independence, the support of your tranquillity at home, your peace abroad, of your safety, of your prosperity, of that very liberty which you so highly prize. But as it is easy to foresee that from different causes and from different quarters much pains will be taken, many artifices employed, to weaken in your minds the conviction of this truth, as this is the point in your political fortress against which the batteries of internal and external enemies will be most constantly and actively (though often covertly and insidiously) directed, it is of definite moment that you should properly estimate the immense value of your national union to your collective and individual happiness; that you should cherish a cordial, habitual, and immovable attachment to it; accustoming your-selves to think and speak of it as of the palladium of your political safety and prosperity; watching for its preservation with jealous anxiety; discountenancing whatever may suggest even a suspicion that it can in any event be abandoned, and indignantly frowning upon the first dawning of every attempt to alienate any portion of our country from the rest or to enfeeble the sacred ties which now link together the various parts.

For this you have every inducement of sympathy and interest. Citizens by birth or choice of a common country, that country has a right to concentrate your affections. The name of American, which belongs to you in your national capacity, must always exalt the just pride of patriotism more than any appellation derived from local discriminations. With slight shades of difference, you have the same religion, manners, habits, and political principles. You have in a common cause fought and triumphed together. The independence and liberty you possess are the work of joint councils and joint efforts, of common dangers, sufferings, and successes.

But these considerations, however powerfully they address themselves to your sensibility, are greatly outweighed by those which apply more immediately to your interest. Here every portion of our country finds the most commanding motives for carefully guarding and preserving the union of the whole.

The *North*, in an unrestrained intercourse with the *South*, protected by the equal laws of a common government, finds in the productions of the latter great additional resources of maritime and commercial enterprise and precious materials of manufacturing industry. The *South*, in the same intercourse, benefiting by the same agency of the *North*, sees its agriculture grow and its commerce expand. Turning partly into its own channels the seamen of the *North*, it finds its particular navigation invigorated; and while it contributes in different ways to nourish and increase the general mass of the national navigation, it looks forward to the protection of a maritime strength to which itself is unequally adapted. The *East*, in a like intercourse with the *West*, already finds, and in the progressive improvement of interior communications by land and water will more and more find, a valuable vent for the commodities which it brings from abroad or manufactures at home. The *West* derives from the *East* supplies requisite to its growth and comfort, and what is perhaps of still greater consequence, it must of necessity owe the *secure* enjoyment of indispensable *outlets* for its own productions to the weight, influence, and the future maritime strength of the Atlantic side of the Union, directed by an indissoluble community of interest as *one nation*. Any other tenure by which the *West* can hold this essential advantage, whether derived from its own separate strength or from an apostate and unnatural connection with any foreign power, must be intrinsically precarious.

While, then, every part of our country thus feels an immediate and particular interest in union, all the parts combined can not fail to find in the united mass of means and efforts greater strength, greater resource, proportionably greater security from external danger, a less frequent, interruption of their peace by foreign nations, and what is of inestimable value, they must derive from union an exemption from those broils and wars between themselves which so frequently afflict neighboring countries not tied together by the same governments, which their own rivalships alone would be sufficient to produce, but which opposite foreign alliances, attachments, and intrigues would stimulate and imbitter. Hence, likewise, they will avoid the necessity of those overgrown military establishments which, under any form of government, are inauspicious to liberty, and which are to be regarded as particularly hostile to republican liberty. In this sense it is that your union ought to be considered as a main prop of your liberty, and that the love of the one ought to endear to you the preservation of the other.

These considerations speak a persuasive language to every reflecting and virtuous mind, and exhibit the continuance of the union as a primary object of patriotic desire. Is there a doubt whether a common government can embrace so large a sphere? Let experience solve it. To listen to mere speculation in such a case were criminal. We are authorized to hope that a proper organization of the whole, with the auxiliary agency of governments for the respective subdivisions, will afford a happy issue to the experiment. It is well worth a fair and full experiment. With such powerful and obvious motives to union affecting all parts of our country, while experience shall not have demonstrated its impracticability, there will always be reason to distrust the patriotism of those who in any quarter may endeavor to weaken its bands.

In contemplating the causes which may disturb our union it occurs as matter of serious concern that any ground should have been furnished for characterizing parties by *geographical* discriminations—*Northern* and *Southern, Atlantic* and *Western*—whence designing men may endeavor to excite a belief that there is a real difference of local interests and views. One of the expedients of party to acquire influence within particular districts is to misrepresent the opinions and aims of other districts. You can not shield yourselves too much against the jealousies and heart-burnings which spring from these misrepresentations; they tend to render alien to each other those who ought to be bound together by fraternal affection. The inhabitants of our Western country have lately had a useful lesson on this head. They have seen in the negotiation by the Executive and in the unanimous ratification by the Senate of the treaty with Spain, and in the universal satisfaction at that event throughout the United States, a decisive proof how unfounded were the suspicions propagated among them of a policy in the General Government and in the Atlantic States unfriendly to their interests in regard to the Mississippi. They have been witnesses to the formation of two treaties—that with Great Britain and that with Spain—which secure to them everything they could desire in respect to our foreign relations toward confirming their prosperity. Will it not be their wisdom to rely for the preservation of these advantages on the union by which they were procured? Will they not henceforth be deaf to those advisers, if such there are, who would sever them from their brethren and connect them with aliens?

To the efficacy and permanency of your union a government for the whole is indispensable. No alliances, however strict, between the parts can be an adequate substitute. They must inevitably experience the infractions and interruptions which all alliances in all times have experienced. Sensible of this momentous truth, you have improved upon your first essay by the adoption of a Constitution of Government better calculated than your former for an intimate union and for the efficacious management of your common concerns. This Government, the offspring of your own choice, uninfluenced and unawed, adopted upon full investigation and mature deliberation, completely free in its principles, in the distribution of its powers, uniting security with energy, and containing within itself a provision for its own amendment, has a just claim to your confidence and your support. Respect for its authority, compliance with its laws, acquiescence in its measures, are duties enjoined by the fundamental maxims of true liberty. The basis of our political systems is the right of the people to make and to alter their constitutions of government. But the constitution which at any time exists till changed by an explicit and authentic act of the whole people is sacredly obligatory upon all. The very idea of the power and the right of the people to establish government presupposes the duty of every individual to obey the established government.

All obstructions to the execution of the laws, all combinations and associations, under whatever plausible character, with the real design to direct, control, counteract, or awe the regular deliberation and action of the constituted authorities, are destructive of this fundamental principle and of fatal tendency. They serve to organize faction; to give it an artificial and extraordinary force; to put in the place of the delegated will of the nation the will of a party, often a small but artful and enterprising minority of the community, and, according to the alternate triumphs of different parties, to make the public administration the mirror of the ill-concerted and incongruous projects of faction rather than the organ of consistent and wholesome plans, digested by common counsels and modified by mutual interests.

However combinations or associations of the above description may now and then answer popular ends, they are likely in the course of time and things to become potent engines by which cunning, ambitious, and unprincipled men will be enabled to subvert the power of the people, and to usurp for themselves the reins of government, destroying afterwards the very engines which have lifted them to unjust dominion.

Toward the preservation of your Government and the permanency of your present happy state, it is requisite not only that you steadily discountenance irregular oppositions to its acknowledged authority, but also that you resist with care the spirit of innovation upon its principles, however specious the pretexts. One method of assault may be to effect in the forms of the Constitution alterations which will impair the energy of the system, and thus to undermine what can not be directly overthrown. In all the changes to which you may be invited remember that time and habit are at least as necessary to fix the true character of governments as of other human institutions; that experience is the surest standard by which to test the real tendency of the existing constitution of a country; that facility in changes upon the credit of mere hypothesis and opinion exposes to perpetual change, from the endless variety of hypothesis and opinion; and remember especially that for the efficient management of your common interests in a country so extensive as ours a government of as much vigor as is consistent with the perfect security of liberty is indispensable. Liberty itself will find in such a government, with powers properly distributed and adjusted, its surest guardian. It is, indeed, little else than a name where the government is too feeble to withstand the enterprises of faction, to confine each member of the society within the limits prescribed by the laws, and to maintain all in the secure and tranquil enjoyment of the rights of person and property.

I have already intimated to you the danger of parties in the State, with particular reference to the founding of them on geographical discriminations. Let me now take a more comprehensive view, and warn you in the most solemn manner against the baneful effects of the spirit of party generally.

This spirit, unfortunately, is inseparable from our nature, having its root in the strongest passions of the human mind. It exists under different shapes in all governments, more or less stifled, controlled, or repressed; but in those of the popular form it is seen in its greatest rankness and is truly their worst enemy.

The alternate domination of one faction over another, sharpened by the spirit of revenge natural to party dissension, which in different ages and countries has perpetrated the most horrid enormities, is itself a frightful despotism. But this leads at length to a more formal and permanent despotism. The disorders and miseries which result gradually incline the minds of men to seek security and repose in the absolute power of an individual, and sooner or later the chief of some prevailing faction, more able or more fortunate than his competitors, turns this disposition to the purposes of his own elevation on the ruins of public liberty.

Without looking forward to an extremity of this kind (which nevertheless ought not to be entirely out of sight), the common and continual mischiefs of the spirit of party are sufficient to make it the interest and duty of a wise people to discourage and restrain it.

It serves always to distract the public councils and enfeeble the public administration. It agitates the community with ill-founded jealousies and false alarms; kindles the animosity of one part against another; foments occasionally riot and insurrection. It opens the door to foreign influence and corruption, which find a facilitated access to the government itself through the channels of party passion. Thus the policy and the will of one country are subjected to the policy and will of another.

There is an opinion that parties in free countries are useful checks upon the administration of the government, and serve to keep alive the spirit of liberty. This within certain limits is probably true; and in governments of a monarchical cast patriotism may look with indulgence, if not with favor, upon the spirit of party. But in those of the popular character, in governments purely elective, it is a spirit not to be encouraged. From their natural tendency it is certain there will always be enough of that spirit for every salutary purpose; and there being constant danger of excess, the effort ought to be by force of public opinion to mitigate and assuage it. A fire not to be quenched, it demands a uniform vigilance to prevent its bursting into a flame, lest, instead of warming, it should consume.

It is important, likewise, that the habits of thinking in a free country should inspire caution in those intrusted with its administration to confine themselves within their respective constitutional spheres, avoiding in the exercise of the powers of one department to encroach upon another. The spirit of encroachment tends to consolidate the powers of all the departments in one, and thus to create, whatever the form of government, a real despotism. A just estimate of that love of power and proneness to abuse it which predominates in the human heart is sufficient to satisfy us of the truth of this position. The necessity of reciprocal checks in the exercise of political power, by dividing and distributing it into different depositories, and constituting each the guardian of the public weal against invasions by the others, has been evinced by experiments ancient and modern, some of them in our country and under our own eyes. To preserve them must be as necessary as to institute them. If in the opinion of the people the distribution or modification of the constitutional powers be in any particular wrong, let it be corrected by an amendment in the way which the Constitution designates. But let there be no change by usurpation; for though this in one instance may be the instrument of good, it is the customary weapon by which free governments are destroyed. The precedent must always greatly overbalance in permanent evil any partial or transient benefit which the use can at any time yield.

Of all the dispositions and habits which lead to political prosperity, religion and morality are indispensable supports. In vain would that man claim the tribute of patriotism who should labor to subvert these great pillars of human happiness—these firmest props of the duties of men and citizens. The mere politician, equally with the pious man, ought to respect and to cherish them. A volume could not trace all their connections with private and public felicity. Let it simply be asked, Where is the security for property, for reputation, for life, if the sense of religious obligation *desert* the oaths which are the instruments of investigation in courts of justice? And let us with caution indulge the supposition that morality can be maintained without religion. Whatever may be conceded to the influence of refined education on minds of peculiar structure, reason and experience both forbid us to expect that national morality can prevail in exclusion of religious principle.

It is substantially true that virtue or morality is a necessary spring of popular government. The rule indeed extends with more or less force to every species of free government. Who that is a sincere friend to it can look with indifference upon attempts to shake the foundation of the fabric? Promote, then, as an object of primary importance, institutions for the general diffusion of knowledge. In proportion as the structure of a government gives force to public opinion, it is essential that public opinion should be enlightened.

As a very important source of strength and security, cherish public credit. One method of preserving it is to use it as sparingly as possible, avoiding occasions of expense by cultivating peace, but remembering also that timely disbursements to prepare for danger frequently prevent much greater disbursements to repel it; avoiding likewise the accumulation of debt, not only by shunning occasions of expense, but by vigorous exertions in time of peace to discharge the debts which unavoidable wars have occasioned, not ungenerously throwing upon posterity the burthen which we ourselves ought to bear. The execution of these maxims belongs to your representatives; but it is necessary that public opinion should cooperate. To facilitate to them the performance of their duty it is essential that you should practically bear in mind that toward the payment of debts there must be revenue; that to have revenue there must be taxes; that no taxes can be devised which are not more or less inconvenient and unpleasant; that the intrinsic embarrassment inseparable from the selection of the proper objects (which is always a choice of difficulties), ought to be a decisive motive for a candid construction of the conduct of the Government in making it, and for a spirit of acquiescence in the measures for obtaining revenue which the public exigencies may at any time dictate.

Observe good faith and justice toward all nations. Cultivate peace and harmony with all. Religion and morality enjoin this conduct. And can it be that good policy does not equally enjoin it? It will be worthy of a free, enlightened, and at no distant period a great nation to give to mankind the magnanimous and too novel example of a people always guided by an exalted justice and benevolence. Who can doubt that in the course of time and things the fruits of such a plan would richly repay any temporary advantages which might be lost by a steady adherence to it? Can it be that Providence has not connected the permanent felicity of a nation with its virtue? The experiment, at least, is recommended by every sentiment which ennobles human nature. Alas! is it rendered impossible by its vices?

In the execution of such a plan nothing is more essential than that permanent, inveterate antipathies against particular nations and passionate attachments for others should be excluded, and that in place of them

203

just and amicable feelings toward all should be cultivated. The nation which indulges toward another an habitual hatred or an habitual fondness is in some degree a slave. It is a slave to its animosity or to its affection, either of which is sufficient to lead it astray from its duty and its interest. Antipathy in one nation against another disposes each more readily to offer insult and injury, to lay hold of slight causes of umbrage, and to be haughty and intractable when accidental or trifling occasions of dispute occur.

Hence frequent collisions, obstinate, envenomed, and bloody contests. The nation prompted by ill will and resentment sometimes impels to war the government contrary to the best calculations of policy. The government sometimes participates in the national propensity, and adopts through passion what reason would reject. At other times it makes the animosity of the nation subservient to projects of hostility, instigated by pride, ambition, and other sinister and pernicious motives. The peace often, sometimes perhaps the liberty, of nations has been the victim.

So, likewise, a passionate attachment of one nation for another produces a variety of evils. Sympathy for the favorite nation, facilitating the illusion of an imaginary common interest in cases where no real common interest exists, and infusing into one the enmities of the other, betrays the former into a participation in the quarrels and wars of the latter without adequate inducement or justification. It leads also to concessions to the favorite nation of privileges denied to others, which is apt doubly to injure the nation making the concessions by unnecessarily parting with what ought to have been retained, and by exciting jealousy, ill-will, and a disposition to retaliate in the parties from whom equal privileges are withheld; and it gives to ambitious, corrupted, or deluded citizens (who devote themselves to the favorite nation) facility to betray or sacrifice the interests of their own country without odium, sometimes even with popularity, gilding with the appearances of a virtuous sense of obligation, a commendable deference for public opinion, or a laudable zeal for public good the base or foolish compliances of ambition, corruption, or infatuation.

As avenues to foreign influence in innumerable ways, such attachments are particularly alarming to the truly enlightened and independent patriot. How many opportunities do they afford to tamper with domestic factions, to practice the arts of seduction, to mislead public opinion, to influence or awe the public councils! Such an attachment of a small or weak toward a great and powerful nation dooms the former to be the satellite of the latter. Against the insidious wiles of foreign influence (I conjure you to believe me, fellow-citizens) the jealousy of a free people ought to be *constantly* awake, since history and experience prove that foreign influence is one of the most baneful foes of republican government. But that jealousy, to be useful, must be impartial, else it becomes the instrument of the very influence to be avoided, instead of a defense against it. Excessive partiality for one foreign nation and excessive dislike of another cause those whom they actuate to see danger only on one side, and serve to veil and even second the arts of influence on the other. Real patriots who may resist the intrigues of the favorite are liable to become suspected and odious, while its tools and dupes usurp the applause and confidence of the people to surrender their interests.

The great rule of conduct for us in regard to foreign nations is, in extending our commercial relations to have with them as little *political* connection as possible. So far as we have already formed engagements let them be fulfilled with perfect good faith. Here let us stop.

Europe has a set of primary interests which to us have none or a very remote relation. Hence she must be engaged in frequent controversies, the causes of which are essentially foreign to our concerns. Hence, therefore, it must be unwise in us to implicate ourselves by artificial ties in the ordinary vicissitudes of her politics or the ordinary combinations and collisions of her friendships or enmities.

Our detached and distant situation invites and enables us to pursue a different course. If we remain one people, under an efficient government, the period is not far off when we may defy material injury from external annoyance; when we may take such an attitude as will cause the neutrality we may at any time resolve upon to be scrupulously respected; when belligerent nations, under the impossibility of making acquisitions upon us, will not lightly hazard the giving us provocation; when we may choose peace or war, as our interest, guided by justice, shall counsel.

Why forego the advantages of so peculiar a situation? Why quit our own to stand upon foreign ground? Why, by interweaving our destiny with that of any part of Europe, entangle our peace and prosperity in the toils of European ambition, rivalship, interest, humor, or caprice?

It is our true policy to steer clear of permanent alliances with any portion of the foreign world, so far, I mean, as we are now at liberty to do it; for let me not be understood as capable of patronizing infidelity to existing engagements. I hold the maxim no less applicable to public than to private affairs that honesty is always the best policy. I repeat, therefore, let those engagements be observed in their genuine sense. But in my opinion it is unnecessary and would be unwise to extend them.

Taking care always to keep ourselves by suitable establishments on a respectable defensive posture, we may safely trust to temporary alliances for extraordinary emergencies.

Harmony, liberal intercourse with all nations are recommended by policy, humanity, and interest. But even our commercial policy should hold an equal and impartial hand, neither seeking nor granting exclusive favors or preferences; consulting the natural course of things; diffusing and diversifying by gentle means the streams of commerce, but forcing nothing; establishing with powers so disposed, in order to give trade a stable course, to define the rights of our merchants, and to enable the Government to support them, conventional rules of intercourse, the best that present circumstances and mutual opinion will permit, but temporary and liable to be from time to time abandoned or varied as experience and circumstance shall dictate; constantly keeping in view that it is folly in one nation to look for disinterested favors from another; that it must pay with a portion of its independence for whatever it may accept under that character; that by such acceptance it may place itself in the condition of having given equivalents for nominal favors, and yet of being reproached with ingratitude for not giving more. There can be no greater error than to expect or calculate upon real favors from nation to nation. It is an illusion which experience must cure, which a just pride ought to discard.

In offering to you, my countrymen, these counsels of an old and affectionate friend I dare not hope they will make the strong and lasting impression I could wish—that they will control the usual current of the passions or prevent our nation from running the course which has hitherto marked the destiny of nations. But if I may even flatter myself that they may be productive of some partial benefit, some occasional good—that they may now and then recur to moderate the fury of party spirit, to warn against the mischiefs of foreign intrigue, to guard against the impostures of pretended patriotism—this hope will be a full recompense for the solicitude for your welfare by which they have been dictated.

How far in the discharge of my official duties I have been guided by the principles which have been delineated the public records and other evidences of my conduct must witness to you and to the world. To myself, the assurance of my own conscience is that I have at least believed myself to be guided by them.

In relation to the still subsisting war in Europe my proclamation of the 22d of April, 1793, is the index to my plan. Sanctioned by your approving voice and by that of your representatives in both Houses of Congress, the spirit of that measure has continually governed me, uninfluenced by any attempts to deter or divert me from it.

After deliberate examination, with the aid of the best lights I could obtain, I was well satisfied that our country, under all the circumstances of the case, had a right to take, and was bound in duty and interest to take, a neutral position. Having taken it, I determined as far as should depend upon me to maintain it with moderation, perseverance, and firmness.

The considerations which respect the right to hold this conduct it is not necessary on this occasion to detail. I will only observe that, according to my understanding of the matter, that right, so far from being denied by any of the belligerent powers, has been virtually admitted by all.

The duty of holding a neutral conduct may be inferred, without anything more, from the obligation which justice and humanity impose on every nation, in cases in which it is free to act, to maintain inviolate the relations of peace and amity toward other nations.

The inducements of interest for observing that conduct will best be referred to your own reflections and experience. With me a predominant motive has been to endeavor to gain time to our country to settle and mature its yet recent institutions, and to progress without interruption to that degree of strength and consistency which is necessary to give it, humanly speaking, the command of its own fortunes.

Though in reviewing the incidents of my Administration I am unconscious of intentional error, I am nevertheless too sensible of my defects not to think it probable that I may have committed many errors. Whatever they may be, I fervently beseech the Almighty to avert or mitigate the evils to which they may tend. I shall also carry with me the hope that my country will never cease to view them with indulgence, and that, after forty-five years of my life dedicated to its service with an upright zeal, the faults of incompetent abilities will be consigned to oblivion, as myself must soon be to the mansions of rest.

Relying on its kindness in this as in other things, and actuated by that fervent love toward it which is so natural to a man who views in it the native soil of himself and his progenitors for several generations, I anticipate with pleasing expectation that retreat in which I promise myself to realize without alloy the sweet enjoyment of partaking in the midst of my fellow-citizens the benign influence of good laws under a free government—the ever-favorite object of my heart, and the happy reward, as I trust, of our mutual cares, labors, and dangers.

G.° WASHINGTON

Written after the style of eighteenth-century European statesmen, Washington's political testament had far more durability than that of Frederick the Great or other monarchs who fancied this form of address to their respective nations. Not all portions of Washington's address were equally durable, however. His injunction against political factionalism did not prevent the rise of a two-party system, nor did his prophetic warning of the dangers of sectionalism deter civil war between North and South. What did survive was his "Great Rule," his guide lines for American foreign policy. This did not in fact represent a change in policy, but rather it gave literary articulation to the big decisions which had already been made in his Administration to avoid entanglement in the European war which came in the wake of the French Revolution. These decisions had been embodied in Washington's Proclamation of Neutrality and in Jay's Treaty with Great Britain, which gave the young nation a necessary breathing spell.

The "Great Rule" foreshadowed the end of the French alliance, terminated in the Administration of Washington's successor, John Adams. It was Jefferson, not Washington, who gave the "Great Rule" a more distinctively isolationist tinge. In his First Inaugural Address President Jefferson counseled his fellow citizens to enjoy "peace, commerce, and honest friendship with all nations, entangling alliances with none." Washington had not included that phrase in his "Farewell Address," but in the nation's memory the injunctions of the two Presidents have become intermingled and indistinguishable.

Washington's "Great Rule" later took concrete form in the Monroe Doctrine, which expressed the notion of two separate spheres of political action. The United States would abstain from involvement in European politics; Europe was to abstain from interfering in the political affairs of the independent states of the New World. President Jackson's Secretary of State, John Forsyth, epitomized America's foreign policy as a "national reserve," a deliberate abstention from the political relationships entered into by most states. Thus, when, in the mid-nineteenth century, interventionists sought to have America give aid to Europe's revolutionary movements and called for the abandonment of isolation, they were met with arguments from statesmen like John Quincy Adams, who insisted that America could save the world only if it remained free to save itself. This policy was broadly construed to involve the avoidance of any entangling alliances or commitments; the United States would refrain from intervening or participating in European politics and even from acting jointly with other powers. The Monroe Doctrine was a unilateral action.

In essence, Washington's "Great Rule" was adhered to until the Spanish-American War involved the United States at once in both European and Asiatic political questions. Although the conquest of the Philippines may have seemed a violent departure from the injunctions of the Farewell Address and the Monroe Doctrine, it did not forecast an abrupt reversal from traditional isolationism. Wilson's studied neutrality in the early years of World War I voiced the strength of that tradition, as did the refusal of the Senate to ratify a postwar military alliance with France, or to enter the League of Nations or the World Court. Indeed, by the 1920's isolationism, in addition to its other historic connotations, involved avoiding the placing of limits on what some deemed to be "essential" rights of national sovereignty. The isolationist mood fitted America's postwar disenchantment about the goals of European states, and found concrete expression in the neutrality legislation of the 1930's.

The perils which totalitarianism seemed to pose to the civilization of the West, combined with the rude shock of Pearl Harbor, uprooted isolationism. The foreign policy of the United States had to be drastically refashioned, as America assumed a vastly enlarged role in world affairs. America's active participation in the United Nations and her broad system of alliances may seem a far cry from the "Great Rule," until it is remembered that Washington's concern was to formulate a policy of prudence which would allow the new nation a twenty-year period to gain strength and power through the avoidance of war. Washington was too realistic a statesman to imagine that rules of behavior appropriate for an infant republic, separated by what was then a vast distance from Europe's power struggles, could apply with equal force as that nation grew larger and more powerful. By mid-twentieth century the revolution of science and technology and a multitude of other interests had tied the United States to all the other peoples on the face of this planet.

Thomas Jefferson
First Inaugural Address
1801

EDITED BY DUMAS MALONE

The inaugural address which Thomas Jefferson delivered on March 4, 1801, was the first ever made by a President in Washington, whither the federal government had transferred from Philadelphia a few months earlier, during the Presidency of John Adams. Jefferson made the address in the Senate Chamber of the original Capitol, the only part of that structure then completed. His inauguration was also notable in that it was the first to mark a change in the control of the government from one party to another. The election preceding it was one of the most heated in American history; and, while it left no doubt that the Federalists had been defeated by the Republicans, there was grave doubt until February 17 whether Jefferson or Aaron Burr would be President. Under the system then in operation, the electors voted for two men without designating either specifically for the first or second office; and in this case the accidental result was a tie which, according to the Constitution, had to be resolved by the House of Representatives. In that body the Federalists supported Burr, while the Republicans loyally stood by Jefferson, who was obviously the popular choice. For a time the possibility existed that there would be no legally elected President to inaugurate, and as things turned out Jefferson had only a little more than two weeks in which to write his speech.

He wrote it, without secretarial assistance, at Conrad and McMunn's boarding house, where he was staying. The most pressing need of which he was conscious at this point was that of restoring unity to the country. Since the intransigent Federalist congressmen already stood rebuked by the outcome which they had succeeded only in delaying, his immediate purpose was to reassure his countrymen, whom he believed to be predominantly moderate, patriotic, and freedom-loving. In this respect his address was notably successful. He also took this occasion to set forth the principles on which he would conduct the government and the general lines of policy he expected to follow. Since he had made no speeches and issued no public statements in the recent campaign, his views had often been distorted and misrepresented. In private he had made frequent reference to the "spirit of 1776," and what he really meant by republicanism, as he now made clear in public, was loyalty to the ideals of the American Revolution. At the same time he also strongly advocated federalism, which to him was support of the Constitution and the federal principle underlying it. He sought to unite and rally the country by emphasizing the compatibility of the two ideas.

FRIENDS AND FELLOW-CITIZENS.

CALLED upon to undertake the duties of the first executive office of our country, I avail myself of the presence of that portion of my fellow citizens which is here assembled to express my grateful thanks for the favor with which they have been pleased to look toward me, to declare a sincere consciousness that the task is above my talents, and that I approach it with those anxious and awful presentiments which the greatness of the charge and the weakness of my powers so justly inspire. A rising nation, spread over a wide and fruitful land, traversing all the seas with the rich productions of their industry, engaged in commerce with nations who feel power and forget right, advancing rapidly to destinies beyond the reach of mortal eye—when I

The text given here is that printed in the *National Intelligencer* at the time of the inauguration, from a copy provided the editor by Jefferson. This differs little from the texts printed in the journals of the legislative and executive proceedings of the United States Senate. Later editors made more changes, and one of these, in capitalization, was particularly unfortunate. In Jefferson's own draft a famous sentence reads as follows: "We are all republicans: we are all federalists." In the earliest printed versions the key words remain in lower case. By capitalizing them, later editors have caused the sentence to seem more paradoxical than it was.

contemplate these transcendent objects, and see the honor, the happiness, and the hopes of this beloved country committed to the issue and the auspices of this day, I shrink from the contemplation, and humble myself before the magnitude of the undertaking. Utterly indeed should I despair did not the presence of many whom I here see remind me that in the other high authorities provided by our Constitution I shall find resources of wisdom, of virtue, and of zeal on which to rely under all difficulties. To you then, gentlemen, who are charged with the sovereign functions of legislation, and to those associated with you, I look with encouragement for that guidance and support which may enable us to steer with safety the vessel in which we are all embarked amidst the conflicting elements of a troubled world.

During the contest of opinion through which we have past the animation of discussions and of exertions has sometimes worn an aspect which might impose on strangers unused to think freely and to speak and to write what they think. But this being now decided by the voice of the nation, enounced according to the rules of the constitution, all will of course arrange themselves under the will of the law, and unite in common efforts for the common good. All too will bear in mind this sacred principle, that though the will of the majority is in all cases to prevail, that will, to be rightful, must be reasonable; that the minority possess their equal rights, which equal laws must protect, and to violate would be oppression. Let us then, fellow citizens, unite with one heart and one mind, let us restore to social intercourse that harmony and affection without which liberty and even life itself are but dreary things. And let us reflect that, having banished from our land that religious intolerance under which mankind so long bled and suffered, we have yet gained little if we countenance a political intolerance as despotic, as wicked, and capable of as bitter and bloody persecutions. During the throes and convulsions of the ancient world, during the agonizing spasms of infuriated man, seeking through blood and slaughter his long lost liberty, it was not wonderful that the agitation of the billows should reach even this distant and peaceful shore; that this should be more felt and feared by some and less by others, and should divide opinions as to measures of safety; but every difference of opinion is not a difference of principle. We have called by different names brethren of the same principle. We are all republicans: we are all federalists. If there be any among us who wish to dissolve this Union or to change its republican form, let them stand undisturbed, as monuments of the safety with which error of opinion may be tolerated where reason is left free to combat it. I know, indeed, that some honest men fear that a republican government cannot be strong, that this government is not strong enough. But would the honest partriot, in the full tide of successful experiment, abandon a government which has so far kept us free and firm on the theoretic and visionary fear that this government, the world's best hope, may, by possibility, want energy to preserve itself? I trust not. I believe this, on the contrary, the strongest government on earth. I believe it the only one where every man, at the call of the law, would fly to the standard of the law, and would meet invasions of the public order as his own personal concern. Sometimes it is said that man cannot be trusted with the government of himself. Can he, then, be trusted with the government of others? Or have we found angels in the form of kings to govern him? Let history answer this question.

Let us then pursue with courage and confidence our own federal and republican principles, our attachment to union and representative government. Kindly separated by nature, and a wide ocean, from the exterminating havoc of one quarter of the globe; too high-minded to endure the degradations of the others; possessing a chosen country, with room enough for our descendants to the thousandth and thousandth generation; entertaining a due sense of our equal right to the use of our own faculties, to the acquisitions of our own industry, to honor and confidence from our fellow citizens, resulting not from birth, but from our actions and their sense of them; enlightened by a benign religion, professed, indeed, and practiced in various forms, yet all of them inculcating honesty, truth, temperance, gratitude, and the love of man; acknowledging and adoring an overruling providence, which by all its dispensations proves that it delights in the happiness of man here and his greater happiness hereafter—with all these blessings, what more is necessary to make us a happy and a prosperous people? Still one thing more, fellow citizens—a wise and frugal government, which shall restrain men from injuring one another, shall leave them otherwise free to regulate their own pursuits of industry and improvement, and shall not take from the mouth of labor the bread it has earned. This is the sum of good government, and this is necessary to close the circle of our felicities.

About to enter, fellow citizens, on the exercise of duties which comprehend everything dear and valuable to you, it is proper you should understand what I deem the essential principles of this government, and consequently those which ought to shape its administration. I will compress them in the narrowest compass they will bear, stating the general principle, but not all its limitations. Equal and exact justice to all men, of whatever state or persuasion, religious or political; peace, commerce, and honest friendship with all nations, entangling alliances with none; the support of the state governments in all their rights, as the most competent administrations for our domestic concerns and the surest bulwarks against anti-republican tendencies; the preservation of the general government in its whole constitutional vigor, as the sheet anchor of our peace at home and safety abroad; a jealous care of the right of election by the people, a mild and safe corrective of abuses which are lopped by the sword of revolution where peaceable remedies are unprovided; absolute acquiescence in the decisions of the majority, the vital principle of republics from which is no appeal but to force, the vital principle and immediate parent of despotism; a well disciplined militia, our best reliance in peace and for the first moments of war, till regulars may relieve them; the supremacy of the civil over the military authority; economy in the public expence, that labor may be lightly burthened; the honest payment of our debts and sacred preservation of the public faith; encouragement of agriculture, and of commerce as its handmaid; the diffusion of information and arraignment of all abuses at the bar of the public reason; freedom of religion; freedom of the press, and freedom of person under the protection of the habeas corpus, and trial by juries impartially selected. These principles form the bright constellation which has gone before us and guided our steps through an age of revolution and reformation. The wisdom of our sages and blood of our heroes have been devoted to their attainment. They should be the creed of our political faith, the text of civic instruction, the touchstone by which to try the services of those we trust; and should we wander from them in moments of error or of alarm, let us hasten to retrace our steps and to regain the road which alone leads to peace, liberty, and safety.

I repair, then, fellow-citizens, to the post you have assigned me. With experience enough in subordinate stations to know the difficulties of this the greatest of all, I have learnt to expect that it will rarely fall to the lot of imperfect man to retire from this station with the reputation and the favor which bring him into it. Without pretensions to that high confidence you reposed in our first and greatest revolutionary character, whose preeminent services had entitled him to the first place in his country's love and destined for him the fairest page in the volume of faithful history, I ask so much confidence only as may give firmness and effect to the legal administration of your affairs. I shall often go wrong through defect of judgment. When right, I shall often be thought wrong by those whose positions will not command a view of the whole ground. I ask your indulgence for my own errors, which will never be intentional, and your support against the errors of others, who may condemn what they would not if seen in all its parts. The approbation implied by your suffrage is a great consolation to me for the past, and my future solicitude will be to retain the good opinion of those who have bestowed it in advance, to conciliate that of others by doing them all the good in my power, and to be instrumental to the happiness and freedom of all.

Relying, then, on the patronage of your good will, I advance with obedience to the work, ready to retire from it whenever you become sensible how much better choices it is in your power to make. And may that infinite power which rules the destinies of the universe lead our councils to what is best, and give them a favorable issue for your peace and prosperity.

March 4, 1801.

It is partly because of the historical significance of Jefferson's accession to the Presidency, and the felicitous language of his address on taking office, that this document is memorable. But the chief reason for its continuing appeal is that much of it has seemed timeless. Since his day there has been no necessity, except in 1860 and perhaps in 1876, to point out that a defeated group must accept the result of a national election. No one now questions the right of an opposition party to exist, and, if it can command the votes, to replace an Administration. After the verdict at the polls, political conflict in the United States has generally been resolved in a mood of sportsmanship. Political triumph has never been followed by the liquidation of enemy chieftains, and rarely if ever on a national scale by sweeping and vindictive proscription. By word and deed Jefferson taught his countrymen an unforgettable lesson in the peaceful transfer of authority. In this address he did more: he set forth ideals which still challenge us. With the maxim that the will of the majority

must prevail, he coupled the "sacred principle" that this will "to be rightful, must be reasonable," that the minority must always be protected. He virtually recapitulated the provisions of the Bill of Rights, and in matchless phrase proclaimed the inviolability of the individual and of his opinions. Such words and thoughts will never be out of date so long as self-governing society persists on earth.

The same cannot be claimed for what he said in the first year of the nineteenth century about the policies he proposed to follow; and the chief abuses of his First Inaugural have resulted from a failure to distinguish between these dated policies and the abiding principles of self-government which he proclaimed. Within the memory of men now living, advocates of national isolation have sought to buttress their position by quoting things he said about foreign policy in a wholly different world situation. Jefferson was indubitably wise in disavowing "entangling alliances" in 1801, and actually the policy of noninvolvement in Old World affairs had validity for a century and more, but it has been necessarily repudiated in our day. The third President was charting a wise course for his country when it was young and weak and needed nothing so much as time to grow.

Another anachronism is the continued citation of Jefferson's views on the operations and limitations of government. He pronounced those views in an age which was not only prenuclear but which in America was virtually preindustrial. Common sense requires that allowance be made for changed circumstances; American society has been so transformed since Jefferson's inauguration that almost the only factors common to that time and this are those of topography, climate, and human nature. A good government, as he described it in 1801, should be "a wise and frugal government, which shall restrain men from injuring one another, shall leave them otherwise free to regulate their own pursuits of industry and improvement, and shall not take from the mouth of labor the bread it has earned." These terms are susceptible of amplification, but Jefferson undoubtedly wanted to keep the sum of government very small. His contemporaries Alexander Hamilton and John Marshall thought it dangerously small, but his basically negative domestic policy was well adapted to the conditions of the country at the time, and it was immensely popular. To follow that policy under the conditions of a much later time would be manifestly impossible. It is unimaginable that a man of Jefferson's intelligence would defend it now, and, in fairness to the memory of this great champion of freedom and apostle of enlightenment, we must recognize that his views about the limits of governmental power, and also about the relations between the states and the nation, are now quite irrelevant. Indeed, they have long been so. The first person to concede this would be the Jefferson who said: "The earth belongs always to the living generation." In his day he distrusted power as a potential instrument of tyranny; circumstances had not yet taught him, as they have taught us, that it is an indispensable weapon in defense of freedom. We cannot now learn from him the "how" of government, but we can learn the "why."

Jacob Henry
On Religion and Elective Office
1809

EDITED BY JOSEPH L. BLAU

Article 34 of the constitution of the state of North Carolina, adopted in 1776, forbade the establishment of "any one religious church or denomination . . . in preference to any other," and maintained that "all persons shall be at liberty to exercise their own mode of worship." The Declaration of Rights adopted by North Carolina in the same year included both the acknowledgment that freedom of worship is an inalienable right of man and, in its forty-fourth article, the assertion that the Declaration of Rights had authority superior to that of the constitution. In the event of contradiction between the Declaration of Rights and the constitution, the constitution had to give way. Yet, in Article 32 of the constitution, the following provision appeared:

That no person, who shall deny the being of God or the truth of the Protestant religion, or the divine authority either of the Old or New Testaments, or who shall hold religious principles incompatible with the freedom and safety of the State, shall be capable of holding any office or place of trust or profit in the civil department within this State.

This contradiction set the stage for a most interesting and important defense of the principle that civil rights are independent of religious affiliation.

In 1809, Jacob Henry was elected to the lower house of the legislature of North Carolina as a representative of Carteret County. When Mr.

Henry had first been given this honor by his fellow citizens, one year earlier, his right to sit in the House of Commons went unchallenged. On his re-election, however, the question of his eligibility was raised, on the ground that Jacob Henry was a Jew. As a Jew he did not subscribe to the "divine authority" of the New Testament, nor did he accept "the truth of the Protestant religion." For Jacob Henry to hold the seat to which he had been elected violated Article 32 of the state constitution. For him to be denied his seat violated Article 34 of the same document, as well as refusing him a civil right apparently granted by the Declaration of Rights. As a special privilege, Mr. Henry was permitted to take part in the ensuing debate over his right to his elective office. The speech he delivered was soon recognized as a masterpiece of American oratory. It was often reprinted in collections of American public speeches after *1814.* Its immediate effect was to lead the House of Commons to vote to sustain Henry's right to the seat to which he had been elected.

Little biographical information about Jacob Henry has been found. At one time it was suggested that he was a member of the famous Gratz family that spread out from Philadelphia to other parts of the country, but this suggestion lacks supporting evidence. With so little knowledge it is difficult to appraise the report, presented by the author of a major history of North Carolina, that the speech was "ghosted" for Jacob Henry by Attorney-General John Louis Taylor, a Roman Catholic. Undoubtedly it was to the interest of the Roman Catholics of the state that the question of the right of non-Protestants to hold elective office should be decided. If the right of a Jew to such a position could be vindicated, then the Catholic right would be even more certainly established.

I CERTAINLY, Mr. Speaker, know not the design of the Declaration of Rights made by the people of this State in the year 1776, if it was not to consecrate certain great and fundamental rights and principles which even the Constitution cannot impair; for the 44th section of the latter instrument declares that the Declaration of Rights ought

---

Henry's speech is reprinted from John H. Wheeler, *Historical Sketches of North Carolina from 1584 to 1851* (Philadelphia, 1851), II, 74–76. The earliest reprinting probably appeared in a collection of addresses, *The American Speaker* (Philadelphia, 1814).

never to be violated, on any pretence whatever; if there is any apparent difference between the two instruments, they ought, if possible, to be reconciled; but if there is a final repugnance between them, the Declaration of Rights must be considered paramount; for I believe it is to the Constitution, as the Constitution is to law; it controls and directs it absolutely and conclusively. If, then, a belief in the Protestant religion is required by the Constitution, to qualify a man for a seat in this house, and such qualification is dispensed with by the Declaration of Rights, the provision of the Constitution must be altogether inoperative; as the language of the Bill of Rights is, "that all men have a natural and inalienable right to worship ALMIGHTY GOD according to the dictates of their own consciences." It is undoubtedly a natural right, and when it is declared to be an inalienable one by the people in their sovereign and original capacity, any attempt to alienate either by the Constitution or by law, must be vain and fruitless.

It is difficult to conceive how such a provision crept into the Constitution, unless it is from the difficulty the human mind feels in suddenly emancipating itself from fetters by which it has long been enchained: and how adverse it is to the feelings and manners of the people of the present day every gentleman may satisfy himself by glancing at the religious belief of the persons who fill the various offices in this State: there are Presbyterians, Lutherans, Calvinists, Mennonists, Baptists, Trinitarians, and Unitarians. But, as far as my observation extends, there are fewer Protestants, in the strict sense of the word, used by the Constitution, than of any other persuasion; for I suppose that they meant by it, the Protestant religion as established by the law in England. For other persuasions we see houses of worship in almost every part of the State, but very few of the Protestant; so few, that indeed I fear that the people of this State would for some time remain unrepresented in this House, if that clause of the Constitution is supposed to be in force. So far from believing in the Thirty-nine Articles, I will venture to assert that a majority of the people never have read them.

If a man should hold religious principles incompatible with the freedom and safety of the State, I do not hesitate to pronounce that he should be excluded from the public councils of the same; and I trust if I know myself, no one would be more ready to aid and assist than myself. But I should really be at a loss to specify any known religious principles which are thus dangerous. It is surely a question between a man and his Maker, and requires more than human attributes to pronounce which of the numerous sects prevailing in the world is most acceptable to the Deity. If a man fulfills the duties of that religion, which his education or his conscience has pointed to him as the true one, no person, I hold, in this our land of liberty, has a right to arraign him at the bar of any inquisition: and the day, I trust, has long passed, when principles merely speculative were propagated by force; when the sincere and pious were made victims, and the light-minded bribed into hypocrites.

The purest homage man could render to the Almighty was the sacrifice of his passions and the performance of his duties. That the ruler of the universe would receive with equal benignity the various offerings of man's adoration, if they proceeded from the heart. Governments only concern the actions and conduct of man, and not his speculative notions. Who among us feels himself so exalted above his fellows as to have a right to dictate to them any mode of belief? Will you bind the conscience in chains, and fasten conviction upon the mind in spite of the conclusions of reason and of those ties and habitudes which are blended with every pulsation of the heart? Are you prepared to plunge at once from the sublime heights of moral legislation into the dark and gloomy caverns of superstitious ignorance? Will you drive from your shores and from the shelter of your constitution, all who do not lay their oblations on the same altar, observe the same ritual, and subscribe to the same dogmas? If so, which, among the various sects into which we are divided, shall be the favored one?

I should insult the understanding of this House to suppose it possible that they could ever assent to such absurdities; for all know that persecution in all its shapes and modifications, is contrary to the genius of our government and the spirit of our laws, and that it can never produce any other effect than to render men hypocrites or martyrs.

When Charles V., Emperor of Germany, tired of the cares of government, resigned his crown to his son, he retired to a monastery, where he amused the evening of his life in regulating the movements of watches, endeavoring to make a number keep the same time; but, not being able to make any two go exactly alike, it led him to reflect upon the folly and crimes he had committed, in attempting the impossibility of making men think alike!

Nothing is more easily demonstrated than that the conduct alone is the subject of human laws, and that man ought to suffer civil disqualification for what he does, and not for what he thinks. The mind can receive laws only from Him, of whose Divine essence it is a portion;

He alone can punish disobedience; for who else can know its movements, or estimate their merits? The religion I profess, inculcates every
duty which men owes to his fellow men; it enjoins upon its votaries the
practice of every virtue, and the detestation of every vice; it teaches them
to hope for the favor of heaven exactly in proportion as their lives have
been directed by just, honorable, and beneficent maxims. This, then,
gentlemen, is my creed, it was impressed upon my infant mind; it has
been the director of my youth, the monitor of my manhood, and will, I
trust, be the consolation of my old age. At any rate, Mr. Speaker, I am
sure that you cannot see anything in this Religion, to deprive me of my
seat in this house. So far as relates to my life and conduct, the
examination of these I submit with cheerfulness to your candid and
liberal construction. What may be the religion of him who made this
objection against me, or whether he has any religion or not I am unable
to say. I have never considered it my duty to pry into the belief of other
members of this house. If their actions are upright and conduct just, the
rest is for their own consideration, not for mine. I do not seek to make
converts to my faith, whatever it may be esteemed in the eyes of my
officious friend, nor do I exclude any one from my esteem or friendship,
because he and I differ in that respect. The same charity, therefore, it is
not unreasonable to expect, will be extended to myself, because in all
things that relate to the State and to the duties of civil life, I am bound
by the same obligations with my fellow-citizens, nor does any man
subscribe more sincerely than myself to the maxim, "whatever ye would
that men should do unto you do ye so even unto them, for such is the
law and the prophets."

*The government of the United States, from its beginnings, was based
upon an organic law that outlawed civil discrimination because of
religious differences. Some of the older states, however, retained in their
constitutions disqualifications of Jews, Roman Catholics, and members
of other minority groups. Many years of conflict and struggle were
needed before the promise of a religiously open society, as set forth in the
federal Constitution, was to be realized. Only gradually were the
constitutions of the states modified or rewritten. Massachusetts, for
example, did not disestablish the Congregational Church until 1833. In*

North Carolina years after Jacob Henry's magnificent defense of the right of a member of a religious minority to hold office a change was finally made. At the constitutional convention of 1835 Roman Catholics were fully enfranchised by the changing of the word "Protestant" in Article 34 to "Christian." The status of the Jews of North Carolina remained anomalous. This legal disability of the Jews was not eliminated until after the Civil War, in a Reconstruction revision of the state constitution in 1868.

In Maryland, where the same sort of contradiction between the constitution of the state and its Bill of Rights existed, the interpretation was so narrow that no Jew could even enter upon a career as a lawyer, because a lawyer is, by definition, an officer of the court and therefore an occupant of a state office. A campaign of almost thirty years' duration was necessary before the passage of a bill in 1826 specifically exempted Jews from the operation of a clause requiring a test oath. This exemption did not end all discrimination on religious grounds in Maryland, for its constitution still required that all persons who might be elected or appointed to any office within the state must subscribe to a special oath affirming their belief in God. As a result, the agnostic, the atheist, or the person whose conscience would not permit his subscribing to such an oath was debarred from office in Maryland. This requirement of the Maryland constitution was put to a legal test by Roy Torcaso, an applicant for certification as a notary public. Denied his certification on the sole ground that he would not sign the oath affirming his belief in God, Torcaso appealed, first, to the highest court of Maryland, and then, when this appeal was denied, to the Supreme Court of the United States. In June, 1961, the Supreme Court, in a forceful opinion written by Justice Hugo Black, unanimously declared that "this Maryland religious test for public office unconstitutionally invades the appellant's freedom of belief and religion and therefore cannot be enforced against him." The principle for which Jacob Henry had argued in 1809, that the civil rights of American citizens may not be abridged in any respect because of their religious affiliation or beliefs, was finally vindicated and definitively established just over a century and a half after Henry's defense of it.

Public attitudes are never altogether identical with legal principles. At times, the attitudes of the public are in advance of the formal requirements of the law. So it was, for example, among those neighbors of Jacob Henry in Carteret County who elected him in 1808 and re-elected him in 1809. Knowing that Henry was Jewish, they still chose him as their representative because, presumably, they liked and trusted him. Even though the law of their state retained expressions of outdated ideas, Henry's constituents were prepared to consider him on his own personal merits, as a unique individual, rather than as a member of a stereotyped group. There have been many other instances in the history of the American states in which the people have been ahead of their legal systems and have elected members not only of the Jewish minority but also of other minorities as their representatives, whatever the law might say.

In other cases, however, the law has been in advance of public opinion. This was notoriously the case in the presidential election of 1928, in which a major factor entering into the defeat of Alfred E. Smith, the Democratic Party's nominee for the Presidency, was his membership in the Roman Catholic Church. Whatever weight may be granted to the special circumstances of the age—especially to the turning away from American ideals in the name of American ideals that followed the disappointments of American participation in World War I—it still remains clear that the election campaign of 1928 brought out the most backward and bigoted elements in American public opinion. That the 1928 offenses against human decency were unsuccessfully and ineffectively repeated in the 1960 election campaign, in which there was again a Roman Catholic candidate for the Presidency, does not mean that the forces which use such appeals have been finally defeated. But it does indicate that there has been a measure of progress in the development of American public opinion. The election of John F. Kennedy is convincing evidence that a large section of the American electorate is willing to consider nominees for even the highest of offices on the grounds of their personal qualifications and their programs.

In recent years a growing appreciation of the contributions of minority groups to the development of all aspects of American life and culture has begun to appear in the work of historians and educators. This is, certainly, a consequence of the increasingly urban character of American society. In the urban communities of our nation, there is much more opportunity for man to meet man across the barriers of race, color, class, ethnic derivation, and religion. In the actuality of these many meetings, it becomes more and more difficult to maintain the traditional stereotypes that are so easy to hold in the isolation of rural life, where one's contacts may be largely—even exclusively—with other members of one's own group. Our cosmopolitan cities hold forth the hope that our citizens may become more cosmopolitan, not just in the externals of life, but at its core. When such a genuine and deep-seated cosmopolitanism has developed in America, Jacob Henry's battle will have been completely won, not for the Jews alone, but for all members of minorities within American culture.

John Adams
What Do We Mean by the American Revolution?
1818

EDITED BY L. H. BUTTERFIELD

John Adams spent much of his retirement at Quincy after his Presidency refighting old battles. First came his episodic Autobiography, written between 1802 and 1807 and broken off in order to put Mercy Warren straight on mistakes in her recently published History of the American Revolution. Then followed, from 1809 to 1812, the extraordinary outpouring of his letters to the Boston Patriot, in effect a second autobiography, which overwhelmed both the printers and the readers of that paper with material drawn from his old letterbooks, hastily copied, uncorrected, and held together by a thin but coruscating thread of commentary. The reminiscences Adams sent to his friends Dr. Benjamin Rush and former President Jefferson are gentler in tone, but he was still fighting the Revolution and complaining that nothing resembling a true history of it had yet been written—indeed ever would or could be written.

Meanwhile he did his best for those who applied to him for information by replying with impetuous and copious generosity. Among a number of inquirers who hit the jackpot was Hezekiah Niles of Baltimore. Publisher of the first American news magazine and a thoroughgoing, even sentimental, nationalist, Niles had long made his Weekly Register a repository for documents on current affairs. In 1816, with the close of the second war with England and with the approach of the fiftieth anniversaries of important Revolutionary events, he appealed to the survivors of America's heroic age for their recollections, for unpublished letters and papers, for inspirational matter of every sort to satisfy a public suddenly grown as proud of its short past as it was confident of its long future. Adams replied serially by sending Niles his own early pamphlet publications for reprinting, long letters of reminiscence, copies of letters he had received from Revolutionary celebrities, and finally, since he had no clerical help, a great bundle of original letters addressed to him during the earliest years of the conflict. He was to regret this last step, for Niles did not print them all and never returned the irreplaceable originals.

What touched off John Adams' final account of the beginnings of the American Revolution in Massachusetts—of which the present letter to Niles is only one installment among many—was the appearance in 1817 of a phenomenal book, William Wirt's Sketches of the Life and Character of Patrick Henry. With the meagerest of materials and in some respects the most intractable of subjects, Wirt had in a stroke converted the Virginia stump orator into an American folk hero, lazily stretching his limbs like the young nation itself and bidding defiance to Old World tyranny "in a voice of thunder, and with the look of a god." John Adams read the Sketches with the same delight with which he read the novels of Sir Walter Scott and Jane Porter. He wrote Wirt to tell him so, but he added that, although he envied Virginia none of its "well merited glories," he was at the same time "Jealous, very jealous, of the honour of Massachusetts." He wished he were young enough to undertake a volume of "Sketches of the Life and writings of James Otis of Boston," in which he would demonstrate that Otis' services in resisting "the British System for Subjugating the Colonies" had begun earlier and been substantially greater than Patrick Henry's. Warming to his work, he sent off to Niles on January 14, 1818, a sketch of Otis for publication, in which he declared "in the most solemn manner that Mr. Otis's Oration against Writts of Assistance" in 1761—antedating by four years Henry's speech against the Stamp Act—"breathed into the Nation the Breath of Life." Here indeed was a Massachusetts Roland for Virginia's Oliver!

Adams' next letter to Niles, that of February 13, 1818, furnished Otis with a band of intrepid colleagues and vividly described their exploits. But it is Adams' leading question—"What do We mean by the American Revolution?"—and his grand answering assertions that lift *this letter above mere reminiscence or, for that matter, above the liveliest historical narrative.*

Quincy, February 13th. 1818

MR. NILES

THE AMERICAN REVOLUTION was not a common Event. It's Effects and Consequences have already been Awful over a great Part of the Globe. And when and where are they to cease?

But what do We mean by the American Revolution? Do we mean the American War? The Revolution was effected before the War commenced. The Revolution was in the Minds and Hearts of the People. A Change in their Religious Sentiments of their Duties and Obligations. While the King, and all in Authority under him, were believed to govern, in Justice and Mercy according to the Laws and Constitutions derived to them from the God of Nature, and transmitted to them by their Ancestors: they thought themselves bound to pray for the King and Queen and all the Royal Family, and all the Authority under them, as Ministers ordained of God for their good. But when they saw those Powers renouncing all the Principles of Authority, and bent upon the destruction of all the Securities of their Lives, Liberties and Properties, they thought it their Duty to pray for the Continental Congress and all the thirteen State Congresses, &c.

There might be, and there were others, who thought less about Religion and Conscience, but had certain habitual Sentiments of Allegiance and Loyalty derived from their Education; but believing Allegiance and Protection to be reciprocal, when Protection was withdrawn, they thought Allegiance was dissolved.

Adams' letter is here for the first time printed faithfully from the manuscript. The original, owned by the Maryland Historical Society, runs to nine pages and is entirely in John Adams' hand. The hand is still firm, but the manuscript is marred by careless blots and other marks of haste. No letterbook copy was made for retention in Adams' files. At the head of the text, crossed out, is the name "Samuel Adams," as if this letter were to have been devoted to that subject; it was not, but see its final paragraph. Scattered words, phrases, and sentences in the manuscript are underscored or doubly underscored in different hands, one of them doubtless that of Niles, but only what are believed to be John Adams' marks of emphasis are followed in the present text. Someone, very likely Niles himself, inked out a passage of fifteen words concerning Oxenbridge Thacher that he thought in doubtful taste. To restore this passage it has been necessary to guess at two words.

Another Alteration was common to all. The People of America had been educated in an habitual Affection for England as their Mother-Country; and while they thought her a kind and tender Parent (erroneously enough, however, for she never was such a Mother,) no Affection could be more sincere. But when they found her a cruel Beldam, willing, like Lady Macbeth, to "dash their Brains out," it is no Wonder if their fillial Affections ceased and were changed into Indignation and horror.

This radi[c]al Change in the Principles, Opinions, Sentiments and Affections of the People, was the real American Revolution.

By what means, this great and important Alteration in the religious, moral, political and social Character of the People of thirteen Colonies, all distinct, unconnected and independent of each other, was begun, pursued and accomplished, it is surely interesting to Humanity to investigate, and perpetuate to Posterity.

To this End it is greatly to be desired that Young Gentlemen of Letters in all the States, especially in the thirteen Original States, would undertake the laborious, but certainly interesting and amusing Task, of searching and collecting all the Records, Pamphlets, Newspapers and even hand-Bills, which in any Way contributed to change the Temper and Views of The People and compose them into an independent Nation.

The Colonies had grown up under Constitutions of Government, so different, there was so great a Variety of Religions, they were composed of so many Nations, their Customs, Manners and Habits had so little resemblance, and their Intercourse had been so rare and their Knowledge of each other so imperfect, that to unite them in the same Principles in Theory and the same System of Action was certainly a very difficult Enterprize. The compleat Accomplishment of it, in so short a time and by such simple means, was perhaps a singular Example in the History of Mankind. Thirteen Clocks were made to strike together; a perfection of Mechanism which no Artist had ever before effected.

In this Research, the Glorioroles of Individual Gentlemen and of separate States is of little Consequence. The Means and the Measures are the proper Objects of Investigation. These may be of Use to Posterity, not only in this Nation, but in South America, and all other Countries. They may teach Mankind that Revolutions are no Trifles; that they ought never to be undertaken rashly; nor without deliberate Consideration and sober Reflection; nor without a solid, immutable, eternal foundation of Justice and Humanity; nor without a People possessed of Intelligence, Fortitude and Integrity sufficient to carry them with Steadiness, Patience, and Perseverance, through all the Vicissitudes of fortune, the fiery Tryals and melancholly Disasters they may have to encounter.

The Town of Boston early instituted an annual Oration on the fourth of July, in commemoration of the Principles and Feelings which contributed to produce the Revolution. Many of those Orations I have heard, and all that I could obtain I have read. Much Ingenuity and Eloquence appears upon every Subject, except those Principles and Feelings. That of my honest and amiable Neighbour, Josiah Quincy, appeared to me, the most directly to the purpose of the Institution. Those Principles and Feelings ought to be traced back for Two hundred Years, and sought in the history of the Country from the first Plantations in America. Nor should the Principles and Feelings of the English and Scotch towards the Colonies, through that whole Period ever be forgotten. The perpetual discordance between British Principles and Feelings and those of America, the next Year after the Suppression of the French Power in America, came to a Crisis, and produced an Explosion.

It was not till after the Annihilation of the French Dominion in America, that any British Ministry had dared to gratify their own Wishes, and the desire of the Nation, by projecting a formal Plan for raising a national Revenue from America by Parliamentary Taxation. The first great Manifestation of this design, was by the Order to carry into strict Execution those Acts of Parliament which were well known by the Appelation of the Acts of Trade, which had lain a dead Letter, unexecuted for half a Century, and some of them I believe for nearly a whole one.

This produced, in 1760 and 1761, An Awakening and a Revival of American Principles and Feelings, with an Enthusiasm which went on increasing till in 1775 it burst out in open Violence, Hostility and Fury.

The Characters, the most conspicuous, the most ardent and influential, in this Revival, from 1760 to 1766, were—First and Foremost, before all, and above all, James Otis; Next to him was Oxenbridge Thatcher; next to him Samuel Adams; next to him John Hancock; then Dr. Mayhew, then Dr. Cooper and his Brother. Of Mr. Hancock's Life, Character, generous Nature, great disinterested Sacrifices, and important Services, if

I had forces, I should be glad to write a Volume. But this I hope will be done by some younger and abler hand. Mr. Thatcher, because his Name and Merits are less known, must not be wholly omitted. This Gentleman was an eminent Barrister at Law, in as large practice as any one in Boston. There was not a Citizen of that Town more universally beloved for his Learning, Ingenuity, every domestic & social Virtue, and conscientious Conduct in every Relation of Life. His Patriotism was as ardent as his Progenitors had been ancient and illustrious in this Country. Hutchinson often said "Thatcher was not born a Plebeian, but he was determined to die one." In May 1763, I beleive, he was chosen by the Town of Boston one of their Representatives in the Legislature, a Colleague with Mr. Otis, who had been a Member from May 1761, and he continued to be reelected annually till his Death in 1765, when Mr. Samuel Adams was elected to fill his place, in the Absence of Mr. Otis, then attending the Congress at New York. Thatcher had long been jealous of the unbounded Ambition of Mr. Hutchinson, but when he found him not content with the Office of Lieutenant Governor, the Command of the Castle and its Emoluments, of Judge of Probate for the County of Suffolk, a Seat in his Majesty's Council in the Legislature, his Brother-in-Law Secretary of State by the Kings Commission, a Brother of that Secretary of State a Judge of the Superiour Court and a Member of Council, now in 1760 and 1761, soliciting and accepting the Office of the Chief Justice of the Superior Court of Judicature, he concluded as Mr. Otis did, and as every other enlightened Friend of his Country did, that he sought that Office with the determined Purpose of determining all Causes in favour of the Ministry at Saint James's and their servile Parliament.

His Indignation against him henceforward, to 1765, when he died, knew no bounds but Truth. I speak from personal Knowledge and with [*one word effaced by an accidental blot*]. For, from 1758 to 1765, I attended every Superiour and Inferiour Court in Boston, and recollect not one in which he did not invite me home to spend Evenings with him, when he made me converse with him as well as I could on all Subjects of Religion, Morals, Law, Politicks, History, Phylosophy, Belle Letters, Theology, Mythology, Cosmogony, Metaphysicks, Lock, Clark, Leibnits, Bolinbroke, Berckley, the Preestablished Harmony of the Universe, the Nature of Matter and Spirit, and the eternal Establishment of Coincidences between their Operations; Fate, foreknowledge, absolute—and We reasoned on such unfathomable Subjects as high as

Milton's Gentry in Pandemonium; and We understood them as well as they did, and no better. To such mighty Mysteries he added the News of the day, and the Tittle Tattle of the Town. But his favourite Subject was Politicks, and the impending threatening System of Parliamentary Taxation and Universal Government over the Colonies. On this Subject he was so anxious and agitated that I have no doubt it occasioned his premature death. From the time when he argued the question of Writts of Assistance to his death, he considered the King, Ministry, Parliament and Nation of Great Britain as determined to new model the Colonies from the Foundation; to annul all their Charters, to constitute them all Royal Governments; to raise a Revenue in America by Parliamentary Taxation; to apply that Revenue to pay the Salaries of Governors, Judges and all other Crown Officers; and, after all this, to raise as large a Revenue as they pleased to be applied to National Purposes at the Exchequer in England; and farther to establish Bishops and the whole System of the Church of England, Tythes and all, throughout all British America. This System, he said, if it was suffered to prevail would extinguish the Flame of Liberty all over the World; that America would be employed as an Engine to batter down all the miserable remains of Liberty in Great Britain and Ireland, where only any Semblance of it was left in the World. To this System he considered Hutchinson, the Olivers and all their Connections, dependants, adherents, Shoelickers— and another Epithet with which I will not [pollute?] my page nor [tarnish?] his memory, to be entirely devoted. He asserted that they were all engaged with all the Crown Officers in America and the Understrappers of the Ministry in England, in a deep and treasonable Conspiracy to betray the Liberties of their Country, for their own private personal and family Aggrandisement. His Philippicks against the unprincipled Ambition and Avarice of all of them, but especially of Hutchinson, were unbridled; not only in private, confidential Conversations, but in all Companies and on all Occasions. He gave Hutchinson the Sobriquet of "Summa Potestas," and rarely mentioned him but by the Name of "Summa." His Liberties of Speech were no Secrets to his Enemies. I have sometimes wondered that they did not throw him over the Barr, as they did soon afterwards Major Hawley. For they hated him worse than they did James Otis or Samuel Adams, and they feared him more,— because they had no Revenge for a Father's disappointment of a Seat on the Superiour Bench to impute to him as they did to Otis; and Thatcher's Character through Life had been so modest, decent, unassuming,—his Morals so pure, and his Religion so venerated, that they dared not attack him. In his Office were educated to the Barr two eminent Characters, the late Judge Lowell and Josiah Quincy, aptly called the Boston Cicero. Mr. Thatcher's frame was slender, his Constitution delicate; whether his Physicians overstrained his Vessels with Mercury, when he had the Small Pox by Inoculation at the Castle, or whether he was overplyed by publick Anxieties and Exertions, the Small Pox left him in a Decline from which he never recovered. Not long before his death he sent for me to commit to my care some of his Business at the Barr. I asked him whether he had seen the Virginia Resolves.—"Oh yes.—They are Men! They are noble Spirits! It kills me to think of the Leathargy and Stupidity that prevails here. I long to be out. I will go out. I will go out. I will go into Court, and make a Speech which shall be read after my death as my dying Testimony against this infernal Tyrany they are bringing upon us." Seeing the violent Agitation into which it threw him, I changed the Subject as soon as possible, and retired. He had been confined for some time. Had he been abroad among the People he would not have complained so pathetically of the "Lethargy and Stupidity that prevailed," for Town and Country were all Alive; and in August became active enough and some of the People proceeded to unwarrantable Excesses, which were more lamented by the Patriots than by their Enemies. Mr. Thatcher soon died, deeply lamented by all the Friends of their Country.

Another Gentleman who had great influence in the Commencement of the Revolution, was Doctor Jonathan Mayhew, a descendant of the ancient Governor of Martha's Vineyard. This Divine had raised a great Reputation both in Europe and America by the publication of a Volume of seven Sermons in the Reign of King George the Second, 1749, and by many other Writings, particularly a Sermon in 1750, on the thirtieth of January, on the Subject of Passive Obedience and Non Resistance; in which the Saintship and Martyrdom of King Charles the first are considered, seasoned with Witt and Satyre, superior to any in Swift or Franklin. It was read by every Body, celebrated by Friends, and abused by Enemies. During the Reigns of King George the first and King George the second, the Reigns of the Stewarts, the Two Jameses, and the two Charleses were in general disgrace in England. In America they had always been held in Abhorrence. The Persecutions and Cruelties suffered by their Ancestors under those Reigns, had been transmitted by History and Tradition, and Mayhew seemed to be raised up to revive all their Animosity against Tyranny, in Church and State, and at the same time to destroy their Bigotry, Fanaticism and Inconsistency. David Hume's plausible, elegant, fascinating and fallacious Apology in which he varnished over the Crimes of the Stewarts had not then appeared. To draw the Character of Mayhew would be to transcribe a dozen Volumes. This transcendant Genius threw all the Weight of his great Fame into the Scale of his Country in 1761, and maintained it there with Zeal and Ardour till his death in 1766. In 1763 appeared the Controversy between him and Mr. Apthorp, Mr. Caner, Dr. Johnson and Archbishop Secker, on the Charter and Conduct of the Society for propagating the Gospel in foreign Parts. To form a Judgment of this debate I beg leave to refer to a Review of the whole, printed at the time, and written by Samuel Adams, though by some, very absurdly and erroneously, ascribed to Mr. Apthorp. If I am not mistaken, it will be found a Model of Candour, Sagacity, Impartiality and close correct reasoning.

If any Gentleman supposes this Controversy to be nothing to the present purpose, he is grossly mistaken. It spread an Universal Alarm against the Authority of Parliament. It excited a general and just Apprehension that Bishops and Dioceses and Churches, and Priests and Tythes, were to be imposed upon Us by Parliament. It was known that neither King nor Ministry nor Archbishops could appoint Bishops in America without an Act of Parliament; and if Parliament could Tax Us they could establish the Church of England with all its Creeds, Articles, Tests, Ceremonies and Tythes, and proscribe all other Churches as Conventicles and Schism Shops.

Nor must Mr. Cushing be forgotten. His good Sense and sound Judgment, the Urbanity of his Manners, his universal good Character, his numerous Friends and Connections and his continual intercourse with all Sorts of People, added to his constant Attachment to the Liberties of his Country, gave him a great and salutary influence from the beginning in 1760.

Let me recommend these hints to the Consideration of Mr. Wirt, whose Life of Mr. Henry I have read with great delight. I think, that after mature investigation, he will be convinced that Mr. Henry did not "give the first impulse to the Ball of Independence," and that Otis, Thatcher, Samuel Adams, Mayhew, Hancock, Cushing and thousands of others were labouring for several Years at the Wheel before the Name of Mr. Henry was heard beyond the limits of Virginia.

If you print this, I will endeavour to send You some thing concerning Samuel Adams, who was destined to a longer Career, and to act a more conspicuous and, perhaps, a more important Part than any other Man. But his Life would require a Volume. If you decline printing this Letter I pray to return it as soon as possible to

Sir, your humble Servant
JOHN ADAMS

Mr. Niles.

Niles made prompt use of both of John Adams' letters on the great issue of writs of assistance in Massachusetts. That of January 14, 1818, on Otis, he printed in his Weekly Register for January 31, and the present letter, on Otis' collaborators, in the Register for March 7. But Adams was not content to let matters rest there. For the benefit of the "Young Gentlemen of Letters" who he hoped would investigate the origins of the American Revolution, he published in the following year a collected edition of Daniel Leonard's "Massachusettensis" papers and his own "Novanglus" papers in reply to Leonard. To this republication of newspaper pieces written in 1774–75 he appended the whole suite of his letters addressed in 1818 to Niles, Wirt, and William Tudor on this (to him, at least) inexhaustibly fascinating subject. By far the greatest number of the letters—about two dozen, some of them very long indeed —he addressed to Tudor, his old friend and former law clerk, for Tudor's son William planned to write the "Sketches of the Life and Writings of James Otis of Boston," which Adams had told Wirt that he himself was too old to write, and he was determined that young Tudor should neither lack materials nor fail to show Otis' primacy among the founders of independence. In one of the first and longest of these letters (April 5, 1818), Adams related an incident that occurred in the Massachusetts House of Representatives in 1762, when Otis was rebuked by a supporter of the Crown for including treasonable language toward the King of Great Britain in a remonstrance to the royal governor. "Why," Adams demanded, "has the sublime Compliment of 'Treason! Treason!' made to Mr. Henry in 1765 been so celebrated, when that to Mr. Otis in 1762, three Years before, has been totally forgotten?" As usual, he answered his own question: "Because the Virginia Patriot has

had many Trumpetters and very loud ones; but the Massachusetts Patriot none"—or, as Adams had said elsewhere, with George Washington in mind, "Virginia Geese are all Swans."

But most of the cataract of letters to Tudor dealt with a single subject —Otis as "a flame of Fire" in the first hearing on the legality of writs of assistance, held before Chief Justice Hutchinson and the other judges of the Massachusetts Superior Court of Judicature in February, 1761. As an accurate reconstruction of Otis' four- or five-hour argument, these epistolary reminiscences, so charged with learning and emotion alike, have long since been discredited by legal and historical scholars. The verdict of Adams' grandson, Charles Francis Adams, is as good as any. In a note at the end of the series, this usually highly restrained editor observed (Works of John Adams, X, 362): "By comparison of this sketch of Mr. Otis's speech with that taken at the time, vol. ii. pp. 521–525, as well as with Mr. Otis's published writings, it is difficult to resist the belief that Mr. Adams insensibly infused into this work much of the learning and of the breadth of views belonging to himself. It looks a little as Raphael's labor might be supposed to look, if he had undertaken to show how Perugino painted."

But it was the tableaux painted by "Raphael" Adams that fired the popular imagination and became fixed in the American mind (scholarly opinion to the contrary notwithstanding) as the way the Revolution really began. Tudor's Life of Otis, published in 1823, drew heavily and uncritically on Adams' highly colored narrative. According to George Ticknor, whom one might suppose a discriminating judge, Tudor's book gave "the best representation possible, and, indeed what might be called a kind of dramatic exhibition, of the state of feeling in New England out of which the Revolution was produced. There is nothing like it in print, . . . nor could such a book be made twenty years from hence, for then all the traditions will have perished with the old men from whose graves he has just rescued them. It takes prodigiously here, and will, I think, do much good by promoting an inquiry into the most interesting and important period of our history." The immediate and long-range effects of both Adams' letters and Tudor's rendering of them may be seen in the subsequent Fourth of July orations that were a Boston municipal institution and were published collectively in 1852 as The Hundred Boston Orators—a volume distributed free by a Boston philanthropist to every school in the city, every academy in the state, and every college in the United States.

Through these and countless other channels, Adams' letters helped shape the nineteenth-century pantheon of Massachusetts heroes in the struggle for independence and contributed to the new secular religion of American nationalism. Of the things he remembered, some had never happened except in his own excited recollection of those brave days. His own earlier opinions of some of these heroes—notably Otis, Hancock, and Cushing—were utterly at variance with his tributes to them in 1818. But no matter. The way he remembered and felt about both the characters and events of the Revolution in his old age was the way his countrymen wanted to feel about and to celebrate them. According to his and their view, the American Revolution was a grand but wholly foreordained action, midway between two others equally grand. The earlier one, the full meaning of which the Revolution itself had made clear, was the peopling of America with men determined to govern themselves. The later action, now just beginning but bound to follow the Revolution as inevitably as the Revolution had followed the planting of North America, was awesome in its implications for world history. Study of the "MEANS AND THE MEASURES" applied in the winning of American independence would enable men "of Intelligence, Fortitude and Integrity" to throw off the chains of the regnant legitimacies and assume self-government over the whole surface of the globe.

All this was implicit in John Adams' appraisal of the collective role of Otis, Mayhew, Sam Adams, Thacher, Hancock, and the rest of the radical leaders in the Bay Colony on the eve of the Revolution. No wonder these men took on for him—and, before long, for others—more than human proportions. All this became explicit in nineteenth-century America's view of itself and its destiny. It was, and in the twentieth century still is, the core of America's continuing sense of mission, the most driving force in our national consciousness.

John Marshall
M'Culloch v. Maryland
1819

EDITED BY ROBERT G. MCCLOSKEY

John Marshall's opinion in M'Culloch v. Maryland *is by almost universal assent his paramount state paper and, as William D. Lewis has said, "perhaps the most celebrated Judicial utterance in the annals of the English speaking world." And the opinion is surely Marshall's own in a genuine and important sense, for it is stamped from first to last with his unique rhetorical gifts—the capacity to condense and elucidate an enormously complex issue, the instinct for a memorable phrase, the black-and-white approach to right and wrong that made many of his arguments so hard to answer. Yet in another sense any Supreme Court opinion is the work of many authors, and this one is no exception. The writer's colleagues who concur in his pronouncements may help to decide what he says, although their precise influence is seldom easy to discern because of the privacy of the judicial conference. In this case we can only guess that such strong-minded justices as Joseph Story and William Johnson may have played a part in shaping the composition even of "the Great Chief Justice." A second influence is less conjectural. The arguments of counsel before the Court have often provided the judges with ideas and phrases, and counsel for M'Culloch (i.e., for the Bank of the United States) consisted of three of the best courtroom lawyers who have ever adorned the American bar—William Pinckney, William Wirt, and Daniel Webster. Marshall's famous statement "the power to tax involves the power to destroy" was, for example, foreshadowed in*

Webster's oral argument, although Webster had said that an "unlimited" tax power involves the power to destroy and Marshall, characteristically, omitted the qualification. Thirdly, Marshall's prose here contains echoes of the famous opinion of Story in Martin v. Hunter's Lessee in 1816, a case involving a related question of national power. Fourthly and most important of all, Marshall was drawing on Alexander Hamilton's 1791 opinion on the constitutionality of the Bank, an opinion composed at President Washington's request when the bill establishing the first Bank was under consideration. Marshall's great rule for judging the extent of the implied powers ("Let the end be legitimate. . . .") is simply a restatement of language used by Hamilton; and the discussion of the meaning of the word "necessary" is also heavily dependent on Hamilton's paper. Finally it is worth noting that the general viewpoint expressed in M'Culloch had been anticipated as long ago as 1786 by James Wilson in his defense of the Bank of North America.

Nevertheless, to say that Marshall must share his glory is not to detract from it; form and substance are often inseparable. His opinion surpasses its sources in the way that a successful poem surpasses a paraphrase. The thing is not only said; it is said with a rightness, a persuasiveness, a vividness that make it unforgettable.

For three decades America had been debating the momentous issue of national versus state power; but the issue was still gravely in doubt. Indeed there was reason to believe in 1819 that the states' rights tide, which had seemed to ebb a few years before, was flowing again more strongly than ever.

The M'Culloch case involved a heavy Maryland tax on the issuance of bank notes by any bank which Maryland herself had not chartered (the Bank of the United States had been chartered by Congress). M'Culloch was cashier of the Baltimore branch of the Bank; he issued notes without paying the tax; Maryland brought an action to recover penalties for nonpayment. The Baltimore County Court rendered judgment for the state, and the Maryland Court of Appeals affirmed. M'Culloch then urged the Supreme Court to pronounce the Maryland tax unconstitutional. Maryland, on the other hand, argued that the congressional act incorporating the Bank was itself invalid, that in passing it Congress had extended its powers beyond those granted by the Constitution.

Marshall was a passionate defender of national prerogatives, and the revival of state challenges to those prerogatives filled him with dread. He hoped that his argument in M'Culloch would influence the contemporary debate. But he also hoped that it would ring in the ears of posterity as the classic justification for national sovereignty and as a lasting barrier to state encroachments. To fulfill these hopes it was necessary for him to muster, as never before, his splendid talents. When he actually composed the opinion is uncertain. It is one of his longest, and he read it aloud before the Court on March 6, 1819, only three days after the oral arguments had ended. Perhaps, as has been suggested, he had written most of it at his home in Richmond during the preceding months, and the three-day interval was used to polish and sharpen the draft. Yet this inference is not inevitable. The opinion, like most of Marshall's, is unencumbered by citation; it is an essay, not a pandect. To write this much prose in three days is a formidable assignment. But it does not seem an insuperable one when we reflect that the author had been, with the help of his generation, preparing himself to write it for almost thirty years.

I N THE CASE now to be determined, the defendant, a sovereign State, denies the obligation of a law enacted by the legislature of the Union, and the plaintiff, on his part, contests the validity of an act which has been passed by the legislature of that State. The constitution of our country, in its most interesting and vital parts, is to be considered; the conflicting powers of the government of the Union and of its members, as marked in that constitution, are to be discussed; and an opinion given, which may essentially influence the great operations of the government. No tribunal can approach such a question without a deep sense of its importance, and of the awful responsibility involved in its decision. But it must be decided peacefully, or remain a source of hostile legislation, perhaps of hostility of a still more serious nature; and if it is to be so decided, by this tribunal alone can the decision be made. On the Supreme Court of the United States has the constitution of our country devolved this important duty.

The first question made in the cause is, has Congress power to incorporate a bank?

. . . In discussing this question, the counsel for the State of Maryland

---

The opinion is reprinted from 4 Wheaton 316 (1819).

have deemed it of some importance, in the construction of the constitution, to consider that instrument not as emanating from the people, but as the act of sovereign and independent States. The powers of the general government, it has been said, are delegated by the States, who alone are truly sovereign; and must be exercised in subordination to the States, who alone possess supreme dominion.

It would be difficult to sustain this proposition. The Convention which framed the constitution was indeed elected by the State legislatures. But the instrument, when it came from their hands, was a mere proposal, without obligation, or pretensions to it. It was reported to the then existing Congress of the United States, with a request that it might "be submitted to a Convention of Delegates, chosen in each State by the people thereof, under the recommendation of its Legislature, for their assent and ratification." This mode of proceeding was adopted; and by the Convention, by Congress, and by the State Legislatures, the instrument was submitted to the people. They acted upon it in the only manner in which they can act safely, effectively, and wisely, on such a subject, by assembling in Convention. It is true, they assembled in their several States—and where else should they have assembled? No political dreamer was ever wild enough to think of breaking down the lines which separate the States, and of compounding the American people into one common mass. Of consequence, when they act, they act in their States. But the measures they adopt do not, on that account, cease to be the measures of the people themselves, or become the measures of the State governments.

From these Conventions the constitution derives its whole authority. The government proceeds directly from the people; is "ordained and established" in the name of the people; and is declared to be ordained, "in order to form a more perfect union, establish justice, ensure domestic tranquillity, and secure the blessings of liberty to themselves and to their posterity." The assent of the States, in their sovereign capacity, is implied in calling a Convention, and thus submitting that instrument to the people. But the people were at perfect liberty to accept or reject it; and their act was final. It required not the affirmance, and could not be negatived, by the State governments. The constitution, when thus adopted, was of complete obligation, and bound the State sovereignties.

It has been said, that the people had already surrendered all their powers to the State sovereignties, and had nothing more to give. But, surely, the question whether they may resume and modify the powers granted to government does not remain to be settled in this country. Much more might the legitimacy of the general government be doubted, had it been created by the States. The powers delegated to the State sovereignties were to be exercised by themselves, not by a distinct and independent sovereignty, created by themselves. To the formation of a league, such as was the confederation, the State sovereignties were certainly competent. But when, "in order to form a more perfect union," it was deemed necessary to change this alliance into an effective government, possessing great and sovereign powers, and acting directly on the people, the necessity of referring it to the people, and of deriving its powers directly from them, was felt and acknowledged by all.

The government of the Union, then, (whatever may be the influence of this fact on the case,) is, emphatically, and truly, a government of the people. In form and in substance it emanates from them. Its powers are granted by them, and are to be exercised directly on them, and for their benefit.

This government is acknowledged by all to be one of enumerated powers. The principle, that it can exercise only the powers granted to it, would seem too apparent to have required to be enforced by all those arguments which its enlightened friends, while it was depending before the people, found it necessary to urge. That principle is now universally admitted. But the question respecting the extent of the powers actually granted, is perpetually arising, and will probably continue to arise, as long as our system shall exist.

In discussing these questions, the conflicting powers of the general and State governments must be brought into view, and the supremacy of their respective laws, when they are in opposition, must be settled.

If any one proposition could command the universal assent of mankind, we might expect it would be this—that the government of the Union, though limited in its powers, is supreme within its sphere of action. This would seem to result necessarily from its nature. It is the government of all; its powers are delegated by all; it represents all, and acts for all. Though any one State may be willing to control its operations, no State is willing to allow others to control them. The nation, on those subjects on which it can act, must necessarily bind its component parts. But this question is not left to mere reason: the people have, in express terms, decided it, by saying, "this constitution, and the laws of the United States, which shall be made in pursuance thereof," "shall be the supreme law of the land," and by requiring that the members of the State legislatures, and the officers of the executive and judicial departments of the States, shall take the oath of fidelity to it.

The government of the United States, then, though limited in its powers, is supreme; and its laws, when made in pursuance of the constitution, form the supreme law of the land, "any thing in the constitution or laws of any State to the contrary notwithstanding."

Among the enumerated powers, we do not find that of establishing a bank or creating a corporation. But there is no phrase in the instrument which, like the articles of confederation, excludes incidental or implied powers; and which requires that every thing granted shall be expressly and minutely described. Even the 10th amendment, which was framed for the purpose of quieting the excessive jealousies which had been excited, omits the word "expressly," and declares only that the powers "not delegated to the United States, nor prohibited to the States, are reserved to the States or to the people;" thus leaving the question, whether the particular power which may become the subject of contest has been delegated to the one government, or prohibited to the other, to depend on a fair construction of the whole instrument. The men who drew and adopted this amendment had experienced the embarrassments resulting from the insertion of this word in the articles of confederation, and probably omitted it to avoid those embarrassments. A constitution, to contain an accurate detail of all the subdivisions of which its great powers will admit, and of all the means by which they may be carried into execution, would partake of the prolixity of a legal code, and could scarcely be embraced by the human mind. It would probably never be understood by the public. Its nature, therefore, requires, that only its great outlines should be marked, its important objects designated, and the minor ingredients which compose those objects be deduced from the nature of the objects themselves. . . . In considering this question, then, we must never forget, that it is *a constitution* we are expounding.

Although, among the enumerated powers of government, we do not find the word "bank" or "incorporation," we find the great powers to lay and collect taxes; to borrow money; to regulate commerce; to declare and conduct a war; and to raise and support armies and navies. The sword and the purse, all the external relations, and no inconsiderable portion of the industry of the nation, are entrusted to its government. It can never be pretended that these vast powers draw after them others of inferior importance, merely because they are inferior. Such an idea can never be advanced. But it may with great reason be contended, that a government, entrusted with such ample powers, on the due execution of which the happiness and prosperity of the nation so vitally depends, must also be entrusted with ample means for their execution. The power being given, it is the interest of the nation to facilitate its execution. It can never be their interest, and cannot be presumed to have been their intention, to clog and embarrass its execution by withholding the most appropriate means. Throughout this vast republic, from the St. Croix to the Gulph of Mexico, from the Atlantic to the Pacific, revenue is to be collected and expended, armies are to be marched and supported. The exigencies of the nation may require that the treasure raised in the north should be transported to the south, *that* raised in the east conveyed to the west, or that this order should be reversed. Is that construction of the constitution to be preferred which would render these operations difficult, hazardous, and expensive? Can we adopt that construction, (unless the words imperiously require it,) which would impute to the framers of that instrument, when granting these powers for the public good, the intention of impeding their exercise by withholding a choice of means? If, indeed, such be the mandate of the constitution, we have only to obey; but that instrument does not profess to enumerate the means by which the powers it confers may be executed; nor does it prohibit the creation of a corporation, if the existence of such a being be essential to the beneficial exercise of those powers. It is, then, the subject of fair inquiry, how far such means may be employed.

It is not denied, that the powers given to the government imply the ordinary means of execution. That, for example, of raising revenue, and applying it to national purposes, is admitted to imply the power of conveying money from place to place, as the exigencies of the nation may require, and of employing the usual means of conveyance. But it is denied that the government has its choice of means; or, that it may employ the most convenient means, if, to employ them, it be necessary to erect a corporation.

 . . . The power of creating a corporation, though appertaining to sovereignty, is not, like the power of making war, or levying taxes, or of regulating commerce, a great substantive and independent power, which cannot be implied as incidental to other powers, or used as a means of executing them. It is never the end for which other powers are exercised, but a means by which other objects are accomplished. . . . The power

245

of creating a corporation is never used for its own sake, but for the purpose of effecting something else. No sufficient reason is, therefore, perceived, why it may not pass as incidental to those powers which are expressly given, if it be a direct mode of executing them.

But the constitution of the United States has not left the right of Congress to employ the necessary means, for the execution of the powers conferred on the government, to general reasoning. To its enumeration of powers is added that of making "all laws which shall be necessary and proper, for carrying into execution the foregoing powers, and all other powers vested by this constitution, in the government of the United States, or in any department thereof."

The counsel for the State of Maryland have urged various arguments, to prove that this clause, though in terms a grant of power, is not so in effect; but is really restrictive of the general right, which might otherwise be implied, of selecting means for executing the enumerated powers.

In support of this proposition, they have found it necessary to contend, that this clause was inserted for the purpose of conferring on Congress the power of making laws. That, without it, doubts might be entertained, whether Congress could exercise its powers in the form of legislation.

But could this be the object for which it was inserted? . . . That a legislature, endowed with legislative powers, can legislate, is a proposition too self-evident to have been questioned.

But the argument on which most reliance is placed, is drawn from the peculiar language of this clause. Congress is not empowered by it to make all laws, which may have relation to the powers conferred on the government, but such only as may be *"necessary and proper"* for carrying them into execution. The word *"necessary,"* is considered as controlling the whole sentence, and as limiting the right to pass laws for the execution of the granted powers, to such as are indispensable, and without which the power would be nugatory. That it excludes the choice of means, and leaves to Congress, in each case, that only which is most direct and simple.

Is it true, that this is the sense in which the word "necessary" is always used? Does it always import an absolute physical necessity, so strong, that one thing, to which another may be termed necessary, cannot exist without that other? We think it does not. If reference be had to its use, in the common affairs of the world, or in approved authors, we find that

246

it frequently imports no more than that one thing is convenient, or useful, or essential to another. To employ the means necessary to an end, is generally understood as employing any means calculated to produce the end, and not as being confined to those single means, without which the end would be entirely unattainable. Such is the character of human language, that no word conveys to the mind, in all situations, one single definite idea; and nothing is more common than to use words in a figurative sense. Almost all compositions contain words, which, taken in their rigorous sense, would convey a meaning different from that which is obviously intended. It is essential to just construction, that many words which import something excessive, should be understood in a more mitigated sense—in that sense which common usage justifies. The word "necessary" is of this description. It has not a fixed character peculiar to itself. It admits of all degrees of comparison; and is often connected with other words, which increase or diminish the impression the mind receives of the urgency it imports. A thing may be necessary, very necessary, absolutely or indispensably necessary. To no mind would the same idea be conveyed, by these several phrases. . . . This word, then, like others, is used in various senses; and, in its construction, the subject, the context, the intention of the person using them, are all to be taken into view.

Let this be done in the case under consideration. The subject is the execution of those great powers on which the welfare of a nation essentially depends. It must have been the intention of those who gave these powers, to insure, as far as human prudence could insure, their beneficial execution. This could not be done by confiding the choice of means to such narrow limits as not to leave it in the power of Congress to adopt any which might be appropriate, and which were conducive to the end. This provision is made in a constitution intended to endure for ages to come, and, consequently, to be adapted to the various *crises* of human affairs. To have prescribed the means by which government should, in all future time, execute its powers, would have been to change, entirely, the character of the instrument, and give it the properties of a legal code. It would have been an unwise attempt to provide, by immutable rules, for exigencies which, if foreseen at all, must have been seen dimly, and which can be best provided for as they occur. To have declared that the best means shall not be used, but those alone without which the power given would be nugatory, would have been to

247

deprive the legislature of the capacity to avail itself of experience, to exercise its reason, and to accommodate its legislation to circumstances. . . .

But the argument which most conclusively demonstrates the error of the construction contended for by the counsel for the State of Maryland, is founded on the intention of the Convention, as manifested in the whole clause. To waste time and argument in proving that, without it, Congress might carry its powers into execution, would be not much less idle than to hold a lighted taper to the sun. As little can it be required to prove, that in the absence of this clause, Congress would have some choice of means. That it might employ those which, in its judgment, would most advantageously effect the object to be accomplished. That any means adapted to the end, any means which tended directly to the execution of the constitutional powers of the government, were in themselves constitutional. This clause, as construed by the State of Maryland, would abridge, and almost annihilate this useful and necessary right of the legislature to select its means. That this could not be intended, is, we should think, had it not been already controverted, too apparent for controversy. We think so for the following reasons:

1st. The clause is placed among the powers of Congress, not among the limitations on those powers.

2nd. Its terms purport to enlarge, not to diminish the powers vested in the government. It purports to be an additional power, not a restriction on those already granted. No reason has been, or can be assigned for thus concealing an intention to narrow the discretion of the national legislature under words which purport to enlarge it. The framers of the constitution wished its adoption, and well knew that it would be endangered by its strength, not by its weakness. Had they been capable of using language which would convey to the eye one idea, and, after deep reflection, impress on the mind another, they would rather have disguised the grant of power, than its limitation. . . .

The result of the most careful and attentive consideration bestowed upon this clause is, that if it does not enlarge, it cannot be construed to restrain the powers of Congress, or to impair the right of the legislature to exercise its best judgment in the selection of measures to carry into execution the constitutional powers of the government. If no other motive for its insertion can be suggested, a sufficient one is found in the desire to remove all doubts respecting the right to legislate on that vast mass of incidental powers which must be involved in the constitution, if that instrument be not a splendid bauble.

We admit, as all must admit, that the powers of the government are limited, and that its limits are not to be transcended. But we think the sound construction of the constitution must allow to the national legislature that discretion, with respect to the means by which the powers it confers are to be carried into execution, which will enable that body to perform the high duties assigned to it, in the manner most beneficial to the people. Let the end be legitimate, let it be within the scope of the constitution, and all means which are appropriate, which are plainly adapted to that end, which are not prohibited, but consist with the letter and spirit of the constitution, are constitutional.

. . . If a corporation may be employed indiscriminately with other means to carry into execution the powers of the government, no particular reason can be assigned for excluding the use of a bank, if required for its fiscal operations. To use one, must be within the discretion of Congress, if it be an appropriate mode of executing the powers of government. That it is a convenient, a useful, and essential instrument in the prosecution of its fiscal operations, is not now a subject of controversy. . . . The time has passed away when it can be necessary to enter into any discussion in order to prove the importance of this instrument, as a means to effect the legitimate objects of the government.

But, were its necessity less apparent, none can deny its being an appropriate measure; and if it is, the degree of its necessity, as has been very justly observed, is to be discussed in another place. Should Congress, in the execution of its powers, adopt measures which are prohibited by the constitution; or should Congress, under the pretext of executing its powers, pass laws for the accomplishment of objects not entrusted to the government; it would become the painful duty of this tribunal, should a case requiring such a decision come before it, to say that such an act was not the law of the land. But where the law is not prohibited, and is really calculated to effect any of the objects entrusted to the government, to undertake here to inquire into the degree of its necessity, would be to pass the line which circumscribes the judicial department, and to tread on legislative ground. This court disclaims all pretensions to such a power.

. . . After the most deliberate consideration, it is the unanimous and decided opinion of this Court, that the act to incorporate the Bank of the United States is a law made in pursuance of the constitution, and is a part of the supreme law of the land.

. . . It being the opinion of the Court, that the act incorporating the bank is constitutional; and that the power of establishing a branch in the State of Maryland might be properly exercised by the bank itself, we proceed to inquire—

. . . Whether the State of Maryland may, without violating the constitution, tax that branch?

That the power of taxation is one of vital importance; that it is retained by the States; that it is not abridged by the grant of a similar power to the government of the Union; that it is to be concurrently exercised by the two governments: are truths which have never been denied. But, such is the paramount character of the constitution, that its capacity to withdraw any subject from the action of even this power, is admitted. The States are expressly forbidden to lay any duties on imports or exports, except what may be absolutely necessary for executing their inspection laws. If the obligation of this prohibition must be conceded—if it may restrain a State from the exercise of its taxing power on imports and exports; the same paramount character would seem to restrain, as it certainly may restrain, a State from such other exercise of this power, as is in its nature incompatible with, and repugnant to, the constitutional laws of the Union. A law, absolutely repugnant to another, as entirely repeals that other as if express terms of repeal were used.

On this ground the counsel for the bank place its claim to be exempted from the power of a State to tax its operations. There is no express provision for the case, but the claim has been sustained on a principle which so entirely pervades the constitution, is so intermixed with the materials which compose it, so interwoven with its web, so blended with its texture, as to be incapable of being separated from it, without rending it into shreds.

This great principle is, that the constitution and the laws made in pursuance thereof are supreme; that they control the constitution and laws of the respective States, and cannot be controlled by them. From this, which may be almost termed an axiom, other propositions are deduced as corollaries, on the truth or error of which, and on their application to this case, the cause has been supposed to depend. These are, 1st. that a power to create implies a power to preserve. 2nd. That a power to destroy, if wielded by a different hand, is hostile to, and incompatible with these powers to create and to preserve. 3d. That where this repugnancy exists, that authority which is supreme must control, not yield to that over which it is supreme.

These propositions, as abstract truths, would, perhaps, never be controverted. Their application to this case, however, has been denied; and, both in maintaining the affirmative and the negative, a splendor of eloquence, and strength of argument, seldom, if ever, surpassed, have been displayed.

The power of Congress to create, and of course to continue, the bank, was the subject of the preceding part of this opinion; and is no longer to be considered as questionable.

That the power of taxing it by the States may be exercised so as to destroy it, is too obvious to be denied. But taxation is said to be an absolute power, which acknowledges no other limits than those expressly prescribed in the constitution, and like sovereign power of every other description, is trusted to the discretion of those who use it. . . .

The argument on the part of the State of Maryland, is, not that the States may directly resist a law of Congress, but that they may exercise their acknowledged powers upon it, and that the constitution leaves them this right in the confidence that they will not abuse it.

. . . That the power to tax involves the power to destroy; that the power to destroy may defeat and render useless the power to create; that there is a plain repugnance, in conferring on one government a power to control the constitutional measures of another, which other, with respect to those very measures, is declared to be supreme over that which exerts the control, are propositions not to be denied. But all inconsistencies are to be reconciled by the magic of the word CONFIDENCE. Taxation, it is said, does not necessarily and unavoidably destroy. To carry it to the excess of destruction would be an abuse, to presume which, would banish that confidence which is essential to all government.

But is this a case of confidence? Would the people of any one State trust those of another with a power to control the most insignificant operations of their State government? We know they would not. Why, then, should we suppose that the people of any one State should be willing to trust those of another with a power to control the operations of a government to which they have confided their most important and most valuable interests? In the legislature of the Union alone, are all represented. The legislature of the Union alone, therefore, can be

251

trusted by the people with the power of controlling measures which concern all, in the confidence that it will not be abused. This, then, is not a case of confidence, and we must consider it as it really is.

If we apply the principle for which the State of Maryland contends, to the constitution generally, we shall find it capable of changing totally the character of that instrument. We shall find it capable of arresting all the measures of the government, and of prostrating it at the foot of the States. The American people have declared their constitution, and the laws made in pursuance thereof, to be supreme; but this principle would transfer the supremacy, in fact, to the States.

If the States may tax one instrument, employed by the government in the execution of its powers, they may tax any and every other instrument. They may tax the mail; they may tax the mint; they may tax patent rights; they may tax the papers of the custom-house; they may tax judicial process; they may tax all the means employed by the government, to an excess which would defeat all the ends of government. This was not intended by the American people. They did not design to make their government dependent on the States.

. . . It has also been insisted, that, as the power of taxation in the general and State governments is acknowledged to be concurrent, every argument which would sustain the right of the general government to tax banks chartered by the States, will equally sustain the right of the States to tax banks chartered by the general government.

But the two cases are not on the same reason. The people of all the States have created the general government, and have conferred upon it the general power of taxation. The people of all the States, and the States themselves, are represented in Congress, and, by their representatives, exercise this power. When they tax the chartered institutions of the States, they tax their constituents; and these taxes must be uniform. But, when a State taxes the operations of the government of the United States, it acts upon institutions created, not by their own constituents, but by people over whom they claim no control. It acts upon the measures of a government created by others as well as themselves, for the benefit of others in common with themselves. The difference is that which always exists, and always must exist, between the action of the whole on a part, and the action of a part on the whole— between the laws of a government declared to be supreme, and those of a government which, when in opposition to those laws, is not supreme.

. . . The Court has bestowed on this subject its most deliberate consideration. The result is a conviction that the States have no power, by taxation or otherwise, to retard, impede, burden, or in any manner control, the operations of the constitutional laws enacted by Congress to carry into execution the powers vested in the general government. This is, we think, the unavoidable consequence of that supremacy which the constitution has declared.

We are unanimously of opinion, that the law passed by the legislature of Maryland, imposing a tax on the Bank of the United States, is unconstitutional and void.

Marshall's biographer, Albert Beveridge, once said that the M'Culloch opinion "has done more for the American Nation than any single utterance of any other one man, excepting only the Farewell Address of Washington." Beveridge was uncritically enamored of his great subject: perhaps he overstated the case. But there can be no doubt that Marshall's words have had a vital and continuing influence on the history of the Republic.

Their immediate result was, indeed, to excite a barrage of retaliatory tirades from the states' rights party. Spencer Roane and John Taylor of Virginia attacked the opinion bitterly and at length in the press; the legislatures of Virginia and Ohio passed resolutions damning it. Pennsylvania, Indiana, Illinois, and Tennessee joined in the assault. Marshall was chagrined and discouraged, and with some reason if he had hoped to slay the hydra of states' rights with a single stroke. This was too much to expect; no pen, not even Marshall's, was capable of that. Yet the very vehemence of the counterattack suggested that he had struck a telling blow, though not a mortal one. Insofar as logic and rhetoric could affect the contemporary debate, his opinion had done so, and his opponents found it easier to denounce the "crafty chief judge" (Jefferson's phrase) than to refute his reasoning.

The full greatness of the opinion, however, was to be revealed not in its own time but in the "ages to come" of which Marshall spoke. The marching logic, the infectious phrases reached out to a future in which changing historical circumstances were turning America toward the nationhood he had envisioned. Then the opinion, especially the first part with its classic defense of the national government's powers, could come into its own. The essential argument—that the people, not the states, created that government and endowed it with supremacy—was echoed by Webster in 1830 in the Reply to Hayne; it probably helped to form Lincoln's ideas about the nature of the Union; the outcome of the Civil War made it a dogma. The resulting principle—that the authority of the Union as construed by the Supreme Court overrides the authority of the states—did not in Marshall's day command the "universal assent of mankind" which he claimed for it, and it is still sometimes challenged in political rhetoric. But the Chief Justice's early assertion of the principle in decisions like M'Culloch has helped in the long run to insure that those challenges would lack the support of the American people. "Let the end be legitimate . . . ," Marshall's expansive rule for judging the scope of the implied powers, is surely one of the most frequently cited sentences in constitutional annals. In 1819 and for some decades thereafter Congress was little disposed to exercise the vast range of power this rule bestows. But when it began, in the late nineteenth century, to pass national regulatory laws, the rule was ready as a justification for them, and it continues as the constitutional mainstay of national power to the present day. Even the terse statement "we must never forget, that it is a constitution we are expounding" is as pregnant today as in 1819, for it summarizes aphoristically what has come to be the dominant conception of the nature of the Constitution.

The second part of the opinion, explaining why Maryland's tax on the Bank was unconstitutional, also has enjoyed an eventful, though very different, history. Marshall's words "the power to tax involves the power to destroy" were instrumental in promoting his nationalist purposes. Since the power to tax carries such a potential, we cannot concede a state's power to tax an agency of the national government; for that would mean that an inferior state could destroy its superior, that the part could frustrate the whole. But the phrase also had the epigrammatic, truistic ring that sometimes turns sentences into maxims and endows them with lives of their own. Its implications were seized by later judges to support the doctrine of "intergovernmental tax immunity"—that neither the states nor the nation could tax the instrumentalities of the other. For generations judges and lawyers elaborated this doctrine that had its origin in Marshall's special taste for sweeping language. It was only in the 1930's that the Supreme Court finally repudiated most of the inferences from his epigram by adopting in considerable degree the counter-epigram of Justice Holmes: "the power to tax is not the power to destroy while this court sits."

James Monroe
The Monroe Doctrine
1823

EDITED BY DEXTER PERKINS

The Monroe Doctrine, embodied in President James Monroe's message to Congress of December 2, 1823, had a dual origin.

On the one hand, it was related to the controversy between Russia and the United States over the northwest coast of America. The Russians claimed this coast from the Behring Straits south to an undetermined line on the Pacific Coast, and in February of 1821 the Russian government issued a ukase forbidding foreign ships to approach within one hundred miles of the shore. The American government contested this decree. In the course of discussions with the Russian minister in Washington, Secretary of State John Quincy Adams declared that "we should assume distinctly the principle that the American continents are no longer subjects for any new colonial establishments." Adams also suggested that a declaration to this effect be made in the presidential message of 1823, and his language was taken over by the President.

The second question that gave rise to the Monroe Doctrine was that of the Spanish-American colonies, most of which had revolted and attained independence by 1823, and some of which the United States had recognized. At this time continental Europe was in the grip of reaction, and the continental powers, loosely known as the Holy Alliance (Russia, France, Austria, and Prussia), had intervened to put down revolution in Naples (1821) and Spain (1823). In the summer of 1823 conversations between the British Foreign Secretary, George Canning, and the American minister at London, Richard Rush, seemed to suggest the possibility of similar repressive action in Latin America. Only a little later the language of the Russian Tsar with regard to the colonies suggested that intervention to restore the colonies to Spain might be under consideration.

In lengthy Cabinet discussions in November Monroe and his advisers went over the whole question. Should the United States join with Great Britain, as Canning had suggested, in some common declaration of interest in the independence of the Spanish-American colonies? Or should it act unilaterally? Jefferson and Madison, whom Monroe had informed of the British overture, favored common action. But Monroe, on his own initiative, determined to deal with the problem in his message to Congress. His original draft, which included references to European repressive policies in Spain, and an expression of sympathy with the Greek rebels, was sharply criticized by Adams. The Secretary declared it necessary to "make an American cause and adhere inflexibly to that." He and Monroe accordingly revised the message, drawing a sharp line between the New World and the Old. Thus both the President and the Secretary deserve credit for the enunciation of the Monroe Doctrine.

. . . At the proposal of the Russian imperial government, made through the minister of the Emperor residing here, a full power and instructions have been transmitted to the Minister of the United States at St. Petersburgh, to arrange, by amicable negotiation, the respective rights and interests of the two nations on the northwest coast of this continent. A similar proposal has been made by his Imperial Majesty to the government of Great Britain, which has likewise been acceded to. The government of the United States has been desirous, by this friendly proceeding, of manifesting the great value which they have invariably attached to the friendship of the emperor, and their solicitude to cultivate the best understanding with his government. In the discussions to which this interest has given rise, and in the arrangements by which they may terminate, the occasion has been judged proper for

---

Monroe's draft of the message is in the National Archives. Senate and House versions of the text vary slightly. About one-sixth of the House version is reprinted here from *House Documents, Eighteenth Congress, First Session, 1823–1824*, Vol. I, No. 2 (Washington, D.C.: Gales and Seaton, 1823), December 2, 1823, pp. 3–15.

asserting, as a principle in which the rights and interests of the United States are involved, that the American continents, by the free and independent condition which they have assumed and maintain, are henceforth not to be considered as subjects for future colonization by any European powers.

. . . It was stated at the commencement of the last session, that a great effort was then making in Spain and Portugal, to improve the condition of the people of those countries; and that it appeared to be conducted with extraordinary moderation. It need scarcely be remarked, that the result has been, so far, very different from what was then anticipated. Of events in that quarter of the globe, with which we have so much intercourse, and from which we derive our origin, we have always been anxious and interested spectators. The citizens of the United States cherish sentiments the most friendly, in favor of the liberty and happiness of their fellow men on that side of the Atlantic. In the wars of the European powers, in matters relating to themselves, we have never taken any part, nor does it comport with our policy so to do. It is only when our rights are invaded, or seriously menaced, that we resent injuries, or make preparation for our defence. With the movements in this hemisphere, we are, of necessity, more immediately connected, and by causes which must be obvious to all enlightened and impartial observers. The political system of the allied powers is essentially different, in this respect, from that of America. This difference proceeds from that which exists in their respective governments. And to the defence of our own, which has been achieved by the loss of so much blood and treasure, and matured by the wisdom of their most enlightened citizens, and under which we have enjoyed unexampled felicity, this whole nation is devoted. We owe it, therefore, to candor, and to the amicable relations existing between the United States and those powers, to declare, that we should consider any attempt on their part to extend their system to any portion of this hemisphere, as dangerous to our peace and safety. With the existing colonies or dependencies of any European power, we have not interfered, and shall not interfere. But, with the governments who have declared their independence, and maintained it, and whose independence we have, on great consideration, and on just principles, acknowledged, we could not view any interposition for the purpose of oppressing them, or controlling, in any other manner, their destiny, by any European power, in any other light than as the manifestation of an unfriendly disposition towards the United States. In the war between these new governments and Spain, we

declared our neutrality at the time of their recognition, and to this we
have adhered, and shall continue to adhere, provided no change shall
occur, which, in the judgment of the competent authorities of this
government, shall make a corresponding change, on the part of the
United States, indispensable to their security.

The late events in Spain and Portugal, shew that Europe is still
unsettled. Of this important fact, no stronger proof can be adduced
than that the allied powers should have thought it proper, on any
principle satisfactory to themselves, to have interposed, by force, in the
internal concerns of Spain. To what extent such interposition may be
carried, on the same principle, is a question, in which all independent
powers, whose governments differ from theirs, are interested; even
those most remote, and surely none more so than the United States. Our
policy, in regard to Europe, which was adopted at an early stage of the
wars which have so long agitated that quarter of the globe, nevertheless remains the same, which is, not to interfere in the internal concerns
of any of its powers; to consider the government *de facto* as the
legitimate government for us; to cultivate friendly relations with it, and
to preserve those relations by a frank, firm, and manly policy, meeting, in
all instances, the just claims of every power; submitting to injuries from
none. But, in regard to those continents, circumstances are eminently
and conspicuously different. It is impossible that the allied powers
should extend their political system to any portion of either continent,
without endangering our peace and happiness; nor can any one believe
that our Southern Brethren, if left to themselves, would adopt it of their
own accord. It is equally impossible, therefore, that we should behold
such interposition, in any form, with indifference. If we look to the
comparative strength and resources of Spain and those new governments, and their distance from each other, it must be obvious that she
can never subdue them. It is still the true policy of the United States, to
leave the parties to themselves, in the hope that other powers will
pursue the same course. . . .

*The practical effects of the message of 1823 were not great. It is now
known that there was no danger whatsoever of the reconquest of the
Spanish-American colonies by the Holy Alliance. As early as October,*

1823, France, whose cooperation would have been essential to the enterprise, had assured the British government that no such project was contemplated. Without exception, the continental powers ignored Monroe's message in public, and condemned it in private. Metternich, the Austrian Chancellor, described it as an "indecent declaration"; and the Russian Foreign Minister declared that it merited the "most profound contempt." The physical power of the United States was quite inadequate to oppose a serious enterprise of reconquest.

Nor did the paragraph on the northwest coast have any impact. It was ignored by the Russian government; Russia and the United States later reached a compromise settlement on the northwest-coast controversy without any reference to Monroe's message.

Finally, the message was received with mixed emotions in Great Britain. British liberals applauded it, but Canning was chagrined that the American President had beaten him to the punch in issuing a public declaration in defense of the Latin-Americans, and was also displeased by the noncolonization principle.

The message did not, we now know, stave off European action against the colonies; no such action had been intended. It was not immediately accepted as a great declaration of principle—a "doctrine." And though discussed in 1824–26, it nearly faded from sight for almost twenty years thereafter. It was strikingly revived by President James K. Polk in his message of December 2, 1845, when he used Monroe's statement to support the American stand against British policy with regard to Texas and Oregon, and against suspected British designs on California, then a province of Mexico. It was frequently cited in the early 1850's in connection with Anglo-American rivalry in Central America.

By 1853 the phrase "Monroe Doctrine" appears, though more frequently among the Democrats than the Whigs. In the Civil War, and the years just after, the declaration was invoked in opposition to the French intervention in Mexico, which had as its object the establishment of the Austrian Archduke Maximilian as Emperor (though Secretary of State Seward never mentioned the Monroe Doctrine by name in his correspondence with the French). By the end of the sixties it had become a national dogma. It was broadened by President Grant to forbid the transfer of European territory in the New World from one power to another. President Hayes extended it still further, asserting the principle that any interoceanic canal should be under American control. Grover Cleveland, in one of the most extraordinary assertions of the Monroe principle, insisted upon the arbitration of a boundary dispute between Great Britain and Venezuela over the limits of British Guiana. By the end of the nineteenth century the Doctrine had become a deeply cherished principle of American foreign policy.

Down to this time the United States had never protested when European powers took punitive action against American states, so long as no question of territorial occupation was involved. In 1902 the British and German governments instituted a blockade against Venezuela, to force the Venezuelan government to give redress for damages suffered by their nationals. We know today that no more than this purpose was intended. But a vigorous movement of protest developed in the United States, and the Roosevelt Administration, though it had not originally objected to the British and German action, was influenced to extend the Monroe Doctrine. Fearing new interventions, Theodore Roosevelt enunciated in 1905 the principle that "chronic wrong-doing, or an impotence resulting in a general loosening of the ties of civilized society on the part of a country in the Western Hemisphere" might require the United States to exercise an international police power. This declaration has become known as the "Roosevelt Corollary."

The solicitude of the United States over its interests in the Caribbean was naturally increased by the construction of the Panama Canal. The Roosevelt Corollary seemed to fit this situation. Unsettled conditions in Nicaragua, in Haiti, and in the Dominican Republic also led to interventions on the part of the United States.

This extension of the Monroe Doctrine proved profoundly unpopular in Latin America. American troops withdrew from the Dominican Republic in 1924. By 1928 the United States was put very definitely on the defensive at the Havana meeting of the Pan-American Conference. In 1929, the Senate, in ratifying the Kellogg-Briand Pact for the renunciation of war, appended a gloss which dissociated the Corollary from the Doctrine. The pressure continued. By 1933, at the next Pan-American Conference, the United States put its name to a protocol which formally forbade intervention by any state in the domestic or foreign affairs of another. In 1936, at a special conference at Buenos Aires, the same principle was reasserted in still more binding form. These two protocols were overwhelmingly ratified by the Senate of the United States.

In the period since 1933, the Monroe Doctrine has been frequently invoked by American publicists, and by American politicians, as the need has arisen. But there has been a disposition on the part of the government itself to refer to the principle of Pan-American solidarity, rather than to use the language of Monroe. Thus the principles of 1823 have been sustained without giving offense to the sensitive pride of the Latin Americans, to whom the Doctrine has always seemed touched with a claim on the part of the United States to hegemony or domination.

During World War II, the United States made skillful use of the Grant doctrine without directly appealing to it. After the Germans conquered Holland and France, apprehension arose that they might seize Dutch or French colonies in the New World. At the Pan-American Conference in the summer of 1940, the principle was reasserted that no territory in the New World could be transferred from one power to another, and the United States was authorized, in an emergency, to act unilaterally to enforce this principle.

A further application of Monroe's principles is to be found in the agreements made by the United States and the Latin-American states against European aggression. The first of these agreements was made at Lima in 1938; more important and far-reaching compacts were made at Chapultepec in 1945 and at Rio de Janeiro in 1947. These agreements called for collective action in the event of direct attack from abroad. They do not touch the question of internal subversion, or of the establishment of Communist or proto-Communist regimes. Such a regime appeared in Guatemala in 1954. It was overthrown by Guatemalans themselves, but only after many references to the Doctrine in the press, and sub rosa assistance from the United States. At the time the other Latin-American states, devoted as they are to the principle of nonintervention, cannot be said to have been vigorous in support of the United States government.

A much more serious situation arose a few years later in Cuba. A Communist government was installed there in 1959. In 1962 that government, under Fidel Castro, accepted from the Russians missile weapons which threatened the southern United States and northern Latin America. President Kennedy instituted a blockade of Cuba, and demanded of the Kremlin the withdrawal of the weapons. After several days of crisis, the Russians yielded. In this confrontation the United States was supported by the Latin-American states. No mention was made of the Monroe Doctrine, but the principles of the Doctrine were brilliantly upheld.

In 1965 new difficulties in the Caribbean occurred. In the Dominican

Republic a revolutionary movement, with certain Communist elements behind it, threatened the safety of the American residents. For the first time in a generation, the American government landed the Marines. But it sought to associate other Latin-American states with the occupation, and several such states accepted. As in the Cuban case, no mention was made of the Monroe Doctrine; the episode raises the question whether the nonintervention principle will be modified or abandoned when what is at stake is the Communization of a New World state.

The Monroe Doctrine has had a long existence, and it is still cherished by the American people. Its fundamental principle is sound: that is, the defense of the American continents against alien doctrine or conquest. But in the practice of diplomacy, it has been deemed more expedient to avoid reference to the Doctrine, which sometimes wounds Latin-American susceptibilities, and to rely, wherever possible, on the principle of self-defense and on the solidarity of the Americas.

Andrew Jackson
The Majority Is To Govern
1829

EDITED BY JOHN WILLIAM WARD

Because one of its premises was an implicit trust in the common sense of the common man, Jacksonian democracy lacks its philosopher. But a characteristic statement which asserts "the first principle" of Jacksonian democracy is Andrew Jackson's first message to Congress upon becoming President. Here he speaks for the principle which has kept his name alive in the historical memory of the American people: the will of the people is the fundamental source of all power. Power is responsible finally to the majority.

In 1824, Jackson had received a plurality of the popular and electoral vote in a four-cornered race for the Presidency, followed by John Quincy Adams, William Crawford, and Henry Clay. Since no candidate had a majority, selection devolved on the House of Representatives, where choice, according to the provision of the Constitution, lay among the three leading candidates. Clay, now excluded as a candidate, threw his political influence behind Adams, and after Adams became President he named Clay his Secretary of State, placing him in the office which to that time had been the conventional stepping stone to the Presidency. Immediately Jacksonian partisans raised the cry of a "corrupt bargain" between Adams and Clay and began the campaign which was to bring Jackson to the White House in 1828.

James Parton, Jackson's contemporary and first and still best biographer, tells how Jackson went about preparing his messages. He used to begin, says Parton, some months beforehand, gathering ideas and jotting down notes, and when the time came all were turned over to his private secretary, Andrew Jackson Donelson, who then put them in order. Unlike his predecessors in the office of President, Jackson did not use his Cabinet as a council of state. He relied more on a personal staff of advisers in the White House, the "Kitchen Cabinet," and tended to treat Cabinet members as administrative officers. When Donelson had drafted a message, Jackson would consult informally with his own intimate staff before arriving at a final version. Characteristically, a Jackson message was a collective effort, but the ideas were always Jackson's.

Against the background of the "corrupt bargain" Jackson, in his first presidential address to Congress, catechized the legislative branch on the principles of democratic government. In the course of his message, delivered on December 8, 1829, he laid bare the major assumptions of his democratic faith.

FELLOW CITIZENS OF THE SENATE, AND
HOUSE OF REPRESENTATIVES:

IT AFFORDS me pleasure to tender my friendly greetings to you on the occasion of your assembling at the Seat of Government, to enter upon the important duties to which you have been called by the voice of our countrymen. The task devolves on me, under a provision of the Constitution, to present to you, as the Federal Legislature of twenty-four sovereign States, and twelve millions of happy people, a view of our affairs; and to propose such measures as, in the discharge of my official functions, have suggested themselves as necessary to promote the objects of our Union.

In communicating with you for the first time, it is, to me, a source of unfeigned satisfaction, calling for mutual gratulation and devout thanks to a benign Providence, that we are at peace with all mankind; and that

---

The text is reproduced here from *Message from the President of the United States to the Two Houses of Congress at the Commencement of the First Session of the Twenty-first Congress, December 8, 1829* (Washington: Printed by Duff Green, 1829). Jackson's speech may also be found in *Senate Documents* (1829–30), I, Document 1. Approximately two-fifths of the speech appears here.

our country exhibits the most cheering evidence of general welfare and progressive improvement. Turning our eyes to other nations, our great desire is to see our brethren of the human race secured in the blessings enjoyed by ourselves, and advancing in knowledge, in freedom, and in social happiness.

Our foreign relations, although in their general character pacific and friendly, present subjects of difference between us and other Powers, of deep interest, as well to the country at large as to many of our citizens. To effect an adjustment of these shall continue to be the object of my earnest endeavors; and notwithstanding the difficulties of the task, I do not allow myself to apprehend unfavorable results. Blessed as our country is with every thing which constitutes national strength, she is fully adequate to the maintenance of all her interests. In discharging the responsible trust confided to the Executive in this respect, it is my settled purpose to ask nothing that is not clearly right, and to submit to nothing that is wrong; and I flatter myself, that, supported by the other branches of the Government, and by the intelligence and patriotism of the People, we shall be able, under the protection of Providence, to cause all our just rights to be respected. . . .

I consider it one of the most urgent of my duties to bring to your attention the propriety of amending that part of our Constitution which relates to the election of President and Vice President. Our system of government was, by its framers, deemed an experiment; and they, therefore, consistently provided a mode of remedying its defects.

To the People belongs the right of electing their Chief Magistrate: it was never designed that their choice should, in any case, be defeated, either by the intervention of electoral colleges, or by the agency confided, under certain contingencies, to the House of Representatives. Experience proves, that, in proportion as agents to execute the will of the People are multiplied, there is danger of their wishes being frustrated. Some may be unfaithful: all are liable to err. So far, therefore, as the People can, with convenience, speak, it is safer for them to express their own will.

The number of aspirants to the Presidency, and the diversity of the interests which may influence their claims, leave little reason to expect a choice in the first instance: and, in that event, the election must devolve on the House of Representatives, where, it is obvious, the will of the People may not be always ascertained; or, if ascertained, may not be regarded. From the mode of voting by States, the choice is to be made by twenty-four votes; and it may often occur, that one of these will be controlled by an individual representative. Honors and offices are at the disposal of the successful candidate. Repeated ballotings may make it apparent that a single individual holds the cast in his hand. May he not be tempted to name his reward? But even without corruption—supposing the probity of the Representative to be proof against the powerful motives by which it may be assailed—the will of the People is still constantly liable to be misrepresented. One may err from ignorance of the wishes of his constituents; another, from a conviction that it is his duty to be governed by his own judgment of the fitness of the candidates: finally, although all were inflexibly honest—all accurately informed of the wishes of their constituents—yet, under the present mode of election, a minority may often elect the President; and when this happens, it may reasonably be expected that efforts will be made on the part of the majority to rectify this injurious operation of their institutions. But although no evil of this character should result from such a perversion of the first principle of our system—*that the majority is to govern*—it must be very certain that a President elected by a minority cannot enjoy the confidence necessary to the successful discharge of his duties.

In this, as in all other matters of public concern, policy requires that as few impediments as possible should exist to the free operation of the public will. Let us, then, endeavor so to amend our system, that the office of Chief Magistrate may not be conferred upon any citizen but in pursuance of a fair expression of the will of the majority.

I would therefore recommend such an amendment of the Constitution as may remove all intermediate agency in the election of President and Vice President. The mode may be so regulated as to preserve to each State its present relative weight in the election; and a failure in the first attempt may be provided for, by confining the second to a choice between the two highest candidates. In connexion with such an amendment, it would seem advisable to limit the service of the Chief Magistrate to a single term, of either four or six years. If, however, it should not be adopted, it is worthy of consideration whether a provision disqualifying for office the Representatives in Congress on whom such an election may have devolved, would not be proper.

While members of Congress can be constitutionally appointed to offices of trust and profit, it will be the practice, even under the most conscientious adherence to duty, to select them for such stations as they are believed to be better qualified to fill than other citizens; but the purity of our Government would doubtless be promoted, by their exclusion from all appointments in the gift of the President in whose election they may have been officially concerned. The nature of the judicial office, and the necessity of securing in the Cabinet and in diplomatic stations of the highest rank, the best talents and political experience, should, perhaps, except these from the exclusion.

There are perhaps few men who can for any great length of time enjoy office and power, without being more or less under the influence of feelings unfavorable to the faithful discharge of their public duties. Their integrity may be proof against improper considerations imme- diately addressed to themselves; but they are apt to acquire a habit of looking with indifference upon the public interests, and of tolerating conduct from which an unpractised man would revolt. Office is consid- ered as a species of property; and Government, rather as a means of promoting individual interests, than as an instrument created solely for the service of the People. Corruption in some, and, in others, a perversion of correct feelings and principles, divert Government from its legitimate ends, and make it an engine for the support of the few at the expense of the many. The duties of all public officers are, or, at least, admit of being made, so plain and simple, that men of intelligence may readily qualify themselves for their performance; and I cannot but believe that more is lost by the long continuance of men in office, than is generally to be gained by their experience. I submit therefore to your consideration, whether the efficiency of the Government would not be promoted, and official industry and integrity better secured, by a general extension of the law which limits appointments to four years.

In a country where offices are created solely for the benefit of the People, no one man has any more intrinsic right to official station than another. Offices were not established to give support to particular men, at the public expense. No individual wrong is therefore done by removal, since neither appointment to, nor continuance in, office, is matter of right. The incumbent became an officer with a view to public benefits; and when these require his removal, they are not to be sacrificed to private interests. It is the People, and they alone, who have a right to complain, when a bad officer is substituted for a good one. He who is removed has the same means of obtaining a living, that are enjoyed by the millions who never held office. The proposed limitation would destroy the idea of property, now so generally connected with official station; and although individual distress may be sometimes produced, it would, by promoting that rotation which constitutes a leading principle in the republican creed, give healthful action to the system.

No very considerable change has occurred, during the recess of Congress, in the condition of either our Agriculture, Commerce, or Manufactures. . . .

. . . To regulate its conduct, so as to promote equally the prosperity of these three cardinal interests, is one of the most difficult tasks of Government; and it may be regretted that the complicated restrictions which now embarrass the intercourse of nations, could not by common consent be abolished; and commerce allowed to flow in those channels to which individual enterprise—always its surest guide—might direct it. . . . Frequent legislation in regard to any branch of industry, affecting its value, and by which its capital may be transferred to new channels, must always be productive of hazardous speculation and loss.

In deliberating, therefore, on these interesting subjects, local feelings and prejudices should be merged in the patriotic determination to promote the great interests of the whole. All attempts to connect them with the party conflicts of the day are necessarily injurious, and should be discountenanced. Our action upon them should be under the control of higher and purer motives. Legislation, subjected to such influences, can never be just; and will not long retain the sanction of a People, whose active patriotism is not bounded by sectional limits, nor insensible to that spirit of concession and forbearance, which gave life to our political compact, and still sustains it. Discarding all calculations of political ascendancy, the North, the South, the East, and the West, should unite in diminishing any burthen, of which either may justly complain.

The agricultural interest of our country is so essentially connected with every other, and so superior in importance to them all, that it is scarcely necessary to invite to it your particular attention. It is principally as manufactures and commerce tend to increase the value of agricultural productions, and to extend their application to the wants and comforts of society, that they deserve the fostering care of Government. . . .

[The] state of the finances exhibits the resources of the nation in an aspect highly flattering to its industry; and auspicious of the ability of Government, in a very short time, to extinguish the public debt. When this shall be done, our population will be relieved from a considerable portion of its present burthens; and will find, not only new motives to patriotic affection, but additional means for the display of individual enterprise. The fiscal power of the States will also be increased; and may be more extensively exerted in favor of education and other public objects: while ample means will remain in the Federal Government to promote the general weal, in all the modes permitted to its authority.

After the extinction of the public debt, it is not probable that any adjustment of the tariff, upon principles satisfactory to the People of the Union, will, until a remote period, if ever, leave the Government without a considerable surplus in the Treasury, beyond what may be required for its current service. As then the period approaches when the application of the revenue to the payment of debt will cease, the disposition of the surplus will present a subject for the serious deliberation of Congress; and it may be fortunate for the country that it is yet to be decided. . . .

. . . It appears to me that the most safe, just, and federal disposition which could be made of the surplus revenue, would be its apportionment among the several States according to their ratio of representation; and should this measure not be found warranted by the Constitution, that it would be expedient to propose to the States an amendment authorizing it. I regard an appeal to the source of power, in cases of real doubt, and where its exercise is deemed indispensable to the general welfare, as among the most sacred of all our obligations. Upon this country, more than any other, has, in the providence of God, been cast the special guardianship of the great principle of adherence to written constitutions. If it fail here, all hope in regard to it will be extinguished. That this was intended to be a Government of limited and specific, and not general powers, must be admitted by all; and it is our duty to preserve for it the character intended by its framers. If experience points out the necessity for an enlargement of these powers, let us apply for it to those for whose benefit it is to be exercised; and not undermine the whole system by a resort to overstrained constructions. The scheme has worked well. It has exceeded the hopes of those who devised it, and become an object of admiration to the world. We are responsible to our country, and to the glorious cause of self-government, for the preservation of so great a good. The great mass of legislation relating to our internal affairs, was intended to be left where the Federal Convention found it—in the State Governments. Nothing is clearer, in my view, than that we are chiefly indebted for the success of the Constitution under which we are now acting, to the watchful and auxiliary operation of the State authorities. This is not the reflection of a day, but belongs to the most deeply rooted convictions of my mind. I cannot, therefore, too strongly or too earnestly, for my own sense of its importance, warn you against all encroachments upon the legitimate sphere of State sovereignty. Sustained by its healthful and invigorating influence, the Federal system can never fall. . . .

. . . I would suggest, also, an inquiry, whether the provisions of the act of Congress, authorizing the discharge of the persons of debtors to the Government, from imprisonment, may not, consistently with the public interest, be extended to the release of the debt, where the conduct of the debtor is wholly exempt from the imputation of fraud. Some more liberal policy than that which now prevails, in reference to this unfortunate class of citizens, is certainly due to them, and would prove beneficial to the country. The continuance of the liability, after the means to discharge it have been exhausted, can only serve to dispirit the debtor; or, where his resources are but partial, the want of power in the Government to compromise and release the demand, instigates to fraud, as the only resource for securing a support to his family. He thus sinks into a state of apathy, and becomes a useless drone in society, or a vicious member of it, if not a feeling witness of the rigor and inhumanity of his country. All experience proves, that oppressive debt is the bane of enterprise; and it should be the care of a Republic not to exert a grinding power over misfortune and poverty. . . .

The condition and ulterior destiny of the Indian Tribes within the limits of some of our States, have become objects of much interest and importance. It has long been the policy of Government to introduce among them the arts of civilization, in the hope of gradually reclaiming them from a wandering life. This policy has, however, been coupled with another, wholly incompatible with its success. Professing a desire to civilize and settle them, we have, at the same time, lost no opportunity to purchase their lands, and thrust them further into the wilderness. By this means they have not only been kept in a wandering state, but been led to look upon us as unjust and indifferent to their fate. Thus, though lavish in its expenditures upon the subject, Government has constantly defeated its own policy; and the Indians, in general, receding further and further to the West, have retained their savage habits. A portion, however, of the Southern tribes, having mingled much with the whites, and made some progress in the arts of civilized life, have lately attempted to erect an independent government, within the limits of Georgia and Alabama. These States, claiming to be the only Sovereigns within their territories, extended their laws over the Indians; which induced the latter to call upon the United States for protection.

Under these circumstances, the question presented was, whether the General Government had a right to sustain those people in their pretensions? The Constitution declares, that "no new State shall be formed or erected within the jurisdiction of any other State," without the consent of its legislature. If the General Government is not permitted to tolerate the erection of a confederate State within the territory of one of the members of this Union, against her consent; much less could it allow a foreign and independent government to establish itself there. Georgia became a member of the Confederacy which eventuated in our Federal Union, as a sovereign State, always asserting her claim to certain limits; which having been originally defined in her colonial charter, and subsequently recognised in the treaty of peace, she has ever since continued to enjoy, except as they have been circumscribed by her own voluntary transfer of a portion of her territory to the United States, in the articles of cession of 1802. Alabama was admitted into the Union on the same footing with the original States, with boundaries which were prescribed by Congress. There is no constitutional, conventional, or legal provision, which allows them less power over the Indians within their borders, than is possessed by Maine or New York. Would the People of Maine permit the Penobscot tribe to erect an Independent Government within their State? and unless they did, would it not be the duty of the General Government to support them in resisting such a measure? Would the People of New York permit each remnant of the Six Nations within her borders, to declare itself an independent people under the protection of the United States? Could the Indians establish a separate republic on each of their reservations in Ohio? and if they were so disposed, would it be the duty of this Government to protect them in the attempt? If the principle involved in the obvious answer to these questions be abandoned, it will follow that the objects of this Government are reversed; and that it has become a part of its duty to aid in destroying the States which it was established to protect.

Actuated by this view of the subject, I informed the Indians inhabiting parts of Georgia and Alabama, that their attempt to establish an independent government would not be countenanced by the Executive of the United States; and advised them to emigrate beyond the Mississippi, or submit to the laws of those States.

Our conduct towards these people is deeply interesting to our national character. Their present condition, contrasted with what they once were, makes a most powerful appeal to our sympathies. Our ancestors found them the uncontrolled possessors of these vast regions. By persuasion and force, they have been made to retire from river to river, and from mountain to mountain; until some of the tribes have become extinct, and others have left but remnants, to preserve, for a while, their once terrible names. Surrounded by the whites, with their arts of civilization, which, by destroying the resources of the savage, doom him to weakness and decay; the fate of the Mohegan, the Narragansett, and the Delaware, is fast overtaking the Choctaw, the Cherokee, and the Creek. That this fate surely awaits them, if they remain within the limits of the States, does not admit of a doubt. Humanity and national honor demand that every effort should be made to avert so great a calamity. It is too late to inquire whether it was just in the United States to include them and their territory within the bounds of new States whose limits they could control. That step cannot be retraced. A State cannot be dismembered by Congress, or restricted in the exercise of her constitutional power. But the people of those States, and of every State, actuated by feelings of justice and a regard for our national honor, submit to you the interesting question, whether something cannot be done, consistently with the rights of the States, to preserve this much injured race?

As a means of effecting this end, I suggest, for your consideration, the propriety of setting apart an ample district West of the Mississippi, and without the limits of any State or Territory, now formed, to be guarantied to the Indian tribes, as long as they shall occupy it: each tribe having a distinct control over the portion designated for its use. There they may be secured in the enjoyment of governments of their own choice, subject to no other control from the United States than such as may be necessary to preserve peace on the frontier, and between the several tribes. There the benevolent may endeavor to teach them the arts of civilization; and, by promoting union and harmony among them, to raise up an interesting commonwealth, destined to perpetuate the race, and to attest the humanity and justice of this Government.

This emigration should be voluntary: for it would be as cruel as unjust to compel the aborigines to abandon the graves of their fathers, and seek a home in a distant land. But they should be distinctly informed that, if they remain within the limits of the States, they must be subject to their laws. In return for their obedience, as individuals, they will, without doubt, be protected in the enjoyment of those possessions which they have improved by their industry. But it seems to me visionary to suppose, that, in this state of things, claims can be allowed on tracts of country on which they have neither dwelt nor made improvements, merely because they have seen them from the mountain, or passed them in the chace. Submitting to the laws of the States, and receiving, like other citizens, protection in their persons and property, they will, ere long, become merged in the mass of our population. . . .

I now commend you, fellow-citizens, to the guidance of Almighty God, with a full reliance on his merciful providence for the maintenance of our free institutions; and with an earnest supplication, that, whatever errors it may be my lot to commit, in discharging the arduous duties which have devolved on me, will find a remedy in the harmony and wisdom of your counsels.

ANDREW JACKSON

The good society for which Jackson spoke embodied three themes: rule by the will of the people, the avoidance of corruption, and simplicity of government. When Jackson says "the first principle of our system" is "that the majority is to govern," he is himself on uncertain historical ground. The Constitution to which Jackson appeals is not a document devised to implement a thoroughgoing domination by the majority in politics. Jackson, in saying it is, seems to be verging toward the majoritarian position whose probable consequences so concerned Alexis de Tocqueville in his analysis of democracy in the America of Jackson's time. But as one watches the development of Jackson's argument, one sees him avoid in an astonishing way the tyranny of the majority which Tocqueville feared.

The premise of Jackson's message is a trust in the will of a virtuous and competent people. As far as they can, the "People" should act directly. But "experience proves," as for Jackson it clearly did in 1824, that agents trusted with the power of translating the will of the people into reality will, inevitably, be corrupted by that power: "Office is considered as a species of property; and Government, rather as a means of promoting individual interests, than as an instrument created solely for the service of the People." To avoid such corruption, Jackson spoke for limited tenure for the President and rotation in all appointive offices. Later generations would stigmatize the principle by remembering it only as the "spoils system." It is true that Jackson was enough of a politician to recognize the uses of patronage, but he embraced the system as a species of reform. His rejection of a trained and experienced class of civil servants, a gesture which made Jackson's memory a curse to reformers who came after him, was possible only on the assumption that the work of government was essentially so plain and simple that the average intelligent man could do the job. Jackson's solution to the paradox of politics, the corruption of the selfless will of the people by the power necessary to enact that will, was no less than to dismiss the need for power in politics at all. If power corrupts, then America was in the happy state of having no need for power.

Jackson's ideal in politics was the limited state of classical liberalism. The chief action of government was not to act, and the major issues of Jackson's Presidency bear witness to his ideal. His extensive use of the veto power, his removals from office, his attack on the Second Bank of the United States, and his denial of the propriety of federal participation in internal improvements were all designed to strip the central government of the accretions of power. Jackson's only positive assertion of federal power was his Proclamation against the doctrine of nullification in 1832 when South Carolina threatened the very existence of the Union. Paradoxically, Jackson's vigorous Presidency schooled subsequent Presidents in the power of the office, but his own intention ran in the opposite direction. It ran in the direction of a purely administrative state which beyond the minimal preservation of law and order left the business of society "to flow in those channels to which individual enterprise—always its surest guide—might direct it."

If the particular occasion of Jackson's address is important, the larger occasion, the general economic and social context in which he spoke, is even more so. Jackson assumed that the best way to serve the general interest of society was to have a simple and limited government which would leave each individual free to pursue his own self-interest. He could make this assumption only in the context of conditions of general equality in an agrarian society, unhampered by debt and untroubled by the threat of foreign enemies, supported by the seemingly limitless expanse of a virgin continent whose Indians posed the chief problem for the American conscience. Looked at from the vantage point of our own present, the age of Jackson has a pastoral air about it. The consequence Jackson did not foresee, and which we see so clearly because we have experienced it, was that to dismiss power from the realm of politics left power unhampered and unchecked in other areas of society, especially the economic.

"In elective government," wrote Frederick Grimké, a contemporary of Andrew Jackson, "public men may be said to be the representatives of the ideas of the age, as well as of the grosser interests with which they have to deal; and to give those ideas a visible form, is the most certain way of commanding public attention, and of stimulating inquiry." Because of Andrew Jackson's dramatic success in giving the ideas of his age a visible form, we remember that age by his very name. But the ideals he once acted out in politics seem still to speak to us, who live in a drastically different age.

"To most of us," said Franklin D. Roosevelt in a radio broadcast from Washington in 1936, "Andrew Jackson appropriately has become the symbol of certain great ideals." The ideal which Roosevelt saw embodied in Jackson's career bore upon the "real issue" still before the American people: "the right of the average man and woman to lead a finer, a better and a happier life." Yet long before Roosevelt discovered a use for the sanctions of the Jacksonian heritage, other Americans, also living in years of change and economic and social disorder, had looked to Jackson to find a meaning quite different from the one Roosevelt was to find. In 1883, the president of the Western Union Telegraph Company, arguing in behalf of the "laws of supply and demand" and against "legislative interference," said, "I am a believer in that old maxim of General Jackson: 'That people is governed best which is governed least.'" Intellectuals of the time agreed, just as intellectuals later were to agree with Roosevelt. William Graham Sumner argued that Jackson was, although by instinct rather than thought, a better political philosopher for America than Alexander Hamilton, because Jackson firmly opposed positive action by the state in the affairs of society. Intellectuals of the age of Roosevelt found Jackson to mean that government, acting on behalf of the common man, should intervene in the social and economic order and discipline the business community to make it conform to the interests of the majority.

William Lloyd Garrison
Prospectus for the "Liberator"
1831

EDITED BY KENNETH M. STAMPP

Emerson once asked: "What is man born for but to be a Reformer, a Remaker of what man has made; a renouncer of lies; a restorer of truth and good . . . ?" Many of Emerson's New England contemporaries agreed with him and devoted their lives to various movements for moral uplift or social reform, but none more fervently than William Lloyd Garrison.

Born in Newburyport, Massachusetts, in 1805, Garrison experienced both poverty and insecurity in his childhood. His father, a sailor, deserted the family when Garrison was an infant; his mother, an austere, pious Baptist, made her son aware of the prevalence of sin in the world but offered him neither warmth nor understanding. As a youth Garrison learned the printer's trade and developed a taste for polemical newspaper writing. He had considerable talent, and with it he combined a strong ambition to win public recognition—in order, as he once said, to have his name known "in a praiseworthy manner."

Reform journalism was Garrison's road to fame. In 1828 he went first to Boston to edit the National Philanthropist, a temperance weekly, then to Bennington, Vermont, to edit the Journal of the Times, in whose columns he preached temperance, world peace, and the gradual abolition of slavery. The survival of slavery in the southern states, he told a Boston audience on July 4, 1829, was a "glaring contradiction" of the American creed of liberty and equality. The free states had a right to demand gradual emancipation, because as long as slavery existed "they participate in the guilt thereof." Soon after making this speech, Garrison abandoned gradualism and began to demand the immediate abolition of slavery. Since slaveholding was a sin, to advocate gradual emancipation was like asking a thief gradually to abandon a life of crime.

In August, 1829, Garrison moved to Baltimore to join the gentle Quaker Benjamin Lundy in editing an antislavery newspaper, the Genius of Universal Emancipation. Two months later, in one of his editorials, Garrison violently upbraided Francis Todd, a Newburyport shipowner, for transporting a cargo of slaves from Baltimore to New Orleans. Men such as Todd, he said, were "enemies of their own species—highway robbers and murderers," and they deserved to be punished with solitary confinement for life. For this editorial a Baltimore grand jury indicted Garrison for libel, and he was tried, convicted, and fined $50. Since he could pay neither the fine nor court costs, he was jailed from April 17 to June 5, 1830.

After his release from jail, Garrison returned to Boston determined to awaken the northern people to the evils of slavery. "A few white victims must be sacrificed to open the eyes of this nation," wrote the young martyr. "I expect and am willing to be persecuted, imprisoned and bound for advocating African rights." Thus, at the age of twenty-five, Garrison was prepared for his life's work. On January 1, 1831, in a dingy room on the third floor of Merchants' Hall in Boston, he began to publish a weekly abolitionist newspaper, the Liberator. The prospectus, printed below, appeared in the first issue.

IN THE MONTH of August, I issued proposals for publishing *The Liberator* in Washington city; but the enterprise, though hailed in different sections of the country, was palsied by public indifference. Since that time, the removal of the *Genius of Universal Emancipation* to the Seat of Government has rendered less imperious the establishment of a similar periodical in that quarter.

During my recent tour for the purpose of exciting the minds of the people by a series of discourses on the subject of slavery, every place that

---

The text is reprinted here as it originally appeared in the *Liberator* of January 1, 1831.

I visited gave fresh evidence of the fact, that a greater revolution in public sentiment was to be effected in the free states—*and particularly in New-England*—than at the south. I found contempt more bitter, opposition more active, detraction more relentless, prejudice more stubborn, and apathy more frozen, than among the slave owners themselves. Of course, there were individual exceptions to the contrary. This state of things afflicted, but did not dishearten me. I determined, at every hazard, to lift up the standard of emancipation in the eyes of the nation, *within sight of Bunker Hill and in the birth place of liberty.* That standard is now unfurled; and long may it float, unhurt by the spoliations of time or the missiles of a desperate foe—yea, till every chain be broken, and every bondman set free! Let southern oppressors tremble—let their secret abettors tremble—let their northern apologists tremble—let all the enemies of the persecuted blacks tremble.

I deem the publication of my original Prospectus * unnecessary, as it has obtained a wide circulation. The principles therein inculcated will be steadily pursued in this paper, excepting that I shall not array myself as the political partisan of any man. In defending the great cause of human rights, I wish to derive the assistance of all religions and of all parties.

Assenting to the "self-evident truth" maintained in the American Declaration of Independence, "that all men are created equal, and endowed by their Creator with certain inalienable rights—among which are life, liberty and the pursuit of happiness," I shall strenuously contend for the immediate enfranchisement of our slave population. In Park-street Church, on the Fourth of July, 1829, in an address on slavery, I unreflectingly assented to the popular but pernicious doctrine of *gradual* abolition. I seize this opportunity to make a full and unequivocal recantation, and thus publickly to ask pardon of my God, of my country, and of my brethren the poor slaves, for having uttered a sentiment so full of timidity, injustice and absurdity. A similar recantation, from my pen, was published in the *Genius of Universal Emancipation* at Baltimore, in September, 1829. My conscience is now satisfied.

I am aware that many object to the severity of my language; but is there not cause for severity? I *will be* as harsh as truth, and as uncompromising as justice. On this subject, I do not wish to think, or

---

* I would here offer my grateful acknowledgments to those editors who so promptly and generously inserted my Proposals. They must give me an available opportunity to repay their liberality.

speak, or write, with moderation. No! no! Tell a man whose house is on fire, to give a moderate alarm; tell him to moderately rescue his wife from the hands of the ravisher; tell the mother to gradually extricate her babe from the fire into which it has fallen;—but urge me not to use moderation in a cause like the present. I am in earnest—I will not equivocate—I will not excuse—I will not retreat a single inch—AND I WILL BE HEARD. The apathy of the people is enough to make every statue leap from its pedestal, and to hasten the resurrection of the dead.

It is pretended, that I am retarding the cause of emancipation, by the coarseness of my invective, and the precipitancy of my measures. *The charge is not true.* On this question my influence,—humble as it is,—is felt at this moment to a considerable extent, and shall be felt in coming years—not perniciously, but beneficially—not as a curse, but as a blessing; and posterity will bear testimony that I was right. I desire to thank God, that he enables me to disregard "the fear of man which bringeth a snare," and to speak his truth in its simplicity and power.

And here I close with this fresh dedication:

> "Oppression! I have seen thee, face to face,
> And met thy cruel eye and cloudy brow;
> But thy soul-withering glance I fear not now—
> For dread to prouder feelings doth give place
> Of deep abhorrence! Scorning the disgrace
> Of slavish knees that at thy footstool bow,
> I also kneel—but with far other bow
> Do hail thee and thy herd of hirelings base:—
> I swear, while life-blood warms my throbbing veins,
> Still to oppose and thwart, with heart and hand,
> Thy brutalizing sway—'till Afric's chains
> Are burst, and Freedom rules the rescued land,—
> Trampling Oppression and his iron rod:
> *Such is the vow I take*—SO HELP ME GOD!"

The crusade that Garrison thus helped to launch lasted until 1865, when the Thirteenth Amendment finally abolished slavery and the Liberator was discontinued. In the intervening years many abolitionists proved to be better organizers, leaders, and strategists than Garrison, but none

could match him as an agitator or polemicist. None ever penned a manifesto as stirring as the one that appeared in the first issue of the Liberator, and no other abolitionist document is so well remembered.

Garrison's severe indictment of slavery was hardly calculated to win converts among the slaveholders of the South. It was not meant to. Rather, the appearance of the Liberator and the organization of a northern abolitionist movement represented the abandonment of hope that slaveholders would voluntarily accept a program of gradual emancipation. With slavery flourishing in the South and spreading to the Southwest, few masters would tolerate criticism, however moderate, of the "peculiar institution." It can hardly be said that Garrison set back the cause of emancipation in the South, for there was no cause to set back.

Garrison's aim was to create massive moral indignation in the North, to isolate the slaveholders, to make the name slaveholder itself a reproach. But most Northerners were indifferent about slavery—"slumbering in the lap of moral death"—at the time the Liberator first appeared. In defense of Garrison, the Kentucky abolitionist James G. Birney expressed the belief that "nothing but a rude and almost ruffianlike shake could rouse . . . [the nation] to a contemplation of her danger."

Though Garrison's language was harsh, it was not his intention to achieve his goal by violence. Like most abolitionists he was a pacifist, and the New England Antislavery Society that he organized promised not to "operate on the existing relations of society by other than peaceful and lawful means." The violence was all in Garrison's words. He cried down slavery as the revivalist preachers of his day cried down other forms of sin. In the end, in spite of his pacifism, Garrison's chief contribution to the antislavery cause was to help give Northerners the moral strength to endure four years of civil war. That slavery died in the agony of this great conflict was in part due to the fact that Garrison had indeed been heard.

The prospectus for the Liberator is one among many protests against injustice that have from time to time been issued in the long and still unfinished struggle to achieve freedom and equality for American Negroes. This is a problem about which most white Americans have usually been apathetic, and whose solution they prefer to put off to a more convenient time. Each advance has usually been preceded by the shrill voice of a Garrison reminding us of the contradictions between American theory and practice. To this day it makes us uneasy to read Garrison, and few historians have shown much admiration for him.

Garrison was a man of immense conceit, of overbearing dogmatism, of irritating self-righteousness. But he was also a man who gave himself wholly to the cause of the slave and who practiced the racial equality that he preached. He was, no doubt, a "fanatic."

Garrison's message has been a constant reminder to us as individuals of our moral responsibility in society. It was characteristic of the reformers of his age to feel directly involved in social injustices and to feel a personal obligation to work for their removal. What Garrison told his northern contemporaries was that there was no relief from guilt until slavery was destroyed. Today, in our mass society, the individual finds an escape from responsibility through a belief in his powerlessness. What possible difference could his small voice make? But Garrison tells us that as long as some men are not free all are bound with them. Each man must speak out for the sake of his own conscience, "till every chain be broken, and every bondman set free!"

Ralph Waldo Emerson
The American Scholar
1837

EDITED BY ROBERT E. SPILLER

It must have been a surprise to the young clergyman Ralph Waldo Emerson when, in the spring of 1837, he received an invitation, previously declined by the Reverend Jonathan Wainwright, to deliver the annual oration to the Harvard chapter of the national honorary fraternity Phi Beta Kappa, of which he was then not even a member. The occasion was a formal one which had commanded the best oratorical talent of the day, including Edward Everett, and the topic and the title "The American Scholar" were more or less assigned. When the officers and members of the Society and the faculty and students of the College filed into the white Meeting House in Harvard Square at noon on the last day of August, 1837, they were prepared to hear reaffirmed to one more group of picked young men their duty to the life of the mind and to the traditional culture of the race.

Emerson could not himself answer to any such definition of the scholar. As a student in both the College and the Divinity School, he had been rated by the faculty as no better than average, and he had, a few years previously, resigned his charge at the Second (Unitarian) Church in Boston because he found it too confining spiritually. Doubtless, his recent series of public lectures in the Masonic Temple in Boston on "Human Culture" and related topics had brought him repute as an effective if unsensational speaker. Although a thoughtful man and a

282

constant user of books, he was so far the author of only one slim volume, Nature (1836), a poetical exhortation to the life of the spirit.

What his audience probably did not realize on that day—at least before his hour-and-a-quarter address had been heard—was that here was a man who had had the courage, in the moment of his first maturity, to face illness, deaths in his family, and apparent professional defeat only to rebuild his life from its foundations. He was now ready to accept the challenge of the occasion, but to attack rather than to defend the system of values which it represented.

On July 29, when he began his preparation, he found his notebooks filled with ideas on self-reliance, on the misuse of history for escape into the past, on the duties of the free individual to rediscover life, and on the vital roles of nature and action, as well as books, in the shaping of character, both personal and national. "If the Allwise would give me light," he noted (MS Journal "C," p. 100), "I should write for the Cambridge men a theory of the Scholar's office. . . . he must be able to read in all books . . . the one incorruptible text of truth." From that text he had faced the crisis in his own career, and he now made it a crisis in the history of American scholarship from which the American mind has fortunately never quite recovered.

MR. PRESIDENT, AND GENTLEMEN,

I GREET you on the re-commencement of our literary year. Our anniversary is one of hope, and, perhaps, not enough of labor. We do not meet for games of strength or skill, for the recitation of histories, tragedies and odes, like the ancient Greeks; for parliaments of love and poesy, like the Troubadours; nor for the advancement of science, like our contemporaries in the British and European capitals. Thus far, our holiday has been simply a friendly sign of the survival of the love of letters amongst a people too busy to give to letters any more. As such, it is precious as the sign of an indestructible instinct. Perhaps the time is already come, when it ought to be, and will be something else; when the

---

The text is reproduced from the copy of the first edition in the library of Morton Perkins, now in the Harvard College Library. It was published in 1837 by James Monroe and Company, Boston, under the title *An Oration, Delivered Before the Phi Beta Kappa Society, at Cambridge, August 31, 1837.*

sluggard intellect of this continent will look from under its iron lids and fill the postponed expectation of the world with something better than the exertions of mechanical skill. Our day of dependence, our long apprenticeship to the learning of other lands, draws to a close. The millions that around us are rushing into life, cannot always be fed on the sere remains of foreign harvests. Events, actions arise, that must be sung, that will sing themselves. Who can doubt that poetry will revive and lead in a new age, as the star in the constellation Harp which now flames in our zenith, astronomers announce, shall one day be the pole-star for a thousand years.

In the light of this hope, I accept the topic which not only usage, but the nature of our association, seems to prescribe to this day,—the AMERICAN SCHOLAR. Year by year, we come up hither to read one more chapter of his biography. Let us inquire what new lights, new events and more days have thrown on his character, his duties and his hopes.

It is one of those fables, which out of an unknown antiquity, convey an unlooked for wisdom, that the gods, in the beginning, divided Man into men, that he might be more helpful to himself; just as the hand was divided into fingers, the better to answer its end.

The old fable covers a doctrine ever new and sublime; that there is One Man,—present to all particular men only partially, or through one faculty; and that you must take the whole society to find the whole man. Man is not a farmer, or a professor, or an engineer, but he is all. Man is priest, and scholar, and statesman, and producer, and soldier. In the *divided* or social state, these functions are parcelled out to individuals, each of whom aims to do his stint of the joint work, whilst each other performs his. The fable implies that the individual to possess himself, must sometimes return from his own labor to embrace all the other laborers. But unfortunately, this original unit, this fountain of power, has been so distributed to multitudes, has been so minutely subdivided and peddled out, that it is spilled into drops, and cannot be gathered. The state of society is one in which the members have suffered amputation from the trunk, and strut about so many walking monsters, —a good finger, a neck, a stomach, an elbow, but never a man.

Man is thus metamorphosed into a thing, into many things. The planter, who is Man sent out into the field to gather food, is seldom cheered by any idea of the true dignity of his ministry. He sees his bushel and his cart, and nothing beyond, and sinks into the farmer, instead of Man on the farm. The tradesman scarcely ever gives an ideal worth to his work, but is ridden by the routine of his craft, and the soul is subject to dollars. The priest becomes a form; the attorney, a statute-book; the mechanic, a machine; the sailor, a rope of a ship.

In this distribution of functions, the scholar is the delegated intellect. In the right state, he is, *Man Thinking*. In the degenerate state, when the victim of society, he tends to become a mere thinker, or, still worse, the parrot of other men's thinking.

In this view of him, as Man Thinking, the whole theory of his office is contained. Him nature solicits, with all her placid, all her monitory pictures. Him the past instructs. Him the future invites. Is not, indeed, every man a student, and do not all things exist for the student's behoof? And, finally, is not the true scholar the only true master? But, as the old oracle said, "All things have two handles. Beware of the wrong one." In life, too often, the scholar errs with mankind and forfeits his privilege. Let us see him in his school, and consider him in reference to the main influences he receives.

I. The first in time and the first in importance of the influences upon the mind is that of nature. Every day, the sun; and, after sunset, night and her stars. Ever the winds blow; ever the grass grows. Every day, men and women, conversing, beholding and beholden. The scholar must needs stand wistful and admiring before this great spectacle. He must settle its value in his mind. What is nature to him? There is never a beginning, there is never an end to the inexplicable continuity of this web of God, but always circular power returning into itself. Therein it resembles his own spirit, whose beginning, whose ending he never can find—so entire, so boundless. Far, too, as her splendors shine, system on system shooting like rays, upward, downward, without centre, without circumference,—in the mass and in the particle nature hastens to render account of herself to the mind. Classification begins. To the young mind, every thing is individual, stands by itself. By and by, it finds how to join two things, and see in them one nature; then three, then three thousand; and so, tyrannized over by its own unifying instinct, it goes on tying things together, diminishing anomalies, discovering roots running under ground, whereby contrary and remote things cohere, and flower out from one stem. It presently learns, that, since the dawn of history, there has been a constant accumulation and classifying of facts. But what is classification but the perceiving that these objects are not chaotic, and are not foreign, but have a law which is also a law of the human mind? The astronomer discovers that geometry, a pure abstraction of the human mind, is the measure of planetary motion. The chemist finds proportions and intelligible method throughout matter: and science is nothing but the finding of analogy, identity in the most remote parts. The ambitious soul sits down before each refractory fact; one after another, reduces all strange constitutions, all new powers, to their class and their law, and goes on forever to animate the last fibre of organization, the outskirts of nature, by insight.

Thus to him, to this school-boy under the bending dome of day, is suggested, that he and it proceed from one root; one is leaf and one is flower; relation, sympathy, stirring in every vein. And what is that Root? Is not that the soul of his soul?—A thought too bold—a dream too wild. Yet when this spiritual light shall have revealed the law of more earthly natures,—when he has learned to worship the soul, and to see that the natural philosophy that now is, is only the first gropings of its gigantic hand, he shall look forward to an ever expanding knowledge as to a becoming creator. He shall see that nature is the opposite of the soul, answering to it part for part. One is seal, and one is print. Its beauty is the beauty of his own mind. Its laws are the laws of his own mind. Nature then becomes to him the measure of his attainments. So much of nature as he is ignorant of, so much of his own mind does he not yet possess. And, in fine, the ancient precept, "Know thyself," and the modern precept, "Study nature," become at last one maxim.

II. The next great influence into the spirit of the scholar, is, the mind of the Past,—in whatever form, whether of literature, of art, of institutions, that mind is inscribed. Books are the best type of the influence of the past, and perhaps we shall get at the truth—learn the amount of this influence more conveniently—by considering their value alone.

The theory of books is noble. The scholar of the first age received into him the world around; brooded thereon; gave it the new arrangement of his own mind, and uttered it again. It came into him—life; it went out from him—truth. It came to him—short-lived actions; it went out from him—immortal thoughts. It came to him—business; it went from him—poetry. It was—dead fact; now, it is quick thought. It can stand, and it can go. It now endures, it now flies, it now inspires. Precisely in proportion to the depth of mind from which it issued, so high does it soar, so long does it sing.

Or, I might say, it depends on how far the process had gone, of transmuting life into truth. In proportion to the completeness of the

286

distillation, so will the purity and imperishableness of the product be. But none is quite perfect. As no air-pump can by any means make a perfect vacuum, so neither can any artist entirely exclude the conventional, the local, the perishable from his book, or write a book of pure thought that shall be as efficient, in all respects, to a remote posterity, as to cotemporaries, or rather to the second age. Each age, it is found, must write its own books; or rather, each generation for the next succeeding. The books of an older period will not fit this.

Yet hence arises a grave mischief. The sacredness which attaches to the act of creation,—the act of thought,—is instantly transferred to the record. The poet chanting, was felt to be a divine man. Henceforth the chant is divine also. The writer was a just and wise spirit. Henceforward it is settled, the book is perfect; as love of the hero corrupts into worship of his statue. Instantly, the book becomes noxious. The guide is a tyrant. We sought a brother, and lo, a governor. The sluggish and perverted mind of the multitude, always slow to open to the incursions of Reason, having once so opened, having once received this book, stands upon it, and makes an outcry, if it is disparaged. Colleges are built on it. Books are written on it by thinkers, not by Man Thinking; by men of talent, that is, who start wrong, who set out from accepted dogmas, not from their own sight of principles. Meek young men grow up in libraries, believing it their duty to accept the views which Cicero, which Locke, which Bacon have given, forgetful that Cicero, Locke and Bacon were only young men in libraries when they wrote these books.

Hence, instead of Man Thinking, we have the bookworm. Hence, the book-learned class, who value books, as such; not as related to nature and the human constitution, but as making a sort of Third Estate with the world and the soul. Hence, the restorers of readings, the emendators, the bibliomaniacs of all degrees.

This is bad; this is worse than it seems. Books are the best of things, well used; abused, among the worst. What is the right use? What is the one end which all means go to effect? They are for nothing but to inspire. I had better never see a book than to be warped by its attraction clean out of my own orbit, and made a satellite instead of a system. The one thing in the world of value, is, the active soul,—the soul, free, sovereign, active. This every man is entitled to; this every man contains within him, although in almost all men, obstructed, and as yet unborn. The soul active sees absolute truth; and utters truth, or creates. In this action, it is genius; not the privilege of here and there a favorite, but the sound estate of every man. In its essence, it is progressive. The book, the college, the school of art, the institution of any kind, stop with some past utterance of genius. This is good, say they,—let us hold by this. They pin me down. They look backward and not forward. But genius always looks forward. The eyes of man are set in his forehead, not in his hindhead. Man hopes. Genius creates. To create,—to create,—is the proof of a divine presence. Whatever talents may be, if the man create not, the pure efflux of the Deity is not his:—cinders and smoke, there may be, but not yet flame. There are creative manners, there are creative actions, and creative words; manners, actions, words, that is, indicative of no custom or authority, but springing spontaneous from the mind's own sense of good and fair.

On the other part, instead of being its own seer, let it receive always from another mind its truth, though it were in torrents of light, without periods of solitude, inquest and self-recovery, and a fatal disservice is done. Genius is always sufficiently the enemy of genius by over-influence. The literature of every nation bear me witness. The English dramatic poets have Shakspearized now for two hundred years.

Undoubtedly there is a right way of reading,—so it be sternly subordinated. Man Thinking must not be subdued by his instruments. Books are for the scholar's idle times. When he can read God directly, the hour is too precious to be wasted in other mens' transcripts of their readings. But when the intervals of darkness come, as come they must,—when the soul seeth not, when the sun is hid, and the stars withdraw their shining,—we repair to the lamps which were kindled by their ray to guide our steps to the East again, where the dawn is. We hear that we may speak. The Arabian proverb says, "A fig tree looking on a fig tree, becometh fruitful."

It is remarkable, the character of the pleasure we derive from the best books. They impress us ever with the conviction that one nature wrote and the same reads. We read the verses of one of the great English poets, of Chaucer, of Marvell, of Dryden, with the most modern joy,—with a pleasure, I mean, which is in great part caused by the abstraction of all *time* from their verses. There is some awe mixed with the joy of our surprise, when this poet, who lived in some past world, two or three hundred years ago, says that which lies close to my own soul, that which I also had well nigh thought and said. But for the evidence thence afforded to the philosophical doctrine of the identity of all minds, we should suppose some pre-established harmony, some foresight of souls that were to be, and some preparation of stores for their future wants, like the fact observed in insects, who lay up food before death for the young grub they shall never see.

I would not be hurried by any love of system, by any exaggeration of instincts, to underrate the Book. We all know, that as the human body can be nourished on any food, though it were boiled grass and the broth of shoes, so the human mind can be fed by any knowledge. And great and heroic men have existed, who had almost no other information than by the printed page. I only would say, that it needs a strong head to bear that diet. One must be an inventor to read well. As the proverb says, "He that would bring home the wealth of the Indies, must carry out the wealth of the Indies." There is then creative reading, as well as creative writing. When the mind is braced by labor and invention, the page of whatever book we read becomes luminous with manifold allusion. Every sentence is doubly significant, and the sense of our author is as broad as the world. We then see, what is always true, that as the seer's hour of vision is short and rare among heavy days and months, so is its record, perchance, the least part of his volume. The discerning will read in his Plato or Shakspeare, only that least part,—only the authentic utterances of the oracle,—and all the rest he rejects, were it never so many times Plato's and Shakspeare's.

Of course, there is a portion of reading quite indispensable to a wise man. History and exact science he must learn by laborious reading. Colleges, in like manner, have their indispensable office,—to teach elements. But they can only highly serve us, when they aim not to drill, but to create; when they gather from far every ray of various genius to their hospitable halls, and, by the concentrated fires, set the hearts of their youth on flame. Thought and knowledge are natures in which apparatus and pretension avail nothing. Gowns, and pecuniary foundations, though of towns of gold, can never countervail the least sentence or syllable of wit. Forget this, and our American colleges will recede in their public importance whilst they grow richer every year.

III. There goes in the world a notion that the scholar should be a recluse, a valetudinarian,—as unfit for any handiwork or public labor, as a penknife for an axe. The so called "practical men" sneer at speculative men, as if, because they speculate or *see*, they could do nothing. I have heard it said that the clergy,—who are always more universally than any other class, the scholars of their day,—are addressed as women: that the rough, spontaneous conversation of men they do not hear, but only a mincing and diluted speech. They are often virtually disfranchised; and, indeed, there are advocates for their celibacy. As far as this is true of the studious classes, it is not just and wise. Action is with the scholar subordinate, but it is essential. Without it, he is not yet man. Without it, thought can never ripen into truth. Whilst the world hangs before the eye as a cloud of beauty, we can not even see its beauty. Inaction is cowardice, but there can be no scholar without the heroic mind. The preamble of thought, the transition through which it passes from the unconscious to the conscious, is action. Only so much do I know, as I have lived. Instantly we know whose words are loaded with life, and whose not.

The world,—this shadow of the soul, or *other me*, lies wide around. Its attractions are the keys which unlock my thoughts and make me acquainted with myself. I launch eagerly into this resounding tumult. I grasp the hands of those next me, and take my place in the ring to suffer and to work, taught by an instinct that so shall the dumb abyss be vocal with speech. I pierce its order; I dissipate its fear; I dispose of it within the circuit of my expanding life. So much only of life as I know by experience, so much of the wilderness have I vanquished and planted, or so far have I extended my being, my dominion. I do not see how any man can afford, for the sake of his nerves and his nap, to spare any action in which he can partake. It is pearls and rubies to his discourse. Drudgery, calamity, exasperation, want, are instructers in eloquence and wisdom. The true scholar grudges every opportunity of action past by, as a loss of power.

It is the raw material out of which the intellect moulds her splendid products. A strange process too, this, by which experience is converted into thought, as a mulberry leaf is converted into satin. The manufacture goes forward at all hours.

The actions and events of our childhood and youth are now matters of calmest observation. They lie like fair pictures in the air. Not so with our recent actions,—with the business which we now have in hand. On this we are quite unable to speculate. Our affections as yet circulate through it. We no more feel or know it, than we feel the feet, or the hand, or the brain of our body. The new deed is yet a part of life,— remains for a time immersed in our unconscious life. In some contemplative hour, it detaches itself from the life like a ripe fruit, to become a thought of the mind. Instantly, it is raised, transfigured; the corruptible has put on incorruption. Always now it is an object of beauty, however base its origin and neighborhood. Observe, too, the impossibility of antedating this act. In its grub state, it cannot fly, it cannot shine,—it is a dull grub. But suddenly, without observation, the selfsame thing unfurls beautiful wings, and is an angel of wisdom. So is there no fact, no event, in our private history, which shall not, sooner or later, lose its adhesive inert form, and astonish us by soaring from our body into the empyrean. Cradle and infancy, school and playground, the fear of boys, and dogs, and ferules, the love of little maids and berries, and many another fact that once filled the whole sky, are gone already; friend and relative, profession and party, town and country, nation and world, must also soar and sing.

Of course, he who has put forth his total strength in fit actions, has the richest return of wisdom. I will not shut myself out of this globe of action and transplant an oak into a flower pot, there to hunger and pine; nor trust the revenue of some single faculty, and exhaust one vein of thought, much like those Savoyards, who, getting their livelihood by carving shepherds, shepherdesses, and smoking Dutchmen, for all Europe, went out one day to the mountain to find stock, and discovered that they had whittled up the last of their pine trees. Authors we have in numbers, who have written out their vein, and who, moved by a commendable prudence, sail for Greece or Palestine, follow the trapper into the prairie, or ramble round Algiers to replenish their merchantable stock.

If it were only for a vocabulary the scholar would be covetous of action. Life is our dictionary. Years are well spent in country labors; in town—in the insight into trades and manufactures; in frank intercourse with many men and women; in science; in art; to the one end of mastering in all their facts a language, by which to illustrate and embody our perceptions. I learn immediately from any speaker how much he has already lived, through the poverty or the splendor of his speech. Life lies behind us as the quarry from whence we get tiles and copestones for the masonry of to-day. This is the way to learn grammar. Colleges and books only copy the language which the field and the workyard made.

But the final value of action, like that of books, and better than books, is, that it is a resource. That great principle of Undulation in nature, that shows itself in the inspiring and expiring of the breath; in desire and satiety; in the ebb and flow of the sea, in day and night, in heat and cold, and as yet more deeply ingrained in every atom and every fluid, is known to us under the name of Polarity,—these "fits of easy transmission and reflection," as Newton called them, are the law of nature because they are the law of spirit.

The mind now thinks; now acts; and each fit reproduces the other. When the artist has exhausted his materials, when the fancy no longer paints, when thoughts are no longer apprehended, and books are a weariness,—he has always the resource *to live*. Character is higher than intellect. Thinking is the function. Living is the functionary. The stream retreats to its source. A great soul will be strong to live, as well as strong to think. Does he lack organ or medium to impart his truths? He can still fall back on this elemental force of living them. This is a total act. Thinking is a partial act. Let the grandeur of justice shine in his affairs. Let the beauty of affection cheer his lowly roof. Those "far from fame" who dwell and act with him, will feel the force of his constitution in the doings and passages of the day better than it can be measured by any public and designed display. Time shall teach him that the scholar loses no hour which the man lives. Herein he unfolds the sacred germ of his instinct screened from influence. What is lost in seemliness is gained in strength. Not out of those on whom systems of education have exhausted their culture, comes the helpful giant to destroy the old or to build the new, but out of unhandselled savage nature, out of terrible Druids and Berserkirs, come at last Alfred and Shakspear.

I hear therefore with joy whatever is beginning to be said of the dignity and necessity of labor to every citizen. There is virtue yet in the hoe and the spade, for learned as well as for unlearned hands. And labor is every where welcome; always we are invited to work; only be this limitation observed, that a man shall not for the sake of wider activity sacrifice any opinion to the popular judgments and modes of action.

I have now spoken of the education of the scholar by nature, by books, and by action. It remains to say somewhat of his duties.

They are such as become Man Thinking. They may all be comprised in self-trust. The office of the scholar is to cheer, to raise, and to guide men by showing them facts amidst appearances. He plies the slow, unhonored, and unpaid task of observation. Flamsteed and Herschel, in their glazed observatory, may catalogue the stars with the praise of all men, and, the results being splendid and useful, honor is sure. But he, in his private observatory, cataloguing obscure and nebulous stars of the human mind, which as yet no man has thought of as such,—watching days and months, sometimes, for a few facts; correcting still his old records;—must relinquish display and immediate fame. In the long period of his preparation, he must betray often an ignorance and shiftlessness in popular arts, incurring the disdain of the able who shoulder him aside. Long he must stammer in his speech; often forego the living for the dead. Worse yet, he must accept—how often! poverty and solitude. For the ease and pleasure of treading the old road, accepting the fashions, the education, the religion of society, he takes the cross of making his own, and, of course, the self accusation, the faint heart, the frequent uncertainty and loss of time which are the nettles and tangling vines in the way of the self-relying and self-directed; and the state of virtual hostility in which he seems to stand to society, and especially to educated society. For all this loss and scorn, what offset? He is to find consolation in exercising the highest functions of human nature. He is one who raises himself from private considerations, and breathes and lives on public and illustrious thoughts. He is the world's eye. He is the world's heart. He is to resist the vulgar prosperity that retrogrades ever to barbarism, by preserving and communicating heroic sentiments, noble biographies, melodious verse, and the conclusions of history. Whatsoever oracles the human heart in all emergencies, in all solemn hours has uttered as its commentary on the world of actions, —these he shall receive and impart. And whatsoever new verdict Reason from her inviolable seat pronounces on the passing men and events of to-day,—this he shall hear and promulgate.

These being his functions, it becomes him to feel all confidence in himself, and to defer never to the popular cry. He and he only knows the world. The world of any moment is the merest appearance. Some great decorum, some fetish of a government, some ephemeral trade, or war, or man, is cried up by half mankind and cried down by the other half, as if all depended on this particular up or down. The odds are that the whole question is not worth the poorest thought which the scholar has lost in listening to the controversy. Let him not quit his belief that a popgun is a popgun, though the ancient and honorable of the earth affirm it to be the crack of doom. In silence, in steadiness, in severe abstraction, let him hold by himself; add observation to observation; patient of neglect, patient of reproach, and bide his own time,—happy enough if he can satisfy himself alone that this day he has seen something truly. Success treads on every right step. For the instinct is sure that prompts him to tell his brother what he thinks. He then learns that in going down into the secrets of his own mind, he has descended into the secrets of all minds. He learns that he who has mastered any law in his private thoughts, is master to that extent of all men whose language he speaks, and of all into whose language his own can be translated. The poet in utter solitude remembering his spontaneous thoughts and recording them, is found to have recorded that which men in "cities vast" find true for them also. The orator distrusts at first the fitness of his frank confessions,—his want of knowledge of the persons he addresses,—until he finds that he is the complement of his hearers;—that they drink his words because he fulfils for them their own nature; the deeper he dives into his privatest secretest presentiment,—to his wonder he finds, this is the most acceptable, most public, and universally true. The people delight in it; the better part of every man feels, This is my music: this is myself.

In self-trust, all the virtues are comprehended. Free should the scholar be,—free and brave. Free even to the definition of freedom, "without any hindrance that does not arise out of his own constitution." Brave; for fear is a thing which a scholar by his very function puts behind him. Fear always springs from ignorance. It is a shame to him if his tranquillity, amid dangerous times, arise from the presumption that like children and women, his is a protected class; or if he seek a temporary peace by the diversion of his thoughts from politics or vexed questions, hiding his head like an ostrich in the flowering bushes, peeping into microscopes, and turning rhymes, as a boy whistles to keep his courage up. So is the danger a danger still: so is the fear worse. Manlike let him turn and face it. Let him look into its eye and search its nature, inspect its origin—see the whelping of this lion,—which lies no great way back; he will then find in himself a perfect comprehension of its nature and extent; he will have made his hands meet on the other side, and can henceforth defy it, and pass on superior. The world is his who can see through its pretension. What deafness, what stone-blind custom, what overgrown error you behold, is there only by sufferance,—by your sufferance. See it to be a lie, and you have already dealt it its mortal blow.

Yes, we are the cowed,—we the trustless. It is a mischievous notion that we are come late into nature; that the world was finished a long time ago. As the world was plastic and fluid in the hands of God, so it is ever to so much of his attributes as we bring to it. To ignorance and sin, it is flint. They adapt themselves to it as they may; but in proportion as a man has anything in him divine, the firmament flows before him, and takes his signet and form. Not he is great who can alter matter, but he who can alter my state of mind. They are the kings of the world who give the color of their present thought to all nature and all art, and persuade men by the cheerful serenity of their carrying the matter, that this thing which they do, is the apple which the ages have desired to pluck, now at last ripe, and inviting nations to the harvest. The great man makes the great thing. Wherever Macdonald sits, there is the head of the table. Linnæus makes botany the most alluring of studies and wins it from the farmer and the herb-woman. Davy, chemistry: and Cuvier, fossils. The day is always his, who works in it with serenity and great aims. The unstable estimates of men crowd to him whose mind is filled with a truth, as the heaped waves of the Atlantic follow the moon.

For this self-trust, the reason is deeper than can be fathomed,—darker than can be enlightened. I might not carry with me the feeling of my audience in stating my own belief. But I have already shown the ground of my hope, in adverting to the doctrine that man is one. I believe man has been wronged: he has wronged himself. He has almost lost the light that can lead him back to his prerogatives. Men are become of no account. Men in history, men in the world of to-day are bugs, are spawn, and are called "the mass" and "the herd." In a century, in a millenium, one or two men; that is to say—one or two approximations to the right state of every man. All the rest behold in the hero or the poet their own green and crude being—ripened; yes, and are content to be less, so *that* may attain to its full stature. What a testimony—full of grandeur, full of pity, is borne to the demands of his own nature, by the poor clansman, the poor partisan, who rejoices in the glory of his chief. The poor and the low find some amends to their immense moral capacity, for their acquiescence in a political and social inferiority. They are content to be brushed like flies from the path of a great person, so that justice shall be done by him to that common nature which it is the dearest desire of all to see enlarged and glorified. They sun themselves in the great man's light, and feel it to be their own element. They cast the dignity of man from their downtrod selves upon the shoulders of a hero, and will perish to add one drop of blood to make that great heart beat, those giant sinews combat and conquer. He lives for us, and we live in him.

Men such as they are, very naturally seek money or power; and power because it is as good as money,—the "spoils," so called, "of office." And why not? for they aspire to the highest, and this, in their sleep-walking, they dream is highest. Wake them, and they shall quit the false good and leap to the true, and leave governments to clerks and desks. This revolution is to be wrought by the gradual domestication of the idea of Culture. The main enterprise of the world for splendor, for extent, is the upbuilding of a man. Here are the materials strown along the ground. The private life of one man shall be a more illustrious monarchy,—more formidable to its enemy, more sweet and serene in its influence to its friend, than any kingdom in history. For a man, rightly viewed, comprehendeth the particular natures of all men. Each philosopher, each bard, each actor, has only done for me, as by a delegate, what one day I can do for myself. The books which once we valued more than the apple of the eye, we have quite exhausted. What is that but saying that we have come up with the point of view which the universal mind took through the eyes of that one scribe; we have been that man, and have passed on. First, one; then, another; we drain all cisterns, and waxing greater by all these supplies, we crave a better and more abundant food. The man has never lived that can feed us ever. The human mind cannot be enshrined in a person who shall set a barrier on any one side to this unbounded, unboundable empire. It is one central fire which flaming now out of the lips of Etna, lightens the capes of Sicily; and now out of the throat of Vesuvius, illuminates the towers and vineyards of Naples. It is one light which beams out of a thousand stars. It is one soul which animates all men.

But I have dwelt perhaps tediously upon this abstraction of the Scholar. I ought not to delay longer to add what I have to say, of nearer reference to the time and to this country.

Historically, there is thought to be a difference in the ideas which predominate over successive epochs, and there are data for marking the genius of the Classic, of the Romantic, and now of the Reflective or Philosophical age. With the views I have intimated of the oneness or the identity of the mind through all individuals, I do not much dwell on these differences. In fact, I believe each individual passes through all three. The boy is a Greek; the youth, romantic; the adult, reflective. I deny not, however, that a revolution in the leading idea may be distinctly enough traced.

Our age is bewailed as the age of Introversion. Must that needs be evil? We, it seems, are critical. We are embarrassed with second thoughts. We cannot enjoy any thing for hankering to know whereof

296

the pleasure consists. We are lined with eyes. We see with our feet. The time is infected with Hamlet's unhappiness,—

"Sicklied o'er with the pale cast of thought."

Is it so bad then? Sight is the last thing to be pitied. Would we be blind? Do we fear lest we should outsee nature and God, and drink truth dry? I look upon the discontent of the literary class as a mere announcement of the fact that they find themselves not in the state of mind of their fathers, and regret the coming state as untried; as a boy dreads the water before he has learned that he can swim. If there is any period one would desire to be born in,—is it not the age of Revolution; when the old and the new stand side by side, and admit of being compared; when the energies of all men are searched by fear and by hope; when the historic glories of the old, can be compensated by the rich possibilities of the new era? This time, like all times, is a very good one, if we but know what to do with it.

I read with joy some of the auspicious signs of the coming days as they glimmer already through poetry and art, through philosophy and science, through church and state.

One of these signs is the fact that the same movement which effected the elevation of what was called the lowest class in the state, assumed in literature a very marked and as benign an aspect. Instead of the sublime and beautiful, the near, the low, the common, was explored and poetised. That which had been negligently trodden under foot by those who were harnessing and provisioning themselves for long journies into far countries, is suddenly found to be richer than all foreign parts. The literature of the poor, the feelings of the child, the philosophy of the street, the meaning of household life, are the topics of the time. It is a great stride. It is a sign—is it not? of new vigor, when the extremities are made active, when currents of warm life run into the hands and the feet. I ask not for the great, the remote, the romantic; what is doing in Italy or Arabia; what is Greek art, or Provencal Minstrelsy; I embrace the common, I explore and sit at the feet of the familiar, the low. Give me insight into to-day, and you may have the antique and future worlds. What would we really know the meaning of? The meal in the firkin; the milk in the pan; the ballad in the street; the news of the boat; the glance of the eye; the form and the gait of the body;—show me the ultimate

297

reason of these matters;—show me the sublime presence of the highest spiritual cause lurking, as always it does lurk, in these suburbs and extremities of nature; let me see every trifle bristling with the polarity that ranges it instantly on an eternal law; and the shop, the plough, and the ledger, referred to the like cause by which light undulates and poets sing;—and the world lies no longer a dull miscellany and lumber room, but has form and order; there is no trifle; there is no puzzle; but one design unites and animates the farthest pinnacle and the lowest trench.

This idea has inspired the genius of Goldsmith, Burns, Cowper, and, in a newer time, of Goethe, Wordsworth, and Carlyle. This idea they have differently followed and with various success. In contrast with their writing, the style of Pope, of Johnson, of Gibbon, looks cold and pedantic. This writing is blood-warm. Man is surprised to find that things near are not less beautiful and wondrous than things remote. The near explains the far. The drop is a small ocean. A man is related to all nature. This perception of the worth of the vulgar, is fruitful in discoveries. Goethe, in this very thing the most modern of the moderns, has shown us, as none ever did, the genius of the ancients.

There is one man of genius who has done much for this philosophy of life, whose literary value has never yet been rightly estimated;—I mean Emanuel Swedenborg. The most imaginative of men, yet writing with the precision of a mathematician, he endeavored to engraft a purely philosophical Ethics on the popular Christianity of his time. Such an attempt, of course, must have difficulty which no genius could surmount. But he saw and showed the connexion between nature and the affections of the soul. He pierced the emblematic or spiritual character of the visible, audible, tangible world. Especially did his shade-loving muse hover over and interpret the lower parts of nature; he showed the mysterious bond that allies moral evil to the foul material forms, and has given in epical parables a theory of insanity, of beasts, of unclean and fearful things.

Another sign of our times, also marked by an analogous political movement is, the new importance given to the single person. Every thing that tends to insulate the individual,—to surround him with barriers of natural respect, so that each man shall feel the world is his, and man shall treat with man as a sovereign state with a sovereign state; —tends to true union as well as greatness. "I learned," said the melancholy Pestalozzi, "that no man in God's wide earth is either willing or able to help any other man." Help must come from the bosom alone. The scholar is that man who must take up into himself all the ability of the time, all the contributions of the past, all the hopes of the future. He must be an university of knowledges. If there be one lesson more than another which should pierce his ear, it is, The world is nothing, the man is all; in yourself is the law of all nature, and you know not yet how a globule of sap ascends; in yourself slumbers the whole of Reason; it is for you to know all, it is for you to dare all. Mr. President and Gentlemen, this confidence in the unsearched might of man, belongs by all motives, by all prophecy, by all preparation, to the American Scholar. We have listened too long to the courtly muses of Europe. The spirit of the American freeman is already suspected to be timid, imitative, tame. Public and private avarice make the air we breathe thick and fat. The scholar is decent, indolent, complaisant. See already the tragic consequence. The mind of this country taught to aim at low objects, eats upon itself. There is no work for any but the decorous and the complaisant. Young men of the fairest promise, who begin life upon our shores, inflated by the mountain winds, shined upon by all the stars of God, find the earth below not in unison with these,— but are hindered from action by the disgust which the principles on which business is managed inspire, and turn drudges, or die of disgust,— some of them suicides. What is the remedy? They did not yet see, and thousands of young men as hopeful now crowding to the barriers for the career, do not yet see, that if the single man plant himself indomitably on his instincts, and there abide, the huge world will come round to him. Patience—patience;—with the shades of all the good and great for company; and for solace, the perspective of your own infinite life; and for work, the study and the communication of principles, the making those instincts prevalent, the conversion of the world. Is it not the chief disgrace in the world, not to be an unit;—not to be reckoned one character;—not to yield that peculiar fruit which each man was created to bear, but to be reckoned in the gross, in the hundred, or the thousand, of the party, the section, to which we belong; and our opinion predicted geographically, as the north, or the south. Not so, brothers and friends, —please God, ours shall not be so. We will walk on our own feet; we will work with our own hands; we will speak our own minds. Then shall man be no longer a name for pity, for doubt, and for sensual indulgence. The dread of man and the love of man shall be a wall of defence and a wreath of love around all. A nation of men will for the first time exist, because each believes himself inspired by the Divine Soul which also inspires all men.

The immediate reception of Emerson's academic heresies was somewhat mixed, but it was far more cordial than was that of his theological heresies in the Divinity School Address of the next year. The young men in his audience were enthusiastic, and he was praised and toasted at the dinner after the ceremony. James Russell Lowell, then a student, recalled the event thirty years later as "without parallel in our literary annals." Carlyle wrote, "I could have wept to read that speech," and O. W. Holmes, Sr., later declared it "our intellectual Declaration of Independence." The pamphlet edition of five hundred copies was soon sold out and the collected edition of 1849 found its place as Volume I of the "complete" works thereafter. No anthology of American literature or thought could afford to omit it.

An intellectual Declaration of Independence it assuredly was—although not the first. Freneau, Bryant, Cooper, Irving, Channing, and many lesser men had begun to publish exhortations to literary nationalism almost before the ink was dry on the political document of 1776. But Emerson was cautious; he had already warned of nationalism as such. When he now proclaimed that "Our day of dependence, our long apprenticeship to the learning of other lands draws to a close," he was firing a double-barreled charge. Certainly the vigorous new nation must gain and assert its cultural independence; but only to give the world a new concept of freedom for the mind in any time or place. In the right state, he made it clear, "the scholar is the delegated intellect, . . . Man Thinking. In the degenerate state, when the victim of society, he tends to become a mere thinker, or still worse, the parrot of other men's thinking."

"If the single man plant himself indomitably on his instincts, and there abide, the huge world will come round to him." From this focus on self-reliance, waves of influence moved out into all American life. To Emerson, scholarship was a dynamic force, a continuing process, a function of the whole personality, a way of life. Specialization for him became a function rather than a limitation of the activities of the mind. From this emphasis on the present, on experience, on the individual, it

was easy to take the next steps with C. S. Peirce, William James, and John Dewey toward a wholly empirical approach to all knowledge. Learning springs from living and is tested by doing. A pragmatism based on idealistic premises became and remains the distinctive American philosophy.

To attribute to Emerson alone the freedom of inquiry that is characteristic of American science, the freedom of speech that inspires American journalism, and the freedom of learning that opens the schools to all young Americans would be going much too far. But we can say that his focus on the free individual as the beginning and end of wisdom was a principal agent in translating the political ideals of the American Revolution into the whole of American culture. Like most great documents, Emerson's oration created nothing; it condensed and focused the otherwise kaleidescopic American faith in the possibilities of the human mind and spirit. "It is for you to know all; it is for you to dare all."

Lemuel Shaw
Commonwealth v. Hunt
1842

EDITED BY LEONARD W. LEVY

Judge Peter O. Thacher, charging the jury that tried the members of the Bootmakers' Society in Boston's Municipal Court in 1840, practically directed a verdict of guilty. The jury obliged, after deliberating twenty minutes. They were apparently persuaded by Thacher's frenetic forebodings: if unions became widespread, he had declared, free enterprise would be at an end, property insecure, the rich and poor pitted against each other in class warfare, and a "frightful despotism would soon be erected on the ruins of this free and happy commonwealth."

Technically the crime for which the union had been convicted was criminal conspiracy. The indictment luridly accused the little trade union of having conspired to maintain what a later age would call a "closed shop." Another count in the indictment charged a conspiracy to impoverish both employers and fellow employees who did not acquiesce in union regulations. The case had arisen when the union insisted on the firing of a shoemaker whom it had expelled for violating union rules; the employer, anxious to avoid a strike, complied: he knew the union's rule that its members would not work for anyone employing a nonmember whose discharge had been demanded. The prosecution, initiated on the complaint of the disgruntled worker, not of the employer, had depended upon a great many English and American precedents which stigmatized as an unlawful conspiracy virtually all union tactics and objectives—specifically, joining together to obtain higher wages, shorter hours, or

302

improved conditions of employment. The conviction had been expected: convictions in such cases were routine.

But Robert Rantoul, Jr., the union's counsel, appealed the case after objecting to points of law in Thacher's charge. In the Supreme Judicial Court of the Commonwealth, Rantoul argued that the "tyrannical" common law of conspiracies was not in force in Massachusetts. In support of his radical position, he added that the indictment was defective because the "combination" that it described was not per se a conspiracy. The court that heard this argument was presided over by Lemuel Shaw, a man of formidable and majestic reputation who gave the impression, it was said, of having "the absolute power of a crag vitalized by a human spirit." During his thirty years of service as Chief Justice of the Massachusetts court, Shaw wrote a record number of opinions—over 2,200, only one of which was a dissent—imbuing hoary doctrines with a fresh spirit as, he once said, "the advancement of civilization may require."

Commonwealth v. Hunt, despite the precedents, was the first case of its kind in Massachusetts. Shaw's tendency, even in a routine case, as a Senator who had once practiced before him recalled, was "to unlimber the heavy artillery of his mind, go down to the roots of the question, consider the matter in all possible relations, and deal with it as if he were besieging a fortress." In this, his best-known opinion, handed down in the March term of 1842, Shaw spoke, as usual, not only for himself but also for all his associates—Samuel S. Wilde, Charles A. Dewey, and Samuel Hubbard. They were Whigs all, but jurists who saw, in this little case against the shoemaker Hunt and his fellow unionists, momentous issues: in a free, competitive society, are not combinations, whether of workers or entrepreneurs, inevitable; and does not society itself stand to gain from the competition between interest groups?

CONSIDERABLE time has elapsed since the argument of this case. It has been retained long under advisement, partly because we were desirous of examining, with some attention, the great number of cases cited at the argument, and others which have presented themselves in course, and partly because we considered it a question of

Shaw's opinion is reprinted from 4 Metcalf 111 (1842).

great importance to the Commonwealth, and one which had been much examined and considered by the learned judge of the municipal court.

We have no doubt, that by the operation of the constitution of this Commonwealth, the general rules of the common law, making conspiracy an indictable offence, are in force here, and that this is included in the description of laws which had, before the adoption of the constitution, been used and approved in the Province, Colony, or State of Massachusetts Bay, and usually practised in the courts of law. . . . Still, it is proper in this connexion to remark, that although the common law in regard to conspiracy in this Commonwealth is in force, yet it will not necessarily follow that every indictment at common law for this offence is a precedent for a similar indictment in this State. The general rule of the common law is, that it is a criminal and indictable offence, for two or more to confederate and combine together, by concerted means, to do that which is unlawful or criminal, to the injury of the public, or portions or classes of the community, or even to the rights of an individual. This rule of law may be equally in force as a rule of the common law, in England and in this Commonwealth; and yet it must depend upon the local laws of each country to determine, whether the purpose to be accomplished by the combination, or the concerted means of accomplishing it, be unlawful or criminal in the respective countries. All those laws of the parent country, whether rules of the common law, or early English statutes, which were made for the purpose of regulating the wages of laborers, the settlement of paupers, and making it penal for any one to use a trade or handicraft to which he had not served a full apprenticeship—not being adapted to the circumstances of our colonial condition—were not adopted, used or approved, and therefore do not come within the description of the laws adopted and confirmed by the provision of the constitution already cited. This consideration will do something towards reconciling the English and American cases, and may indicate how far the principles of the English cases will apply in this Commonwealth, and show why a conviction in England, in many cases, would not be a precedent for a like conviction here. . . .

But the rule of law, that an illegal conspiracy, whatever may be the facts which constitute it, is an offence punishable by the laws of this Commonwealth, is established as well by legislative as by judicial authority. Like many other cases, that of murder, for instance, it leaves the definition or description of the offence to the common law, and provides modes for its prosecution and punishment. . . .

But the great difficulty is, in framing any definition or description, to be drawn from the decided cases, which shall specifically identify this offence—a description broad enough to include all cases punishable under this description, without including acts which are not punishable. Without attempting to review and reconcile all the cases, we are of opinion, that as a general description, though perhaps not a precise and accurate definition, a conspiracy must be a combination of two or more persons, by some concerted action, to accomplish some criminal or unlawful purpose, or to accomplish some purpose, not in itself criminal or unlawful, by criminal or unlawful means. We use the terms criminal or unlawful, because it is manifest that many acts are unlawful, which are not punishable by indictment or other public prosecution; and yet there is no doubt, we think, that a combination by numbers to do them would be an unlawful conspiracy, and punishable by indictment. . . .

Several rules upon the subject seem to be well established,—to wit, that the unlawful agreement constitutes the gist of the offence, and therefore that it is not necessary to charge the execution of the unlawful agreement. *Commonwealth v. Judd*, 2 Mass. 337. And when such execution is charged, it is to be regarded as proof of the intent, or as an aggravation of the criminality of the unlawful combination.

Another rule is a necessary consequence of the former, which is, that the crime is consummate and complete by the fact of unlawful combination, and, therefore, that if the execution of the unlawful purpose is averred, it is by way of aggravation, and proof of it is not necessary to conviction; and therefore the jury may find the conspiracy, and negative the execution, and it will be a good conviction.

And it follows, as another necessary legal consequence, from the same principle, that the indictment must—by averring the unlawful purpose of the conspiracy, or the unlawful means by which it is contemplated and agreed to accomplish a lawful purpose, or a purpose not of itself criminally punishable—set out an offence complete in itself, without the aid of any averment of illegal acts done in pursuance of such an agreement; and that an illegal combination, imperfectly and insufficiently set out in the indictment, will not be aided by averments of acts done in pursuance of it.

From this view of the law respecting conspiracy, we think it an offence which especially demands the application of that wise and humane rule of the common law, that an indictment shall state, with as much certainty as the nature of the case will admit, the facts which constitute the crime intended to be charged. This is required, to enable the defendant to meet the charge and prepare for his defence, and, in case of acquittal or conviction, to show by the record the identity of the charge, so that he may not be indicted a second time for the same offence. It is also necessary, in order that a person, charged by the grand jury for one offence, may not substantially be convicted, on his trial, of another. This fundamental rule is confirmed by the Declaration of Rights, which declares that no subject shall be held to answer for any crime or offence, until the same is fully and plainly, substantially and formally described to him.

From these views of the rules of criminal pleading, it appears to us to follow, as a necessary legal conclusion, that when the criminality of a conspiracy consists in an unlawful agreement of two or more persons to compass or promote some criminal or illegal purpose, that purpose must be fully and clearly stated in the indictment; and if the criminality of the offence, which is intended to be charged, consists in the agreement to compass or promote some purpose, not of itself criminal or unlawful, by the use of fraud, force, falsehood, or other criminal or unlawful means, such intended use of fraud, force, falsehood, or other criminal or unlawful means, must be set out in the indictment. Such, we think, is, on the whole, the result of the English authorities, although they are not quite uniform. . . .

With these general views of the law, it becomes necessary to consider the circumstances of the present case, as they appear from the indictment itself, and from the bill of exceptions filed and allowed.

One of the exceptions, though not the first in the order of time, yet by far the most important, was this:

The counsel for the defendants contended, and requested the court to instruct the jury, that the indictment did not set forth any agreement to do a criminal act, or to do any lawful act by any specified criminal means, and that the agreements therein set forth did not constitute a conspiracy indictable by any law of this Commonwealth. But the judge refused so to do, and instructed the jury, that the indictment did, in his opinion, describe a confederacy among the defendants to do an unlawful act, and to effect the same by unlawful means; that the society, organized and associated for the purposes described in the indictment, was an unlawful conspiracy, against the laws of this Commonwealth; and that if the jury believed, from the evidence in the case, that the defendants, or any of them, had engaged in such a confederacy, they were bound to find such of them guilty.

We are here carefully to distinguish between the confederacy set forth in the indictment, and the confederacy or association contained in the constitution of the Boston Journeymen Bootmakers' Society, as stated in the little printed book, which was admitted as evidence on the trial. Because, though it was thus admitted as evidence, it would not warrant a conviction for any thing not stated in the indictment. It was proof, as far as it went to support the averments in the indictment. If it contained any criminal matter not set forth in the indictment, it is of no avail. The question then presents itself in the same form as on a motion in arrest of judgment.

The first count set forth, that the defendants, with divers others unknown, on the day and at the place named, being workmen, and journeymen, in the art and occupation of bootmakers, unlawfully, perniciously and deceitfully designing and intending to continue, keep up, form, and unite themselves, into an unlawful club, society and combination, and make unlawful by-laws, rules and orders among themselves, and thereby govern themselves and other workmen, in the said art, and unlawfully and unjustly to exhort sums of money by means thereof, did unlawfully assemble and meet together, and being so assembled, did unjustly and corruptly conspire, combine, confederate and agree together, that none of them should thereafter, and that none of them would, work for any master or person whatsoever, in the said art, mystery and occupation, who should employ any workman or journeyman, or other person, in the said art, who was not a member of said club, society or combination, after notice given him to discharge such workman, from the employ of such master; to the great damage and oppression, &c.

Now it is to be considered, that the preamble and introductory matter in the indictment—such as unlawfully and deceitfully designing and intending unjustly to extort great sums, &c.—is mere recital, and not traversable, and therefore cannot aid an imperfect averment of the facts constituting the description of the offence. The same may be said of the concluding matter, which follows the averment, as to the great damage and oppression not only of their said masters, employing them in said art and occupation, but also of divers other workmen in the same art, mystery and occupation, to the evil example, &c. If the facts averred constitute the crime, these are properly stated as the legal inferences to be drawn from them. If they do not constitute the charge of such an offence, they cannot be aided by these alleged consequences.

Stripped then of these introductory recitals and alleged injurious consequences, and of the qualifying epithets attached to the facts, the averment is this; that the defendants and others formed themselves into a society, and agreed not to work for any person, who should employ any journeyman or other person, not a member of such society, after notice given him to discharge such workman.

The manifest intent of the association is, to induce all those engaged in the same occupation to become members of it. Such a purpose is not unlawful. It would give them a power which might be exerted for useful and honorable purposes, or for dangerous and pernicious ones. If the latter were the real and actual object, and susceptible of proof, it should have been specially charged. Such an association might be used to afford each other assistance in times of poverty, sickness and distress; or to raise their intellectual, moral and social condition; or to make improvement in their art; or for other proper purposes. Or the association might be designed for purposes of oppression and injustice. But in order to charge all those, who become members of an association, with the guilt of a criminal conspiracy, it must be averred and proved that the actual, if not the avowed object of the association, was criminal. An association may be formed, the declared objects of which are innocent and laudable, and yet they may have secret articles, or an agreement communicated only to the members, by which they are banded together for purposes injurious to the peace of society or the rights of its members. Such would undoubtedly be a criminal conspiracy, on proof of the fact, however meritorious and praiseworthy the declared objects might be. The law is not to be hoodwinked by colorable pretences. It looks at truth and reality, through whatever disguise it may assume. But to make such an association, ostensibly innocent, the subject of prosecution as a criminal conspiracy, the secret agreement, which makes it so, is to be averred and proved as the gist of the offence. But when an association is formed for purposes actually innocent, and afterwards its powers are abused, by those who have the control and management of it, to purposes of oppression and injustice, it will be criminal in those who thus misuse it, or give consent thereto, but not in the other members of the association. In this case, no such secret agreement, varying the objects of the association from those avowed, is set forth in this count of the indictment.

Nor can we perceive that the objects of this association, whatever they may have been, were to be attained by criminal means. The means which they proposed to employ, as averred in this count, and which, as we are now to presume, were established by the proof, were, that they would not work for a person, who, after due notice, should employ a journeyman not a member of their society. Supposing the object of the association to be laudable and lawful, or at least not unlawful, are these means criminal? The case supposes that these persons are not bound by contract, but free to work for whom they please, or not to work, if they so prefer. In this state of things, we cannot perceive, that it is criminal for men to agree together to exercise their own acknowledged rights, in such a manner as best to subserve their own interests. One way to test this is, to consider the effect of such an agreement, where the object of the association is acknowledged on all hands to be a laudable one. Suppose a class of workmen, impressed with the manifold evils of intemperance, should agree with each other not to work in a shop in which ardent spirit was furnished, or not to work in a shop with any one who used it, or not to work for an employer, who should, after notice, employ a journeyman who habitually used it. The consequences might be the same. A workman, who should still persist in the use of ardent spirit, would find it more difficult to get employment; a master employing such an one might, at times, experience inconvenience in his work, in losing the services of a skilful but intemperate workman. Still it seems to us, that as the object would be lawful, and the means not unlawful, such an agreement could not be pronounced a criminal conspiracy.

From this count in the indictment, we do not understand that the agreement was, that the defendants would refuse to work for an employer, to whom they were bound by contract for a certain time, in violation of that contract; nor that they would insist that an employer should discharge a workman engaged by contract for a certain time, in violation of such contract. It is perfectly consistent with every thing stated in this count, that the effect of the agreement was, that when they were free to act, they would not engage with an employer, or continue in his employment, if such employer, when free to act, should engage with a workman, or continue a workman in his employment, not a member of

309

the association. If a large number of men, engaged for a certain time, should combine together to violate their contract, and quit their employment together, it would present a very different question. Suppose a farmer, employing a large number of men, engaged for the year, at fair monthly wages, and suppose that just at the moment that his crops were ready to harvest, they should all combine to quit his service, unless he would advance their wages, at a time when other laborers could not be obtained. It would surely be a conspiracy to do an unlawful act, though of such a character, that if done by an individual, it would lay the foundation of a civil action only, and not of a criminal prosecution. It would be a case very different from that stated in this count.

The second count, omitting the recital of unlawful intent and evil disposition, and omitting the direct averment of an unlawful club or society, alleges that the defendants, with others unknown, did assemble, conspire, confederate and agree together, not to work for any master or person who should employ any workman not being a member of a certain club, society or combination, called the Boston Journeymen Bootmaker's Society, or who should break any of their by-laws, unless such workmen should pay to said club, such sum as should be agreed upon as a penalty for the breach of such unlawful rules, &c; and that by means of said conspiracy they did compel one Isaac B. Wait, a master cordwainer, to turn out of his employ one Jeremiah Horne, a journeyman boot-maker, &c. in evil example, &c. So far as the averment of a conspiracy is concerned, all the remarks made in reference to the first count are equally applicable to this. It is simply an averment of an agreement amongst themselves not to work for a person, who should employ any person not a member of a certain association. It sets forth no illegal or criminal purpose to be accomplished, nor any illegal or criminal means to be adopted for the accomplishment of any purpose. It was an agreement, as to the manner in which they would exercise an acknowledged right to contract with others for their labor. It does not aver a conspiracy or even an intention to raise their wages; and it appears by the bill of exceptions, that the case was not put upon the footing of a conspiracy to raise their wages. Such an agreement, as set forth in this count, would be perfectly justifiable under the recent English statute, by which this subject is regulated. *St.* 6 Geo. IV. *c.* 129. See Roscoe Crim. Ev. (2d Amer. ed.) 368, 369.

As to the latter part of this count, which avers that by means of said conspiracy, the defendants did compel one Wait to turn out of his employ one Jeremiah Horne, we remark, in the first place, that as the acts done in pursuance of a conspiracy, as we have before seen, are stated by way of aggravation, and not as a substantive charge; if no criminal or unlawful conspiracy is stated, it cannot be aided and made good by mere matter of aggravation. If the principal charge falls, the aggravation falls with it. *State* v. *Rickey*, 4 Halst. 293.

But further; if this is to be considered as a substantive charge, it would depend altogether upon the force of the word "compel," which may be used in the sense of coercion, or duress, by force or fraud. It would therefore depend upon the context and the connexion with other words, to determine the sense in which it was used in the indictment. If, for instance, the indictment had averred a conspiracy, by the defendants, to compel Wait to turn Horne out of his employment, and to accomplish that object by the use of force or fraud, it would have been a very different case; especially if it might be fairly construed, as perhaps in that case it might have been, that Wait was under obligation, by contract, for an unexpired term of time, to employ and pay Horne. As before remarked, it would have been a conspiracy to do an unlawful, though not a criminal act, to induce Wait to violate his engagement, to the actual injury of Horne. To mark the difference between the case of a journeyman or a servant and master, mutually bound by contract, and the same parties when free to engage anew, I should have before cited the case of the *Boston Glass Co.* v. *Binney*, 4 Pick. 425. In that case, it was held actionable to entice another person's hired servant to quit his employment, during the time for which he was engaged; but not actionable to treat with such hired servant, whilst actually hired and employed by another, to leave his service, and engage in the employment of the person making the proposal, when the term for which he is engaged shall expire. It acknowledges the established principle, that every free man, whether skilled laborer, mechanic, farmer or domestic servant, may work or not work, or work or refuse to work with any company or individual, at his own option, except so far as he is bound by contract. But whatever might be the force of the word "compel," unexplained by its connexion, it is disarmed and rendered harmless by the precise statement of the means, by which such compulsion was to be effected. It was the agreement not to work for him, by which they compelled Wait to decline employing Horne longer. On both of these grounds, we are of opinion that the statement made in this second count, that the unlawful agreement was carried into execution, makes no essential difference between this and the first count.

The third count, reciting a wicked and unlawful intent to impoverish one Jeremiah Horne, and hinder him from following his trade as a boot-maker, charges the defendants, with others unknown, with an unlawful conspiracy, by wrongful and indirect means, to impoverish said Horne and to deprive and hinder him, from his said art and trade and getting his support thereby, and that, in pursuance of said unlawful combination, they did unlawfully and indirectly hinder and prevent, &c. and greatly impoverish him.

If the fact of depriving Jeremiah Horne of the profits of his business, by whatever means it might be done, would be unlawful and criminal, a combination to compass that object would be an unlawful conspiracy, and it would be unnecessary to state the means. . . .

Suppose a baker in a small village had the exclusive custom of his neighborhood, and was making large profits by the sale of his bread. Supposing a number of those neighbors, believing the price of his bread too high, should propose to him to reduce his prices, or if he did not, that they would introduce another baker; and on his refusal, such other baker should, under their encouragement, set up a rival establishment, and sell his bread at lower prices; the effect would be to diminish the profit of the former baker, and to the same extent to impoverish him. And it might be said and proved, that the purpose of the associates was to diminish his profits, and thus impoverish him, though the ultimate and laudable object of the combination was to reduce the cost of bread to themselves and their neighbors. The same thing may be said of all competition in every branch of trade and industry; and yet it is through that competition, that the best interests of trade and industry are promoted. It is scarcely necessary to allude to the familiar instances of opposition lines of conveyance, rival hotels, and the thousand other instances, where each strives to gain custom to himself, by ingenious improvements, by increased industry, and by all the means by which he may lessen the price of commodities, and thereby diminish the profits of others.

We think, therefore, that associations may be entered into, the object of which is to adopt measures that may have a tendency to impoverish another, that is, to diminish his gains and profits, and yet so far from being criminal or unlawful, the object may be highly meritorious and public spirited. The legality of·such an association will therefore depend upon the means to be used for its accomplishment. If it is to be carried into effect by fair or honorable and lawful means, it is, to say the least, innocent; if by falsehood or force, it may be stamped with the character of conspiracy. It follows as a necessary consequence, that if criminal and indictable, it is so by reason of the criminal means intended to be employed for its accomplishment; and as a further legal consequence, that as the criminality will depend on the means, those means must be stated in the indictment. If the same rule were to prevail in criminal, which holds in civil proceedings—that a case defectively stated may be aided by a verdict—then a court might presume, after verdict, that the indictment was supported by proof of criminal or unlawful means to effect the object. But it is an established rule in criminal cases, that the indictment must state a complete indictable offence, and cannot be aided by the proof offered at the trial. . . .

The fourth count avers a conspiracy to impoverish Jeremiah Horne, without stating any means; and the fifth alleges a conspiracy to impoverish employers, by preventing and hindering them from employing persons, not members of the Bootmakers' Society; and these require no remarks, which have not been already made in reference to the other counts. . . .

It appears by the bill of exceptions, that it was contended on the part of the defendants, that this indictment did not set forth any agreement to do a criminal act, or to do any lawful act by criminal means, and that the agreement therein set forth did not constitute a conspiracy indictable by the law of this State, and that the court was requested so to instruct the jury. This the court declined doing, but instructed the jury that the indictment did describe a confederacy among the defendants to do an unlawful act, and to effect the same by unlawful means—that the society, organized and associated for the purposes described in the indictment, was an unlawful conspiracy against the laws of this State, and that if the jury believed, from the evidence, that the defendants or any of them had engaged in such confederacy, they were bound to find such of them guilty.

In this opinion of the learned judge, this court, for the reasons stated, cannot concur. Whatever illegal purpose can be found in the constitution of the Bootmakers' Society, it not being clearly set forth in the indictment, cannot be relied upon to support this conviction. So if any facts were disclosed at the trial, which, if properly averred, would have given a different character to the indictment, they do not appear in the bill of exceptions, nor could they, after verdict, aid the indictment. But looking solely at the indictment, disregarding the qualifying epithets, recitals and immaterial allegations, and confining ourselves to facts so averred as to be capable of being traversed and put in issue, we cannot perceive that it charges a criminal conspiracy punishable by law. The exceptions must, therefore, be sustained, and the judgment arrested.

Commonwealth v. Hunt, by removing the stigma of criminality from labor organizations, became the Magna Carta of American trade unionism. Shaw was a tough and fair-minded realist who understood that the conspiracy doctrine, if not restricted, might throttle industrial development and professional organizations as well as unions. He was tolerant of unionism even beyond approving the right of workers to organize. It was the legality of the union's activities, its methods and purposes, not just the lawfulness of its existence, that constituted the issue in the case. The express holding was that a combination of workers to establish and maintain a closed shop by the employment of peaceable coercion is not an indictable conspiracy. Even after more than a century, this holding still implies a latitudinarian attitude toward unions. Shaw also indicated that a strike for the purpose of raising wages was not a crime. Because the dicta as well as the holding demonstrated his belief that the common law should not penalize normal union activities, Shaw made it legally possible for unions to operate and grow. This fact has given his opinion its enduring significance. Without repudiating the conspiracy doctrine, he narrowed its applicability though leaving it available for use in future labor cases. His means-ends formulation of the doctrine became the definitive one; it has been cited hundreds of times by American courts. For two generations Commonwealth v. Hunt dominated the American law of labor combinations. A New Jersey decision of 1867 is notable only as the exception that proved the rule, a case in which a court did not come to the same conclusion as Shaw did; yet in that case the judge contrived an explanation for his decision after he was forced to allege his complete concurrence in the principles of Commonwealth v. Hunt.

Shaw's opinion was destined to survive as the leading statement of the law even in our own time. Yet it passed through a period of oblivion or, rather, judicial circumvention. The conspiracy doctrine, like the crime it

314

described, remained inherently nebulous, so that courts could still discover criminality in some labor activity that was personally repugnant to the judges sitting. The letter of Shaw's opinion could be satisfied, if not its spirit, by the naming of ends or means as illegal. Picketing or boycotting, for example, were judicially regarded as acts of violence in many states, and often the purpose of a strike was deemed an unwarrantable interference with private property. In the late nineteenth century and well into the twentieth, when judges were acting on the presupposition that the Fourteenth Amendment protected only entrepreneurial liberty, Shaw's opinions in this and other cases seemed faintly socialistic. His name was respected, even revered, but Commonwealth v. Hunt was politely evaded.

American law, from the late nineteenth century to the ultimate victory of Holmesian jurisprudence, became a deathbed for general-welfare or public-interest doctrines. In the meanwhile, doctrines of vested rights dominated, the conspiracy doctrine enjoyed a revival, and only a few states responded to labor's protest by enacting statutes half-heartedly intended to nullify labor's common law crimes. After the passage of the Sherman Act of 1890, with its prohibitions on combinations and conspiracies in restraint of trade, courts found in this "antitrust" legislation an effective weapon against unions. Almost any union activity could be speedily enjoined as a conspiracy in restraint of trade. The issuance of an injunction, the law's new and streamlined antilabor instrument, was often rationalized on the basis of the old conspiracy doctrine. Few successors to Lemuel Shaw—dispassionate and beholden to no special interests; concerned for the integrity of the law and of the judicial process; towering in stature and influence—were on the scene to protest.

In 1896, for example, when Justice Oliver Wendell Holmes of the Massachusetts Supreme Judicial Court invoked Shaw's name and decried the use of an injunction against peaceful picketing, he spoke in dissent. Holmes made explicit an implication that he found in Shaw: conflict between employers and employed is a form of competition. "If," declared Holmes, "the policy on which our law is founded is too narrowly expressed in the term free competition, we may substitute free struggle for life. Certainly, the policy is not limited to struggles between persons of the same class, competing for the same end. It applies to all conflicts of temporal interests." That it was lawful for a union to benefit itself even at the expense of injuring its antagonists was "decided as long

315

ago as 1842 by the good sense of Chief Justice Shaw, in Com. v. Hunt, 4 Metc. (Mass.) 111." Holmes relied on Shaw's belief that benefits to the public would accrue from the contest between unions and employers. He explained his position by advancing the proposition that "free competition is worth much more to society than it costs, and that on this ground the infliction of the damage is privileged. Commonwealth v. Hunt, 4 Metc. 111, 134." A young Massachusetts attorney, Louis Dembitz Brandeis, subscribed to the same view of the matter, indeed, made it a commitment to which he passionately dedicated himself. Together Holmes and Brandeis, most often in dissent from the Court's majority opinion, gave continued life to Shaw's vision of the law as a means of releasing the energies and range of choices for all Americans who utilized the right of association to advance their interests.

In the time of the New Deal, national law embodied protections to labor unions that had been foreshadowed in a tentative, groping way by Lemuel Shaw almost a century earlier. In the passage of the Wagner Labor Relations Act of 1936, Commonwealth v. Hunt received its greatest vindication. The first great victory for labor in the courts of this nation has today become so deeply accepted that it has been accorded the ultimate honor: it is taken for granted. Long a courageous, trail-blazing opinion, it is now a historical antique that bears the same relationship to modern labor law as the tin lizzie does to the new vehicles of space travel. The opinion continues, however, to bear witness to the estimate of Shaw by Justice Holmes, who remarked on his "accurate appreciation of the requirements of the community." Few have lived, thought Holmes, "who were his equals in their understanding of the grounds of public policy to which all laws must be ultimately referred. It was this which made him . . . the greatest magistrate which this country has produced."

Henry David Thoreau
Civil Disobedience
1846

EDITED BY FREDERICK B. TOLLES

A legend is not history. By definition it is a story that cannot be documented. Some legends nevertheless are too good not to be true. It is so with a conversation Ralph Waldo Emerson is said to have had with his friend Henry David Thoreau, whom, one evening in July, 1846, he was surprised to find locked up in the town jail at Concord, Massachusetts.

"Henry, why are you there?"

"Waldo, why are you not here?"

Now Emerson really didn't need to ask his question. He should have known why his friend was in jail. Thoreau was, like himself, a Transcendentalist, a philosophical individualist, yes, an anarchist, resistant on principle to civil government whenever it trenched upon his private life or made him support measures of which he morally disapproved. Resistant in practice, too, as on that very afternoon. He was living in his one-room hut on Walden Pond. He had gone there with a purpose: to live "deliberately, to front only the essential facts of life . . . to drive life into a corner," and find out what it really was. He had strolled into town, that afternoon, to pick up a repaired shoe at the cobbler's. Sam Staples, the town constable, had stopped him, reminded him that his poll tax was overdue. For three years Thoreau had declined to pay his poll tax. But now, in the summer of 1846, the United States was at war with Mexico. Like other abolitionists, he was convinced that the war was being fought to extend the area of slaveholding. To pay his tax would be to *imply his approval. He had told Sam Staples that he would not pay his poll tax. So off to jail he went. If Emerson did come by and asked why he was there, how else could he have replied but by asking, "Why are you not here?"*

Next morning, to his annoyance, he was set free. A veiled woman—probably his Aunt Maria—had gone to Staples' house after nightfall and paid the tax. The constable told her that, having taken off his boots for the evening, he would not go back to release his prisoner. So Thoreau spent one night in jail.

To explain his motives to his fellow townsmen, he wrote out and delivered at the Concord Lyceum a lecture entitled "The Relation of the Individual to the State." A few years later, in 1849, Elizabeth Peabody published it in the one issue of her periodical Aesthetic Papers under the title "Resistance to Civil Government." Later reprints carried the title "On the Duty of Civil Disobedience." But it is best known simply as "Civil Disobedience."

I HEARTILY accept the motto—"That government is best which governs least;" and I should like to see it acted up to more rapidly and systematically. Carried out, it finally amounts to this, which also I believe,—"That government is best which governs not at all;" and when men are prepared for it, that will be the kind of government which they will have. Government is at best but an expedient; but most governments are usually, and all governments are sometimes, inexpedient. The objections which have been brought against a standing army, and they are many and weighty, and deserve to prevail, may also at last be brought against a standing government. The standing army is only an arm of the standing government. The government itself, which is only the mode which the people have chosen to execute their will, is equally liable to be abused and perverted before the people can act through it. Witness the present Mexican war, the work of comparatively a few individuals using the standing government as their tool; for, in the outset, the people would not have consented to this measure.

This American government,—what is it but a tradition, though a recent one, endeavoring to transmit itself unimpaired to posterity, but

The essay is given here as it appeared in *Aesthetic Papers* (Boston, 1849).

each instant losing some of its integrity? It has not the vitality and force of a single living man; for a single man can bend it to his will. It is a sort of wooden gun to the people themselves; and, if ever they should use it in earnest as a real one against each other, it will surely split. But it is not the less necessary for this; for the people must have some complicated machinery or other, and hear its din, to satisfy that idea of government which they have. Governments show thus how successfully men can be imposed on, even impose on themselves, for their own advantage. It is excellent, we must all allow; yet this government never of itself furthered any enterprise, but by the alacrity with which it got out of its way. *It* does not keep the country free. *It* does not settle the West. *It* does not educate. The character inherent in the American people has done all that has been accomplished; and it would have done somewhat more, if the government had not sometimes got in its way. For government is an expedient by which men would fain succeed in letting one another alone; and, as has been said, when it is most expedient, the governed are most let alone by it. Trade and commerce, if they were not made of india rubber, would never manage to bounce over the obstacles which legislators are continually putting in their way; and, if one were to judge these men wholly by the effects of their actions, and not partly by their intentions, they would deserve to be classed and punished with those mischievous persons who put obstructions on the railroads.

But, to speak practically and as a citizen, unlike those who call themselves no-government men, I ask for, not at once no government, but *at once* a better government. Let every man make known what kind of government would command his respect, and that will be one step toward obtaining it.

After all, the practical reason why, when the power is once in the hands of the people, a majority are permitted, and for a long period continue, to rule, is not because they are most likely to be in the right, nor because this seems fairest to the minority, but because they are physically the strongest. But a government in which the majority rule in all cases cannot be based on justice, even as far as men understand it. Can there not be a government in which majorities do not virtually decide right and wrong, but conscience?—in which majorities decide only those questions to which the rule of expediency is applicable? Must the citizen ever for a moment, or in the least degree, resign his conscience to the legislator? Why has every man a conscience, then? I think that we should be men first, and subjects afterward. It is not desirable to cultivate a respect for the law, so much as for the right. The only obligation which I have a right to assume, is to do at any time what I think right. It is truly enough said, that a corporation has no conscience; but a corporation of conscientious men is a corporation *with* a conscience. Law never made men a whit more just; and, by means of their respect for it, even the well-disposed are daily made the agents of injustice. A common and natural result of an undue respect for law is, that you may see a file of soldiers, colonel, captain, corporal, privates, powder-monkeys and all, marching in admirable order over hill and dale to the wars, against their wills, aye, against their common sense and consciences, which makes it very steep marching indeed, and produces a palpitation of the heart. They have no doubt that it is a damnable business in which they are concerned; they are all peaceably inclined. Now, what are they? Men at all? or small moveable forts and magazines, at the service of some unscrupulous man in power? Visit the Navy Yard, and behold a marine, such a man as an American government can make, or such as it can make a man with its black arts, a mere shadow and reminiscence of humanity, a man laid out alive and standing, and already, as one may say, buried under arms with funeral accompaniments, though it may be

> "Not a drum was heard, nor a funeral note,
>   As his corse to the ramparts we hurried;
> Not a soldier discharged his farewell shot
>   O'er the grave where our hero we buried."

The mass of men serve the State thus, not as men mainly, but as machines, with their bodies. They are the standing army, and the militia, jailers, constables, *posse comitatus*, &c. In most cases there is no free exercise whatever of the judgment or of the moral sense; but they put themselves on a level with wood and earth and stones; and wooden men can perhaps be manufactured that will serve the purpose as well. Such command no more respect than men of straw, or a lump of dirt. They have the same sort of worth only as horses and dogs. Yet such as these even are commonly esteemed good citizens. Others, as most legislators, politicians, lawyers, ministers, and office-holders, serve the State chiefly with their heads; and, as they rarely make any moral distinctions, they are as likely to serve the devil, without intending it, as God. A very few, as heroes, patriots, martyrs, reformers in the great sense, and *men* serve the State with their consciences also, and so necessarily resist it for the most part; and they are commonly treated by it as enemies. A wise man will only be useful as a man, and will not submit to be "clay," and "stop a hole to keep the wind away," but leave that office to his dust at least:—

> "I am too high-born to be propertied,
> To be a secondary at control,
> Or useful serving-man and instrument
> To any sovereign state throughout the world."

He who gives himself entirely to his fellow-men appears to them useless and selfish; but he who gives himself partially to them is pronounced a benefactor and philanthropist.

How does it become a man to behave toward this American government to-day? I answer that he cannot without disgrace be associated with it. I cannot for an instant recognize that political organization as *my* government which is the *slave's* government also.

All men recognize the right of revolution; that is, the right to refuse allegiance to and to resist the government, when its tyranny or its inefficiency are great and unendurable. But almost all say that such is not the case now. But such was the case, they think, in the Revolution of '75. If one were to tell me that this was a bad government because it taxed certain foreign commodities brought to its ports, it is most probable that I should not make an ado about it, for I can do without them: all machines have their friction; and possibly this does enough good to counterbalance the evil. At any rate, it is a great evil to make a stir about it. But when the friction comes to have its machine, and oppression and robbery are organized, I say, let us not have such a machine any longer. In other words, when a sixth of the population of a nation which has undertaken to be the refuge of liberty are slaves, and a whole country is unjustly overrun and conquered by a foreign army, and subjected to military law, I think that it is not too soon for honest men to rebel and revolutionize. What makes this duty the more urgent is the fact, that the country so overrun is not our own, but ours is the invading army.

Paley, a common authority with many on moral questions, in his chapter on the "Duty of Submission to Civil Government," resolves all civil obligation into expediency; and he proceeds to say, "that so long as the interest of the whole society requires it, that is, so long as the established government cannot be resisted or changed without public inconveniency, it is the will of God that the established government be obeyed,—and no longer. This principle being admitted, the justice of every particular case of resistance is reduced to a computation of the quantity of the danger and grievance on the one side, and of the probability and expense of redressing it on the other." Of this, he says, every man shall judge for himself. But Paley appears never to have contemplated those cases to which the rule of expediency does not apply, in which a people, as well as an individual, must do justice, cost what it may. If I have unjustly wrested a plank from a drowning man, I must restore it to him though I drown myself. This, according to Paley, would be inconvenient. But he that would save his life, in such a case, shall lose it. This people must cease to hold slaves, and to make war on Mexico, though it cost them their existence as a people.

In their practice, nations agree with Paley; but does any one think that Massachusetts does exactly what is right at the present crisis?

> "A drab of state, a cloth-o'-silver slut,
>   To have her train borne up, and her soul trail in the dirt."

Practically speaking, the opponents to a reform in Massachusetts are not a hundred thousand politicians at the South, but a hundred thousand merchants and farmers here, who are more interested in commerce and agriculture than they are in humanity, and are not prepared to do justice to the slave and to Mexico, *cost what it may*. I quarrel not with far-off foes, but with those who, near at home, co-operate with, and do the bidding of those far away, and without whom the latter would be harmless. We are accustomed to say, that the mass of men are unprepared; but improvement is slow, because the few are not materially wiser or better than the many. It is not so important that many should be as good as you, as that there be some absolute goodness somewhere; for that will leaven the whole lump. There are thousands who are *in opinion* opposed to slavery and to the war, who yet in effect do nothing to put an end to them; who, esteeming themselves children of Washington and Franklin, sit down with their hands in their pockets, and say that they know not what to do, and do nothing; who even postpone the question of freedom to the question of free-trade, and quietly read the prices-current along with the latest advices from Mexico, after dinner, and, it may be, fall asleep over them both. What is the price-current of an honest man and patriot to-day? They hesitate, and they regret, and sometimes they petition; but they do nothing in earnest and with effect.

They will wait, well disposed, for others to remedy the evil, that they may no longer have it to regret. At most, they give only a cheap vote, and a feeble countenance and God-speed, to the right, as it goes by them. There are nine hundred and ninety-nine patrons of virtue to one virtuous man; but it is easier to deal with the real possessor of a thing than with the temporary guardian of it.

All voting is a sort of gaming, like chequers or backgammon, with a slight moral tinge to it, a playing with right and wrong, with moral questions; and betting naturally accompanies it. The character of the voters is not staked. I cast my vote, perchance, as I think right; but I am not vitally concerned that that right should prevail. I am willing to leave it to the majority. Its obligation, therefore, never exceeds that of expediency. Even voting *for the right* is *doing* nothing for it. It is only expressing to men feebly your desire that it should prevail. A wise man will not leave the right to the mercy of chance, nor wish it to prevail through the power of the majority. There is but little virtue in the action of masses of men. When the majority shall at length vote for the abolition of slavery, it will be because they are indifferent to slavery, or because there is but little slavery left to be abolished by their vote. *They* will then be the only slaves. Only *his* vote can hasten the abolition of slavery who asserts his own freedom by his vote.

I hear of a convention to be held at Baltimore, or elsewhere, for the selection of a candidate for the Presidency, made up chiefly of editors, and men who are politicians by profession; but I think, what is it to any independent, intelligent, and respectable man what decision they may come to, shall we not have the advantage of his wisdom and honesty, nevertheless? Can we not count upon some independent votes? Are there not many individuals in the country who do not attend conventions? But no: I find that the respectable man, so called, has immediately drifted from his position, and despairs of his country, when his country has more reason to despair of him. He forthwith adopts one of the candidates thus selected as the only *available* one, thus proving that he is himself *available* for any purposes of the demagogue. His vote is of no more worth than that of any unprincipled foreigner or hireling native, who may have been bought. Oh for a man who is a *man*, and, as my neighbor says, has a bone in his back which you cannot pass your hand through! Our statistics are at fault: the population has been returned too large. How many *men* are there to a square thousand miles in this country? Hardly one. Does not America offer any inducement for men to settle here? The American has dwindled into an Odd Fellow,—one who may be known by the development of his organ of gregariousness, and a manifest lack of intellect and cheerful self-reliance; whose first and chief concern, on coming into the world, is to see that the almshouses are in good repair; and, before yet he has lawfully donned the virile garb, to collect a fund for the support of the widows and orphans that may be; who, in short, ventures to live only by the aid of the mutual insurance company, which has promised to bury him decently.

It is not a man's duty, as a matter of course, to devote himself to the eradication of any, even the most enormous wrong; he may still properly have other concerns to engage him; but it is his duty, at least, to wash his hands of it, and, if he gives it no thought longer, not to give it practically his support. If I devote myself to other pursuits and contemplations, I must first see, at least, that I do not pursue them sitting upon another man's shoulders. I must get off him first, that he may pursue his contemplations too. See what gross inconsistency is tolerated. I have heard some of my townsmen say, "I should like to have them order me out to help put down an insurrection of the slaves, or to march to Mexico,—see if I would go;" and yet these very men have each, directly by their allegiance, and so indirectly, at least, by their money, furnished a substitute. The soldier is applauded who refuses to serve in an unjust war by those who do not refuse to sustain the unjust government which makes the war; is applauded by those whose own act and authority he disregards and sets at naught; as if the State were penitent to that degree that it hired one to scourge it while it sinned, but not to that degree that it left off sinning for a moment. Thus, under the name of order and civil government, we are all made at last to pay homage to and support our own meanness. After the first blush of sin, comes its indifference; and from immoral it becomes, as it were, *un*moral, and not quite unnecessary to that life which we have made.

The broadest and most prevalent error requires the most disinterested virtue to sustain it. The slight reproach to which the virtue of patriotism is commonly liable, the noble are most likely to incur. Those who, while they disapprove of the character and measures of a government, yield to it their allegiance and support are undoubtedly its most conscientious supporters, and so frequently the most serious obstacles to reform. Some are petitioning the State to dissolve the Union, to disregard the requisitions of the President. Why do they not dissolve it themselves,—the union between themselves and the State,—and refuse to pay their quota into its treasury? Do not they stand in the same relation to the State that the State does to the Union? And have not the same reasons prevented the State from resisting the Union, which have prevented them from resisting the State?

How can a man be satisfied to entertain an opinion merely, and enjoy *it?* Is there any enjoyment in it, if his opinion is that he is aggrieved? If you are cheated out of a single dollar by your neighbor, you do not rest satisfied with knowing that you are cheated, or with saying that you are cheated, or even with petitioning him to pay you your due; but you take effectual steps at once to obtain the full amount, and see that you are never cheated again. Action from principle,—the perception and the performance of right,—changes things and relations; it is essentially revolutionary, and does not consist wholly with any thing which was. It not only divides states and churches, it divides families; aye, it divides the *individual*, separating the diabolical in him from the divine.

Unjust laws exist: shall we be content to obey them, or shall we endeavor to amend them, and obey them until we have succeeded, or shall we transgress them at once? Men generally, under such a government as this, think that they ought to wait until they have persuaded the majority to alter them. They think that, if they should resist, the remedy would be worse than the evil. But it is the fault of the government itself that the remedy *is* worse than the evil. *It* makes it worse. Why is it not more apt to anticipate and provide for reform? Why does it not cherish its wise minority? Why does it cry and resist before it is hurt? Why does it not encourage its citizens to be on the alert to point out its faults, and *do* better than it would have them? Why does it always crucify Christ, and excommunicate Copernicus and Luther, and pronounce Washington and Franklin rebels?

One would think, that a deliberate and practical denial of its authority was the only offence never contemplated by government; else, why has it not assigned its definite, its suitable and proportionate penalty? If a man who has no property refuses but once to earn nine shillings for the State, he is put in prison for a period unlimited by any law that I know, and determined only by the discretion of those who placed him there; but if he should steal ninety times nine shillings from the State, he is soon permitted to go at large again.

If the injustice is part of the necessary friction of the machine of government, let it go, let it go: perchance it will wear smooth,—certainly the machine will wear out. If the injustice has a spring, or a pulley, or a rope, or a crank, exclusively for itself, then perhaps you may consider whether the remedy will not be worse than the evil; but if it is of such a nature that it requires you to be the agent of injustice to another, then, I say, break the law. Let your life be a counter friction to stop the machine. What I have to do is to see, at any rate, that I do not lend myself to the wrong which I condemn.

As for adopting the ways which the State has provided for remedying the evil, I know not of such ways. They take too much time, and a man's life will be gone. I have other affairs to attend to. I came into this world, not chiefly to make this a good place to live in, but to live in it, be it good or bad. A man has not every thing to do, but something; and because he cannot do *every thing*, it is not necessary that he should do *something* wrong. It is not my business to be petitioning the governor or the legislature any more than it is theirs to petition me; and if they should not hear my petition, what should I do then? But in this case the State has provided no way: its very Constitution is the evil. This may seem to be harsh and stubborn and unconciliatory; but it is to treat with the utmost kindness and consideration the only spirit that can appreciate or deserves it. So is all change for the better, like birth and death which convulse the body.

I do not hesitate to say, that those who call themselves abolitionists should at once effectually withdraw their support, both in person and property, from the government of Massachusetts, and not wait till they constitute a majority of one, before they suffer the right to prevail through them. I think that it is enough if they have God on their side, without waiting for that other one. Moreover, any man more right than his neighbors constitutes a majority of one already.

I meet this American government, or its representative the State government, directly, and face to face, once a year, no more, in the person of its tax-gatherer; this is the only mode in which a man situated as I am necessarily meets it; and it then says distinctly, Recognize me; and the simplest, the most effectual, and, in the present posture of affairs, the indispensablest mode of treating with it on this head, of expressing your little satisfaction with and love for it, is to deny it then. My civil neighbor, the tax-gatherer, is the very man I have to deal with, —for it is, after all, with men and not with parchment that I quarrel,— and he has voluntarily chosen to be an agent of the government. How shall he ever know well what he is and does as an officer of the government, or as a man, until he is obliged to consider whether he shall treat me, his neighbor, for whom he has respect, as a neighbor and well-disposed man, or as a maniac and disturber of the peace, and see if he can get over this obstruction to his neighborliness without a ruder and more impetuous thought or speech corresponding with his action? I know this well, that if one thousand, if one hundred, if ten men whom I could name,—if ten *honest* men only,—aye, if *one* HONEST man, in this State of Massachusetts, *ceasing to hold slaves*, were actually to withdraw from this copartnership, and be locked up in the county jail therefor, it would be the abolition of slavery in America. For it matters not how small the beginning may seem to be: what is once well done is done for ever. But we love better to talk about it: that we say is our mission. Reform keeps many scores of newspapers in its service, but not one man. If my esteemed neighbor, the State's ambassador, who will devote his days to the settlement of the question of human rights in the Council Chamber, instead of being threatened with the prisons of Carolina, were to sit down the prisoner of Massachusetts, that State which is so anxious to foist the sin of slavery upon her sister,—though at present she can discover only an act of inhospitality to be the ground of a quarrel with her,—the Legislature would not wholly waive the subject the following winter.

Under a government which imprisons any unjustly, the true place for a just man is also in prison. The proper place to-day, the only place which Massachusetts has provided for her freer and less desponding spirits, is in her prisons, to be put out and locked out of the State by her own act, as they have already put themselves out by their principles. It is there that the fugitive slave, and the Mexican prisoner on parole, and the Indian come to plead the wrongs of his race, should find them; on that separate, but more free and honorable ground, where the State places those who are not *with* her, but *against* her,—the only house in a slave-state in which a free man can abide with honor. If any think that their influence would be lost there, and their voices no longer afflict the ear of the State, that they would not be as an enemy within its walls, they do not know by how much truth is stronger than error, nor how much more eloquently and effectively he can combat injustice who has experienced a little in his own person. Cast your whole vote, not a strip of paper merely, but your whole influence. A minority is powerless while it conforms to the majority; it is not even a minority then; but it is irresistible when it clogs by its whole weight. If the alternative is to keep all just men in prison, or give up war and slavery, the State will not hesitate which to choose. If a thousand men were not to pay their tax-bills this year, that would not be a violent and bloody measure, as it would be to pay them, and enable the State to commit violence and shed innocent blood. This is, in fact, the definition of a peaceable revolution, if any such is possible. If the tax-gatherer, or any other public officer, asks me, as one has done, "But what shall I do?" my answer is, "If you really wish to do any thing, resign your office." When the subject has refused allegiance, and the officer has resigned his office, then the revolution is accomplished. But even suppose blood should flow. Is there not a sort of blood shed when the conscience is wounded? Through this wound a man's real manhood and immortality flow out, and he bleeds to an everlasting death. I see this blood flowing now.

I have contemplated the imprisonment of the offender, rather than the seizure of his goods,—though both will serve the same purpose,—because they who assert the purest right, and consequently are most dangerous to a corrupt State, commonly have not spent much time in accumulating property. To such the State renders comparatively small service, and a slight tax is wont to appear exorbitant, particularly if they are obliged to earn it by special labor with their hands. If there were one who lived wholly without the use of money, the State itself would hesitate to demand it of him. But the rich man—not to make any invidious comparison—is always sold to the institution which makes him rich. Absolutely speaking, the more money, the less virtue; for money comes between a man and his objects, and obtains them for him; and it was certainly no great virtue to obtain it. It puts to rest many questions which he would otherwise be taxed to answer; while the only new question which it puts is the hard but superfluous one, how to spend it. Thus his moral ground is taken from under his feet. The opportunities of living are diminished in proportion as what are called the "means" are increased. The best thing a man can do for his culture when he is rich is to endeavour to carry out those schemes which he entertained when he was poor. Christ answered the Herodians according to their condition. "Show me the tribute-money," said he;—and one took a penny out of his pocket;—if you use money which has the image of Caesar on it, and which he has made current and valuable, that is, *if you are men of the State*, and gladly enjoy the advantages of Caesar's government, then pay him back some of his own when he demands it. "Render therefore to Caesar that which is Caesar's, and to God those things which are God's,"—leaving them no wiser than before as to which was which; for they did not wish to know.

When I converse with the freest of my neighbors, I perceive that, whatever they may say about the magnitude and seriousness of the question, and their regard for the public tranquillity, the long and the short of the matter is, that they cannot spare the protection of the existing government, and they dread the consequences of disobedience to it to their property and families. For my own part, I should not like to think that I ever rely on the protection of the State. But, if I deny the authority of the State when it presents its tax-bill, it will soon take and waste all my property, and so harass me and my children without end. This is hard. This makes it impossible for a man to live honestly, and at the same time comfortably in outward respects. It will not be worth the while to accumulate property; that would be sure to go again. You must hire or squat somewhere, and raise but a small crop, and eat that soon. You must live within yourself, and depend upon yourself, always tucked up and ready for a start, and not have many affairs. A man may grow rich in Turkey even, if he will be in all respects a good subject of the Turkish government. Confucius said,—"If a State is governed by the principles of reason, poverty and misery are subjects of shame; if a State is not governed by the principles of reason, riches and honors are the subjects of shame." No: until I want the protection of Massachusetts to be extended to me in some distant southern port, where my liberty is endangered, or until I am bent solely on building up an estate at home by peaceful enterprise, I can afford to refuse allegiance to Massachusetts, and her right to my property and life. It costs me less in every sense to incur the penalty of disobedience to the State than it would to obey. I should feel as if I were worth less in that case.

Some years ago, the State met me in behalf of the church, and commanded me to pay a certain sum toward the support of a clergyman whose preaching my father attended, but never I myself. "Pay it," it said, "or be locked up in the jail." I declined to pay. But, unfortunately, another man saw fit to pay it. I did not see why the schoolmaster should be taxed to support the priest, and not the priest the schoolmaster; for I was not the State's schoolmaster, but I supported myself by voluntary subscription. I did not see why the lyceum should not present its tax-bill, and have the State to back its demand, as well as the church. However, at the request of the selectmen, I condescended to make some such statement as this in writing:—"Know all men by these presents, that I, Henry Thoreau, do not wish to be regarded as a member of any incorporated society which I have not joined." This I gave to the town-clerk; and he has it. The State, having thus learned that I did not wish to be regarded as a member of that church, has never made a like demand on me since; though it said that it must adhere to its original presumption that time. If I had known how to name them, I should then have signed off in detail from all the societies which I never signed on to; but I did not know where to find a complete list.

I have paid no poll-tax for six years. I was put into a jail once on this account, for one night; and, as I stood considering the walls of solid stone, two or three feet thick, the door of wood and iron, a foot thick, and the iron grating which strained the light, I could not help being struck with the foolishness of that institution which treated me as if I were mere flesh and blood and bones, to be locked up. I wondered that it should have concluded at length that this was the best use it could put me to, and had never thought to avail itself of my services in some way. I saw that, if there was a wall of stone between me and my townsmen, there was a still more difficult one to climb or break through, before they could get to be as free as I was. I did not for a moment feel confined, and the walls seemed a great waste of stone and mortar. I felt as if I alone of all my townsmen had paid my tax. They plainly did not know how to treat me, but behaved like persons who are underbred. In every threat and in every compliment there was a blunder; for they thought that my chief desire was to stand the other side of that stone wall. I could not but smile to see how industriously they locked the door on my meditations, which followed them out again without let or hinderance, and *they* were really all that was dangerous. As they could not reach me, they had resolved to punish my body; just as boys, if they cannot come at some person against whom they have a spite, will abuse his dog. I saw that the State was half-witted, that it was timid as a lone woman with her silver spoons, and that it did not know its friends from its foes, and I lost all my remaining respect for it, and pitied it.

Thus the State never intentionally confronts a man's sense, intellectual or moral, but only his body, his senses. It is not armed with superior wit or honesty, but with superior physical strength. I was not born to be forced. I will breathe after my own fashion. Let us see who is the strongest. What force has a multitude? They only can force me who obey a higher law than I. They force me to become like themselves. I do not hear of *men* being *forced* to live this way or that by masses of men. What sort of life were that to live? When I meet a government which says to me, "Your money or your life," why should I be in haste to give it my money? It may be in a great strait, and not know what to do: I cannot help that. It must help itself; do as I do. It is not worth the while to snivel about it. I am not responsible for the successful working of the machinery of society. I am not the son of the engineer. I perceive that, when an acorn and a chestnut fall side by side, the one does not remain inert to make way for the other, but both obey their own laws, and spring and grow and flourish as best they can, till one, perchance, overshadows and destroys the other. If a plant cannot live according to its nature, it dies; and so a man.

The night in prison was novel and interesting enough. The prisoners in their shirt-sleeves were enjoying a chat and the evening air in the door-way, when I entered. But the jailer said, "Come, boys, it is time to lock up;" and so they dispersed, and I heard the sound of their steps returning into the hollow apartments. My room-mate was introduced to me by the jailer, as "a first-rate fellow and a clever man." When the door was locked, he showed me where to hang my hat, and how he managed matters there. The rooms were whitewashed once a month; and this one, at least, was the whitest, most simply furnished, and probably the neatest apartment in the town. He naturally wanted to know where I came from, and what brought me there; and, when I had told him, I asked him in my turn how he came there, presuming him to be an honest man, of course; and, as the world goes, I believe he was. "Why," said he, "they accuse me of burning a barn; but I never did it." As near as I could discover, he had probably gone to bed in a barn when drunk, and smoked his pipe there; and so a barn was burnt. He had the reputation of being a clever man, had been there some three months waiting for his trial to come on, and would have to wait as much longer: but he was quite domesticated and contented, since he got his board for nothing, and thought that he was well treated.

He occupied one window, and I the other; and I saw, that, if one stayed there long, his principal business would be to look out the window. I had soon read all the tracts that were left there, and examined where former prisoners had broken out, and where a grate had been sawed off, and heard the history of the various occupants of that room; for I found that even here there was a history and a gossip which never circulated beyond the walls of the jail. Probably this is the only house in

331

the town where verses are composed, which are afterward printed in a circular form, but not published. I was shown quite a long list of verses which were composed by some young men who had been detected in an attempt to escape, who avenged themselves by singing them.

I pumped my fellow-prisoner as dry as I could, for fear I should never see him again; but at length he showed me which was my bed, and left me to blow out the lamp.

It was like travelling into a far country, such as I had never expected to behold, to lie there for one night. It seemed to me that I never had heard the town-clock strike before, nor the evening sounds of the village; for we slept with the windows open, which were inside the grating. It was to see my native village in the light of the middle ages, and our Concord was turned into a Rhine stream, and visions of knights and castles passed before me. They were the voices of old burghers that I heard in the streets. I was an involuntary spectator and auditor of whatever was done and said in the kitchen of the adjacent village-inn,— a wholly new and rare experience to me. It was a closer view of my native town. I was fairly inside of it. I never had seen its institutions before. This is one of its peculiar institutions; for it is a shire town. I began to comprehend what its inhabitants were about.

In the morning, our breakfasts were put through the hole in the door, in small oblong-square tin pans, made to fit, and holding a pint of chocolate, with brown bread, and an iron spoon. When they called for the vessels again, I was green enough to return what bread I had left; but my comrade seized it, and said that I should lay that up for lunch or dinner. Soon after, he was let out to work at haying in a neighboring field, whither he went every day, and would not be back till noon; so he bade me good-day, saying that he doubted if he should see me again.

When I came out of prison,—for some one interfered, and paid the tax,—I did not perceive that great changes had taken place on the common, such as he observed who went in a youth and emerged a tottering and gray-headed man; and yet a change had to my eyes come over the scene,—the town, and State and country,—greater than any that mere time could effect. I saw yet more distinctly the State in which I lived. I saw to what extent the people among whom I lived could be trusted as good neighbors and friends; that their friendship was for summer weather only; that they did not greatly purpose to do right; that they were a distinct race from me by their prejudices and superstitions, as the Chinamen and Malays are; that, in their sacrifices to humanity, they ran no risks, not even to their property; that, after all, they were not so noble but they treated the thief as he had treated them, and hoped, by a certain outward observance and a few prayers, and by walking in a particular straight though useless path from time to time, to save their souls. This may be to judge my neighbors harshly; for I believe that most of them are not aware that they have such an institution as the jail in their village.

It was formerly the custom in our village, when a poor debtor came out of jail, for his acquaintances to salute him, looking through their fingers, which were crossed to represent the grating of a jail window, "How do ye do?" My neighbors did not thus salute me, but first looked at me, and then at one another, as if I had returned from a long journey. I was put into jail as I was going to the shoemaker's to get a shoe which was mended. When I was let out the next morning, I proceeded to finish my errand, and, having put on my mended shoe, joined a huckleberry party, who were impatient to put themselves under my conduct; and in half an hour,—for the horse was soon tackled,—was in the midst of a huckleberry field, on one of our highest hills, two miles off; and then the State was nowhere to be seen.

This is the whole history of "My Prisons."

I have never declined paying the highway tax, because I am as desirous of being a good neighbor as I am of being a bad subject; and as for supporting schools, I am doing my part to educate my fellow-countrymen now. It is for no particular item in the tax-bill that I refuse to pay it. I simply wish to refuse allegiance to the State, to withdraw and stand aloof from it effectually. I do not care to trace the course of my dollar, if I could, till it buys a man, or a musket to shoot one with,—the dollar is innocent,—but I am concerned to trace the effects of my allegiance. In fact, I quietly declare war with the State, after my fashion, though I will still make what use and get what advantage of her I can, as is usual in such cases.

If others pay the tax which is demanded of me, from a sympathy with the State, they do but what they have already done in their own case, or rather they abet injustice to a greater extent than the State requires. If they pay the tax from a mistaken interest in the individual taxed, to save his property or prevent his going to jail, it is because they have not considered wisely how far they let their private feelings interfere with the public good.

333

This, then, is my position at present. But one cannot be too much on his guard in such a case, lest his action be biassed by obstinacy or an undue regard for the opinions of men. Let him see that he does only what belongs to himself and to the hour.

I think sometimes, Why, this people mean well; they are only ignorant; they would do better if they knew how: why give your neighbors this pain to treat you as they are not inclined to? But I think, again, this is no reason why I should do as they do, or permit others to suffer much greater pain of a different kind. Again, I sometimes say to myself, When many millions of men, without heat, without ill-will, without personal feeling of any kind, demand of you a few shillings only, without the possibility, such is their constitution, of retracting or altering their present demand, and without the possibility, on your side, of appeal to any other millions, why expose yourself to this overwhelming brute force? You do not resist cold and hunger, the winds and the waves, thus obstinately; you quietly submit to a thousand similar necessities. You do not put your head into the fire. But just in proportion as I regard this as not wholly a brute force, but partly a human force, and consider that I have relations to those millions as to so many millions of men, and not of mere brute or inanimate things, I see that appeal is possible, first and instantaneously, from them to the Maker of them, and, secondly, from them to themselves. But if I put my head deliberately into the fire, there is no appeal to fire or to the Maker of fire, and I have only myself to blame. If I could convince myself that I have any right to be satisfied with men as they are, and to treat them accordingly, and not according, in some respects, to my requisitions and expectations of what they and I ought to be, then, like a good Mussulman and fatalist, I should endeavor to be satisfied with things as they are, and say it is the will of God. And, above all, there is this difference between resisting this and a purely brute or natural force, that I can resist this with some effect; but I cannot expect, like Orpheus, to change the nature of the rocks and trees and beasts.

I do not wish to quarrel with any man or nation. I do not wish to split hairs, to make fine distinctions, or set myself up as better than my neighbors. I seek rather, I may say, even an excuse for conforming to the laws of the land. I am but too ready to conform to them. Indeed I have reason to suspect myself on this head; and each year, as the tax-gatherer comes round, I find myself disposed to review the acts and position of the general and state governments, and the spirit of the people, to discover a pretext for conformity. I believe that the State will soon be able to take all my work of this sort out of my hands, and then I shall be no better a patriot than my fellow-countrymen. Seen from a lower point of view, the Constitution, with all its faults, is very good; the law and the courts are very respectable; even this State and this American government are, in many respects, very admirable and rare things, to be thankful for, such as a great many have described them; but seen from a point of view a little higher, they are what I have described them; seen from a higher still, and the highest, who shall say what they are, or that they are worth looking at or thinking of at all?

However, the government does not concern me much, and I shall bestow the fewest possible thoughts on it. It is not many moments that I live under a government, even in this world. If a man is thought-free, fancy-free, imagination-free, that which *is not* never for a long time appearing *to be* to him, unwise rulers or reformers cannot fatally interrupt him.

I know that most men think differently from myself; but those whose lives are by profession devoted to the study of these or kindred subjects, content me as little as any. Statesmen and legislators, standing so completely within the institution, never distinctly and nakedly behold it. They speak of moving society, but have no resting-place without it. They may be men of a certain experience and discrimination, and have no doubt invented ingenious and even useful systems, for which we sincerely thank them; but all their wit and usefulness lie within certain not very wide limits. They are wont to forget that the world is not governed by policy and expediency. Webster never goes behind government, and so cannot speak with authority about it. His words are wisdom to those legislators who contemplate no essential reform in the existing government; but for thinkers, and those who legislate for all time, he never once glances at the subject. I know of those whose serene and wise speculations on this theme would soon reveal the limits of his mind's range and hospitality. Yet, compared with the cheap professions of most reformers, and the still cheaper wisdom and eloquence of politicians in general, his are almost the only sensible and valuable words, and we thank Heaven for him. Comparatively, he is always strong, original, and, above all, practical. Still his quality is not wisdom, but prudence. The lawyer's truth is not Truth, but consistency or a consistent expediency. Truth is always in harmony with herself, and is not concerned chiefly to reveal the justice that may consist with wrong-doing. He well deserves to be called, as he has been called, the Defender of the Constitution. There are really no blows to be given by him but defensive ones. He is not a leader, but a follower. His leaders are the men of '87. "I have never made an effort," he says, "and never propose to make an effort; I have never countenanced an effort, and never mean to countenance an effort, to disturb the arrangement as originally made, by which the various States came into the Union." Still thinking of the sanction which the Constitution gives to slavery, he says, "Because it was a part of the original compact,—let it stand." Notwithstanding his special acuteness and ability, he is unable to take a fact out of its merely political relations, and behold it as it lies absolutely to be disposed of by the intellect,—what, for instance, it behoves a man to do here in America to-day with regard to slavery, but ventures, or is driven, to make some such desperate answer as the following, while professing to speak absolutely, and as a private man,—from which what new and singular code of social duties might be inferred?—"The manner," says he, "in which the governments of those States where slavery exists are to regulate it, is for their own consideration, under their responsibility to their constituents, to the general laws of propriety, humanity, and justice, and to God. Associations formed elsewhere, springing from a feeling of humanity, or any other cause, have nothing whatever to do with it. They have never received any encouragement from me, and they never will." *

They who know of no purer sources of truth, who have traced up its stream no higher, stand, and wisely stand, by the Bible and the Constitution, and drink at it there with reverence and humility; but they who behold where it comes trickling into this lake or that pool, gird up their loins once more, and continue their pilgrimage toward its fountainhead.

No man with a genius for legislation has appeared in America. They are rare in the history of the world. There are orators, politicians, and eloquent men, by the thousand; but the speaker has not yet opened his mouth to speak, who is capable of settling the much-vexed questions of the day. We love eloquence for its own sake, and not for any truth which it may utter, or any heroism it may inspire. Our legislators have not yet learned the comparative value of free-trade and of freedom, of union, and of rectitude, to a nation. They have no genius or talent for

---

* These extracts have been inserted since the Lecture was read.

comparatively humble questions of taxation and finance, commerce and manufactures and agriculture. If we were left solely to the wordy wit of legislators in Congress for our guidance, uncorrected by the seasonable experience and the effectual complaints of the people, America would not long retain her rank among the nations. For eighteen hundred years, though perchance I have no right to say it, the New Testament has been written; yet where is the legislator who has wisdom and practical talent enough to avail himself of the light which it sheds on the science of legislation?

The authority of government, even such as I am willing to submit to, —for I will cheerfully obey those who know and can do better than I, and in many things even those who neither know nor can do so well,—is still an impure one: to be strictly just, it must have the sanction and consent of the governed. It can have no pure right over my person and property but what I concede to it. The progress from an absolute to a limited monarchy, from a limited monarchy to a democracy, is a progress toward a true respect for the individual. Is a democracy, such as we know it, the last improvement possible in government? Is it not possible to take a step further towards recognizing and organizing the rights of man? There will never be a really free and enlightened State, until the State comes to recognize the individual as a higher and independent power, from which all its own power and authority are derived, and treats him accordingly. I please myself with imagining a State at last which can afford to be just to all men, and to treat the individual with respect as a neighbor; which even would not think it inconsistent with its own repose, if a few were to live aloof from it, not meddling with it, nor embraced by it, who fulfilled all the duties of neighbors and fellowmen. A State which bore this kind of fruit, and suffered it to drop off as fast as it ripened, would prepare the way for a still more perfect and glorious State, which also I have imagined, but not yet anywhere seen.

His protest made, Thoreau went cheerily off to pick huckleberries. His essay in Aesthetic Papers *did not cause much comment. Perhaps it only confirmed the common belief that he was, after all, either a wild man who lived in the woods or a conceited fool who delighted, said James*

Russell Lowell, in perversity of thought. Even Emerson told Bronson Alcott that Thoreau's action had been "mean and skulking, and in bad taste." But privately to his journal Emerson confided that at least Thoreau was different from Daniel Webster. Webster had lately warned Congress that the war would be expensive, but had voted for it and sent his son off to it. "They calculated rightly on Mr. Webster." But, he went on, "My friend Mr. Thoreau has gone to jail rather than pay his tax. On him they could not calculate."

Nor could one have calculated in 1849 that his essay would have blossomed into a long and splendid life of world-wide usefulness, continuing long after his death. Around 1900, Leo Tolstoy, in Russia, happened to read it. Tolstoy was a man of intense moral convictions. For him, as for Thoreau, complex problems of state and society resolved themselves into simple, radical, moral imperatives. Having read it, he sat down and wrote a letter to the North American Review: Why, he asked, did Americans listen to their big businessmen and military leaders? Why not to Thoreau? He had wisdom. His mind cut through conventions to the simple truth of things. What he believed, that he did.

Down in South Africa, a few years later, a little-known Hindu lawyer happened to read Thoreau's essay. He was hard at work defending his fellow Indians who had violated the discriminatory Asiatic Registration Act. He found the essay "so convincing and truthful" that he became a lifelong admirer of Thoreau. In the end, by turning Thoreau's individual protest into a mass movement of civil disobedience, he set India free. His name was Mohandas K. Gandhi. On October 26, 1907, he reprinted part of Thoreau's essay in his newspaper, Indian Opinion. Soon after, it appeared in pamphlet form. Readers of Indian Opinion were invited to submit essays in a contest on "The Ethics of Passive Resistance," using Thoreau's essay as one of their sources. When the entries were judged, Gandhi was himself in jail for refusing to register as an Indian. He had started his forty-year campaign of civil disobedience and nonviolent resistance.

With Gandhi civil disobedience was a potent instrument of social action. It required the strictest self-discipline from his followers. Often they were beaten, clubbed, trampled upon; sometimes they died. But always unprotestingly. Always, when the first rank was beaten down, there came a second rank, and a third, and a fourth. And always in the end they won. In 1930, the British government having established a monopoly of salt manufacture, Gandhi led his followers to the seashore to produce salt by evaporating sea water. For this violation of law he was thrown into prison. But Indians by the hundreds, by the thousands, followed his example. They marched up to the stockades around the salt pans to be struck down by policemen with five-foot steel-tipped clubs. But, ultimately, the law was repealed. By similar campaigns Mahatma Gandhi and his faithful followers broke down the traditional restrictions which made the lives of the untouchables almost beyond endurance. By nonviolent civil disobedience, with much suffering but with stoic self-control, the Gandhian movement of mass civil disobedience moved on to achieve in 1947 its ultimate goal—self-government for India.

Gandhi always carried a copy of Thoreau's essay with him, even to jail. So he told Roger Baldwin, the American libertarian. It contained, he said, "the essence of his political philosophy, not only as India's struggle related to the British, but as to his own views of the relation of citizens to government." One might almost say that Henry David Thoreau of Concord freed India, a century after his own night in prison.

All over the world strong-minded individuals have read Thoreau's essay, and it has made a difference to them. In 1898 Robert Blatchford, an English writer, published a book called Merrie England. Its pages were steeped in Thoreau. Its stimulation of a little group of men and women, some have said, led to the founding of the British Labour Party. Emma Goldman, the Russian-born anarchist whose radical activities shocked staid middle-class Americans before and after 1900, drew on Thoreau for some of her ideas. She and novelist Upton Sinclair and Socialist Norman Thomas, each acting independently, have read Thoreau's essay in public in times of tension—and have been arrested for it. When Denmark was occupied by the Nazis in World War II, the essay was widely circulated in the resistance movement. Even King Christian took part in some of the mass acts of civil disobedience. These Thoreau-inspired acts often baffled and frustrated the Nazi occupying forces.

In recent years in the United States, Thoreau's ideas have come to life most fruitfully, chiefly among the Negroes in the South. In Montgomery, Alabama, Negroes steadfastly refused to ride on segregated buses—and gained thereby the right to sit where they chose. In Nashville, Tennessee, and elsewhere they entered white churches in a "kneel-in"—and won the right there to worship God, who is no respecter of persons. And so on through a long list of courageous well-disciplined acts of nonviolent civil disobedience.

The leaders of these movements have left little doubt about the ultimate source of their philosophy. More than twenty years ago, the Reverend James Robinson noted that the abolitionists, a century before, had paid little attention to Thoreau's "Civil Disobedience." But "as one reads the essay," he went on, writing for a Negro audience, "it is impossible not to notice that almost every sentence is loaded with meaning for us today. . . . Substitute the economic, political, and social persecution of American Negroes today where Thoreau condemns Negro slavery—and you will scarcely find half a dozen sentences in the entire essay which you cannot apply to your own actions in the present crisis." Among the readers of Robinson's article were the founders of CORE (the Congress of Racial Equality), one of the organizations which have led the way toward civil rights for Negroes in the United States.

And the Reverend Martin Luther King in his autobiographical Stride toward Freedom recalls that early in December, 1955, when he was planning the boycott of segregated buses in Montgomery, Alabama, he suddenly remembered Thoreau's essay, which he had read in college. What he and his fellow Negroes were about to do, he realized, was precisely what Thoreau had done in 1846. "We were simply saying to the white community, 'We can no longer lend our coöperation to an evil system.' . . . From this moment on I conceived of our movement as an act of massive non-coöperation."

Thoreau would have been pleased. His own protest had been purely an individual act. Long after he was dead, it had become the inspiration for a mass movement.

Horace Mann
Report of the Massachusetts Board of Education
1848

EDITED BY RALPH H. GABRIEL

Horace Mann was born and reared in poverty on a farm in Franklin, Massachusetts. As a child he endured winter terms of school which were presided over by ignorant masters, much given to the use of the rod. The hellfire Sunday sermons of his minister caused the sensitive boy many nights of mental anguish. A fortunate contact with an itinerant schoolmaster enabled young Mann to prepare for Brown University, from which he graduated in 1819 with high honors. He completed his training for the law at Tapping Reeve's famous law school at Litchfield, Connecticut. A successful legal practice, first in Dedham and then in Boston, prepared the way for state politics. Mann served first in the Massachusetts House and then in the Senate, becoming president of the latter body. In this capacity he signed a revolutionary educational bill which became law on April 20, 1837. The law, passed for the purpose of improving the quality of public education in the state, created a Board of Education, and empowered it to appoint a secretary and to make annual reports to the legislature.

Moved by the low estate of the schools of the Commonwealth, Mann surprised his friends by abandoning his lucrative practice and his political career to become secretary of the Board of Education at a considerable reduction in income. Traveling over the state, he surveyed a discouraging situation. In 1843 he went abroad to study the school systems of Prussia *and England. The state support of schools in Prussia especially impressed the American, who felt more and more strongly that education should be made available to all citizens. Mann presented his findings in his seventh annual report before the Massachusetts legislature, extolling the virtues not only of tax support but also of graded schools. At the same time, pulling no punches, he discussed the shortcomings of the existing Massachusetts system. The Boston schoolmasters replied with a drumfire attack which finally, together with overwork, impaired Mann's health. In 1848 he wrote his valedictory, the twelfth annual report of the Massachusetts Board of Education. Later that year he resigned, having been elected to the United States House of Representatives to succeed John Quincy Adams.*

GENTLEMEN,—

MASSACHUSETTS may be regarded either as a State by herself, or as a member of a mighty and yet increasing confederacy of States. In the former capacity, she has great and abiding interests, which are mainly dependent upon her own domestic or internal policy. In the latter relation, her fate depends upon the will of her partners in the association. . . .

Now, it is the especial province and function of the statesman and the lawgiver—of all those, indeed, whose influence moulds or modifies public opinion—to study out the eternal principles which conduce to the strength, wisdom, and righteousness of a community; to search for these principles as for hidden riches; to strive for them as one would strive for his life; and then to form public institutions in accordance with them. And he is not worthy to be called a statesman, he is not worthy to be a lawgiver or leader among men, who, either through the weakness of his head or the selfishness of his heart, is incapable of marshalling in his mind the great ideas of knowledge, justice, temperance, and obedience to the laws of God,—on which foundation alone the structure of human welfare can be erected; who is not capable of organizing these ideas into a system, and then of putting that system into operation, as a mechanic does a machine. This only is true statesmanship. . . .

The text is quoted from Mary Mann, ed., *Life and Works of Horace Mann* (Boston, 1868).

Without undervaluing any other human agency, it may be safely affirmed that the common school, improved and energized as it can easily be, may become the most effective and benignant of all the forces of civilization. Two reasons sustain this position. In the first place, there is a universality in its operation, which can be affirmed of no other institution whatever. If administered in the spirit of justice and concilia-tion, all the rising generation may be brought within the circle of its reformatory and elevating influences. And, in the second place, the materials upon which it operates are so pliant and ductile as to be susceptible of assuming a greater variety of forms than any other earthly work of the Creator. The inflexibility and ruggedness of the oak, when compared with the lithe sapling or the tender germ, are but feeble emblems to typify the docility of childhood when contrasted with the obduracy and intractableness of man. It is these inherent advantages of the common school, which, in our own State, have produced results so striking, from a system so imperfect, and an administration so feeble. In teaching the blind and the deaf and dumb, in kindling the latent spark of intelligence that lurks in an idiot's mind, and in the more holy work of reforming abandoned and outcast children, education has proved what it can do by glorious experiments. These wonders it has done in its infancy, and with the lights of a limited experience; but when its faculties shall be fully developed, when it shall be trained to wield its mighty energies for the protection of society against the giant vices which now invade and torment it,—against intemperance, avarice, war, slavery, bigotry, the woes of want, and the wickedness of waste,—then there will not be a height to which these enemies of the race can escape which it will not scale, nor a Titan among them all whom it will not slay.

I proceed, then, in endeavoring to show how the true business of the schoolroom connects itself, and becomes identical, with the great interests of society. The former is the infant, immature state of those interests; the latter their developed, adult state. As "the child is father to the man," so may the training of the schoolroom expand into the institutions and fortunes of the State.

PHYSICAL EDUCATION.

In the worldly prosperity of mankind, health and strength are indispensable ingredients. . . .

Leaving out, then, for the present purpose, all consideration of the pains of sickness and the anguish of bereavement, the momentous truth still remains, that sickness and premature death are positive evils for the

343

statesman and political economist to cope with. The earth, as a hospital for the diseased, would soon wear out the love of life; and, if but the half of mankind were sick, famine, from non-production, would speedily threaten the whole.

Now, modern science has made nothing more certain than that both good and ill health are the direct result of causes mainly within our own control. In other words, the health of the race is dependent upon the conduct of the race. The health of the individual is determined primarily by his parents, secondarily by himself. The vigorous growth of the body, its strength and its activity, its powers of endurance, and its length of life, on the one hand; and dwarfishness, sluggishness, infirmity, and premature death on the other,—are all the subjects of unchangeable laws. These laws are ordained of God; but the knowledge of them is left to our diligence, and the observance of them to our free agency. . . .

My general conclusion, then, under this head, is, that it is the duty of all the governing minds in society—whether in office or out of it—to diffuse a knowledge of these beautiful and beneficent laws of health and life throughout the length and breadth of the State; to popularize them; to make them, in the first place, the common acquisition of all, and, through education and custom, the common inheritance of all, so that the healthful habits naturally growing out of their observance shall be inbred in the people, exemplified in the personal regimen of each individual, incorporated into the economy of every household, observable in all private dwellings, and in all public edifices, especially in those buildings which are erected by capitalists for the residence of their work-people, or for renting to the poorer classes; obeyed, by supplying cities with pure water; by providing public baths, public walks, and public squares; by rural cemeteries; by the drainage and sewerage of populous towns, and by whatever else may promote the general salubrity of the atmosphere: in fine, by a religious observance of all those sanitary regulations with which modern science has blessed the world.

For this thorough diffusion of sanitary intelligence, the common school is the only agency. It is, however, an adequate agency. . . .

INTELLECTUAL EDUCATION AS A MEANS OF REMOVING POVERTY, AND SECURING ABUNDANCE.

. . . According to the European theory, men are divided into classes, —some to toil and earn, others to seize and enjoy. According to the Massachusetts theory, all are to have an equal chance for earning, and equal security in the enjoyment of what they earn. The latter tends to equality of condition; the former, to the grossest inequalities. . . .

But is it not true that Massachusetts, in some respects, instead of adhering more and more closely to her own theory, is becoming emulous of the baneful examples of Europe? The distance between the two extremes of society is lengthening, instead of being abridged. With every generation, fortunes increase on the one hand, and some new privation is added to poverty on the other. We are verging towards those extremes of opulence and of penury, each of which unhumanizes the human mind. A perpetual struggle for the bare necessaries of life, without the ability to obtain them, makes men wolfish. Avarice, on the other hand, sees, in all the victims of misery around it, not objects for pity and succor, but only crude materials to be worked up into more money.

I suppose it to be the universal sentiment of all those who mingle any ingredient of benevolence with their notions on political economy, that vast and overshadowing private fortunes are among the greatest dangers to which the happiness of the people in a republic can be subjected. Such fortunes would create a feudalism of a new kind, but one more oppressive and unrelenting than that of the middle ages. The feudal lords in England and on the Continent never held their retainers in a more abject condition of servitude than the great majority of foreign manufacturers and capitalists hold their operatives and laborers at the present day. The means employed are different; but the similarity in results is striking. What force did then, money does now. The villein of the middle ages had no spot of earth on which he could live, unless one were granted to him by his lord. The operative or laborer of the present day has no employment, and therefore no bread, unless the capitalist will accept his services. The vassal had no shelter but such as his master provided for him. Not one in five thousand of English operatives or farm-laborers is able to build or own even a hovel; and therefore they must accept such shelter as capital offers them. The baron prescribed his own terms to his retainers: those terms were peremptory, and the serf must submit or perish. The British manufacturer or farmer prescribes the rate of wages he will give to his work-people; he reduces these wages under whatever pretext he pleases; and they, too, have no alternative but submission or starvation. In some respects, indeed, the condition of the modern dependant is more forlorn than that of the corresponding serf class in former times. Some attributes of the patriarchal relation did spring up between the lord and his lieges to soften the harsh relations subsisting between them. Hence came some oversight of the condition of children, some relief in sickness, some protection and support in the decrepitude of age. But only in instances comparatively few have kindly offices smoothed the rugged relation between British capital and British labor. The children of the work-people are abandoned to their fate; and notwithstanding the privations they suffer, and the dangers they threaten, no power in the realm has yet been able to secure them an education; and when the adult laborer is prostrated by sickness, or eventually worn out by toil and age, the poor-house, which has all along been his destination, becomes his destiny. . . .

Now, surely nothing but universal education can counterwork this tendency to the domination of capital and the servility of labor. If one class possesses all the wealth and the education, while the residue of society is ignorant and poor, it matters not by what name the relation between them may be called: the latter, in fact and in truth, will be the servile dependants and subjects of the former. But, if education be equably diffused, it will draw property after it by the strongest of all attractions; for such a thing never did happen, and never can happen, as that an intelligent and practical body of men should be permanently poor. Property and labor in different classes are essentially antagonistic; but property and labor in the same class are essentially fraternal. The people of Massachusetts have, in some degree, appreciated the truth, that the unexampled prosperity of the State—its comfort, its competence, its general intelligence and virtue—is attributable to the education, more or less perfect, which all its people have received: but are they sensible of a fact equally important; namely, that it is to this same education that two-thirds of the people are indebted for not being to-day the vassals of as severe a tyranny, in the form of capital, as the lower classes of Europe are bound to in the form of brute force?

Education, then, beyond all other devices of human origin, is the great equalizer of the conditions of men,—the balance-wheel of the social machinery. I do not here mean that it so elevates the moral nature as to make men disdain and abhor the oppression of their fellow-men. This idea pertains to another of its attributes. But I mean that it gives each man the independence and the means by which he can resist the selfishness of other men. It does better than to disarm the poor of their hostility towards the rich: it prevents being poor. Agrarianism is the revenge of poverty against wealth. The wanton destruction of the property of others—the burning of hay-ricks and corn-ricks, the demolition of machinery because it supersedes hand-labor, the sprinkling of vitriol on rich dresses—is only agrarianism run mad. Education prevents both the revenge and the madness. On the other hand, a fellow-feeling for one's class or caste is the common instinct of hearts not wholly sunk in selfish regards for person or for family. The spread of education, by enlarging the cultivated class or caste, will open a wider area over which the social feelings will expand; and, if this education should be universal and complete, it would do more than all things else to obliterate factitious distinctions in society. . . .

In this fact, then, we find a solution of the problem that so long embarrassed inquirers. The reason why the mechanical and useful arts,— those arts which have done so much to civilize mankind, and which have given comforts and luxuries to the common laborer of the present day, such as kings and queens could not command three centuries ago,—the reason why these arts made no progress, and until recently, indeed, can hardly be said to have had any thing more than a beginning, is, that the labor of the world was performed by ignorant men. As soon as some degree of intelligence dawned upon the workman, then a corresponding degree of improvement in his work followed. At first, this intelligence was confined to a very small number, and therefore improvements were few; and they followed each other only after long intervals. They uniformly began in the nations and among the classes where there was most intelligence. The middle classes of England, and the people of Holland and Scotland, have done a hundred times more than all the Eastern hemisphere besides. What single improvement in art, or discovery in science, has ever originated in Spain, or throughout the vast empire of the Russias? But just in proportion as intelligence—that is, education—has quickened and stimulated a greater and a greater number of minds, just in the same proportion have inventions and discoveries increased in their wonderfulness, and in the rapidity of their succession. The progression has been rather geometrical than arithmetical. By the laws of Nature, it must be so. If, among ten well-educated children, the chance is that at least one of them will originate some new and useful process in the arts, or will discover some new scientific principle, or some new application of one, then, among a hundred such well-educated children, there is a moral certainty that there will be more than ten such originators or discoverers of new utilities; for the action of the mind is like the action of fire. One billet of wood will hardly burn alone, though dry as suns and north-west winds can make it, and though placed in the range of a current of air; ten such billets will burn well together; but a hundred will create a heat fifty times as intense as ten, will make a current of air to fan their own flame, and consume even greenness itself.

For the creation of wealth, then,—for the existence of a wealthy people and a wealthy nation,—intelligence is the grand condition. The number of improvers will increase as the intellectual constituency, if I may call it, increases. In former times, and in most parts of the world even at the present day, not one man in a million has ever had such a development of mind as made it possible for him to become a contributor to art or science. Let this development precede, and contributions, numberless, and of inestimable value, will be sure to follow. That political economy, therefore, which busies itself about capital and labor, supply and demand, interest and rents, favorable and unfavorable balances of trade, but leaves out of account the element of a widespread mental development, is nought but stupendous folly. The greatest of all the arts in political economy is to change a consumer into a producer; and the next greatest is to increase the producer's producing power,—an end to be directly attained by increasing his intelligence. For mere delving, an ignorant man is but little better than a swine, whom he so much resembles in his appetites, and surpasses in his powers of mischief. . . .

POLITICAL EDUCATION.

The necessity of general intelligence,—that is, of education (for I use the terms as substantially synonymous, because general intelligence can never exist without general education, and general education will be sure to produce general intelligence),—the necessity of general intelligence under a republican form of government, like most other very important truths, has become a very trite one. It is so trite, indeed, as to have lost much of its force by its familiarity. Almost all the champions of education seize upon this argument first of all, because it is so simple as to be understood by the ignorant, and so strong as to convince the sceptical. Nothing would be easier than to follow in the train of so many writers, and to demonstrate by logic, by history, and by the nature of the case, that a republican form of government, without intelligence in the people, must be, on a vast scale, what a mad-house, without superintendent or keepers, would be on a small one,—the despotism of a few succeeded by universal anarchy, and anarchy by despotism, with no change but from bad to worse. . . .

However elevated the moral character of a constituency may be, however well informed in matters of general science or history, yet they must, if citizens of a republic, understand something of the true nature and functions of the government under which they live. That any one, who is to participate in the government of a country when he becomes a man, should receive no instruction respecting the nature and functions of the government he is afterwards to administer, is a political solecism. In all nations, hardly excepting the most rude and barbarous, the future sovereign receives some training which is supposed to fit him for the exercise of the powers and duties of his anticipated station. Where, by force of law, the government devolves upon the heir while yet in a state of legal infancy, some regency, or other substitute, is appointed to act in his stead until his arrival at mature age; and, in the mean time, he is subjected to such a course of study and discipline as will tend to prepare him, according to the political theory of the time and the place, to assume the reins of authority at the appointed age. If in England, or in the most enlightened European monarchies, it would be a proof of restored barbarism to permit the future sovereign to grow up without any knowledge of his duties,—and who can doubt that it would be such a proof?—then, surely, it would be not less a proof of restored or of never-removed barbarism amongst us to empower any individual to use the elective franchise without preparing him for so momentous a trust. Hence the Constitution of the United States, and of our own State, should be made a study in our public schools. The partition of the powers of government into the three co-ordinate branches,—legislative, judicial, and executive,—with the duties appropriately devolving upon each; the mode of electing or of appointing all officers, with the reasons on which it was founded; and, especially, the duty of every citizen, in a government of laws, to appeal to the courts for redress in all cases of alleged wrong, instead of undertaking to vindicate his own rights by his own arm; and, in a government where the people are the acknowledged sources of power, the duty of changing laws and rulers by an appeal to the ballot, and not by rebellion,—should be taught to all the children until they are fully understood.

Had the obligations of the future citizen been sedulously inculcated upon all the children of this Republic, would the patriot have had to

349

mourn over so many instances where the voter, not being able to accomplish his purpose by voting, has proceeded to accomplish it by violence; where, agreeing with his fellow-citizens to use the machinery of the ballot, he makes a tacit reservation, that, if that machinery does not move according to his pleasure, he will wrest or break it? If the responsibleness and value of the elective franchise were duly appreciated, the day of our state and national elections would be among the most solemn and religious days in the calendar. Men would approach them, not only with preparation and solicitude, but with the sobriety and solemnity with which discreet and religious-minded men meet the great crises of life. No man would throw away his vote through caprice or wantonness, any more than he would throw away his estate, or sell his family into bondage. No man would cast his vote through malice or revenge, any more than a good surgeon would amputate a limb, or a good navigator sail through perilous straits, under the same criminal passions.

But perhaps it will be objected, that the Constitution is subject to different readings, or that the policy of different administrations has become the subject of party strife; and, therefore, if any thing of constitutional or political law is introduced into our schools, there is danger that teachers will be chosen on account of their affinities to this or that political party, or that teachers will feign affinities which they do not feel in order that they may be chosen; and so each schoolroom will at length become a miniature political club-room, exploding with political resolves, or flaming out with political addresses, prepared by beardless boys in scarcely legible hand-writing and in worse grammar.

With the most limited exercise of discretion, all apprehensions of this kind are wholly groundless. There are different readings of the Constitution, it is true; and there are partisan topics which agitate the country from side to side: but the controverted points, compared with those about which there is no dispute, do not bear the proportion of one to a hundred. And, what is more, no man is qualified, or can be qualified, to discuss the disputable questions, unless previously and thoroughly versed in those questions about which there is no dispute. In the terms and principles common to all, and recognized by all, is to be found the only common medium of language and of idea by which the parties can become intelligible to each other; and there, too, is the only common ground whence the arguments of the disputants can be drawn. . . .

. . . Thus may all the children of the Commonwealth receive

instruction in all the great essentials of political knowledge,—in those elementary ideas without which they will never be able to investigate more recondite and debatable questions; thus will the only practicable method be adopted for discovering new truths, and for discarding, instead of perpetuating, old errors; and thus, too, will that pernicious race of intolerant zealots, whose whole faith may be summed up in two articles,—that they themselves are always infallibly right, and that all dissenters are certainly wrong,—be extinguished,—extinguished, not by violence, nor by proscription, but by the more copious inflowing of the light of truth.

MORAL EDUCATION.

Moral education is a primal necessity of social existence. The unrestrained passions of men are not only homicidal, but suicidal; and a community without a conscience would soon extinguish itself. Even with a natural conscience, how often has evil triumphed over good! From the beginning of time, wrong has followed right, as the shadow the substance. . . .

But to all doubters, disbelievers, or despairers in human progress, it may still be said, there is one experiment which has never yet been tried. It is an experiment, which, even before its inception, offers the highest authority for its ultimate success. Its formula is intelligible to all; and it is as legible as though written in starry letters on an azure sky. It is expressed in these few and simple words: *"Train up a child in the way he should go; and, when he is old, he will not depart from it."* This declaration is positive. If the conditions are complied with, it makes no provision for a failure. Though pertaining to morals, yet, if the terms of the direction are observed, there is no more reason to doubt the result than there would be in an optical or a chemical experiment.

But this experiment has never yet been tried. Education has never yet been brought to bear with one-hundredth part of its potential force upon the natures of children, and, through them, upon the character of men and of the race. In all the attempts to reform mankind which have hitherto been made, whether by changing the frame of government, by aggravating or softening the severity of the penal code, or by substituting a government-created for a God-created religion,—in all these attempts, the infantile and youthful mind, its amenability to influences, and the enduring and self-operating character of the influences it receives, have been almost wholly unrecognized. Here, then, is a new agency, whose

351

powers are but just beginning to be understood, and whose mighty energies hitherto have been but feebly invoked; and yet, from our experience, limited and imperfect as it is, we do know, that, far beyond any other earthly instrumentality, it is comprehensive and decisive. . . .

. . . So far as human instrumentalities are concerned, we have abundant means for surrounding every child in the State with preservative and moral influences as extensive and as efficient as those under which the present industrious, worthy, and virtuous members of the community were reared. And as to all those things in regard to which we are directly dependent upon the divine favor, have we not the promise, explicit and unconditional, that the men SHALL NOT depart from the way in which they should go, if the children are trained up in it? It has been overlooked that this promise is not restricted to parents, but seems to be addressed indiscriminately to all, whether parents, communities, states, or mankind. . . .

RELIGIOUS EDUCATION.

But it will be said that this grand result in practical morals is a consummation of blessedness that can never be attained without religion, and that no community will ever be religious without a religious education. Both these propositions I regard as eternal and immutable truths. Devoid of religious principles and religious affections, the race can never fall so low but that it may sink still lower; animated and sanctified by them, it can never rise so high but that it may ascend still higher. And is it not at least as presumptuous to expect that mankind will attain to the knowledge of truth, without being instructed in truth, and without that general expansion and development of faculty which will enable them to recognize and comprehend truth in any other department of human interest as in the department of religion? . . .

. . . That our public schools are not theological seminaries, is admitted. That they are debarred by law from inculcating the peculiar and distinctive doctrines of any one religious denomination amongst us, is claimed; and that they are also prohibited from ever teaching that what they do teach is the whole of religion, or all that is essential to religion or to salvation, is equally certain. But our system earnestly inculcates all Christian morals; it founds its morals on the basis of religion; it welcomes the religion of the Bible; and, in receiving the Bible, it allows it to do what it is allowed to do in no other system,—*to speak for itself.* But here it stops, not because it claims to have compassed all truth, but because it disclaims to act as an umpire between hostile religious opinions.

The very terms "public school" and "common school" bear upon their face that they are schools which the children of the entire community may attend. Every man not on the pauper-list is taxed for their support; but he is not taxed to support them as special religious institutions: if he were, it would satisfy at once the largest definition of a religious establishment. But he is taxed to support them as a *preventive* means against dishonesty, against fraud, and against violence, on the same principle that he is taxed to support criminal courts as a *punitive* means against the same offences. He is taxed to support schools, on the same principle that he is taxed to support paupers,—because a child without education is poorer and more wretched than a man without bread. He is taxed to support schools, on the same principle that he would be taxed to defend the nation against foreign invasion, or against rapine committed by a foreign foe,—because the general prevalence of ignorance, superstition, and vice, will breed Goth and Vandal at home more fatal to the public well-being than any Goth or Vandal from abroad. And, finally, he is taxed to support schools, because they are the most effective means of developing and training those powers and faculties in a child, by which, when he becomes a man, he may understand what his highest interests and his highest duties are, and may be in fact, and not in name only, a free agent. The elements of a political education are not bestowed upon any school child for the purpose of making him vote with this or that political party when he becomes of age, but for the purpose of enabling him to choose for himself with which party he will vote. So the religious education which a child receives at school is not imparted to him for the purpose of making him join this or that denomination when he arrives at years of discretion, but for the purpose of enabling him to judge for himself, according to the dictates of his own reason and conscience, what his religious obligations are, and whither they lead. . . .

I hold it, then, to be one of the excellences, one of the moral beauties, of the Massachusetts system, that there is one place in the land where the children of all the different denominations are brought together for instruction, where the Bible is allowed to speak for itself; one place where the children can kneel at a common altar, and feel that they have a common Father, and where the services of religion tend to create brothers, and not Ishmaelites. . . .

. . . In bidding an official farewell to a system with which I have been so long connected, to which I have devoted my means, my strength, my health, twelve years of time, and, doubtless, twice that number of years from what might otherwise have been my term of life, I have felt bound to submit these brief views in its defence. . . .

Such, then, in a religious point of view, is the Massachusetts system of common schools. Reverently it recognizes and affirms the sovereign rights of the Creator, sedulously and sacredly it guards the religious rights of the creature; while it seeks to remove all hinderances, and to supply all furtherances, to a filial and paternal communion between man and his Maker. In a social and political sense, it is a *free* school-system. It knows no distinction of rich and poor, of bond and free, or between those, who, in the imperfect light of this world, are seeking, through different avenues, to reach the gate of heaven. Without money and without price, it throws open its doors, and spreads the table of its bounty, for all the children of the State. Like the sun, it shines not only upon the good, but upon the evil, that they may become good; and, like the rain, its blessings descend not only upon the just, but upon the unjust, that their injustice may depart from them, and be known no more.

To the great founders of this system we look back with filial reverence and love. Amid the barrenness of the land, and in utter destitution of wealth, they coined the rude comforts, and even the necessaries, of life, into means for its generous support. Though, as laborers by day, they subdued the wilderness, and, as sentinels by night, they guarded the camp, yet they found time for the vigilant administration and oversight of the schools in the day of their infancy and weakness. But for this single institution, into which they transfused so much of their means and of their strength, and of which they have made us the inheritors, how different would our lot and our life have been! Upon us its accumulated blessings have descended. It has saved us from innumerable pains and perils that would otherwise have been our fate,—from the physical wretchedness that is impotent to work out its own relief, from the darkness of the intellect whose wanderings after light so often plunge it into deeper gloom, and from the moral debasement whose pleasures are vices and crimes. It has surrounded us with a profusion of comforts and blessings of which the most poetic imagination would never otherwise have conceived. It has found, not mythologic goddesses, but gigantic and tireless laborers, in every stream; not evil and vindictive spirits, but beneficent and helping ones, in all the elements; and, by a profounder alchemy than the schoolmen ever dreamed of, it transmutes quarries and ice-fields into gold. It has given cunning to the hand of the mechanic, keenness to the artisan's eye, and made a sterile soil grow grateful beneath the skill of the husbandman. Hence the absence of poverty among our native population; hence a competency for the whole people, the means for mental and moral improvement, and for giving embellishment and dignity to life, such as the world has never known before, and such as nowhere else can be found upon the face of the earth. . . .

Horace Mann launched the common school in the United States on a course which has brought public education to that extraordinary tax-supported system now extending from the kindergarten through the university. Laboring in an age when seminal ideas in educational theory and pedagogical practice came from Europe, Mann made no contribution to either. Instead, he worked to persuade the citizens of Massachusetts that the public interest required free schools for all children and that these schools should have the strength which only public funds could give. In carrying out this task he was supported by the lyceum movement inaugurated in 1826 and by the activities of the Western Literary Institute, which after its founding in Cincinnati, Ohio, in 1832 spread rapidly to most of the other states.

Mann's chief contribution to life in his own times lay in his formulation of a broad social philosophy which detailed the significance of universal education. He assumed the importance of the individual person as a unique center of value. He assumed that the institutions of society are instruments to further the welfare of men and women. He began with the problem of health in an age before the development of scientific medicine, when life expectancy was much less than half a century. His hopeful imagination enabled him to visualize an era protected and invigorated by an understanding of the requirements and the practices of public health. He felt the school to be an adequate instrument with which to bring in the new day. His confidence has proved justified; the historical record makes it clear that the role of the school, when the university is included, has been decisive on the issue of public health. The assumption of the importance of the individual person (child or adult) further led Mann to the conclusion that justice demands equality of opportunity for all citizens. He argued to his generation that "education . . . is the great equalizer of the condition of men." The ideal of equality of opportunity has become basic to American thought.

From the humanism and the optimism of the eighteenth-century Enlightenment Mann inherited the concept that man is plastic and improvable. He saw universal education as an instrument for bringing about more fully developed individuals and a more advanced society. Education furnishes the mind of the individual and enables him to further his own material well-being. When Sputnik I went into orbit in 1957, complacent Americans were jolted into a new understanding of Mann's remark in 1848: ". . . in proportion as intelligence—that is education—has quickened and stimulated a greater and greater number of minds, just in the same proportion have inventions and discoveries increased in their wonderfulness, and in the rapidity of their succession." Anxious Americans reacted appropriately.

Mann, working in a decade when universal manhood suffrage represented a new democratic advance, carried on in the tradition of Jefferson and Madison in his insistence that a republican form of government requires a literate and informed electorate. He foresaw the dangers posed to public schools by "the tempest of political strife." The developments in history, social studies, and the social sciences in our public educational establishment have validated his belief that American democracy in essential things can rise above destructive partisanship. Mann believed in reason, in rational analysis of the problems of society, and in rational efforts to achieve their solution. This faith also is fundamental to twentieth-century American thought. Finally, the storm which gathered in the 1960's about the question of religion in the public school demonstrated the importance which vast numbers of Americans attach to Mann's contention (made in 1848) that the Judeo-Christian tradition, which provides the background of American civilization, must have a recognized place in American schools.

356

The Seneca Falls Declaration of
Sentiments and Resolutions
1848

EDITED BY BARBARA M. SOLOMON

At the obscure village of Seneca Falls, New York, in the summer of 1848, five women formulated a Declaration of Sentiments and Resolutions. The adoption of this document at the convention which followed marked the beginning of the organized movement for woman's rights in the United States.

For half a century before their meeting, there had been intellectual discussion of the proper sphere of woman in the new republic. The inherited doctrine of English law expounded in the influential Commentaries of Sir William Blackstone had made the married woman a legal nonentity; this was not consistent with the facts of her evolution. Since the 1600's, wives had been respected partners in American frontier communities. Moreover, religious freedom nurtured the individual conscience and spirit of woman, whether married or single. New opportunities through education and industrialization in the 1800's provided them with new outlets for independent activities.

At the same time, women were part of a nation in which the natural rights of man had been continuously invoked, first to create and then to enlarge the meaning of democracy for its members. By the 1840's, improvement of the whole society was the common element in particular goals, whether reformers worked for temperance, peace, public schools, universal manhood suffrage, or the abolition of human slavery. For those who shared the vision of a perfectible society in America, steps to include women were logical. An important sign of the advancing times was the final passage, in April, 1848, by the New York state legislature of a law giving married women equal property rights. The radical demand for suffrage at Seneca Falls carried the social and political revolution for women into a new era.

The particular impetus for this historic event came from Elizabeth Cady Stanton, a new resident in the remote community. Feeling for the first time the domestic isolation of most housewives, Mrs. Stanton shared her concern with her old colleague, Lucretia Mott, of Philadelphia, who was attending a Friends' Meeting nearby. Eight years earlier, the two had been among the delegates rejected from the Antislavery Convention in London because they were women. Now these feminists recalled their old resolve to hold a convention in America in behalf of their sex. Joined by Mrs. Mott's sister, Martha C. Wright, and two other Quaker friends, Jane Hunt and Mary Ann McClintock, they sent an unsigned notice to the Seneca Falls Courier stating that "a Convention to discuss the social, civil, and religious conditions and rights of woman, will be held on Wednesday and Thursday, the 19th and 20th of July."

Gathering the next day in the McClintocks' parlor to plan the meetings of the convention, the organizers used reports of antislavery and temperance conventions as guides. Still they were perplexed in their search for a convincing framework in which to present their cause to the public. Elizabeth Cady Stanton's reading of the Declaration of Independence to the group provided the solution. Responding to the enthusiasm of this legal-minded woman, daughter of a judge and wife of an abolitionist, the group paraphrased the familiar words of the nation's manifesto, substituting "man" for "King George" as the object of attack. Consulting even their husbands, they worked hard to find, in literal imitation of the great model, eighteen grievances reflecting the tyranny of man. The group then agreed that resolutions were needed to implement the "Declaration of Sentiments" they had composed.

When they dispersed to return for the convention five days later, it was left to Mrs. Stanton to complete the document, which was still in rough form. At home, she drafted the famous ninth resolution, asserting woman's sacred right to the vote. She had not discussed this resolution with the others. Henry Stanton, a journalist and reformer who was usually sympathetic with his wife's aspirations, urged her to abandon so revolutionary a statement. Despite his threat to leave town during the convention, Stanton could not dissuade her. Nor would she accept

358

Lucretia Mott's counsel of moderation. Mrs. Stanton came to the convention determined to gain acceptance of the ninth resolution.

The convention attracted young and old women from outlying farms; and a surprising number of interested men, though uninvited, also appeared at the meeting in the Wesleyan Chapel. Since none of the leaders felt competent to conduct the assembly, James Mott, husband of Lucretia, was called to the chair. During the six sessions held in the two-day period, the audience discussed, amended, and voted upon each part of the "Declaration of Sentiments and Resolutions." Although the majority feared that the demand for suffrage would jeopardize the cause of woman's rights, Frederick Douglass, the emancipated Negro, eloquently defended Mrs. Stanton. After heated debate, the convention voted to acknowledge the right of American women to the elective franchise. When the document had been thoroughly reviewed and approved, Lucretia Mott offered a final resolution at the last session urging men and women to work for professional and vocational equality.

Having adopted the approaches of other reform groups, the feminists envisaged a succession of meetings in the near future. The final paragraph of the "Declaration" outlined their general plan of voluntary action, describing various means by which they hoped to engage wider support in the nation.

At the close of the convention, sixty-eight women and thirty-two men signed the new declaration for woman's rights, though some sources claim that when faced with the ridicule of the press many withdrew their names. One of the signers, Charlotte Woodward Pierce, lived to vote for President of the United States in 1920.

DECLARATION OF SENTIMENTS

W HEN, IN THE course of human events, it becomes necessary for one portion of the family of man to assume among the people of the earth a position different from that which they have hitherto occupied, but one to which the laws of nature and of nature's God entitle them, a decent respect to the opinions of mankind

---

The text used here is the earliest form of the "Declaration of Sentiments and Resolutions of the Seneca Falls Convention," included in the *Report of the Woman's Rights Convention, Held at Seneca Falls, N.Y., July 19th and 20th,*

requires that they should declare the causes that impel them to such a course.

We hold these truths to be self-evident: that all men and women are created equal; that they are endowed by their Creator with certain inalienable rights; that among these are life, liberty, and the pursuit of happiness; that to secure these rights governments are instituted, deriving their just powers from the consent of the governed.—Whenever any form of Government becomes destructive of these ends, it is the right of those who suffer from it to refuse allegiance to it, and to insist upon the institution of a new government, laying its foundation on such principles, and organizing its powers in such form as to them shall seem most likely to effect their safety and happiness. Prudence, indeed, will dictate that governments long established should not be changed for light and transient causes; and accordingly, all experience hath shown that mankind are more disposed to suffer, while evils are sufferable, than to right themselves by abolishing the forms to which they are accustomed. But when a long train of abuses and usurpations, pursuing invariably the same object, evinces a design to reduce them under absolute despotism, it is their duty to throw off such government, and to provide new guards for their future security. Such has been the patient sufferance of the women under this government, and such is now the necessity which constrains them to demand the equal station to which they are entitled.

The history of mankind is a history of repeated injuries and usurpations on the part of man toward woman, having in direct object the establishment of an absolute tyranny over her. To prove this, let facts be submitted to a candid world.

He has never permitted her to exercise her inalienable right to the elective franchise.

1848 (Rochester: North Star Office, 1848). The text differs in a few respects from a better-known version quoted in E. C. Stanton, S. B. Anthony, and M. J. Gage, *History of Woman Suffrage* (New York: Fowler and Wells, 1881), I, 70–73. According to the original *Report*, the resolutions were read the first day of the convention, discussed and approved the second afternoon; and finally at the evening session of the second day Lucretia Mott made the significant addition which was then incorporated permanently as the last resolution. A final statement ("Firmly relying upon the final triumph of the Right and the True, we do this day affix our signatures to this declaration") and an accompanying list of signers were omitted from the later version. Other differences between the 1848 and the 1881 texts, involving minor word changes and variations in punctuation, do not alter the basic meaning of the document.

He has compelled her to submit to laws, in the formation of which she had no voice.

He has withheld from her rights which are given to the most ignorant and degraded men—both natives and foreigners.

Having deprived her of this first right of a citizen, the elective franchise, thereby leaving her without representation in the halls of legislation, he has oppressed her on all sides.

He has made her, if married, in the eye of the law, civilly dead.

He has taken from her all right in property, even to the wages she earns.

He has made her, morally, an irresponsible being, as she can commit many crimes with impunity, provided they be done in the presence of her husband. In the covenant of marriage, she is compelled to promise obedience to her husband, he becoming, to all intents and purposes, her master—the law giving him power to deprive her of her liberty, and to administer chastisement.

He has so framed the laws of divorce, as to what shall be the proper causes of divorce; in case of separation, to whom the guardianship of the children shall be given; as to be wholly regardless of the happiness of women—the law, in all cases, going upon the false supposition of the supremacy of man, and giving all power into his hands.

After depriving her of all rights as a married woman, if single and the owner of property, he has taxed her to support a government which recognizes her only when her property can be made profitable to it.

He has monopolized nearly all the profitable employments, and from those she is permitted to follow, she receives but a scanty remuneration.

He closes against her all the avenues to wealth and distinction, which he considers most honorable to himself. As a teacher of theology, medicine, or law, she is not known.

He has denied her the facilities for obtaining a thorough education—all colleges being closed against her.

He allows her in Church as well as State, but a subordinate position, claiming Apostolic authority for her exclusion from the ministry, and, with some exceptions, from any public participation in the affairs of the Church.

He has created a false public sentiment, by giving to the world a different code of morals for men and women, by which moral delinquencies which exclude women from society, are not only tolerated but deemed of little account in man.

He has usurped the prerogative of Jehovah himself, claiming it as his right to assign for her a sphere of action, when that belongs to her conscience and her God.

He has endeavored, in every way that he could to destroy her confidence in her own powers, to lessen her self-respect, and to make her willing to lead a dependant and abject life.

Now, in view of this entire disfranchisement of one-half the people of this country, their social and religious degradation,—in view of the unjust laws above mentioned, and because women do feel themselves aggrieved, oppressed, and fraudulently deprived of their most sacred rights, we insist that they have immediate admission to all the rights and privileges which belong to them as citizens of these United States.

In entering upon the great work before us, we anticipate no small amount of misconception, misrepresentation, and ridicule; but we shall use every instrumentality within our power to effect our object. We shall employ agents, circulate tracts, petition the State and national Legislatures, and endeavor to enlist the pulpit and the press in our behalf. We hope this Convention will be followed by a series of Conventions, embracing every part of the country.

Firmly relying upon the final triumph of the Right and the True, we do this day affix our signatures to this declaration.

[The names of sixty-eight women and thirty-two men follow.]

RESOLUTIONS

Whereas, the great precept of nature is conceded to be, "that man shall pursue his own true and substantial happiness." Blackstone, in his Commentaries, remarks, that this law of Nature being coeval with mankind, and dictated by God himself, is of course superior in obligation to any other. It is binding over all the globe, in all countries, and at all times; no human laws are of any validity if contrary to this, and such of them as are valid, derive all their force, and all their validity, and all their authority, mediately and immediately, from this original; Therefore,

Resolved, That such laws as conflict, in any way, with the true and substantial happiness of woman, are contrary to the great precept of nature, and of no validity; for this is "superior in obligation to any other."

Resolved, That all laws which prevent woman from occupying such a station in society as her conscience shall dictate, or which place her in a position inferior to that of man, are contrary to the great precept of nature, and therefore of no force or authority.

Resolved, That woman is man's equal—was intended to be so by the Creator, and the highest good of the race demands that she should be recognized as such.

Resolved, That the women of this country ought to be enlightened in regard to the laws under which they live, that they may no longer publish their degradation, by declaring themselves satisfied with their present position, nor their ignorance, by asserting that they have all the rights they want.

Resolved, That inasmuch as man, while claiming for himself intellectual superiority, does accord to woman moral superiority, it is preeminently his duty to encourage her to speak, and teach, as she has an opportunity, in all religious assemblies.

Resolved, That the same amount of virtue, delicacy, and refinement of behavior, that is required of woman in the social state, should also be required of man, and the same transgressions should be visited with equal severity on both man and woman.

Resolved, That the objection of indelicacy and impropriety, which is so often brought against woman when she addresses a public audience, comes with a very ill grace from those who encourage, by their attendance, her appearance on the stage, in the concert, or in the feats of the circus.

Resolved, That woman has too long rested satisfied in the circumscribed limits which corrupt customs and a perverted application of the Scriptures have marked out for her, and that it is time she should move in the enlarged sphere which her great Creator has assigned her.

Resolved, That it is the duty of the women of this country to secure to themselves their sacred right to the elective franchise.

Resolved, That the equality of human rights results necessarily from the fact of the identity of the race in capabilities and responsibilities.

Resolved, therefore, That, being invested by the Creator with the same capabilities, and the same consciousness of responsibility for their exercise, it is demonstrably the right and duty of woman, equally with man, to promote every righteous cause, by every righteous means; and especially in regard to the great subjects of morals and religion, it is self-evidently her right to participate with her brother in teaching them, both in private and in public, by writing and by speaking, by any instrumentalities proper to be used, and in any assemblies proper to be held; and this being a self-evident truth, growing out of the divinely implanted principles of human nature, any custom or authority adverse to it, whether modern or wearing the hoary sanction of antiquity, is to be regarded as self-evident falsehood, and at war with the interests of mankind.

[At the last session Lucretia Mott offered and spoke to the following resolution:]

Resolved, That the speedy success of our cause depends upon the zealous and untiring efforts of both men and women, for the overthrow of the monopoly of the pulpit, and for the securing to woman an equal participation with men in the various trades, professions and commerce.

The authors of the Seneca Falls document succeeded in their immediate purposes. Through their endeavors a group of women and men had met and jointly endorsed a public statement of protest against the inequities experienced by American women in the law, in the economy, and in social and political relations.

Moreover, the convention attracted national attention, for newspapers throughout the country responded to its revolutionary theme with scorn, derision, or, less often, with praise. Retrospectively in 1881, the leaders felt impelled to record in the History of Woman Suffrage that they themselves had been neither " 'sour old maids,' 'childless women,' nor 'divorced wives.' " Each stated that she had been married and, as a "proud, thinking woman," had begun the work for the rights of her sex. In fact, those initiating this movement could not fully interpret their own motives. They acted at Seneca Falls because the possibilities of self-realization for women were growing in the society of which they were a part. They were notable examples of the changing role of women in America.

In 1848, the Seneca Falls "Declaration of Sentiments and Resolutions" went far beyond the expectations of most of the feminists present at the convention. In the perspective of history, however, the insistence upon the right to vote was an accurate forecast of things to come. During the next seventy-two years, the quest for suffrage proved the bond uniting three generations of women who believed with Elizabeth Cady Stanton that only through the exercise of the franchise would they eradicate the existing legal, economic, and social inequalities affecting their sex.

Although in subsequent conventions there were sporadic references to the Seneca Falls "Declaration" and even occasions at which the entire document was read, it never became an official manifesto of the movement. Yet it should be noted that no other document performed this function. Later advocates of woman's rights usually took for granted the philosophic rationale of the "Declaration of Sentiments" even when they tested new assumptions in their efforts to attain the original goals. Only after the passage of the Nineteenth Amendment in 1920 did the document acquire historic value and become a symbol of the pioneering feminist generations.

Even more basic to women's lives than the pursuit of suffrage was the long struggle to eliminate the economic and social grievances equally emphasized in the "Declaration of Sentiments and Resolutions." As the industrial society of democratic America matured during an era affected by three great wars, working women advanced in the professions, in the vocations, and in the labor force. Even though they enjoyed a good measure of achievement and an improved legal status in the 1960's, the psychological and social implications of the grievances of 1848 remained. From the Seneca Falls "Declaration" to the Report of the President's Commission on the Status of Women (October 11, 1963), there was a continuity of themes. The original concern for woman's rights and the attempt to resolve the diverse functions of women's lives still demanded consideration by those who shared, with the original group at Seneca Falls, a high standard of expectations for American women.

Elizabeth Cady Stanton
Address on the Divorce Bill
1861

EDITED BY NELSON M. BLAKE

In February, 1861, the New York legislature had under consideration a bill for liberalizing the state's divorce law. To the one ground—adultery—recognized since 1787, the proposed bill would add the grounds of willful desertion and cruel treatment. The proposal was by no means radical, since practically all the other states allowed divorce on a variety of grounds. Divorce law in America began to diverge from English law during colonial days. Although the mother country made no provision for absolute divorce until 1669 and then permitted it only by special act of Parliament, Puritan Massachusetts and Connecticut soon authorized their regular courts to dissolve marriages. After the Revolution most of the other states had made provision for granting divorce on several grounds. Between 1840 and 1861, reformers made persistent efforts to bring the New York law into line with that of the other states. On several occasions they came close to success, but they were never quite able to push their measures through against the opposition of powerful politicians like Horace Greeley and Thurlow Weed. The most able argument for the divorce bill of 1861 was delivered by Mrs. Elizabeth Cady Stanton at a special session attended not only by the Senate Judiciary Committee but also by a large assemblage of curious politicians and guests.

Then near the midpoint of a remarkable life, Mrs. Stanton was one of the best-known public figures of the day. Born in 1815 in Johnstown, New York, Elizabeth Cady was strongly influenced by her early environment. Her father was Judge Daniel Cady, a shrewd country lawyer and politician; her mother was Margaret Livingston, daughter of a Revolutionary War colonel. Bantering debate with the young law clerks who studied in her father's office sharpened Elizabeth's wits, and two years at the famous Troy Female Seminary of Emma Willard rounded out her formal education. Most stimulating of all was the moral earnestness and passion for reform that Elizabeth encountered in frequent visits to the household of her cousin, the wealthy philanthropist Gerrit Smith. It was here, in the central New York village of Peterboro, that she met her future husband, Henry B. Stanton, ten years her senior and already a well-known abolitionist. Married at the age of twenty-four, she bore seven children. But the responsibilities of a large family did not prevent this strong-minded woman from playing an increasingly active role in the reform movements of the day. She helped organize the first woman's rights convention at Seneca Falls, New York, in 1848, and together with her close friend Susan B. Anthony she exercised leadership over the feminist movement throughout the succeeding years.

Although the right of suffrage was a major goal of the woman's rights movement, it was by no means the only one. Mrs. Stanton regarded contemporary marriage laws as hopelessly archaic, artfully contrived by male moralists and male legislators to bind women in a status not much better than slavery. The feminists won an important victory in 1860 when the New York legislature amended the laws to allow married women to retain their own property and earnings. Equally needed in Mrs. Stanton's eyes was a liberalized divorce law. Although happily married herself, she was filled with indignant compassion at the plight of many other wives deserted or cruelly treated, yet unable to gain their freedom under the harsh New York law.

GENTLEMEN OF THE JUDICIARY—In speaking to you, gentlemen, on such delicate subjects as marriage and divorce, in the revision of laws which are found in your statute books, I must use the language I find there.

The document is reprinted as it originally appeared, under the title *Address of Elizabeth Cady Stanton, on the Divorce Bill, Before the Judiciary Committee of the New York Senate, in the Assembly Chamber, Feb. 8, 1861* (Albany: Weed, Parsons and Company, Printers, 1861).

May I not, without the charge of indelicacy, speak in a mixed assembly of Christian men and women, of wrongs which my daughter may to-morrow suffer in your courts, where there is no woman's heart to pity, and no woman's presence to protect?

I come not before you, gentlemen, at this time, to plead simply the importance of divorce in cases specified in your bill, but the justice of an entire revision of your whole code of laws on marriage and divorce. We claim that here, at least, woman's equality should be recognized. If civilly and politically man must stand supreme, let us at least be equals in our nearest and most sacred relations. . . .

When man suffers from false legislation, he has the remedy in his own hands; but an humble petition, protest or prayer, is all that woman can claim.

The contract of marriage, is by no means equal. From Coke down to Kent, who can cite one law under the marriage contract, where woman has the advantage? The law permits the girl to marry at twelve years of age, while it requires several years more of experience on the part of the boy. In entering this compact, the *man* gives up nothing that he before possessed; he is a *man* still: while the legal existence of the woman is suspended during marriage, and is known but in and through the husband. She is nameless, purseless, childless; though a woman, an heiress, and a mother.

Blackstone says, "the husband and wife are one, and that one is the husband." Kent says, "the legal effects of marriage are generally deducible from the principle of common law by which the husband and wife are regarded as one person, and her legal existence and authority lost or suspended during the continuance of the matrimonial union.". . .

The laws on divorce are quite as unequal as those on marriage; yes, far more so. The advantages seem to be all on one side, and the penalties on the other. In case of divorce, if the husband be the guilty party, he still retains a greater part of the property! If the wife be the guilty party, she goes out of the partnership penniless. . . . In New York, and some other states, the wife of the guilty husband can now sue for a divorce in her own name, and the costs come out of the husband's estate; but in a majority of the states she is still compelled to sue in the name of another, as she has no means of paying costs, even though she may have brought her thousands into the partnership. . . . "Many jurists," says Kent . . . , "are of opinion that the adultery of the husband ought not to be noticed or made subject to the same animadversions as that of the wife, because it is not evidence of such entire depravity, nor equally injurious in its effects upon the morals and good order, and happiness of domestic life." Montesquieu, Pothier, and Dr. Taylor, all insist, that the cases of husband and wife ought to be distinguished, and that the violation of the marriage vow, on the part of the wife, is the most mischievous, and the prosecution ought to be confined to the offense on her part.". . .

Say you, these are but the opinions of men? On what else, I ask, are the hundreds of women depending, who this hour demand in our courts a release from burdensome contracts? Are not these delicate matters left wholly to the discretion of the courts? Are not young women, from our first families, dragged into your public courts—into assemblies of men exclusively? The judges all men, the jurors all men! No true woman there to shield them, by her presence, from gross and impertinent questionings, to pity their misfortunes, or to protest against their wrongs! The administration of justice depends far more on the opinions of eminent jurists, than on law alone, for law is powerless, when at variance with public sentiment.

For years there has been before the legislature of this state, a variety of bills asking for divorce in cases of drunkenness, insanity, desertion, and cruel and brutal treatment, endangering life. My attention was called to this question very early in life, by the sufferings of a friend of my girlhood—a victim of one of those unfortunate unions, called marriage. What my great love for that young girl, and my holy intuitions, then decided to be right, has not been changed by years of experience, observation and reason. I have pondered well these things in my heart, and ever felt the deepest interest in all that has been written and said on this subject; and the most profound respect and loving sympathy for those heroic women, who, in the face of law and public sentiment, have dared to sunder the unholy ties of a joyless, loveless union.

If marriage is a human institution, about which man may legislate, it seems but just that he should treat this branch of his legislation with the same common sense that he applies to all others. If it is a mere legal contract, then should it be subject to the restraints and privileges of all other contracts. A contract, to be valid in law, must be formed between parties of mature age, with an honest intention in said parties to do what they agree. The least concealment, fraud, or intention to deceive, if proved, annuls the contract. A boy cannot contract for an acre of land, or a horse, until he is twenty-one, but he may contract for a wife at fourteen. If a man sell a horse, and the purchaser find in him "great incompatibility of temper"—a disposition to stand still, when the owner is in haste to go—the sale is null and void; the man and his horse part company. But in marriage, no matter how much fraud and deception are practised, nor how cruelly one or both parties have been misled; no matter how young or inexperienced or thoughtless the parties, nor how unequal their condition and position in life, the contract cannot be annulled. . . .

Marriage, as it now exists, must seem to all of you a mere human institution. Look through the universe of matter and mind—all God's arrangements are perfect, harmonious and complete; there is no discord, friction or failure in His eternal plans. Immutability, perfection, beauty, are stamped on all His laws. Love is the vital essence that pervades and permeates from center to circumference—the graduating circle of all thought and action; Love is the talisman of human weal and woe—the "open sesame" to every human soul. Where two human beings are drawn together by the natural laws of likeness and affinity, union and happiness are the result. Such marriages might be divine. But how is it now? You all know our marriage is, in many cases, a mere outward tie, impelled by custom, policy, interest, necessity; founded not even in friendship, to say nothing of love; with every possible inequality of condition and development. In these heterogeneous unions, we find youth and old age, beauty and deformity, refinement and vulgarity, virtue and vice, the educated and the ignorant, angels of grace and goodness with devils of malice and malignity; and the sum of all this is human wretchedness and despair—cold fathers, sad mothers and hapless children, who shiver at the hearthstone, where the fires of love have all gone out. The wide world and the stranger's unsympathizing gaze are not more to be dreaded for young hearts than homes like these. Now, who shall say that it is right to take two beings so unlike, and anchor them right side by side—fast bound—to stay all time, until God, in mercy shall summon one away?

Do wise Christian legislators need any arguments to convince them, that the sacredness of the family relation should be protected at all hazards? The family—that great conservator of national virtue and strength—how can you hope to build it up in the midst of violence, debauchery and excess. Can there be anything sacred, at that family altar, where the chief priest who ministers, makes sacrifice of human beings—of the weak and innocent? where the incense offered up is not to a God of justice and mercy, but those heathen divinities, who best may represent the lost man, in all his grossness and deformity? Call that sacred, where woman, the mother of the race—of a Jesus of Nazareth—unconscious of the true dignity of her nature, of her high and holy destiny, consents to live in legalized prostitution! her whole soul revolting at such gross association! her flesh shivering at the cold contamination of that embrace! held there by no tie but the iron chain of the law, and a false and most unnatural public sentiment? Call that sacred, where innocent children, trembling with fear, fly to the corners and dark places of the house, to hide from the wrath of drunken, brutal fathers, but forgetting their past sufferings, rush out again at their mother's frantic screams, "Help! oh, help!" Behold the agonies of those young hearts, as they see the only being on earth they love, dragged about the room by the hair of her head, kicked and pounded, and left half dead and bleeding on the floor! Call that sacred, where fathers like these have the power and legal right to hand down their natures to other beings, to curse other generations with such moral deformity and death!

Men and brethren! look into your asylums for the blind, the deaf and dumb, the idiot, the imbecile, the deformed, the insane; go out into the by-lanes and dens of your cities, and contemplate the reeking mass of depravity; pause before the terrible revelations, made by statistics, of the rapid increase of all this moral and physical impotency, and learn how fearful a thing it is, to violate the immutable laws of the beneficent Ruler of the Universe; and there behold the sorrowful retributions of your violence on woman. Learn how false and cruel are those institutions, which, with a coarse materialism, set aside the holy instincts of the woman, to seek no union but one of love.

Fathers! do you say, let your daughters pay a lifelong penalty for one unfortunate step? How could they, on the threshold of life, full of joy and hope, believing all things to be as they seemed on the surface, judge of the dark windings of the human soul? How could they foresee that the young man, to-day, so noble, so generous, would, in a few short years, be transformed into a cowardly, mean tyrant, or a foul-mouthed, bloated drunkard? What father could rest at his home by night, knowing that his lovely daughter was at the mercy of a strong man, drunk with wine and passion, and that, do what he might, he was backed up by law and public sentiment? The best interests of the individual, the family, the state, the nation, cry out against these legalized marriages of force and endurance.

There can be no heaven without love; and nothing is sacred in the family and home, but just so far, as it is built up and anchored in purity and peace. Our newspapers teem with startling accounts of husbands and wives having shot or poisoned each other, or committed suicide, choosing death rather than the indissoluble tie, and still worse, the living death of faithless men and women, from the first families in the land, dragged from the privacy of home into the public prints and courts, with all the painful details of sad, false lives.

Now, do you believe, honorable gentlemen, that all these wretched matches were made in heaven? that all these sad, miserable people are bound together by God? But, say you, does not separation cover all these difficulties? No one objects to separation, when the parties are so disposed. To separation, there are two serious objections: first, so long as you insist on marriage as a divine institution, as an indissoluble tie, so long as you maintain your present laws against divorce, you make separation, even, so odious, that the most noble, virtuous and sensitive men and women, choose a life of concealed misery, rather than a partial, disgraceful release. Secondly, those who, in their impetuosity and despair, do, in spite of public sentiment, separate, find themselves, in their new position, beset with many temptations to lead a false, unreal life. This isolation bears especially hard on woman. Marriage is not all of life to a man. His resources for amusement and occupation are boundless. He has the whole world for his home. His business, his politics, his club, his friendships, with either sex, can help to fill up the void, made by an unfortunate union, or separation. But to woman, as she is now educated, marriage is all and everything—her sole object in life—that for which she is taught to live—the all-engrossing subject of all her sleeping and her waking dreams. Now, if a noble girl of seventeen marries, and is unfortunate in her choice, because the cruelty of her husband compels separation, in her dreary isolation, would you drive her to a nunnery, and shall she be a nun indeed? She, innocent child, perchance the victim of a father's pride, or a mother's ambition, betrayed into a worldly union for wealth, or family, or fame, shall the penalty be all visited on the heart of the only guiltless one in the transaction? Henceforth, do you doom this fair young being, just on the threshold of womanhood, to a joyless, loveless solitude? By your present laws you say, though separated, she is married still; indissolubly bound to

one she never loved; by whom she was never wooed or won; but by false
guardians sold. And now, no matter though in the coming time her soul
should, for the first time, wake to love, and one of God's own noblemen,
should echo back her choice, the gushing fountains of her young
affections must all be stayed. Because some man still lives, who once
called her wife, no other man may give to her his love; and if she love
not the tyrant to whom she is legally bound, she shall not love at all.

Think you that human law can set bounds to love? Alas! like faith, it
comes upon us unawares. It is not by an act of will, we believe new
doctrines, nor love what is true and noble in mankind. If you think it
wise to legislate on human affections, pray make your laws with
reference to what our natures are; let them harmonize in some measure
with the immutable laws of God. A very wise father once remarked, that
in the government of his children he forbid as few things as possible: a
wise legislation would do the same. It is folly to make laws on subjects
beyond human prerogative, knowing that in the very nature of things
they must be set aside. To make laws that man cannot, and will not
obey, serves to bring all law into contempt. It is all important in a
republican government that the people should respect the laws: for if we
throw law to the winds, what becomes of civil government?

What do our present divorce laws amount to? Those who wish to
evade them have only to go into another state to accomplish what they
desire. If any of our citizens cannot secure their inalienable rights in
New York state, they may, in Connecticut and Indiana.

Why is it that all contracts, covenants, agreements and partnerships
are left wholly at the discretion of the parties, except that which, of all
others, is considered most holy and important, both for the individual
and the race?

But, say you, what a condition we should soon have in social life, with
no restrictive laws. I ask you, what have we now? Separation and divorce
cases in all your courts; men disposing of their wives in every possible
way; by neglect, cruelty, tyranny, excess, poison, and imprisonment in
insane asylums. We would give the parties greater latitude, rather than
drive either to extreme measures, or crime. If you would make laws for
our protection, give us the power to release from legal conjugal
obligations, all husbands who are unfit for that relation. Woman loses
infinitely more than she gains, by the kind of protection you now
impose; for, much as we love and honor true and noble men, life and
liberty are dearer far to us, than even the legalized slavery of an

indissoluble tie. In this state, are over forty thousand drunkards' wives, earnestly imploring you to grant them deliverance from their fearful bondage. Thousands of sad mothers, too, with helpless children, deserted by faithless husbands, some in California, some in insane asylums, and some in the gutter, all pleading to be released. They ask nothing, but a quit-claim deed to themselves.

Thus far, we have had the man-marriage, and nothing more. From the beginning, man has had the whole and sole regulation of the matter. He has spoken in Scripture, and he has spoken in law. As an individual, he has decided the time and cause for putting away a wife; and as a judge and legislator, he still holds the entire control. In all history, sacred and profane, woman is regarded and spoken of, simply, as the toy of man. She is taken or put away, given or received, bought or sold, just as the interests of the parties might dictate. But the woman has been no more recognized in all these transactions through all the different periods and conditions of the race, than if she had had no part or lot in the whole matter. The right of woman to put away a husband, be he ever so impure, is never hinted at in sacred history.

We cannot take our gauge of womanhood from the past, but from the solemn convictions of our own souls, in the higher development of the race. No parchments, however venerable with the mould of ages, no human institutions, can bound the immortal wants of the royal sons and daughters of the great I Am.

I place man above all governments, all institutions, ecclesiastical and civil, all constitutions and laws. It is a mistaken idea that the same law that oppresses the individual can promote the highest good of society. The best interests of a community never can require the sacrifice of one innocent being, of one sacred right.

In the settlement, then, of any question, we must simply consider the highest good of the individual. It is the inalienable right of all to be happy. It is the highest duty of all to seek those conditions in life, those surroundings, which may develop what is noblest and best, remembering that the lessons of these passing hours are not for time alone, but for the ages of eternity. They tell us, in that future home, the heavenly paradise, that the human family shall be sifted out, and the good and pure shall dwell together in peace. If that be the heavenly order, is it not our duty to render earth as near like heaven as we may? Inasmuch as the greater includes the less, let me repeat, that I come not before you to plead simply the importance of divorce in cases proposed in your bill, but the justice of an entire revision of your whole code of laws on marriage and divorce. In our common law, in our whole system of jurisprudence, we find man's highest idea of right. The object of law is to secure justice. But inasmuch as fallible man is the maker, administrator and adjudicator of law, we must look for many and gross blunders in the application of its general principles to individual cases. The science of theology, of civil, political, moral and social life, all teach the common idea that man ever has been, and ever must be, sacrificed to the highest good of society —the one to the many—the poor to the rich—the weak to the powerful —and all to the institutions of his own creation. Look, what thunderbolts of power man has forged in the ages for his own destruction! at the organizations to enslave himself! And through those times of darkness, those generations of superstition, behold, all along, the relics of his power and skill, that stand like milestones, here and there, to show how far back man was great and glorious. Who can stand in those vast cathedrals of the old world, as the deep-toned organ reverberates from arch to arch, and not feel the grandeur of immortality. Here is the incarnated thought of man, beneath whose stately dome, the man himself, now bows in fear and doubt—knows not himself—and knows not God, a mere slave to symbols—and with holy water signs the cross, while he who died thereon, declared man, God.

In closing, let me submit for your consideration the following propositions:

1st. In the language (slightly varied) of John Milton, "Those who marry intend as little to conspire their own ruin, as those who swear allegiance, and as a whole people is *to an ill government*, so is one man or woman to *an ill marriage*. If a whole people against any authority, covenant or statute, may, by the sovereign edict of charity, save not only their lives, but honest liberties, from unworthy bondage, as well may a married party, against any private covenant, which he or she never entered *to his or her mischief*, be redeemed from unsupportable disturbances to honest peace and just contentment."

2nd. Any constitution, compact or covenant between human beings, that failed to produce or promote human happiness, could not, in the nature of things, be of any force or authority; and it would be not only a right, but a duty to abolish it.

3rd. Though marriage be in itself divinely founded, and is fortified as an institution by innumerable analogies in the whole kingdom of universal nature, still, a true marriage is only known by its results; and

375

like the fountain, if pure, will reveal only pure manifestations. Nor need it ever be said, "What God hath joined together, let not man put asunder," for man could not put it asunder; nor can he any more unite what God and nature have not joined together.

4th. Of all insulting mockeries of heavenly truth and holy law, none can be greater than that *physical impotency* is cause sufficient for divorce, while no amount of mental or moral or spiritual imbecility is ever to be pleaded in support of such a demand.

5th. Such a law was worthy those dark periods when marriage was held by the greatest doctors and priests of the Church to be a *work of the flesh only,* and almost, if not altogether, a defilement; denied wholly to the clergy, and a second time, forbidden to all.

6th. An unfortunate or ill-assorted marriage is ever a calamity, but not ever, perhaps never, a crime; and when society or government, by its laws or customs, compels its continuance, always to the grief of one of the parties, and the actual loss or damage of both, it usurps an authority never delegated to man, nor exercised by God himself.

7th. Observation and experience daily show how incompetent are men, as individuals, or as governments, to select partners in business, teachers for their children, ministers of their religion, or makers, adjudicators or administrators of their laws; and as the same weakness and blindness must attend in the selection of matrimonial partners, the dictates of humanity and common sense alike show that the latter and most important contract should no more be perpetual than either or all of the former.

8th. Children born in these unhappy and unhallowed connections, are in the most solumn sense of *unlawful birth*—the fruit of lust, but not of love; and so not of God, divinely descended, but from beneath, whence proceed all manner of evil and uncleanness.

9th. Next to the calamity of such a birth to the child, is the misfortune of being trained in the atmosphere of a household where love is not the law but where discord and bitterness abound; stamping their demoniac features on the moral nature, with all their odious peculiarities; thus continuing the race in a weakness and depravity that must be a sure precursor of its ruin, as a just penalty of a long violated law.

☆

Elizabeth Cady Stanton must be numbered among the combatants of history who have failed in their immediate objective but have been ultimately vindicated. Although the New York senate voted down the divorce bill of 1861, American attitudes toward divorce moved steadily in the direction of her humane point of view. No matter what the legal hurdles in any particular state, individuals unhappy in their marriages were usually able to find avenues of escape. And in the administration of the laws men and women were at last put upon an equal basis.

By no means daunted by her failure in 1861, Mrs. Stanton continued to agitate the marriage question. The arguments she had used in her address to the Judiciary Committee were repeated again and again in the post–Civil War years. From 1868 to 1870, Mrs. Stanton and Miss Susan B. Anthony published a weekly periodical called the Revolution, in which they advocated among other reforms the need for more rational divorce laws. When financial difficulties terminated this venture, the two women crisscrossed the country on arduous lecture tours. One of Mrs. Stanton's most popular addresses was that on "Marriage and Divorce"— an enlargement of her appeal to the New York legislature. "Women respond to this divorce speech," she declared, "as they never did to suffrage." Shortly before her death in 1902, she submitted to the newspapers her final plea for a more tolerant attitude toward divorce. "The States that have more liberal divorce laws," she wrote, "are for women today what Canada was for the fugitive in the old days of slavery."

By nailing the flag of liberal divorce laws to the staff of woman's rights, Mrs. Stanton provoked bitter controversy. Disagreement on this issue played a major part in splitting the feminist movement into radical and conservative factions for a period of twenty years. Indeed, Mrs. Stanton was waging her campaign in the face of a highly determined counter-movement, led by the many religious leaders who were trying to make divorce more difficult.

Strong though the conservative movement appeared to be, changing economic and social conditions were favoring the more liberal attitude championed by Mrs. Stanton. As women acquired more education and more vocational opportunities, they demanded much more of marriage. Now confident of their ability to make an independent living, they would no longer endure unhappiness in their family affairs. In earlier days the woman who resorted to divorce had encountered a cruel form of social ostracism, but after World War I the harsher taboos were seldom

377

imposed. Since the nation's divorce laws are not materially different today from those of a hundred years ago, the increasing frequency of divorce in our own times is largely to be explained by changing popular attitudes. Resort to the divorce court now appears to be regarded as permissible conduct—except possibly for clergymen and presidential candidates.

Before the nineteenth century divorce had been almost exclusively a masculine prerogative; indeed, the best argument for indissoluble marriage had been that it protected helpless wives against willful husbands who wanted to cast off their old mates and take on new ones. But Mrs. Stanton and like-minded women of the nineteenth century believed that wives were more injured than helped by rigid divorce laws. Husbands who tired of their partners had only to desert them and run away to other parts—often finding female companionship outside the law. But deserted or mistreated wives faced a life of misery unless they could be set free from their oppressors and allowed to marry again. In the late nineteenth and twentieth centuries many more women than men appeared as plaintiffs in divorce actions. The statistics were, to be sure, somewhat misleading, since in cases where husband and wife both wanted the divorce, gallantry usually demanded that the woman be allowed to make the formal accusations. But even when due allowance was made for this practice, it was clear that women more often than men were now the real initiators of divorce proceedings.

It is a measure of the slow response of legislation to changing mores that so much of Mrs. Stanton's criticism of the divorce laws of her day remains relevant a hundred years later. Not until 1966 did the New York legislature finally amend the law to permit divorce on grounds other than adultery. In the end, the logic of Mrs. Stanton's argument could not be denied. "What do our present divorce laws amount to? Those who wish to evade them have only to go into another state to accomplish what they desire."

But the larger implications of Mrs. Stanton's indictment reach much farther than New York State. She believed that marriage was a human institution—divine only to the degree that a particular union contributed to human happiness. When hatred displaced love, she was convinced that it was immoral to continue the relationship. Not only did it chain husband and wife to a life of misery, but it doomed children to be brought up amid discord and bitterness. Divorce, she believed, ought to be like surgery—not to be prescribed unless necessary, but to be performed as cleanly and expeditiously as possible when essential to the well-being of the parties. Even in states with supposedly liberal policies, today's divorce courts perform their function with deplorable inattention and cynicism. Mrs. Stanton would have highly approved the recommendations of contemporary divorce reformers who argue for special family courts. These would abandon the myth of adversary proceedings and make their inquiries with the aid of trained investigators. The filing of embittering charges and countercharges would be eliminated; the possibilities of reconciliation would be explored; the needs of the children would be studied; and a final settlement would be arranged that would protect the interests of all the parties. Thus, in words borrowed by Mrs. Stanton from the Puritan poet John Milton, another great advocate of rational divorce, married parties would be "redeemed from unsupportable disturbances to honest peace and just contentment."

Julia Ward Howe
The Battle Hymn of the Republic
1861

EDITED BY WILLIAM G. MCLOUGHLIN

There is no mystery about the composition of the words of "The Battle Hymn of the Republic," although there is about its music. The words were written by Julia Ward Howe (wife of the then more famous Samuel Gridley Howe) in Willard's Hotel in Washington, D.C., on November 18, 1861, at about five o'clock in the morning. Mrs. Howe, already well known as an abolitionist, a poetess, and a humanitarian reformer, had come to Washington with her husband in connection with his appointment to the United States Sanitary Commission. With them was Governor John Andrew of Massachusetts and the Reverend James Freeman Clarke, noted pastor of the Church of the Disciples (Unitarian) in Boston, which Mrs. Howe attended. On November 17 their party had watched some Army maneuvers south of the Potomac and had sung with the soldiers the popular song "John Brown's body lies a-mouldering in the grave,/His soul is marching on." The Reverend Mr. Clarke suggested, "Mrs. Howe, why do you not write some good words for that stirring tune?" She replied that she had often wished to do so, but "had not yet found in my mind any leading toward it." She went to bed that night pondering the problem and awoke early in the morning to find the words springing spontaneously to her lips. In the gray dawn she wrote out six stanzas almost without hesitation or alteration of a word. Some weeks later she sent the poem to the editor of the Atlantic Monthly, James T. Field. (She omitted the sixth stanza as inferior; it was not printed until

380

1899, and is almost never sung.) He suggested the title and paid her four dollars for the poem. She never received any royalties from it. It appeared, without her name, on the first page of the magazine in February, 1862, in the form in which it has been used ever since.

The first sheet music bearing her words appeared a few months later in Boston; the publisher noted, under the title, that the song was "adapted to the favorite Melody of Glory Hallelujah." Three other sheet-music editions had appeared before the end of 1862. A large part of the song's immediate success lay in the rhythm and melody of the music to which it was written, but although two books have been written on the subject, no one has ever definitively identified the composer. Most authorities attribute the music to one William Steffe of South Carolina, who is said to have written it in 1856. But almost nothing is known about Steffe, and no versions of the melody with his name on it are extant. In later years a composer of popular songs named Thomas Brigham Bishop (among others) claimed the authorship, but there is no proof beyond his own word for this. The versions of the song which appeared prior to "The John Brown Song" (none of them is found before 1858) are contained in various Sunday school hymnbooks with no composer's name; the words usually given are "Say, Brothers, will you meet us, on Canaan's happy shore," and the chorus of "Glory, glory, Hallelujah" ends "For ever, ever more" instead of "His truth is marching on." But the melody of these early versions is essentially the same as that which accompanied Mrs. Howe's words.

Apparently this Sunday school song was known by those soldiers of the 12th Massachusetts Volunteers who were stationed at Fort Warren, Massachusetts, in 1861. A quartet of soldiers in Colonel Fletcher Webster's regiment is given credit for making up the words of "The John Brown Song" in the spring of 1861. The song was published in several sheet-music versions prior to the appearance of "The Battle Hymn of the Republic," and it too was described only as "Sung to the tune of Glory Hallelujah," with no author or composer mentioned.

"The Battle Hymn of the Republic" was praised by Ralph Waldo Emerson, William Cullen Bryant, Henry W. Longfellow, and many of the other leading writers of the day. It is reported that Abraham Lincoln once wept at hearing it sung and told the singer that he had never heard a better song. Many stories have been told about its inspiriting effect upon the soldiers in the Civil War, and Chaplain Charles C. McCabe, later dubbed "The Singing Chaplain," raised thousands of dollars for the

Christian Commission's war work by singing this song at rallies at which he gave his lecture on "The Bright Side of Life in Libby Prison."

Mine eyes have seen the glory of the coming of the Lord:
He is trampling out the vintage where the grapes of wrath are stored;
He hath loosed the fateful lightning of His terrible swift sword:
His truth is marching on.

I have seen Him in the watch-fires of a hundred circling camps;
They have builded Him an altar in the evening dews and damps;
I can read His righteous sentence by the dim and flaring lamps:
His day is marching on.

I have read a fiery gospel writ in burnished rows of steel:
"As ye deal with my contemners, so with you my grace shall deal;
Let the Hero, born of woman, crush the serpent with his heel,
Since God is marching on."

He has sounded forth the trumpet that shall never call retreat;
He is sifting out the hearts of men before His judgment-seat:
Oh, be swift, my soul, to answer Him! be jubilant, my feet!
Our God is marching on.

In the beauty of the lilies Christ was born across the sea,
With a glory in his bosom that transfigures you and me:
As he died to make men holy, let us die to make men free,
While God is marching on.

Born in and of the nation's greatest spiritual and social crisis, "The Battle Hymn of the Republic" is the supreme example of the elementary urge of Americans to equate their religious and their patriotic ideals. Because

---

This is the text of the poem as it originally appeared in the *Atlantic Monthly,* IX (February, 1862), 10. The text in the original sheet-music edition published by Oliver, Ditson Co., Boston, 1862, contains these same words. Later editions often omitted the third verse. The original manuscript in Mrs. Howe's hand is in the Library of Congress.

it is more than a patriotic anthem, it has had a far wider appeal and has been put to more varied uses than such counterparts as "My Country, 'Tis of Thee," "America, the Beautiful," or "The Star-Spangled Banner." In addition to being a patriotic paean, it is also a song of praise to the deity, a resurgent millennial hymn, and a ringing ode to freedom. Appropriately enough, the origin of its music and chorus was a Sunday school song. In the words she wrote to this music (and in her own career) Julia Ward Howe perfectly embodied the whole crusading fervor of the pre–Civil War generation's evangelical activism and moral zeal.

"The Battle Hymn" fuses into a harmonious and eloquent brevity the New World's conviction that here is the chosen land, that Americans are God's chosen people, and that good will eventually triumph over evil. It expresses also some of that moralistic self-righteousness and Old Testament militancy which has been part of the American outlook since the days when the Puritans under John Winthrop determined to make New England a "Citty vpon a Hill." The song is saved from being too self-righteous by the first two lines of its last verse (which are often sung pianissimo in contrast to the thumping martial spirit of the other verses and the chorus). And it is significant that in one of her few revisions Mrs. Howe altered the words "shines out in you and me" to "transfigures you and me." By so doing she unconsciously transcended her own minority (Unitarian) faith in the divinity of man and spoke instead in the evangelical accents of the majority of Americans.

For Mrs. Howe and the Union Army, "The Battle Hymn" was assumed to be a sectional anthem, made so by its final line, which meant to identify the war not (as Lincoln first saw it) as a national effort to preserve the Union but as a Holy War to free the slave. Yet by avoiding any specific mention of slavery or the rebellious South the song transcended its origin. And not the least of many purposes it has since served, strange as it may seem, was the part it played in healing the division between the North and the South. Mrs. Howe was astonished to find when she visited the New Orleans Exposition in 1884 that a southern choir could serenade her with the music of "The Battle Hymn." And as Memorial Day services came to be celebrated in honor of the Blue and the Gray, "The Battle Hymn" itself became a tribute to the dead of both sides and a call for renewed loyalty to a more abstract ideal of freedom than abolition. Participating in a Memorial Day service in Boston in 1899, Mrs. Howe rode in the same carriage with former Confederate General Joseph Wheeler, who himself had risen above sectionalism by volunteering to serve in the United States Army in the Spanish-American War, then in progress. Few failed to see in this occasion a personification of national reunion, as the northern poetess and the southern general waved and sang "The Battle Hymn" along with the crowd. A Philadelphia newspaper reporter, carried away by the occasion, wrote, "If volunteers were really needed for the Philippines, McKinley could have had us all right there."

Because it is both a hymn and a patriotic song, and because its inspirational words lack specificity, "The Battle Hymn" is equally appropriate for church services and Fourth of July parades, for high school commencements and Kiwanis Club luncheons. It can be sung by any group which sees its cause in terms of freedom, of do-goodism, or of the millennial vision. It is suitable for times of national danger, mourning, and rejoicing. It was sung by American soldiers not only during the Civil War but in the Spanish-American War, World War I, and World War II. When a memorial tablet was unveiled in St. Paul's Cathedral in London for the first American soldier killed in World War II, the soldiers who were assembled to honor him sang this song. It has appeared in many of the standard hymnbooks of many denominations as well as in the gospel songbooks used in the revival crusades of D. L. Moody and Billy Sunday; Billy Graham used it as the theme song for his weekly broadcasts in the 1950's. The suffragettes (among whom Julia Ward Howe was a leader) sang it often in their meetings and marches, and so did the prohibitionists. During the Progressive Era it was frequently sung by reformers at political meetings (one notable occasion being at the election of Seth Low as reform mayor of New York in 1901 which overthrew Boss Richard Croker's long Tammany rule over the city). The Bull Moose Party made it virtually a campaign song in 1912 (alternating it with its closest religious counterpart, "Onward Christian Soldiers"). The novelist John Steinbeck took a phrase from the poem (a phrase, incidentally, which must be credited to Mrs. Howe and not to any text in the Bible) and used it to symbolize the plight and ultimate triumph of the common man over the evils of the Great Depression— "the grapes of wrath." A popular recording of "The Battle Hymn" in 1959 sold 200,000 copies within a few weeks. In recent years the song has played a prominent part in demonstrations, marches, and mass meetings on behalf of civil rights for Negroes. It was sadly intoned by an English choir at a memorial service for President John F. Kennedy held in Westminster Abbey on November 24, 1963. And on January 30, 1965, it was sung in St. Paul's Cathedral, London, at the funeral service of Sir Winston Churchill, in accordance with his express wishes.

Perhaps the clearest demonstration of the extent to which this song has come to embody the fundamental religious and patriotic attitudes of the general American public has been the frequently made suggestion, in some places carried into action, that the reading of the hymn be required in daily ceremonies in the public schools to replace recitation of the Lord's Prayer and Bible reading, exercises which the Supreme Court decision of 1963 declared unconstitutional.

Though it has been mercilessly parodied and burlesqued, "The Battle Hymn" has stood the test of time. Americans may no longer be so naively optimistic and buoyantly self-confident as they were fifty or one hundred years ago, but they still continue to believe that their faith in God and their patriotic commitment to American political ideals are and ought to be one and the same. Although, apart from its title, the hymn is not obviously nationalistic (any more than is the "Marseillaise"), nevertheless it has an indefinable quality which marks it as peculiarly American. As an anthem of American hope and faith, as an intonation of belief in the ultimate triumph of freedom and justice for all, and as an inspirational pledge to work for the coming of the millennium, "The Battle Hymn of the Republic" seems destined to live as long as the Republic itself. When it ceases to inspire Americans, something fundamental and elemental will have departed from the national spirit.

The Homestead Act
1862

EDITED BY PAUL W. GATES

The land policy of the United States was originally designed to produce revenue for the government. Its basic features were high minimum prices, competitive bids, and the sale of land only in large tracts. Gradually the representatives of the public-land states succeeded in breaking down this revenue policy and in reshaping the land legislation to make it easier for settlers to acquire ownership of small tracts. In 1820 the minimum price was reduced from $2.00 an acre to $1.25, and in 1854 to as little as 12½¢ for land that had been subject to sale for many years. The smallest tract one could acquire was 40 acres. After 1841 those who settled on public land not yet brought on the market could claim pre-emption rights on a location of 160 acres or less, and could safely begin improving it before they had title. Land newly surveyed continued, however, to be priced at a minimum of $1.25 when first offered for sale, and the West regarded this as excessively high.

The western view was that public land had no value until it was improved by the labor of settlers, by the expenditure of local tax money on roads and public buildings, and by the construction of railroads financed, to a considerable degree, out of public resources. These views became accentuated when settlers began moving into the treeless prairies, where they had to import their lumber for building, even for fuel, and had to expend much capital on fencing, on heavy steel plows and reapers, and on horses and oxen to draw them. Dangerously high farm mortgages and the growth of tenancy resulted, lending support to the view that the government should not compel the pioneer to buy the raw, unimproved land. Also, the West deplored the acquisition of much of the choice land on the frontier by speculators who did nothing to develop it and who withheld it from sale until near-by settlers had improved their tracts and had thereby added to the value of the speculators' holdings. In order to realize the Jeffersonian dream of molding public land policies to bring about a democratic society in which small landowners predominated, free land and curbs on land speculation were needed.

A combination of interests—workingmen's advocates who thought the salvation of the laborer was to migrate to the West and take up public land, sentimentalists who looked to the establishment of an Arcadia in the West, and agrarians—agitated for a free-land policy that would assure everyone who went West to settle and improve land the right to a free quarter-section of 160 acres. Horace Greeley's powerful New York Tribune was the principal spokesman for free land or homestead. The demand was taken up by the Free Soil Party in 1848, and in the 1850's the Republican Party stole the land-reform issue from the Democrats, who up to that time had worked for more liberal policies. In the administrations of Pierce and Buchanan the Democrats actually became hostile to the rapid growth of the West then being encouraged by the increasingly liberal land system. When the land reformers threatened to push through Congress a free-homestead policy, although one that had been shorn of most of the safeguards that Greeley favored, the southern-dominated Democrats made the measure as unpalatable to the reformers as possible before it was approved by Congress, and even then Buchanan vetoed it. This maneuvering wrecked the Democratic Party in the newly developing states and territories and contributed to the success of the Republicans under Lincoln in 1860.

With the South out of the Union in 1862, the Republicans wrote into law the Homestead Act. More than a third of a century of agitation and debate in which workingmen's groups, Greeley, Andrew Johnson of Tennessee, and Galusha Grow of Pennsylvania had played leading parts was finally successful.

Be it enacted by the Senate and House of Representatives of the United States of America in Congress assembled, That any person who is the head of a family, or who has arrived at the age of twenty-one years, and is a citizen of the United States, or who shall have filed his declaration of

---

The Homestead Act, which was approved May 20, 1862, is reprinted from U.S. *Statutes at Large,* XII, 392–93. Its full title is *An Act to secure Homesteads to actual Settlers on the Public Domain.*

intention to become such, as required by the naturalization laws of the United States, and who has never borne arms against the United States Government or given aid and comfort to its enemies, shall, from and after the first January, eighteen hundred and sixty-three, be entitled to enter one quarter section or a less quantity of unappropriated public lands, upon which said person may have filed a preëmption claim, or which may, at the time the application is made, be subject to preëmption at one dollar and twenty-five cents, or less, per acre; or eighty acres or less of such unappropriated lands, at two dollars and fifty cents per acre, to be located in a body, in conformity to the legal subdivisions of the public lands, and after the same shall have been surveyed: *Provided,* That any person owning and residing on land may, under the provisions of this act, enter other land lying contiguous to his or her said land, which shall not, with the land so already owned and occupied, exceed in the aggregate one hundred and sixty acres.

Sec. 2. *And be it further enacted,* That the person applying for the benefit of this act shall, upon application to the register of the land office in which he or she is about to make such entry, make affidavit before the said register or receiver that he or she is the head of a family, or is twenty-one years or more of age, or shall have performed service in the army or navy of the United States, and that he has never borne arms against the Government of the United States or given aid and comfort to its enemies, and that such application is made for his or her exclusive use and benefit, and that said entry is made for the purpose of actual settlement and cultivation, and not either directly or indirectly for the use or benefit of any other person or persons whomsoever; and upon filing the said affidavit with the register or receiver, and on payment of ten dollars, he or she shall thereupon be permitted to enter the quantity of land specified: *Provided, however,* That no certificate shall be given or patent issued therefor until the expiration of five years from the date of such entry; and if, at the expiration of such time, or at any time within two years thereafter, the person making such entry; or, if he be dead, his widow; or in case of her death, his heirs or devisee; or in case of a widow making such entry, her heirs or devisee, in case of her death; shall prove by two credible witnesses that he, she, or they have resided upon or cultivated the same for the term of five years immediately succeeding the time of filing the affidavit aforesaid, and shall make affidavit that no part of said land has been alienated, and that he has borne true allegiance to the Government of the United States; then, in such case, he, she, or they, if at that time a citizen of the United States, shall be entitled to a patent, as in other cases provided for by law; *And provided, further,* That in case of the death of both father and mother, leaving an infant child, or children, under twenty-one years of age, the right and fee shall enure to the benefit of said infant child or children; and the executor, administrator, or guardian may, at any time within two years after the death of the surviving parent, and in accordance with the laws of the State in which such children for the time being have their domicil, sell said land for the benefit of said infants, but for no other purpose; and the purchaser shall acquire the absolute title by the purchase, and be entitled to a patent from the United States, on payment of the office fees and sum of money herein specified.

Sec. 3 *And be it further enacted,* That the register of the land office shall note all such applications on the tract books and plats of his office, and keep a register of all such entries, and make return thereof to the General Land Office, together with the proof upon which they have been founded.

Sec. 4. *And be it further enacted,* That no lands acquired under the provisions of this act shall in any event become liable to the satisfaction of any debt or debts contracted prior to the issuing of the patent therefor.

Sec. 5. *And be it further enacted,* That if, at any time after the filing of the affidavit, as required in the second section of this act, and before the expiration of the five years aforesaid, it shall be proven, after due notice to the settler, to the satisfaction of the register of the land office, that the person having filed such affidavit shall have actually changed his or her residence or abandoned the said land for more than six months at any time, then and in that event the land so entered shall revert to the government.

Sec. 6. *And be it further enacted,* That no individual shall be permitted to acquire title to more than one quarter section under the provisions of this act; and that the Commissioner of the General Land Office is hereby required to prepare and issue such rules and regulations, consistent with this act, as shall be necessary and proper to carry its provisions into effect; and that the registers and receivers of the several land offices shall be entitled to receive the same compensation for any lands entered under the provisions of this act that they are now entitled to receive when the same quantity of land is entered with money, one half to be paid by the person making the application at the time of so doing, and the other half on the issue of the certificate by the person to whom it may be issued; but this shall not be construed to enlarge the maximum of compensation now prescribed by law for any register or receiver: *Provided,* That nothing contained in this act shall be so construed as to impair or interfere in any manner whatever with existing preëmption rights: *And provided, further,* That all persons who may have filed their applications for a preëmption right prior to the passage of this act, shall be entitled to all privileges of this act: *Provided, further,* That no person who has served, or may hereafter serve, for a period of not less than fourteen days in the army or navy of the United States, either regular or volunteer, under the laws thereof, during the existence of an actual war, domestic or foreign, shall be deprived of the benefits of this act on account of not having attained the age of twenty-one years.

Sec. 7. *And be it further enacted,* That the fifth section of the act entitled "An act in addition to an act more effectually to provide for the punishment of certain crimes against the United States, and for other purposes," approved the third of March, in the year eighteen hundred and fifty-seven, shall extend to all oaths, affirmations, and affidavits, required or authorized by this act.

Sec. 8. *And be it further enacted,* That nothing in this act shall be so construed as to prevent any person who has availed him or herself of the benefits of the first section of this act, from paying the minimum price, or the price to which the same may have graduated, for the quantity of land so entered at any time before the expiration of the five years, and obtaining a patent therefor from the government, as in other cases provided by law, on making proof of settlement and cultivation as provided by existing laws granting preëmption rights.

Approved, May 20, 1862.

The Homestead Act promised a grant of 160 acres to any citizen or intended citizen who settled upon a vacant unappropriated area of government land and made specified improvements upon it during the ensuing five years; technically the land itself was free, though the settlers were required to pay certain modest fees to the land officers for recording the applications. Land reformers were disappointed that the Act did not repeal the law permitting cash sale of public land in unlimited amounts

and thus did not halt speculative purchasing. They were also left with a feeling of frustration because much of the best public land was being granted away to railroads and to states, and because the great Indian reservations, as they were cut into and eliminated, were to be sold, not opened to homestead.

Later critics were to maintain that the Act's 160-acre unit was wholly inadequate for farming in the drier portions of the Great Plains beyond the 98th or 100th meridian, and that homesteaders had to resort to fraud to build up holdings sufficient for practicable farming. In fact, Congress had been careful to retain and indeed to strengthen the Preëmption Law of 1841; homesteaders could therefore acquire an additional 160 acres for $200. In 1873, when settlement was moving still farther west into the less humid region of the high plains, Congress adopted the Timber Culture Act which enabled settlers in those areas to gain ownership of a third quarter-section by planting and maintaining trees on 40 acres of it for ten years. In 1877 the Desert Land Act made it possible for settlers to acquire a full section (640 acres) in addition to pre-emption and homestead quarters. Clearly the land system was not as inflexible as some critics maintained.

The rush to take advantage of the Homestead Act was immediate; before the Civil War was over, 26,552 entries had been made. Then came the expected postwar rush of hungry land seekers. The number of homestead filings rose from 15,355 in 1866 to 39,768 in 1871 and 61,638 in 1886. By 1890 a total of 957,902 people had filed entries for homestead land.

In that year the Superintendent of the Census expressed the opinion that the frontier was gone, but land seekers were not troubled by any such false notion. The scramble for the free lands continued unabated, reaching a high figure of 98,829 entries in 1902. Indeed, more than twice as many filings (2,038,558) were made on homesteads after 1890 as before.

By no means all homesteaders who filed original entries won title to their land. Many made poor selections and had to abandon their improvements; others lacked the capital to make necessary improvements and sold relinquishments of their claims to later comers; still others mortgaged their claims when money was abundant and let the mortgage company take over when prices fell and the land appeared to be worth less than the mortgage. Some made their entries without any intention of developing a farm for themselves, commuted their rights to cash purchases six months after filing, as the law allowed, and then sold, usually to a cattle, mining, or timber company. Fraud of this sort was extensive and tended to blacken the reputation of the Homestead Act. Approximately one-half of the original filings were never completed and a considerable portion of the 1,622,107 successful entries that were carried to patent were designed for other than the original entrymen. Notwithstanding this abuse of the Act and the evidence of concentrated ownership in certain areas, far more land went directly into the possession of farmers through the Homestead Act than through any other act of Congress.

In the twentieth century the homestead unit was increased to 320 acres and finally to 640 acres on the assumption that the remaining public lands were suitable for farming only in larger tracts. In 1934 homesteading on public land was practically halted by the adoption of the Taylor Grazing Act, which, with later amendments, withdrew remaining public lands of any value and placed them in organized grazing districts, currently being administered by the Bureau of Land Management.

The Homestead Act was the farmers' act. It contributed mightily to drawing population to the frontier, to making family farm ownership easier, and somewhat to reducing dependence on borrowed capital. This Act, together with the efforts of the states and of the land-grant railroads to promote colonization, greatly accelerated the development of the West. Out of that rapid growth came the agrarian issues of the 1870's. Later generations would look back and wonder that the government had had the wisdom and generosity to help so many people to acquire and develop farms from Florida to California, from Michigan to Washington.

Abraham Lincoln
Second Annual Message to Congress
1862

EDITED BY ROY F. NICHOLS

President Lincoln's means of communication with the public were decidedly limited, compared with those available a century later. He fully realized the value of such contact, however, and made the best use possible of the facilities at hand. He possessed to an unusual degree the capacity to clothe thought in simple and elegant language so that those who received his message could make it their own and cherish it. He could say things that people could not help remembering. The principal avenues available to him were his presidential messages, annual and special, which were printed in all newspapers and given the widest coverage.

As chief magistrate, Lincoln was conscious of the harassing responsibility of war leadership; he also conceived himself a tribune of the people, a statesman with the opportunity and, he came to believe, the responsibility of reordering the social structure of the nation. He was not at first aware of this great duty. At the time of his inauguration he had hoped to avoid war, and when the war came he had hoped to contain it within the lower South and to end it quickly. In order to confine secession and maintain the loyalty of the upper South, he carefully avoided any suggestion of possible interference with the southern social structure, particularly with slavery.

The chief issue at stake, he believed, was proof that a "government . . . conceived in liberty . . . could long endure." As he phrased it in his message to the Special Session of Congress on July 4, 1861, "This is essentially a Peoples' contest. On the side of the Union, it is a struggle for maintaining in the world, that form, and substance of government, whose leading object is, to elevate the condition of men—to lift artificial weights from all shoulders—to clear the paths of laudable pursuit for all —to afford all, an unfettered start, and a fair chance, in the race of life. Yielding to partial, and temporary departures, from necessity, this is the leading object of the government for whose existence we contend. I am most happy to believe that the plain people understand, and appreciate this."

Lincoln pursued this theme further in his First Annual Message, when he supplemented previous arguments in favor of popular institutions with one of greater depth. He referred to an effort which he perceived "to place capital on an equal footing with, if not above labor, in the structure of government."

He believed that there was "not, of necessity, any such thing as the free hired laborer being fixed to that condition for life. Many independent men everywhere in these States, a few years back in their lives, were hired laborers. The prudent, penniless beginner in the world, labors for wages awhile, saves a surplus with which to buy tools or land for himself; then labors on his own account another while, and at length hires another new beginner to help him. . . . No men living are more worthy to be trusted than those who toil up from poverty—none less inclined to take, or touch, aught which they have not honestly earned. Let them beware of surrendering a political power which they already possess, and which, if surrendered, will surely be used to close the door of advancement against such as they, and to fix new disabilities and burdens upon them, till all of liberty shall be lost."

Contrary to Lincoln's early hopes, soon after the war began the question of the future of slavery forced itself upon him. The slaves quite obviously were being used by the Confederacy as active agents in the conflict. Many of them fled to the Union lines or were captured. Congress repealed the Fugitive Slave Act of 1850, which required the return of escaping slaves, and in 1862, passed a Confiscation Act designed to free slaves who were able to reach northern lines or who lived in regions occupied by Union troops. Also, one of the Union commanders, General John C. Frémont, undertook to emancipate slaves in his area of command, the border slave state of Missouri, which was still loyal to the

Union. This cumulation of events, together with the unsatisfactory progress of the war, brought Lincoln to a decision. He revoked Frémont's abolition proclamation, and in his First Annual Message he outlined rather sketchily a policy of his own. The slaves of seceding masters should be made free, with no compensation to be paid for them. He was willing to compensate loyal slave owners for their escaped property, but not to send these Negroes back to bondage. He would free them and would endeavor to colonize all the former slaves in the tropics of the Americas or Africa. He was also working on a plan, which he was talking over with loyal congressmen, to buy the slaves in the border states.

In the course of this consideration, during the winter of 1861–62, he called on the director of the census, Joseph C. G. Kennedy, for runs of statistics. In the midst of trying to get the newly appointed commander, General George B. McClellan, to fight, and of reorganizing the military campaigns, he came to a further decision. Slavery must go. He prescribed this objective first in outline to Congress in messages dated March 6 and July 14, 1862, submitting for the consideration of the lawmakers bills which provided for compensated emancipation. He also held conferences and wrote letters, but he made little progress. Therefore he made a third decision. He would issue a proclamation announcing that in December he would offer his plan in greater detail, with an extended argument in its favor, and if this was not accepted by Congress he would emancipate by his own fiat on January 1, 1863, all slaves within the Confederate lines. He believed that his own plan, which was more gradual, which involved the cooperation of the owners, and which would save them from drastic economic loss, would be much preferable. But if it was not accepted, emancipation by order of the Commander in Chief was the alternative.

In this spirit Lincoln prepared his Second Annual Message, which contains his most elaborate formulation of his economic and social thinking and marks one of the highest points in his statesmanship. He made the usual report on the state of the war and the work of the departments. Then he commented on the operation of two revolutionary laws, providing free homesteads and a subsidy to build a Pacific railroad, and announced the setting up of a Department of Agriculture. Next he introduced his main theme and detailed his argument for emancipation and social reorganization.

☆

I . . . RECALL your attention to what may be called "compensated emancipation."

A nation may be said to consist of its territory, its people, and its laws. The territory is the only part which is of certain durability. "One generation passeth away, and another generation cometh, but the earth abideth forever." It is of the first importance to duly consider, and estimate, this ever-enduring part. That portion of the earth's surface which is owned and inhabited by the people of the United States, is well adapted to be the home of one national family; and it is not well adapted for two, or more. Its vast extent, and its variety of climate and productions, are of advantage, in this age, for one people, whatever they might have been in former ages. Steam, telegraphs, and intelligence, have brought these, to be an advantageous combination, for one united people.

In the inaugural address I briefly pointed out the total inadequacy of disunion, as a remedy for the differences between the people of the two sections. I did so in language which I cannot improve, and which, therefore, I beg to repeat:

"One section of our country believes slavery is right, and ought to be extended, while the other believes it is wrong, and ought not to be extended. This is the only substantial dispute. The fugitive slave clause of the Constitution, and the law for the suppression of the foreign slave trade, are each as well enforced, perhaps, as any law can ever be in a community where the moral sense of the people imperfectly supports the law itself. The great body of the people abide by the dry legal obligation in both cases, and a few break over in each. This, I think, cannot be perfectly cured; and it would be worse in both cases after the separation of the sections, than before. The foreign slave trade, now imperfectly suppressed, would be ultimately revived without restriction in one section; while fugitive slaves, now only partially surrendered, would not be surrendered at all by the other.

"Physically speaking, we cannot separate. We cannot remove our respective sections from each other, nor build an impassable wall between them. A husband and wife may be divorced, and go out of the presence, and beyond the reach of each other; but the different parts of

The message is reprinted from *Collected Works of Abraham Lincoln*, edited by Roy P. Basler (New Brunswick, N.J.: Rutgers University Press, 1953), V, 527–37. The original is in the National Archives, RG 46, Senate 37A F1, except for the first two pages; for this missing portion Mr. Basler followed *House of Representatives Document No. 1*, 37th Cong., 3d sess.

our country cannot do this. They cannot but remain face to face; and intercourse, either amicable or hostile, must continue between them. Is it possible, then, to make that intercourse more advantageous, or more satisfactory, *after* separation than *before?* Can aliens make treaties, easier than friends can make laws? Can treaties be more faithfully enforced between aliens, than laws can among friends? Suppose you go to war, you cannot fight always; and when, after much loss on both sides, and no gain on either, you cease fighting, the identical old questions, as to terms of intercourse, are again upon you."

There is no line, straight or crooked, suitable for a national boundary, upon which to divide. Trace through, from east to west, upon the line between the free and slave country, and we shall find a little more than one-third of its length are rivers, easy to be crossed, and populated, or soon to be populated, thickly upon both sides; while nearly all its remaining length, are merely surveyor's lines, over which people may walk back and forth without any consciousness of their presence. No part of this line can be made any more difficult to pass, by writing it down on paper, or parchment, as a national boundary. The fact of separation, if it comes, gives up, on the part of the seceding section, the fugitive slave clause, along with all other constitutional obligations upon the section seceded from, while I should expect no treaty stipulation would ever be made to take its place.

But there is another difficulty. The great interior region, bounded east by the Alleghanies, north by the British dominions, west by the Rocky mountains, and south by the line along which the culture of corn and cotton meets, and which includes part of Virginia, part of Tennessee, all of Kentucky, Ohio, Indiana, Michigan, Wisconsin, Illinois, Missouri, Kansas, Iowa, Minnesota and the Territories of Dakota, Nebraska, and part of Colorado, already has above ten millions of people, and will have fifty millions within fifty years, if not prevented by any political folly or mistake. It contains more than one-third of the country owned by the United States—certainly more than one million of square miles. Once half as populous as Massachusetts already is, it would have more than seventy-five millions of people. A glance at the map shows that, territorially speaking, it is the great body of the republic. The other parts are but marginal borders to it, the magnificent region sloping west from the rocky mountains to the Pacific, being the deepest, and also the richest, in undeveloped resources. In the production of provisions, grains, grasses, and all which proceed from them, this great interior

397

region is naturally one of the most important in the world. Ascertain from the statistics the small proportion of the region which has, as yet, been brought into cultivation, and also the large and rapidly increasing amount of its products, and we shall be overwhelmed with the magnitude of the prospect presented. An[d] yet this region has no sea-coast, touches no ocean anywhere. As part of one nation, its people now find, and may forever find, their way to Europe by New York, to South America and Africa by New Orleans, and to Asia by San Francisco. But separate our common country into two nations, as designed by the present rebellion, and every man of this great interior region is thereby cut off from some one or more of these outlets, not, perhaps, by a physical barrier, but by embarrassing and onerous trade regulations.

And this is true, *wherever* a dividing, or boundary line, may be fixed. Place it between the now free and slave country, or place it south of Kentucky, or north of Ohio, and still the truth remains, that none south of it, can trade to any port or place north of it, and none north of it, can trade to any port or place south of it, except upon terms dictated by a government foreign to them. These outlets, east, west, and south, are indispensable to the well-being of the people inhabiting, and to inhabit, this vast interior region. *Which* of the three may be the best, is no proper question. All, are better than either, and all, of right, belong to that people, and to their successors forever. True to themselves, they will not ask *where* a line of separation shall be, but will vow, rather, that there shall be no such line. Nor are the marginal regions less interested in these communications to, and through them, to the great outside world. They too, and each of them, must have access to this Egypt of the West, without paying toll at the crossing of any national boundary.

Our national strife springs not from our permanent part; not from the land we inhabit; not from our national homestead. There is no possible severing of this, but would multiply, and not mitigate, evils among us. In all its adaptations and aptitudes, it demands union, and abhors separation. In fact, it would, ere long, force reunion, however much of blood and treasure the separation might have cost.

Our strife pertains to ourselves—to the passing generations of men; and it can, without convulsion, be hushed forever with the passing of one generation.

In this view, I recommend the adoption of the following resolution and articles amendatory to the Constitution of the United States:

"Resolved by the Senate and House of Representatives of the United

States of America in Congress assembled, (two thirds of both houses concurring,) That the following articles be proposed to the legislatures (or conventions) of the several States as amendments to the Constitution of the United States, all or any of which articles when ratified by three-fourths of the said legislatures (or conventions) to be valid as part or parts of the said Constitution, viz:

"Article ——.

"Every State, wherein slavery now exists, which shall abolish the same therein, at any time, or times, before the first day of January, in the year of our Lord one thousand and nine hundred, shall receive compensation from the United States as follows, to wit:

"The President of the United States shall deliver to every such State, bonds of the United States, bearing interest at the rate of —— per cent, per annum, to an amount equal to the aggregate sum of   for each slave shown to have been therein, by the eig[h]th census of the United States, said bonds to be delivered to such State by instalments, or in one parcel, at the completion of the abolishment, accordingly as the same shall have been gradual, or at one time, within such State; and interest shall begin to run upon any such bond, only from the proper time of its delivery as aforesaid. Any State having received bonds as aforesaid, and afterwards reintroducing or tolerating slavery therein, shall refund to the United States the bonds so received, or the value thereof, and all interest paid thereon.

"Article ——.

"All slaves who shall have enjoyed actual freedom by the chances of the war, at any time before the end of the rebellion, shall be forever free; but all owners of such, who shall not have been disloyal, shall be compensated for them, at the same rates as is provided for States adopting abolishment of slavery, but in such way, that no slave shall be twice accounted for.

"Article ——.

"Congress may appropriate money, and otherwise provide, for colonizing free colored persons, with their own consent, at any place or places without the United States."

I beg indulgence to discuss these proposed articles at some length.

Without slavery the rebellion could never have existed; without slavery it could not continue.

Among the friends of the Union there is great diversity, of sentiment, and of policy, in regard to slavery, and the African race amongst us. Some would perpetuate slavery; some would abolish it suddenly, and without compensation; some would abolish it gradually, and with compensation; some would remove the freed people from us, and some would retain them with us; and there are yet other minor diversities. Because of these diversities, we waste much strength in struggles among ourselves. By mutual concession we should harmonize, and act together. This would be compromise; but it would be compromise among the friends, and not with the enemies of the Union. These articles are intended to embody a plan of such mutual concessions. If the plan shall be adopted, it is assumed that emancipation will follow, at least, in several of the States.

As to the first article, the main points are: first, the emancipation; secondly, the length of time for consummating it—thirty-seven years; and thirdly, the compensation.

The emancipation will be unsatisfactory to the advocates of perpetual slavery; but the length of time should greatly mitigate their dissatisfaction. The time spares both races from the evils of sudden derangement—in fact, from the necessity of any derangement—while most of those whose habitual course of thought will be disturbed by the measure will have passed away before its consummation. They will never see it. Another class will hail the prospect of emancipation, but will deprecate the length of time. They will feel that it gives too little to the now living slaves. But it really gives them much. It saves them from the vagrant destitution which must largely attend immediate emancipation in localities where their numbers are very great; and it gives the inspiring assurance that their posterity shall be free forever. The plan leaves to each State, choosing to act under it, to abolish slavery now, or at the end of the century, or at any intermediate time, or by degrees, extending over the whole or any part of the period; and it obliges no two states to proceed alike. It also provides for compensation, and generally the mode of making it. This, it would seem, must further mitigate the dissatisfaction of those who favor perpetual slavery, and especially of those who are to receive the compensation. Doubtless some of those who are to pay, and not to receive will object. Yet the measure is both just and economical. In a certain sense the liberation of slaves is the destruction of property—property acquired by descent, or by purchase, the same as any other property. It is no less true for having been often said, that the people of the south are not more responsible for the original introduction of this property, than are the people of the north; and when it is remembered how unhesitatingly we all use cotton and sugar, and share the profits of dealing in them, it may not be quite safe to say, that the south has been more responsible than the north for its continuance. If then, for a common object, this property is to be sacrificed is it not just that it be done at a common charge?

And if, with less money, or money more easily paid, we can preserve the benefits of the Union by this means, than we can by the war alone, is it not also economical to do it? Let us consider it then. Let us ascertain the sum we have expended in the war since compensated emancipation was proposed last March, and consider whether, if that measure had been promptly accepted, by even some of the slave States, the same sum would not have done more to close the war, than has been otherwise done. If so the measure would save money, and, in that view, would be a prudent and economical measure. Certainly it is not so easy to pay *something* as it is to pay *nothing*; but it is easier to pay a *large* sum than it is to pay a larger one. And it is easier to pay any sum *when* we are able, than it is to pay it *before* we are able. The war requires large sums, and requires them at once. The aggregate sum necessary for compensated emancipation, of course, would be large. But it would require no ready cash; nor the bonds even, any faster than the emancipation progresses. This might not, and probably would not, close before the end of the thirty-seven years. At that time we shall probably have a hundred millions of people to share the burden, instead of thirty one millions, as now. And not only so, but the increase of our population may be expected to continue for a long time after that period, as rapidly as before; because our territory will not have become full. I do not state this inconsiderately. At the same ratio of increase which we have maintained, on an average, from our first national census, in 1790, until that of 1860, we should, in 1900, have a population of 103,208,415. And why may we not continue that ratio far beyond that period? Our abundant room—our broad national homestead—is our ample resource. Were our territory as limited as are the British Isles, very certainly our population could not expand as stated. Instead of receiving the foreign born, as now, we should be compelled to send part of the native born away. But such is not our condition. We have two millions nine hundred and sixty-three thousand square miles. Europe has three millions and eight hundred thousand, with a population averaging seventy-three and one-third persons to the square mile. Why may not our country, at some time, average as many? Is it less fertile? Has it more waste surface, by mountains, rivers, lakes, deserts, or other causes? Is it inferior to Europe in any natural advantage? If, then, we are, at some time, to be as populous as Europe, how soon? As to when this *may* be, we can judge by the past and the present; as to when it *will* be, if ever, depends much on whether we maintain the Union. Several of our States are already above the average of Europe—seventy three and a third to the square mile. Massachusetts has 157; Rhode Island, 133; Connecticut, 99; New York and New Jersey, each, 80; also two other great States, Pennsylvania and Ohio, are not far below, the former having 63, and the latter 59. The States already above the European average, except New York, have increased in as rapid a ratio, since passing that point, as ever before; while no one of them is equal to some other parts of our country, in natural capacity for sustaining a dense population.

Taking the nation in the aggregate, and we find its population and ratio of increase, for the several decennial periods, to be as follows:—

1790	3,929,827		
1800	5,305,937	35.02 per cent.	{ ratio of increase
1810	7,239,814	36.45	"
1820	9,638,131	33.13	"
1830	12,866,020	33.49	"
1840	17,069,453	32.67	"
1850	23,191,876	35.87	"
1860	31,443,790	35.58	"

This shows an average decennial increase of 34.60 per cent. in population through the seventy years from our first, to our last census yet taken. It is seen that the ratio of increase, at no one of these seven periods, is either two per cent. below, or two per cent. above, the average; thus showing how inflexible, and, consequently, how reliable, the law of increase, in our case, is. Assuming that it will continue, gives the following results:—

1870	42,323,341	1910	138,918,526
1880	56,967,216	1920	186,984,335
1890	76,677,872	1930	251,680,914
1900	103,208,415		

These figures show that our country *may* be as populous as Europe now is, at some point between 1920 and 1930—say about 1925—our territory, at seventy-three and a third persons to the square mile, being of capacity to contain 217,186,000.

And we *will* reach this, too, if we do not ourselves relinquish the chance, by the folly and evils of disunion, or by long and exhausting war springing from the only great element of national discord among us. While it cannot be foreseen exactly how much one huge example of secession, breeding lesser ones indefinitely, would retard population, civilization, and prosperity, no one can doubt that the extent of it would be very great and injurious.

The proposed emancipation would shorten the war, perpetuate peace, insure this increase of population, and proportionately the wealth of the country. With these, we should pay all the emancipation would cost, together with our other debt, easier than we should pay our other debt, without it. If we had allowed our old national debt to run at six per cent. per annum, simple interest, from the end of our revolutionary struggle until to day, without paying anything on either principal or interest, each man of us would owe less upon that debt now, than each man owed upon it then; and this because our increase of men, through the whole period, has been greater than six per cent.; has run faster than the interest upon the debt. Thus, time alone relieves a debtor nation, so long as its population increases faster than unpaid interest accumulates on its debt.

This fact would be no excuse for delaying payment of what is justly due; but it shows the great importance of time in this connexion—the great advantage of a policy by which we shall not have to pay until we number a hundred millions, what, by a different policy, we would have to pay now, when we number but thirty one millions. In a word, it shows that a dollar will be much harder to pay for the war, than will be a dollar for emancipation on the proposed plan. And then the latter will cost no blood, no precious life. It will be a saving of both.

As to the second article, I think it would be impracticable to return to bondage the class of persons therein contemplated. Some of them, doubtless, in the property sense, belong to loyal owners; and hence, provision is made in this article for compensating such.

The third article relates to the future of the freed people. It does not oblige, but merely authorizes, Congress to aid in colonizing such as may consent. This ought not to be regarded as objectionable, on the one hand, or on the other, in so much as it comes to nothing, unless by the mutual consent of the people to be deported, and the American voters, through their representatives in Congress.

I cannot make it better known than it already is, that I strongly favor colonization. And yet I wish to say there is an objection urged against free colored persons remaining in the country, which is largely imaginary, if not sometimes malicious.

It is insisted that their presence would injure, and displace white labor and white laborers. If there ever could be a proper time for mere catch arguments, that time surely is not now. In times like the present, men should utter nothing for which they would not willingly be responsible through time and in eternity. Is it true, then, that colored people can displace any more white labor, by being free, than by remaining slaves? If they stay in their old places, they jostle no white laborers; if they leave their old places, they leave them open to white laborers. Logically, there is neither more nor less of it. Emancipation, even without deportation, would probably enhance the wages of white labor, and, very surely, would not reduce them. Thus, the customary amount of labor would still have to be performed; the freed people would surely not do more than their old proportion of it, and very probably, for a time, would do less, leaving an increased part to white laborers, bringing their labor into greater demand, and, consequently, enhancing the wages of it. With deportation, even to a limited extent, enhanced wages to white labor is mathematically certain. Labor is like any other commodity in the market—increase the demand for it, and you increase the price of it. Reduce the supply of black labor, by colonizing the black laborer out of the country, and, by precisely so much, you increase the demand for, and wages of, white labor.

But it is dreaded that the freed people will swarm forth, and cover the whole land? Are they not already in the land? Will liberation make them any more numerous? Equally distributed among the whites of the whole country, and there would be but one colored to seven whites. Could the one, in any way, greatly disturb the seven? There are many communities now, having more than one free colored person, to seven whites; and this, without any apparent consciousness of evil from it. The District of Columbia, and the States of Maryland and Delaware, are all in this condition. The District has more than one free colored to six whites; and yet, in its frequent petitions to Congress, I believe it has never presented the presence of free colored persons as one of its grievances. But why should emancipation south, send the free people north? People, of any color, seldom run, unless there be something to run from. *Heretofore* colored people, to some extent, have fled north from bondage; and *now*, perhaps, from both bondage and destitution. But if gradual emancipation and deportation be adopted, they will have neither to flee from. Their old masters will give them wages at least until new laborers can be procured; and the freed men, in turn, will gladly give their labor for the wages, till new homes can be found for them, in congenial climes, and with people of their own blood and race. This proposition can be trusted on the mutual interests involved. And, in any event, cannot the north decide for itself, whether to receive them?

Again, as practice proves more than theory, in any case, has there been any irruption of colored people northward, because of the abolishment of slavery in this District last spring?

What I have said of the proportion of free colored persons to the whites, in the District, is from the census of 1860, having no reference to persons called contrabands, nor to those made free by the act of Congress abolishing slavery here.

The plan consisting of these articles is recommended, not but that a restoration of the national authority would be accepted without its adoption.

Nor will the war, nor proceedings under the proclamation of September 22, 1862, be stayed because of the *recommendation* of this plan. Its timely *adoption*, I doubt not, would bring restoration and thereby stay both.

And, notwithstanding this plan, the recommendation that Congress provide by law for compensating any State which may adopt emancipation, before this plan shall have been acted upon, is hereby earnestly renewed. Such would be only an advance part of the plan, and the same arguments apply to both.

This plan is recommended as a means, not in exclusion of, but additional to, all others for restoring and preserving the national authority throughout the Union. The subject is presented exclusively in its economical aspect. The plan would, I am confident, secure peace more speedily, and maintain it more permanently, than can be done by force alone; while all it would cost, considering amounts, and manner of payment, and times of payment, would be easier paid than will be the additional cost of the war, if we rely solely upon force. It is much—very much—that it would cost no blood at all.

The plan is proposed as permanent constitutional law. It cannot become such without the concurrence of, first, two-thirds of Congress, and, afterwards, three-fourths of the States. The requisite three-fourths of the States will necessarily include seven of the Slave states. Their concurrence, if obtained, will give assurance of their severally adopting emancipation, at no very distant day, upon the new constitutional terms. This assurance would end the struggle now, and save the Union forever.

I do not forget the gravity which should characterize a paper addressed to the Congress of the nation by the Chief Magistrate of the nation. Nor do I forget that some of you are my seniors, nor that many of you have more experience than I, in the conduct of public affairs. Yet I trust that in view of the great responsibility resting upon me, you will perceive no want of respect to yourselves, in any undue earnestness I may seem to display.

Is it doubted, then, that the plan I propose, if adopted, would shorten the war, and thus lessen its expenditure of money and of blood? Is it doubted that it would restore the national authority and national prosperity, and perpetuate both indefinitely? Is it doubted that we here —Congress and Executive—can secure its adoption? Will not the good people respond to a united, and earnest appeal from us? Can we, can they, by any other means, so certainly, or so speedily, assure these vital objects? We can succeed only by concert. It is not "can any of us imagine better?" but "can we all do better?" Object whatsoever is possible, still the question recurs "can we do better?" The dogmas of the quiet past, are inadequate to the stormy present. The occasion is piled high with difficulty, and we must rise with the occasion. As our case is new, so we must think anew, and act anew. We must disenthrall ourselves, and then we shall save our country.

Fellow-citizens, we cannot escape history. We of this Congress and this administration, will be remembered in spite of ourselves. No personal significance, or insignificance, can spare one or another of us. The fiery trial through which we pass, will light us down, in honor or dishonor, to the latest generation. We say we are for the Union. The world will not forget that we say this. We know how to save the Union. The world knows we do know how to save it. We—even we here—hold the power, and bear the responsibility. In giving freedom to the slave, we assure freedom to the free—honorable alike in what we give, and what we preserve. We shall nobly save, or meanly lose, the last best, hope of earth. Other means may succeed; this could not fail. The way is plain, peaceful, generous, just—a way which, if followed, the world will forever applaud, and God must forever bless.

The end of slavery was not to be achieved gradually by the reasoned plan of cooperation which Lincoln elaborated. His argument brought no response from Congress; so on January 1, 1863, he issued the final Emancipation Proclamation. Time was to demonstrate that Lincoln's analysis of December, 1862, and its predictions were not wholly accurate. His statistical predictions have not been fulfilled. Nor did he reckon properly with the Negroes' tendency to migrate, or with society's resistance to the equalitarian implications of the change and to the reality of the liberty which emancipation was presumed to confer. Argument was to continue over Lincoln's basic premise that without slavery the conflict would not have occurred. Despite these questions, in view of the century of experience since, it can only be regretted that the President's wisdom was given such scant heed.

Because of the method chosen, namely, executive proclamation, quite another path was followed than that set forth in the Second Annual Message. The fiat itself did no more than attempt to destroy a Confederate military resource by freeing slaves within that part of the Confederacy not occupied by Union troops. It in effect advised the slaves to withdraw from the Confederate war effort. Morally the proclamation had tremendous impact. It informed the world and the slave that if the Union won the war that form of human bondage would come to an end. But it had no immediate legal effect, since it proclaimed freedom only in an area that was then outside the jurisdiction of the United States. Even after the South was brought back into the nation, the problem was still to find a means of giving the necessary legal force to Lincoln's proclamation.

Normally state law would define property in the United States, but the southern states could not be expected to emancipate their slaves; local interests and mores were too firmly established. Federal power must be invoked. Since no such federal power existed one must be created by constitutional amendment. The result was the Thirteenth Amendment, which was contrived amid formidable odds in the confused final months of the war and ratified under the dubious procedures characteristic of the early period of Reconstruction. But as events soon demonstrated, emancipation did not insure either civil rights or political privilege, and the Fourteenth and Fifteenth Amendments were inserted in the Constitution by means similar to those which ushered in the Thirteenth Amendment.

With the conclusion of this constitutional revision it became all too clear that the Emancipation Proclamation and the three Amendments had achieved only part of their purpose. Legal human bondage had, it is true, been destroyed, but the social barriers to the "unfettered start and the fair chance" had not been lifted. In fact, some parts of American society began immediately to create new social and legal obstacles to the equality prescribed by the Declaration of Independence and so eloquently reiterated by Lincoln at Gettysburg. The forces of custom, fear, and conscience emphasized a basic incapacity to understand the intricacies of racial difference. Political and legal instruments had been enacted without adequate study, analysis, or social engineering. Therefore, they produced more of the bitter fruits of the two centuries and a half of the "bond-man's . . . unrequited toil." With awful irony they grew ripe in the same vineyard where the nurture of human reason had produced the fine flowering of democracy.

Had Lincoln's suggestions in his Second Annual Message been accepted, the racial tensions of today might have been in some significant part avoided. As it was, there was so much malice and so little charity, that his and following generations have not been able effectively to bind up the nation's wounds. They still bleed.

Abraham Lincoln
The Emancipation Proclamation
1863

EDITED BY JOHN HOPE FRANKLIN

Once the Civil War had begun, there was never a time when the question of freedom for the slaves was not urgent. Abolitionists urged emancipation as a bold humanitarian step. Some military leaders favored it as a logical and necessary war measure. Many citizens, however, thought that the freeing of the slaves was not only inexpedient and impolitic but unconstitutional as well. For the first eighteen months of the war the debate was vigorous; and one delegation after another visited the President to advise him on what action to take.

President Lincoln had long been opposed to slavery, but he had grave doubts, even after the war began, that he possessed the necessary powers to abolish it. Even as he expressed these doubts he was seeking some opportunity and justification for taking action. By the late spring of 1862 he was convinced that he or Congress, perhaps both, should move against slavery. "Things had gone on from bad to worse," he said later, "until I felt that we had reached the end of our rope . . . and must change our tactics, or lose the game!" Action by Congress, in April and June, to abolish slavery in the District of Columbia and in the territories greatly encouraged him.

In June, during his regular visits to the telegraph room of the War Department, the President began to sketch out the main features of the Emancipation Proclamation. By June 18 he had completed a draft; he read this to Vice-President Hannibal Hamlin, who seemed quite pleased.

A few weeks later he told Gideon Welles, Secretary of the Navy, and William H. Seward, Secretary of State, of his decision to issue a proclamation to free the slaves. After Congress passed the Second Confiscation Act on July 17, the President incorporated some of its provisions into his draft.

Within a few days the President was ready to share his plans with his entire Cabinet. On July 22, 1862, he told the members of his decision, made it clear that it was firm, and solicited their suggestions merely regarding language and timing. Some thought it unwise for Lincoln to make the Proclamation at all, while others thought that he should wait to issue it when the military situation was more favorable. The President made no promises, but he waited. When the news came of the limited victory of the Union forces at Antietam on September 17, he felt that the time had come. On that very evening he began reworking the draft and putting it into final form in the quiet of Soldiers' Home near Washington. He returned to the White House on the twentieth, and on the following day he carefully rewrote the document that was the culmination of months of work and worry.

On September 22, at a special meeting of the Cabinet, he read the document and issued it the same day. This document, known as the Preliminary Emancipation Proclamation, announced that on January 1, 1863, all slaves in states or parts of states then in rebellion against the United States would be "thenceforward, and forever free."

For the next hundred days there was discussion throughout the country and in many other parts of the world regarding the possible effect of emancipation by presidential proclamation. Critics were bitter in their strictures. Abolitionists were not altogether happy, but were encouraged at Lincoln's action. There were some who doubted that the President would fulfill his promise to free the slaves; but as the time approached, Lincoln was more determined than ever.

During the week following Christmas Day the Cabinet met almost daily, and Lincoln had many opportunities to discuss with the members the final wording of the Proclamation. At the meeting on December 29 he read a draft of the Emancipation Proclamation on which he had been working, invited criticism, and directed that copies be provided for each member of the Cabinet. During the meetings of December 30 and 31 the Proclamation was one of the main items on the agenda. Several members made suggestions for revision, largely of an editorial nature. During the evening the President began the final writing of the Proclamation. He *completed it on the morning of January 1, 1863, and sent it over to the Department of State for the superscription and closing.*

The New Year's Day reception at the White House had already begun when the Secretary of State and his son, Frederick Seward, the Assistant Secretary, returned with the Proclamation. After the reception the President went up to his study, where, in the presence of a few friends, he signed the Emancipation Proclamation. As he finished writing his signature, he said, "I never, in my life, felt more certain that I was doing right than I do in signing this paper."

January 1, 1863

BY THE PRESIDENT OF THE UNITED STATES OF AMERICA: A PROCLAMATION.

WHEREAS, on the twenty-second day of September, in the year of our Lord one thousand eight hundred and sixty two, a proclamation was issued by the President of the United States, containing, among other things, the following, to wit:

That on the first day of January, in the year of our Lord one thousand eight hundred and sixty-three, all persons held as slaves within any State or designated part of a State, the people whereof shall then be in rebellion against the United States, shall be then, thenceforward, and forever free; and the Executive Government of the United States, including the military and naval authority thereof, will recognize and maintain the freedom of such persons, and will do no act or acts to repress such persons, or any of them, in any efforts they may make for their actual freedom.

That the Executive will, on the first day of January aforesaid, by procla-

---

There are several copies of the December 30 draft of the Emancipation Proclamation. The copies of some members of the Cabinet, Edward Bates, Salmon P. Chase, William H. Seward, and Montgomery Blair, are in the Library of Congress. The draft that the President worked with on December 31 and the morning of New Year's Day is considered the final manuscript draft. Later in the year Lincoln presented it to the women in charge of the Northwestern Fair in Chicago to be sold for the benefit of the Sanitary Commission. The President told the women that he had some desire to retain the paper, "but if it shall contribute to the relief or comfort of the soldiers that will be better." At the fair Thomas B. Bryan purchased it and presented it to the Soldiers' Home in Chicago, of which he was president. It was destroyed in the Great Fire of 1871. Fortunately, four photographic copies of the original had been made. The photograph from which the present copy is printed is in the National Archives.

mation, designate the States and parts of States, if any, in which the people thereof, shall on that day be, in good faith, represented in the Congress of the United States by members chosen thereto at elections wherein a majority of the qualified voters of such State shall have participated, shall in the absence of strong countervailing testimony, be deemed conclusive evidence that such State, and the people thereof, are not then in rebellion against the United States.

Now, therefore, I, Abraham Lincoln, President of the United States, by virtue of the power in me invested as Commander-in-Chief, of the Army and Navy of the United States in time of actual armed rebellion against authority and government of the United States, and as a fit and necessary war measure for suppressing said rebellion, do, on this first day of January, in the year of our Lord one thousand eight hundred and sixty three, and in accordance with my purpose so to do publicly proclaimed for the full period of one hundred days, from the day first above mentioned, order and designate as the States and parts of States wherein the people thereof respectively, are this day in rebellion against the United States, the following towit:

Arkansas, Texas, Louisiana, (except the Parishes of St. Bernard, Plaquemines, Jefferson, St. Johns, St. Charles, St. James, Ascension, Assumption, Terrebone, Lafourche, St. Mary, St. Martin, and Orleans, including the City of New-Orleans) Mississippi, Alabama, Florida, Georgia, South-Carolina, North-Carolina, and Virginia (except the fortyeight counties designated as West Virginia, and also the counties of Berkley, Accomac, Northampton, Elizabeth-City, York, Princess Ann, and Norfolk, including the cities of Norfolk and Portsmouth, and which excepted parts are, for the present, left precisely as if this proclamation were not issued.

And by virtue of the power, and for the purpose aforesaid, I do order and declare that all persons held as slaves within said designated States, and parts of States, are, and henceforward shall be free; and the Executive government of the United States, including the military and naval authorities thereof, will recognize and maintain the freedom of said persons.

And I hereby enjoin upon the people so declared to be free to abstain from all violence, unless in necessary self-defence; and I recommend to them that, in all cases when allowed, they labor faithfully for reasonable wages.

And I further declare and make known that such persons of suitable condition, will be received into the armed service of the United States to garrison forts, positions, stations, and other places, and to man vessels of all sorts in said service.

And upon this act, sincerely believed to be an act of justice, warranted by the Constitution, upon military necessity, I invoke the considerate judgment of mankind, and the gracious favor of Almighty God.

In witness whereof, I have hereunto set my hand and caused the seal of the United States to be affixed.

Done at the City of Washington, the first day of January, in the year of our Lord one thousand eight hundred and sixty three, and of the Independence of the United States of America the eighty-seventh.

By the President: ABRAHAM LINCOLN
WILLIAM H. SEWARD, Secretary of State.

Within a few hours, on the evening of January 1, 1863, the entire country knew that the President had signed the Emancipation Proclamation. Within a few days, the entire world knew that slavery in the United States was doomed. Emancipation celebrations, shared by Negroes and whites alike, were held from Boston to San Francisco. Bells were rung, poems written, hymns composed. One newspaper called the Proclamation "a great moral landmark, a shrine at which future visionaries shall renew their vows, a pillar of fire which shall yet guide other nations out of the night of their bondage . . . ." Almost overnight the war was transformed from a struggle to preserve the Union into one in which the crusade for human freedom became an equally important goal. The Proclamation sharpened the issues of the war. In Europe the opposition to the Union melted before the unequivocal position of the Proclamation. At home the Proclamation provided the moral and humanitarian ingredient that had been lacking in Union attempts to subdue the rebellious South.

In later years the Emancipation Proclamation was to become a significant rallying point for freedom and equality. In pleading for the enfranchisement of the Negro in 1866, Senator Charles Sumner said that in the Proclamation Lincoln had promised to maintain freedom for the Negro "not for any limited period, but for all time." But when real freedom and equality eluded Negroes, some came to believe that gratitude for the Emancipation Proclamation did not require them to remain loyal to a party that had not kept the faith. Nevertheless, if Negroes became disillusioned with the party of Lincoln, they continued to show their gratitude to the man who had issued the Emancipation Proclamation. Throughout the country New Year's Day became and remained a day of commemoration; and the reading of the Emancipation Proclamation became a regular part of scores of annual observances.

As the nation prepared to celebrate the fiftieth anniversary of the Proclamation, many Americans expressed their understanding of the document's continuing importance. One editor of a magazine said, "The emancipation of the Negro race was the act of the American people. The greatness of Abraham Lincoln was the greatness of a statesman who could lead them to that act, who could understand their unexpressed will calling for that act, and who dared to do the act in their name and on their behalf."

The Proclamation has remained, through more than a century, a vital factor in the movement to broaden and deepen the meaning of democracy and equality in the United States. Negroes themselves have always regarded it as a significant beginning of their quest for full citizenship, while the larger community has recognized it as an important milestone in the nation's program to make its early promises of equality meaningful. On many occasions it has been invoked by those who are full of pride for what the nation has achieved, as well as by those who are critical of the nation for what it has not done.

On the occasion of the centennial of the Emancipation Proclamation, most of the nation was acutely conscious of how much was yet to be done in order for all citizens to enjoy equality. On September 22, 1962, the centennial of the Preliminary Emancipation Proclamation, more than 3,000 people gathered at the Lincoln Memorial in Washington. Governor Nelson Rockefeller of New York presented for public view the only known draft of the Preliminary Proclamation in President Lincoln's hand. In making the presentation he said, "May God give us the love, the courage, the understanding to see in perspective ourselves and the times in which we live—and to make the faith that lies behind this Proclamation truly live for all men in all places of our land." In a major address United Nations Ambassador Adlai Stevenson called individual freedom the "great unfinished business of the world today." He observed that the defense of freedom by the United States "will be all the stronger for

414

being based not on illusions but upon the truth about ourselves and our world."

President John F. Kennedy, who sent a special message to the centennial observance, had occasion to refer later to the Emancipation Proclamation when he asked Congress to enact a new civil rights bill in 1963. On that occasion, he said, "No one has been barred on account of his race from fighting for America—there are no 'white' and 'colored' signs on the foxholes and graveyards of battle. Surely, in 1963, one hundred years after emancipation, it should not be necessary for any American to demonstrate in the streets for opportunity to stop at a hotel, or to eat at a lunch counter." Statements like this one and a growing awareness of the unfulfilled promises of the Emancipation Proclamation had much to do with the groundswell for civil rights that reached a new high during the centennial year.

Once the centennial of the Emancipation Proclamation had passed, there remained a sense of urgency to complete the long delayed task of extending equality to Negro Americans. The Civil Rights Act of 1964, with its far-reaching provisions that guaranteed equal enjoyment of public accommodations and facilities and its machinery to accelerate school desegregation, was a result—at least in part—of this sense of urgency. When it became clear that existing legislation was inadequate to guarantee to Negroes their right to vote, President Lyndon B. Johnson urged Congress to enact new laws to eliminate barriers to the right to vote. He showed that he had the unfulfilled promises of the Emancipation Proclamation in mind when he said, "There must be no delay, no hesitation, no compromise with our purpose. We cannot wait another eight months. We have already waited 100 years and more. The time for waiting is gone." Congress agreed, and with the enactment of the voting-rights legislation in 1965 it moved one step closer toward the complete freedom for Negro Americans that the Emancipation Proclamation had begun.

Abraham Lincoln
The Gettysburg Address
1863

EDITED BY ALLAN NEVINS

At nightfall on November 18, 1863, a special train drew into the small station at Gettysburg, Pennsylvania, and President Abraham Lincoln and his party alighted. They were greeted by Judge David Wills, chairman of a committee supervising the dedication of a cemetery nearby, in which the bodies of most of the six thousand men killed in the Civil War battle fought there the preceding July might rest. Few could have dreamed that the President's brief address the following day would be remembered as long as the battle itself. Lincoln slept that night in Judge Wills's house. According to Wills's recollections, set down some years later, the President wrote all or part of his address in his room, then showed it to Secretary of State William H. Seward, who was housed next door, and read it to his audience the next afternoon from the very paper on which his host had seen him writing. But Lincoln's secretary, John G. Nicolay, had a different recollection. He believed that Lincoln had written part of the address in Washington on a sheet of Executive Mansion stationery, and that he took this in his pocket to Gettysburg. Later, in Wills's house, he composed the final part in pencil on a lined bluish sheet. When he read his immortal words it was from the two papers. Though controversy persists, Nicolay's hazy and ragged story appears the more correct, and the authoritative edition of Lincoln's Collected Works, edited by Roy P. Basler, treats as the first draft the text found on the two sheets that Nicolay described.

We have four other surviving holographs of the address, not differing vitally from the first in import or words. One is the so-called second draft, written on the same lined bluish paper that Lincoln used for the second sheet of the first draft, but containing emendations which indicate that its transcription followed the delivery of the speech. The President wrote a third draft for Edward Everett, who wished to bind it with his own long address—also delivered at the Gettysburg ceremonies—in a volume to be sold at the Sanitary Fair in New York in 1864. Lincoln made still another copy for George Bancroft, to be reproduced in facsimile in a book designed for the Baltimore Sanitary Fair, *Autograph Letters of Our Country's Authors*. As this copy proved unsuitable for reproduction, for he had written on the back, Lincoln some time after March 4, 1864, made what is called the final text, for facsimile engraving. This was long held by Alexander Bliss, another member of the Baltimore committee preparing the book of autograph documents. The copies made for Everett, Bancroft, and Bliss differ but slightly. All of them contain minor emendations which Lincoln made after he had consulted press reports of his address, the most important being the insertion of the phrase "under God," which he had uttered extempore, and which the newspapermen caught.

FOURSCORE and seven years ago our fathers brought forth, on this continent, a new nation, conceived in Liberty, and dedicated to the proposition that all men are created equal.

Now we are engaged in a great civil war, testing whether that nation, or any nation so conceived, and so dedicated, can long endure. We are met on a great battlefield of that war. We have come to dedicate a portion of that field, as a final resting-place for those who here gave their lives, that that nation might live. It is altogether fitting and proper that we should do this.

But, in a larger sense, we can not dedicate—we can not consecrate—we can not hallow—this ground. The brave men, living and dead, who struggled here, have consecrated it far above our poor power to add or detract. The world will little note, nor long remember what we say here, but it can never forget what they did here. It is for us the living, rather, to be dedicated here to the unfinished work which they who fought here have thus far so nobly advanced. It is rather for us to be here dedicated to the great task remaining before us—that from these honored dead we take increased devotion to that cause for which they here gave the last full measure of devotion—that we here highly resolve that these dead shall not have died in vain—that this nation, under God, shall have a new birth of freedom—and that government of the people, by the people, for the people, shall not perish from the earth.

November 19, 1863.   ABRAHAM LINCOLN.

The address is quoted here from the "final" or Bliss copy. This long remained in the hands of Alexander Bliss's family, and later was owned by Oscar B. Cintas of Havana, Cuba, former Ambassador to the United States. Mr. Cintas bequeathed the document to the United States, with the understanding that it should be placed in the White House; it is now kept there.

☆

The Associated Press report of Lincoln's address, published in the New York Times, Herald, and Tribune, and in other newspapers throughout the country, was commendably accurate. It departed from the text here given only in minor respects, the most important variant, aside from an obvious typographical error, being that the AP version read "our power to add or detract" instead of "our poor power. . . ." The report in the Chicago Tribune, while defective in various other points, did use "poor." In spite of a few preposterously mangled newspaper records, one of the worst of which defaced the Springfield (Illinois) State Journal, the country thus had an opportunity to judge Lincoln's speech on its clear merits. Only a few papers, like the hostile Springfield State Register, neglected to print the President's address and fixed their attention on his awkward response to a band of serenaders on the evening before the dedication.

It is true that many of the newspapers which printed Lincoln's words, including William Cullen Bryant's Evening Post, Henry J. Raymond's Times, Horace Greeley's Tribune, and Manton Marble's World (all in New York), completely failed to discern the eloquence and force of the address, giving it no editorial notice. The Chicago Tribune placed Everett's oration, Lincoln's address, and a well-sung dirge all on the same level as "moving." The Philadelphia Public Ledger seemed to award the honors of the day to the opening prayer by the Reverend Mr. T. H. Stockton.

On the other hand, the Boston Evening Transcript termed the discourse an impressive illustration of Lincoln's power of reaching and holding every reader. It might seem rough (the paper had a defective report), "but the uncut fragment is full of jewels." The Philadelphia Evening Bulletin declared it a most happy effort. "It is warm, earnest, unaffected, and touching. Thousands . . . will read the President's few words, and not many will do it without a moistening of the eye and a swelling of the heart." A strong eulogy in the Providence Journal can probably be traced to the pen of James Burrill Angell, its editor, later president of the University of Michigan. Harper's Weekly also warmly praised the speech; the comments carried in that publication were probably written by George William Curtis, who was a cultivated literary critic, a polished orator, and a conscientious editor. "The few words of the President," ran the editorial note, "were from the heart to the heart. They cannot be read, even, without kindling emotion. . . . It was as simple and felicitous and earnest a word as was ever spoken."

In short, the frequent statement that Lincoln's masterly address received almost no praise at the time, but either criticism or a slighting inattention, is far from true. Edward Everett's speech, planned as the major oration at the dedication, had felicity and weight. He had given it arduous labor and might well have felt proud of it. Yet on November 20, with unquestioned sincerity, he wrote the President: "Permit me . . . to express my great admiration of the thoughts expressed by you, with such eloquent simplicity and appropriateness, at the consecration of the cemetery. I should be glad, if I could flatter myself, that I came as near to the central idea of the occasion in two hours, as you did in two minutes." Charles A. Dana quotes in his recollections the immediate comment of Edwin M. Stanton, Secretary of War. After lauding the eloquence of Edward Everett, Stanton added that a thousand people would read Lincoln's speech while one read that of the Bostonian, "and it will be remembered as long as anyone's speeches are remembered who speaks in the English language." Only a year or two were to pass before Charles Sumner, if we may believe Lincoln's friend Joshua Speed, characterized the speech as "the most finished piece of oratory he had ever seen." Longfellow in a private letter pronounced the address "admirable."

Little by little, the values of the address sank into the minds not only of Americans but of all English-speaking peoples. Inevitably, from the outset it was republished far and wide, for no thorough account either of Lincoln or of Gettysburg could omit it. Henry J. Raymond, for example, reproduced it in his popular History of the Administration of President Lincoln, published in 1864. By the time that John G. Nicolay and John Hay planned their ten-volume Abraham Lincoln: A History, in the early 1880's, they found a whole chapter on the address necessary. Isaac N. Arnold, bringing out his biography in 1884, reprinted the speech with the comment that it "would be recalled in all future ages, among all peoples; as often as men should be called upon to die for liberty and country." These earlier writers, while perceiving the greatness of the address, judged it primarily as a piece of oratory. Arnold, for example, compared it with the words of Demosthenes on the dead at Marathon, and with Daniel Webster's Bunker Hill oration. When Allen Thorndike Rice in 1885 collected a series of reminiscences of Lincoln by distinguished contemporaries, to be published first in the North American Review and then in book form, one contributor, Ben: Perley Poore, declared that the address had been compared with the Sermon on the Mount! Another, George S.

Boutwell, asserted that it ranked with the noblest productions of antiquity, the works of Pericles, Demosthenes, and Cicero, and with the orations of such moderns as Grattan, Burke, and Webster. This was partial but by no means complete appreciation.

In time men came to see that the address possessed religious, poetic, and philosophical implications which had at first eluded them. Lord Bryce grasped some of them, as an introduction he wrote for a brief selection from Lincoln's writings indicates. Lord Charnwood, in the first full attempt by an Englishman at a study of Lincoln's life, placed the address in a setting which made it a supreme expression of national courage and devotion. Never before had a war demanded such enormous sacrifices of wealth and life as did the Civil War; never before had a country been compelled to reorganize its energies so completely. As another and more titanic conflict ended, James G. Randall in 1945 carried the analysis a step further. To Lincoln, he pointed out, Gettysburg meant the dominant values of human liberty, democracy, the aims of the Fathers, the essence of the Declaration, and the cause of free government in the world. His sense of these values he summed up in a speech which is "the stuff of literature," a speech completely Lincolnian, and completely American.

Carl Sandburg in 1946 hailed the address as one of the great American poems. One may delve deeply into its infolded meanings, he wrote, but its poetic significance carries it far beyond the limits of a state paper. "It curiously incarnates the claims, assurances, and pretences of republican institutions, of democratic procedure, of the rule of the people. It is a timeless psalm in the name of those who fight and do in behalf of great human causes rather than talk, in a belief that men can 'highly resolve' themselves, and can mutually 'dedicate' their lives to a cause."

Abraham Lincoln
Second Inaugural Address
1865

EDITED BY PAUL M. ANGLE

On March 4, 1865, Abraham Lincoln stood on the east portico of the Capitol to take the presidential oath of office for the second time. Four years earlier he had tried, with all the persuasiveness at his command, to prevent a civil war. But the war had come, and had lasted now for nearly four years. It had taken 600,000 lives, and destroyed property valued at somewhere between $5 billion and $10 billion. No one could have computed statistically the heartbreaks of young wives deprived of husbands, the sorrows of parents who had lost sons, the hardships of children whose fathers had been swept into enlistment by personal conviction or by the music of fife and drum and had never come back, or the agonies of men who dragged out their days with empty sleeves or hobbled on stumps of legs.

Lincoln knew, as he approached his second inauguration, that the war could not last much longer. To be sure, Lee with his army was still entrenched at Richmond and Petersburg, but Grant would soon strangle him. Sherman had devastated Georgia and South Carolina, and was meeting only token resistance as he moved into North Carolina. Two months earlier, at Nashville, George H. Thomas, "the Rock of Chickamauga," had smashed Hood's Army of Tennessee and thus eliminated the last serious threat to the Union forces in the West. Only Jefferson Davis could see a prolongation of the conflict.

Throughout the war Lincoln had brooded over the essential nature of

422

the conflict. He could not understand why some men would offer their lives for the continued enslavement of other men, but he took refuge in the biblical admonition, "Judge not, that ye be not judged." Significantly, he spoke of the Confederate forces as "adversaries" rather than as "enemies." He had faith in God, and wanted to do God's will, yet he was never sure that he knew what God's will was.

All his life Lincoln had read the Bible—so assiduously that its doctrines had come to permeate his approach to problems and its cadences to color his literary style. So it was natural that when he rose to speak on March 4, 1865, some of his phrases might have been taken for passages from the King James version of the Old Testament.

FELLOW COUNTRYMEN:

AT THIS second appearing to take the oath of the presidential office, there is less occasion for an extended address than there was at the first. Then a statement, somewhat in detail, of a course to be pursued, seemed fitting and proper. Now, at the expiration of four years, during which public declarations have been constantly called forth on every point and phase of the great contest which still absorbs the attention, and engrosses the energies of the nation, little that is new could be presented. The progress of our arms, upon which all else chiefly depends, is as well known to the public as to myself; and it is, I trust, reasonably satisfactory and encouraging to all. With high hope for the future, no prediction in regard to it is ventured.

On the occasion corresponding to this four years ago, all thoughts were anxiously directed to an impending civil-war. All dreaded it—all sought to avert it. While the inaugural address was being delivered from this place, devoted altogether to *saving* the Union without war, insurgent agents were in the city seeking to *destroy* it without war—seeking to dissolve the Union, and divide effects, by negotiation. Both parties deprecated war; but one of them would *make* war rather than let the

---

The address, the original copy of which is in the Library of Congress, is reprinted from *The Collected Works of Abraham Lincoln*, edited by Roy P. Basler (New Brunswick, N.J.: Rutgers University Press, 1953), VIII, 332–33. Three misspellings in the original document, "enerergies," "inaugeral," and "dissole," have been corrected here.

nation survive; and the other would *accept* war rather than let it perish. And the war came.

One eighth of the whole population were colored slaves, not distributed generally over the Union, but localized in the Southern part of it. These slaves constituted a peculiar and powerful interest. All knew that this interest was, somehow, the cause of the war. To strengthen, perpetuate, and extend this interest was the object for which the insurgents would rend the Union, even by war; while the government claimed no right to do more than to restrict the territorial enlargement of it. Neither party expected for the war, the magnitude, or the duration, which it has already attained. Neither anticipated that the *cause* of the conflict might cease with, or even before, the conflict itself should cease. Each looked for an easier triumph, and a result less fundamental and astounding. Both read the same Bible, and pray to the same God; and each invokes His aid against the other. It may seem strange that any men should dare to ask a just God's assistance in wringing their bread from the sweat of other men's faces; but let us judge not that we be not judged. The prayers of both could not be answered; that of neither has been answered fully. The Almighty has His own purposes. "Woe unto the world because of offences! for it must needs be that offences come; but woe to that man by whom the offence cometh!" If we shall suppose that American Slavery is one of those offences which, in the providence of God, must needs come, but which, having continued through His appointed time, He now wills to remove, and that He gives to both North and South, this terrible war, as the woe due to those by whom the offence came, shall we discern therein any departure from those divine attributes which the believers in a Living God always ascribe to Him? Fondly do we hope—fervently do we pray—that this mighty scourge of war may speedily pass away. Yet, if God wills that it continue, until all the wealth piled by the bond-man's two hundred and fifty years of unrequited toil shall be sunk, and until every drop of blood drawn with the lash, shall be paid by another drawn with the sword, as was said three thousand years ago, so still it must be said "the judgments of the Lord, are true and righteous altogether."

With malice toward none; with charity for all; with firmness in the right, as God gives us to see the right, let us strive on to finish the work we are in; to bind up the nation's wounds; to care for him who shall have borne the battle, and for his widow, and his orphan—to do all which may achieve and cherish a just, and a lasting peace, among ourselves, and with all nations.

Shortly after the inauguration Thurlow Weed complimented Lincoln upon his address. The President replied: "I believe it is not immediately popular. Men are not flattered by being shown that there has been a difference of purpose between the Almighty and them. To deny it, however, in this case, is to deny that there is a God governing the world. It is a truth which I thought needed to be told; and as whatever of humiliation there is in it, falls most directly on myself, I thought others might afford for me to tell it."

Fewer today than in Lincoln's time would subscribe to his interpretation of the war as a punishment inflicted on the people of both sections by an almighty but inscrutable God for the share of both in the sin of human slavery. Nor would many acquiesce, as Lincoln was willing to acquiesce, in the indefinite prolongation of the agony if that were necessary for expiation. Faith today has narrower limits.

In little more than five weeks after Lincoln delivered the Second Inaugural he would be assassinated, and the clemency and effort toward rehabilitation for which he pleaded would be submerged, as far as the North was concerned, in a lust for punishment of the South. Reconstruction, with its excesses, would continue for a decade, and the aftereffects, in the form of suspicion, if not enmity, between the sections would persist much longer.

Yet Lincoln had spoken words that would live. One perceptive critic, Charles Francis Adams, Jr., recognized that fact immediately. Writing to his father, the American Minister to England, on March 7, 1865, Adams said: "What do you think of the inaugural? That rail-splitting lawyer is one of the wonders of the day. Once at Gettysburg and now again on a greater occasion he has shown a capacity for rising to the demands of the hour which we should not expect from orators or men of the schools. This inaugural strikes me in its grand simplicity and directness as being for all time the historical keynote of this war; in it a people seemed to speak in the sublimely simple utterance of ruder times. What will Europe think of this utterance of the rude ruler, of whom they have nourished so lofty a contempt? Not a prince or minister in all Europe could have risen to such an equality with the occasion."

The concluding sentence of the Second Inaugural, "With malice toward none . . . ," has been quoted over the years only less often than the last sentence of the Gettysburg Address. There is a difference, of course, between the parroting of words and the acceptance of what words stand for. No sensible person would contend that the United States has always moved in the spirit of charity for all, or that it has always striven

425

for a just and lasting peace between its citizens and all other nations. Yet the fact remains that Lincoln gave expression to a strain of idealism that is part of the American character. The United States has kept its promise to the Philippines and has endowed that country with independence. Cuba could have been held as a dependency, and would have been held as such by most nations. After World War II what was the Marshall Plan, and much subsequent foreign aid, but a tangible expression of Lincoln's beneficent injunction? What is the whole network of American charity, supporting a maze of welfare societies unequaled in any other nation, but caring for the widow and the orphan? And what of the Peace Corps?

To contend that the attitude which results in these manifestations is universal among the American people would be foolish. To deny that it exists would be to do them less than justice. And is it far-fetched to believe that American benevolence, no matter how embodied, continues to draw nourishment from Lincoln's oft-repeated formulation of its goal?

Ulysses S. Grant
Terms of Surrender for the Army of Northern Virginia
1865

EDITED BY T. HARRY WILLIAMS

On the afternoon of April 9, 1865, General Ulysses S. Grant sat in a chair in the living room of the Wilmer McLean house in the little Virginia village of Appomattox Court House. Seated facing him with serious face and somewhat anxious eyes was General Robert E. Lee. It was for both the end of a bitter and bloody military road. It was also one of the great confrontations of American history—of two great generals and two great gentlemen. Only after some difficult and sometimes devious correspondence had they come together. Grant had proposed that Lee's retreating and dissolving army should surrender, and Lee, after much anguish, had brought himself to go to Grant to ask for terms. Lee went to the meeting formally and faultlessly attired and wearing his sword, in the old way of war. Grant came in from the lines after receiving Lee's last note. He wore his familiar nondescript uniform with only the shoulder straps to denote his rank and looked even more disheveled than usual. Even if he had had time to prepare, he would have still appeared much the same—a technician of the age of modern and industrial war come to deal with a general of that dying warfare of knightly men and waving banners. Lee was accompanied only by his military secretary, Colonel Charles Marshall. Grant had with him his staff and some of his principal officers. They sat now to decide specifically the fate of the Army of

Northern Virginia, but, as both must have known, to determine actually the outcome of the war. For if Lee's army surrendered, all other Confederate forces would follow suit. It was Palm Sunday, and peace, peace for the moment and peace for the long future, hung in the air between the two men in the room at the McLean house.

After some preliminary conversation about their having met in the Mexican War, Lee, for whom the interview was naturally painful, suggested that Grant state his terms of surrender and reduce them to writing. Grant called for his manifold order book, placed it on a small table, and wrote his conditions on two pages. He said later that when he put his pen to the paper he did not know the first word he would use, but that he knew what was in his mind and wanted to make it crystal clear. He also said that as he wrote his eye fell on Lee's sword and this led him to include the provision that the officers would retain their sidearms and horses. The paper was handed to Lee, who put on his spectacles to examine it. As the Confederate read, his facial expression showed that he was touched by the generosity of the terms. When he finished, he exclaimed: "This will have a very happy effect upon my army." Then, after a slight pause, Lee remarked that in the southern service the enlisted men owned their own horses and mules and wondered if they would be able to keep them. Grant replied that the terms regarding animals applied only to officers. But, he went on, as if talking partly to himself, most of the men were probably small farmers and would need their horses to put in a crop; he would pass down an oral order to let each man claiming to own an animal take it home with him. Lee, obviously moved, said this concession would have the best possible effect. With Colonel Marshall's help, he then composed a letter to Grant accepting the terms. Duplicate copies of the two letters were prepared, and shortly Lee departed. Appomattox had become one of the immortal American scenes.

Appomattox C. H., Va.,
Apl 9th, 1865.

Gen. R. E. Lee,
       Comd'g C. S. A.

Gen: In accordance with the substance of my letter to you of the 8th inst., I propose to receive the surrender of the Army of N. Va. on the following terms, to wit: Rolls of all the officers and men to be made in duplicate. One copy to be given to an officer designated by me, the other to be retained by such officer or officers as you may designate. The officers to give their individual paroles not to take up arms against the Government of the United States until properly exchanged, and each company or regimental commander sign a like parole for the men of their commands. The arms, artillery and public property to be parked and stacked, and turned over to the officer appointed by me to receive them. This will not embrace the side-arms of the officers, nor their private horses or baggage. This done, each officer and man will be allowed to return to their homes, not to be disturbed by United States authority so long as they observe their paroles and the laws in force where they may reside.

Very respectfully,
U. S. Grant,
Lt. Gen.

U. S. Grant was a soldier. He thought first and naturally in military terms, in terms of winning a battle or a war. When he went to Appomattox, his primary purpose was to get Lee and Lee's army out of the war. That general and that army constituted the chief resisting power of the Confederacy. If they were removed, all other resistance would shortly cease and the war would be ended. Throughout the negotiations Grant acted on the surface a purely military part. He told Lee in their exchange of notes before the meeting that he had no authority to discuss a general peace but only to conclude a military agreement for the surrender of one army. He did not make the mistake that his friend William T. Sherman made shortly afterward in treating with Joseph E.

Grant's letter is transcribed from *Personal Memoirs of U. S. Grant* (New York: Charles L. Webster and Co., 1885–86), II, opposite p. 496.

Johnston—of agreeing to an inclusive pact that contained political as well as military provisions. Sherman's document was referred to, with substantial accuracy, as a "treaty." Grant would never have concocted a treaty. He was too much the soldier to intervene in the political sphere, too aware that even if he had been so inclined his civil superior, Abraham Lincoln, would not have permitted him or any other general to dictate conditions of peace.

At the same time, Grant, as his actions showed and as his later utterances confirmed, was thinking about the ultimate peace beyond the immediate military ceremony. When he spoke so earnestly to Lee about the common soldiers needing their horses on their farms, he was looking a long way into the future. And on the day after the dramatic meeting he rode to Lee's camp to ask the Confederate leader, without success, to use his great influence to persuade other southern generals to quit the now hopeless struggle. Grant was the very model of a proper democratic soldier; he was always extremely careful not to obtrude his views on the civil authorities. But more than any other general of the time he had a sharp and realistic appreciation of the relation between policy and war. He knew that wars were not fought for their own sake or as an end in themselves but for political objectives. In this particular war the large objective was to restore the Union: to restore it, he hoped, with the least possible violence to the feelings of both sides but with all the vast changes and results wrought by the war affirmed and attested. If satisfactory military rituals could be concluded, without any big talk being indulged in or any specific conditions being required, then men of both sections could proceed to do many things—restore a spirit of national amity, build up the South's shattered economy, and work out a viable plan for the former slaves.

Grant's approach to the problem of peace was startlingly similar to Lincoln's. The President proposed to get the mechanics of Reconstruction under way without discoursing too much about abstract principles. After the process was in motion, the plans and the principles could be fitted in. By somewhat different routes the professional politician and the professional soldier had arrived at the same strategy. Both were worthy representatives of the American pragmatic tradition. Of course, the peace did not develop as either Lincoln or Grant hoped. Perhaps it would have happened much as it did even if Lincoln had lived. Many forces dictated its failure, and Grant himself, as President during the period, has to bear some of the blame. After he left the Presidency he

430

said sadly that neither the North nor the South had acted as he thought each should have. Perhaps, he concluded, it would have been better for both sections and races if the South for a span had remained under military government.

Grant's surrender document did not pass from men's minds with the end of the war. It undoubtedly had some influence on Lee, helping him determine to cast his influence for intersectional harmony. It was often quoted in the South, although generally with the bitter observation that its author had forgotten its spirit. And in the years after Reconstruction and the age of Grant it remained a part of the national consciousness. But there was a tendency to misunderstand the situation in which Grant wrote his terms and therefore to misinterpret his purpose. Men remembered that Grant at Appomattox had acted the part of a generous victor and had given the vanquished generous terms. That was the American way, people said. They said it especially in the disillusioned years after World War I and added that Grant's way was the proper mode to end a war—with terms that the defeated could live with. In World War II American leaders gave an opposite meaning to Grant's peace ideas. Franklin D. Roosevelt recalled that, at Fort Donelson, Grant had demanded of the Confederate garrison "unconditional surrender," and he proposed this formula as a condition to be imposed on the enemies of the Western alliance. Roosevelt forgot that at Donelson Grant was demanding the surrender of a single fort and not of a nation. The Americans of the post–World War I era forgot that at Appomattox Grant was laying down not a peace but a military convention that would make a workable peace possible. He would not punish the South heavily or with revenge, but neither would he give it a blank check to fill in as it pleased.

The war, the exercise in violence, had been brought to a close. But some at least of the political objectives of that exercise had to be attained and could best be attained with pragmatic experimentation in the peace that would follow. Grant was a great soldier, although an indifferent political leader. He had a good stock of common sense, and he was a thoroughly humane man. The terms he wrote at Appomattox have become a symbol of the essential humanity of the American character, and such they will always remain. They should stand too as a reminder of something Americans often forget—the vital and constant relation between war and national objectives.

The Oath of Office
1868

EDITED BY HAROLD M. HYMAN

Framers of the federal Constitution of 1787 and members of the first Congress held under its provisions decided that officeholders of the national government which they were laboring to create should be bound neither by religious tests nor by elaborate loyalty oaths. Instead, they believed that a simple oath of office was adequate.

This decision ran counter to the practice of almost every other government in the world at that time. It reflected the awareness of the men at Philadelphia of certain historical factors which from 1774 through 1783 had helped to initiate and to sustain the revolution against King George III. A century earlier (1640–60 and 1688–89) the ancestors of those men had mounted two successful revolutions, during which they executed one king and exiled another, because England's constitutional law bound inseparably together religious faith and secular allegiance. During the 1770's many colonists rebelled against Britain primarily because royal policy favored establishing the Anglican Church as the official church in America, as it was in England. This would have meant that general taxes would support the Anglican priests and that acquiescence in the Anglican creed would be required of all office-holders. America's religious diversity made dangerous any connection between government and a particular religious organization.

Therefore, the "Federalists" who shaped the 1787 Constitution stated in one of the few presumably unamendable phrases of that document that "no religious Test shall ever be required as a Qualification to any Office or public Trust under the United States" (Article VI). Further

432

to stress the American consensus on this point, the so-called "anti-Federalists" insisted on including, as part of the price of their agreement to the Constitution, the First Amendment's injunction that "Congress shall make no law respecting an establishment of religion, or prohibiting the free exercise thereof."

If religious tests were dangerous, loyalty tests were useless. After all, except for the relatively small number of diehard Tories, every single adult American had switched his allegiance at least once since 1774. Tens of thousands of "patriots" had shifted sides several times during the long course of the Revolution. Little wonder that a suggestion made at Philadelphia in 1787 for the inclusion in the Constitution of a uniform loyalty-oath test for federal and state officers, inquiring into past conduct, received little support. Instead, as Madison recorded it, Pennsylvania's James Wilson spoke for almost everyone at the meeting when he ". . . said that he was never fond of oaths, considering them as a left-handed security only. A good government did not need them and a bad government ought not to be supported."

The framers of the Constitution and the first congressmen agreed, however, that the new government was better off if its servants in national and state offices swore an oath to symbolize individual future commitment to the Constitution. The only office for which the form of the oath was specified in the Constitution was that of the President of the United States (Article II). But an oath requirement faced others in addition to the President; "the Senators and Representatives . . . and the Members of the several State Legislatures, and all executive and judicial officers, shall be bound by Oath or Affirmation, to support the Constitution" (Article VI). The first Congress that met under the ratified Constitution provided the oath form for officers lower than the President: "I, A.B., do solemnly swear or affirm (as the case may be) that I will support the Constitution of the United States" (U.S. Statutes at Large, I, 23).

This remained the standard text of the oath of office for all federal and state employees until 1861. Then the American experiment in political democracy structured in a federal system—unique in the world—split on the rock of slavery. Clearly present danger in the North of homefront disloyalty inspired Congress and many state legislatures to apply loyalty tests widely. Naturally Congress paid special attention to the enlarging number of federal civil and military officers; and on August 6, 1861, it required these men, as a prerequisite to entering on their duties, to swear to their future loyalty "without any mental reservation or evasion whatsoever" (*U.S. Statutes at Large, XII,* 326–27).

Then, on July 2, 1862, the low point in the war for the Union, Congress enacted the so-called "iron-clad test oath." Its lengthy provisions required all federal personnel to swear to their past as well as to their future loyalty (*U.S. Statutes at Large,* 502–8). In its turn the standard text of the federal oath of office, the iron-clad oath expanded its coverage through subsequent congressional enactments. Congressmen themselves, pensioners, claimants, contractors, attorneys practicing in federal courts—in short, anyone having any business with or wanting favors from the national government—had to subscribe it. Although in 1867 the Supreme Court in ex parte Garland (4 Wallace 333) declared unconstitutional this oath requirement for attorneys, the remainder of the oath law's broad coverages remained as before.

During Reconstruction, Republican framers and supporters of the iron-clad oath statute found themselves boxed in by their creation. Reconstruction statutes and the Fourteenth Amendment combined to send to Congress, from the South, delegates-elect who had been pardoned by Congress for past Confederate activity but who could not without perjury swear to the past-loyalty provision of the test oath. After much intra-Republican heartburning, Congress on July 11, 1868, specified a new oath of office for all federal officials caught in this manner between the pardoning provisions of the Fourteenth Amendment and the exclusion clauses of the 1862 oath law. Obviously it was not the purpose of the drafters of the new oath statute to create the text for a permanent oath of office. But, though designed for pardoned ex-rebels, the 1868 oath has served almost without alteration ever since for all government officials.

I A.B., do solemnly swear (or affirm) that I will support and defend the Constitution of the United States against all enemies, foreign and domestic; [that I will bear true faith and allegiance to the same;] that I take this obligation freely, without any mental reservation or purpose of evasion, and that I will well and truthfully discharge the duties of the office on which I am about to enter. So help me God.

Between the closing-off of the Reconstruction effort in 1877 and the choking-off of the Nazi-Fascist-Japanese empire in 1945, matters involving oaths of office and tests of loyalty constituted only a minor theme in America's history. But the onset after 1945 of the "cold war" against the Soviet Union pushed these questions into the forefront of public concern. They remain there still and are likely to keep a prominent place.

An astonishing number of government agencies, national, state, and local, have adopted special disclaimer oaths as standard requirements for office. Industries and other private associations also have plunged into the search for subversives. All this has immensely complicated the problems of national officers who are responsible for maintaining adequate security procedures while refraining from transgressing on the rights of individuals. Amateur efforts do not unearth Soviet agents or American subversives, nor are they likely to do so. The fuss they have raised, however, has permitted opportunistic individuals to exploit the public's concern over internal security. Other Americans, dedicated to protecting and advancing the cause of civil liberty, have carried into the highest courts appeals reminiscent of the Garland case a century past; they contend that oaths of office which also are non-Communist disclaimers offend the Bill of Rights and the constitutional prohibition against ex post facto laws and bills of attainder. On April 18, 1966, the Supreme Court struck down an Arizona law requiring a loyalty oath of all state employees (Elfbrandt v. Russell, 86 Sup. Ct. 1238). The Court, in a 5 to 4 decision, denounced the law as a threat to "the cherished freedom of association protected by the First Amendment."

This is the text of the 1868 statute, with the bracketed phrase indicating what the current code of federal laws has dropped from the older version (U.S. *Statutes at Large*, XV, 85 [1868]; U.S. *Code*, I, 99 [1959]).

Our jurists have not yet found a clear formula by which government may secure itself against disloyalty, through oaths or otherwise, while simultaneously holding to the uncertain but inspiring line set in the Bill of Rights. Scholars in political science, law, philosophy, theology, and history have been no more successful than the jurists. The oath of office will remain a matter of controversy as long as fears remain that disloyalty exists in government offices. Perhaps the issue must boil down to the question whether the men legitimately entrusted with power to take action against disloyalty can employ that power with vigor, sensitivity, and restraint when—but only when—adequate danger exists. A hundred years ago an indignant and unquestionably loyal northerner challenged the legitimacy of Lincoln's employment of stern loyalty tests. The President asked, "Must I shoot a simple-minded soldier boy who deserts, while I must not touch a hair of a wily agitator who induces him to desert?" No, Lincoln replied to his own question: "I think that in such a case, to silence the agitator, and save the boy, is not only constitutional, but, withal, a great mercy."

The Ballad of John Henry
c. 1872

EDITED BY RICHARD M. DORSON

In 1870 workmen on the Chesapeake and Ohio Railroad began blasting through a hump of the Allegheny Mountains in West Virginia. Late in 1872 they completed the Big Bend Tunnel, at that time the longest in the United States, stretching a mile and a quarter under the wild and desolate terrain of Summers County in what was then a frontier wilderness. The tentacles of the transregional and transcontinental railroads were reaching out, in the aftermath of the Civil War, to embrace the nation. The railroad companies joined their trunk lines, standardized their track, patented safety devices like the automatic coupler and the air brake, and speeded up the building of bridges and tunnels. The steam drill made its appearance in these years, as a device to replace the old method of tunneling by hand drillers or "steel drivers." During the construction of the Big Bend Tunnel, reports say that a contest was staged between the newfangled steam drill and a Negro steel driver named John Henry, who defeated the machine, dying on the spot or soon after. From this event grew the most celebrated folk ballad composed on American soil, one whose popularity is still on the increase.

In the Big Bend Tunnel—named for a southerly dip of ten miles the engineers were avoiding along the Greenbrier River—about a thousand laborers, mostly Negro ex-slaves, worked in small gangs driving steel and blasting rock. A steel driver struck a heavy hammer against a steel drill clenched between the legs of another workman, the "turner" or "shaker." The turner twisted the drill slightly every few strokes, to give the steel

437

more cutting edge. When the hole had reached sufficient depth, the turner placed in it a charge of nitroglycerin or other explosive, and set the fuse. As they pounded, the drivers chanted verses, often ribald, or grunted choruses as idle turners sang. Danger and death lurked in the shadows, from falling rock, foul air, and jarring blasts. Most hazardous was the "heading" or upper cross section of the tunnel, which had to be opened before the lower part could be blasted with simple vertical drilling. Turners lay prone in the heading, and the driver drilled sideways. John Henry was supposed to have drilled in the east end of the heading at Big Bend.

A good many workmen, white and Negro, professed to remember John Henry and his contest with the steam drill when investigators interviewed them over half a century later. As with all enduring oral traditions of heroes and events, the details vary widely, even in first-hand reports. One mountaineer claimed John Henry was a black, rawboned man about thirty years old, who had come from North Carolina, was six feet tall, weighed nearly 200 pounds, and had a white—or nearly white—girl friend; he was killed not in the contest but some time after from a blast of rock in the heading, and was secretly buried at night. Another West Virginian remembered John Henry as "yaller-complected," stout, hailing from Virginia, only five feet eight inches tall, no more than 170 pounds in weight, and surviving the tunnel dangers.

And so the conflicting testimony goes, but with a core of agreement. One of the chief witnesses said over half a century after the tunnel was built that he remembered John Henry singing "Can't you drive 'er . . . huh?" A newspaper in nearby Hinton, West Virginia, the Mountain Herald, on January 1, 1874, printed the verse "Can't you drive her home, my boy?" as sung by the tunnel gangs.

In general, the accounts to be found in West Virginia newspapers and county histories point to savagery and violence and frank sexuality in the life of Big Bend tunnelmen. Later recollections likened Big Bend to an inferno, with half-naked men gasping and writhing in the yellow smoke that filled the cavern, while a din as of ten thousand hammers striking anvils beat on their ears. Men died from tunnel sickness, from falls of the crumbly red shale, from knife stabbings, and their bodies were summarily disposed of by the railroad management. Relief was sought in whiskey-drinking, in talk of camp women, in singing. Sexual symbolism found a ready place in song phrases about "driving hard," "piece of steel," "wants my hammer, handle, too."

From this background the ballad of John Henry arose. Its composer is not known, although several workmen at Big Bend possessed a talent for ballad-making. When the tunnel gangs dispersed, they carried with them the folk song about John Henry and distributed it throughout the nation.

John Henry was a very small boy
Setting on his mama's knee.
He picked up a hammer and a little piece of steel,
Said, "The hammer be the death of me,
The hammer be the death of me."

John Henry went upon the mountain,
Came down on the other side.
The mountain was so tall, John Henry was so small,
He laid down his hammer and he cried, "O Lord," etc.

John Henry on the right hand side,
The steam drill on the left,
"Before I'll let your steam drill beat me down,
I'm gonna hammer my fool self to death."

"Oh, look away over yonder, captain,
You can't see like me."
He hollered out in a lonesome cry,
"A hammer be the death of me."

John Henry told the captain,
"When you go to town,
Bring me back a twelve-pound hammer,
I will sho' beat your steam drill down."

The man that invented the steam drill
Thought he was mighty fine.

The ten-stanza version of the ballad is reprinted from Guy B. Johnson, *John Henry: Tracking Down a Negro Legend* (Chapel Hill: University of North Carolina Press, 1929), pp. 115–16; the supplementary stanzas that follow come from Louis W. Chappell, *John Henry: A Folk-Lore Study* (Jena: W. Biedermann, 1933), pp. 104, and 120–21.

John Henry drove his fourteen feet
And the steam drill only made nine.

John Henry told his shaker,
"Shaker, you better pray,
For, if I miss the six-foot steel,
Tomorrow'll be your burying day."

John Henry had a pretty little wife,
Her name was Mary Ann.
He said, "Fix me a place to lay down, child,
I got a roaring in my head."

John Henry had a loving little wife,
The dress she wore was blue.
She walked down the track but never came back,
"John Henry, I've been true to you."

John Henry told the captain
Just before he died,
"Only one favor I ask of you:
Take care of my wife and child."

[One of the most popular "John Henry" stanzas, absent from the above text, is the following:]

John Henry told the captain,
"A man ain't nothin' but a man,
And if I don't beat your steam drill down
I'll die with a hammer in my hand, Lawd, Lawd."

[And these three stanzas appear in yet another text:]

John Henry was a man just six feet in height,
Nearly two feet and a half across the breast.
He'd take a nine-pound hammer and hammer all day long
And never get tired and want to rest, O Lord,
And never get tired and want to rest.

John Henry was a steel-driving man, O Lord,
He drove all over the world.
He come to Big Bend Tunnel on the C. & O. Road
Where he beat the steam drill down, O Lord,
Where he beat the steam drill down.

> The white folks all got scared,
> Thought Big Bend was a-fallin' in;
> John Henry hollered out with a very loud shout,
> "It's my hammer a-fallin' in the wind, O Lord,
> It's my hammer a-fallin' in the wind."

For thirty-seven years after the completion of the Big Bend Tunnel, the tradition of John Henry escaped attention. Then in 1909 it received a short and cryptic note in the Journal of American Folklore. A collector of folk songs from the North Carolina mountains, Louise Rand Bascom, coveted a ballad on "Johnie Henry," of which she possessed the first two lines.

> Johnie Henry was a hard-workin' man,
> He died with his hammer in his hand.

Her informant declared the ballad to be sad, tearful, and sweet, and hoped to secure the rest "when Tobe sees Tom, an' gits him to larn him what he ain't forgot of hit from Muck's pickin'." Apparently Tobe never did see Tom, but the key stanza was enough to guide other collectors.

In the next decade half a dozen contributors to the Journal expanded knowledge of the work song and the ballad carrying the name of John Henry, who at first was confused with John Hardy, a Negro desperado hanged in 1894 in West Virginia. By 1929 a sociologist at the University of North Carolina, Guy B. Johnson, had written a detailed, book-length study, John Henry: Tracking Down a Negro Legend. This was followed in 1933 by another, even more painstaking, inquiry, John Henry: A Folklore Study, by Louis W. Chappell, a professor of English at the University of West Virginia. While Chappell attacked Johnson's handling of evidence, both books persuasively argued for the existence of John Henry and the likelihood that a steam-drilling contest had actually been held at Big Bend Tunnel. Furthermore, they stimulated popular interest in the Negro hero.

Already in his look into the John Henry tradition, Johnson had anticipated its potentialities for the creative arts. "I marvel," he wrote, "that some of the 'new' Negroes with an artistic bent do not exploit the wealth of John Henry lore. Here is material for an epic poem, for a play, for an opera, for a Negro symphony. What more tragic theme than the theme of John Henry's martyrdom?" A response was not long in coming. Within two years a fictionalized story, John Henry, had been published and distributed by the Literary Guild. Its author, Roark Bradford, while not a "new Negro," had grown up on a southern plantation near the Mississippi River, and had seen Negroes closely. (Bradford achieved his greatest success with Ol' Man Adam an' His Chillun [1928], a portrayal of Scripture seen through Negro eyes, which was rendered by Marc Connelly into the Broadway hit The Green Pastures [1930].) In Bradford's John Henry the contest with the machine occupies only 5 out of 223 pages, serving, however, as the dramatic climax for such structure as the book possesses. A cotton-rolling steam winch on the levee replaces the rock-boring steam drill, and New Orleans and the Mississippi River form the locale. John Henry is a cotton-loading roustabout, when he is working; much of the time he is loving and leaving his girl Julie Anne, who follows him to death after his fatal contest with the new machine. At other times he performs great feats of lifting, eating, and brawling. The whole narrative is written in a repetitious, rhythmic stage dialect, interspersed with plaintive little songs, and centering around Negro literary stereotypes. The sporting man, the hell-busting preacher, the woman of easy acquaintance, the old conjure mammy, are all present. John Henry, the frontier boaster, is a new stereotype for the Negro gallery, but a well-established one in other American lore, and he reiterates his tall-tale outcries on nearly every page.

In 1939 an adaptation of John Henry, billed as a play with music, appeared on the Broadway stage. Coauthor with Roark Bradford was Jacques Wolfe, who supplied the musical scores for the song numbers. The play followed closely the original story, which contained obvious elements for a musical drama. Paul Robeson starred as John Henry. The Broadway production closed after a short run.

The book and the play of Roark Bradford, with attendant newspaper reviews and magazine articles, popularized the name of John Henry, and fixed him in the public mind as a Negro Paul Bunyan. In many ways the growth of the John Henry legend and pseudo-legend parallels that of the tales of the giant logger, who was well established as a national property by the 1930's. Bradford's John Henry resembles James Stevens' Paul Bunyan of 1925, as a fictional portrayal of an American "folk" hero based on a slender thread of oral tradition, in one case a few northwoods anecdotes, in the other a single ballad. Bradford, like Stevens, created the

442

picture of a giant strong man, although with a somber rather than a rollicking mien. In 1926 Odum and Johnson called John Henry the "black Paul Bunyan of the Negro workingman." Carl Sandburg made the comparison the following year in The American Songbag, saying both heroes were myths. Newspapers referred to John Henry as the "Paul Bunyan of Negroes," "the Paul Bunyan of his race, a gigantic river roustabout whose Herculean feats of work and living are part of America's folk lore." In the later history of the two traditions, the parallelism persists. Writers, poets, and artists attempted to wrest some deeper meaning from the Paul Bunyan and John Henry legends, and failed. But both figures lived on triumphantly in children's books of American folk heroes and in popular treasuries of American folklore.

The first presentation of John Henry as a folk hero came in 1930, in a chapter of Here's Audacity! American Legendary Heroes, by Frank Shay. His account of "John Henry, the Steel Driving Man," followed Guy B. Johnson's preliminary essay of 1927, "John Henry: A Negro Legend." Shay's formula was repeated by a number of other writers for the juvenile market, all of whom inevitably included the story of John Henry and his contest with the steam drill in their pantheon of American comic demigods. Other authors of children's books found it rewarding to deal individually and serially with America's newfound folk heroes. One product of this trend was John Henry: The Rambling Black Ulysses, by James Cloyd Bowman (1942). Bowman's nearly three hundred pages went far beyond the ballad story to give a full-length improvisation of John Henry's career, from his life as a slave boy on the old plantation through the Civil War to freedom. In this version John Henry encourages unruly freedmen to mine coal, cut corn, pick cotton, and drive railroad ties. He outsmarts confidence men and gamblers, stokes the Robert E. Lee to victory over the Natchez, and at long last dies with his hammer in his hand at the Big Bend Tunnel. But a final chapter presents an alternate report, that John Henry recovered from overwork, and resumed his ramblin' around. In a much briefer story, John Henry and the Double-Jointed Steam Drill, by Irwin Shapiro (1945), John Henry never dies at all, but after beating the steam drill pines away to a ghost, until his old pal John Hardy convinces him that he should learn to use the machine he conquered, and the tale ends with John Henry drilling through the mountain, and the steam drill shivering to pieces in his hands! So for American children John Henry unites the Negroes in faithful service to their white employers, and accepts the machine. In these children's books the full-page illustrations of a sad-faced Negro giant swinging a hammer contributed as much as the printed words to fixing the image of John Henry.

Folklore treasuries and collections of folk songs also continued to keep the story and song steadily before the public. In his best-selling A Treasury of American Folklore (1944), currently in its twenty-third printing, B. A. Botkin reprinted accounts of John Henry in oral hearsay, balladry, and fiction. The lavishly illustrated Life Treasury of American Folklore (1961) offered a picture of John Henry spiking ties on a railroad track rather than driving steel in a tunnel. John A. and Alan Lomax, naturally sympathetic to the ballad hero first presented in a full text by the elder Lomax in 1915, always included John Henry ballads, some adapted and arranged, some recorded in the field, in their popular folksong compilations. "John Henry" was the opening song in their first book, American Ballads and Folksongs (1934), and in Our Singing Country (1941) they called it "probably America's greatest single piece of folk lore." In the latest and most ornate garland, Alan Lomax (the sole author), having meanwhile shifted his emphasis from Marx to Freud, found John Henry equally receptive to his altered insights. The steel-driver shaking the mountain is a phallic image; singers know that John Henry died from love-making, not overwork:

This old hammer—WHAM!
Killed John Henry—WHAM!
Can't kill me—WHAM!
Can't kill me—WHAM!

Thus the hammer song vaunted the sexual virility of the pounder. Lomax has returned full cycle to the psychoanalytic views of Chappell. The steel-driver also appealed to social reformers. In American Folk Songs of Protest (1953, reprinted as a paperback in 1960), John Greenway called "John Henry" the "best-known (and best) Negro ballad, the best-known Negro work song, the best song of protest against imminent technological unemployment. . . ."

The greatest impact of John Henry on American culture has come outside the printed page, through commercial recordings. In 1962 the most widely recorded folk song sold to the public was "John Henry." That year the Phonolog Record Index listed some fifty current renditions of the ballad "John Henry" and fifteen of the work song "Nine Pound

444

Hammer." As many popular singers have made recordings for the general public as have folk singers for collectors in the field. The Library of Congress Copyright Catalogue reveals the publication of over one hundred songs devoted to John Henry from 1916 on, embracing all kinds of musical arrangements from simple melodic line and text to full orchestral composition. Arrangers staking out claims include the well-known American composer Aaron Copland, the Negro song-compiler John W. Work, the musicologist Charles Seeger, the celebrated Negro ex-convict Huddie Ledbetter (Lead Belly), W. C. Handy (the "father of the blues"), concert arranger Elie Siegmeister, and popular singer Bob Gibson.

Popular singers and recording artists have altered the formless sequence of independent stanzas, which comprised the folk ballad, into a swift-moving, tightly knit song story. John Henry has shifted from the sphere of Negro laborers and white mountaineers into the center of the entertainment world of jukebox and hootenanny, radio and television. The earlier texts from tradition show the usual variations characteristic of folklore. John Henry drives steel chiefly on the C & O, but once it is located in Brinton, New Jersey, and he also drives on the A C & L, the Air Line Road, the L & N, and the Georgia Southern Road. He comes from Tennessee most often, but also from eastern Virginia, from Louisiana, and from Mobile, Alabama. His hammer weighs nine, ten, twelve, sixteen, twenty, and thirty pounds; sometimes he carries a hammer in each hand. His girl is named Julie Ann, Polly Ann, Mary Ann, Martha Ann, Nellie Ann, Lizzie Ann, and Mary Magdalene. In one unique text, John Henry's partner kills him with the hammer. Among the visitors to his grave is, in one instance, Queen Elizabeth II.

Today the ballad of John Henry lives on in a form remarkably stable for an anonymous oral composition. It has been refashioned by the urban folk-song revival into a national property, shared by singers and composers, writers and artists, listeners and readers. The ballad commemorates an obscure event in which several lines of American history converged—the growth of the railroads, the rise of the Negro, the struggle of labor. Various interpreters have read in the shadowy figure of John Henry symbols of racial, national, and sexual strivings. The Negro and the white man, teen-ager and tot, professor and performer, have levied upon the John Henry tradition. The explanation for these multiple appeals lies in the dramatic intensity, tragic tension, and simple poetry combined in one unforgettable American folk ballad.

Mary Baker Eddy
Science and Health
1875

EDITED BY MARTIN E. MARTY

The presence of over 250 denominations in the United States is a sign of the religious inventiveness of the American people. But most of these religious groups are direct heirs of European church bodies. Many of them are closely related to each other. Few are original and authentically native products. In 1875 there appeared in Boston a book which ranks with The Book of Mormon as one of the most influential original documents to give birth to an American church body. Entitled Science and Health, it was written by Mrs. Mary Baker Eddy. The book was occasioned by the author's experiences after a fall on ice in 1866. Claiming that she had been abandoned by medical science and that she was rescued by what then was called "faith healing," she reflected upon the spiritual implications of her recovery. The result of these reflections was the book which, through the careful custodianship of the denomination based on it, has formed the religious opinions of hundreds of thousands of Americans.

Mary Baker Eddy was born near Bow, New Hampshire, in 1821. Her earlier years were marked by ill health, the death of a husband, and a later unhappy marital experience. Her generally unfulfilled literary aspirations seemed to predestine her for obscurity; she published nothing of consequence before Science and Health, which appeared when she was

446

well into the sixth decade of her life. During the years before the writing of Science and Health the author seems to have familiarized herself with terms and ideas employed by the New England Transcendentalists, who were experiencing some literary vogue. Later scholars have detected traces of Hegelianism and other European idealistic philosophies casually appropriated into her system of thought. Most important, she was apparently influenced by a faith healer named Phineas P. Quimby. The extent of all these influences upon her writings has been a subject of much controversy—as has almost anything associated with her career. Mrs. Eddy's followers take her word for it that the book was "hopelessly original," and, contending that it was divinely inspired as a revelation of ultimate truth, have withstood those critics who have suggested that some plagiarism was at work in Science and Health.

In 1883 Mary Baker Eddy appended a Key to the Scriptures to the book, which since then has appeared under the combined title. Two admirers of her thought provided funds for publication. Sales were disappointing at first, but increased greatly as the movement founded upon the book grew. Mrs. Eddy revised the book 89 times, and it had passed through 382 editions before her death in 1910. The representative and, indeed, authoritative text is therefore the last one to have been certified by her hand. This version, which bears the copyright date 1906, will remain the permanent source of doctrine and practice for the Church of Christ, Scientist, or "Christian Science," the religious movement founded on Mrs. Eddy's teachings. The rules of the church prevent tampering with the basic text. The book also contains, however, some testimonials by followers to the effects of spiritual healing, and a small number of these have been replaced through the years.

Science and Health was completed in 1875 in a small upstairs room at Lynn, Massachusetts, in austere surroundings which have been preserved by admirers. As Mrs. Eddy's career prospered, she revised the later editions in a more comfortable setting at Concord, New Hampshire, during the years of an energetic retirement. She was active until the end of her long life, spending the last three years near Boston, where she took a leading part in church affairs.

The passage reprinted here from the 700-page work is one of the few which provide some comment on the American setting. The "metaphysical reflections" in the selection are representative of the character of the whole book.

447

MATTER does not express Spirit. God is infinite omnipresent Spirit. If Spirit is *all* and is everywhere, what and where is matter? Remember that truth is greater than error, and we cannot put the greater into the less. Soul is Spirit, and Spirit is greater than body. If Spirit were once within the body, Spirit would be finite, and therefore could not be Spirit.

Soul greater than body

The question, "What is Truth," convulses the world. Many are ready to meet this inquiry with the assurance which comes of understanding; but more are blinded by their old illusions, and try to "give it pause." "If the blind lead the blind, both shall fall into the ditch."

The question of the ages

The efforts of error to answer this question by some *ology* are vain. Spiritual rationality and free thought accompany approaching Science, and cannot be put down. They will emancipate humanity, and supplant unscientific means and so-called laws.

Peals that should startle the slumbering thought from its erroneous dream are partially unheeded; but the last trump has not sounded, or this would not be so. Marvels, calamities, and sin will much more abound as truth urges upon mortals its resisted claims; but the awful daring of sin destroys sin, and foreshadows the triumph of truth. God will overturn, until "He come whose right it is." Longevity is increasing and the power of sin diminishing, for the world feels the alterative effect of truth through every pore.

Heralds of Science

As the crude footprints of the past disappear from the dissolving paths of the present, we shall better understand the Science which governs these changes, and shall plant our feet on firmer ground. Every sensuous pleasure or pain is self-destroyed through suffering. There should be painless progress, attended by life and peace instead of discord and death.

In the record of nineteen centuries, there are sects many but not enough Christianity. Centuries ago religionists were ready to hail an anthropomorphic God, and array His vicegerent with pomp and splendor; but this was not the manner of truth's appearing. Of old the cross was truth's central sign, and it is to-day. The modern lash is less material

Sectarianism and opposition

The text comes from *Science and Health with Key to the Scriptures* (Boston, 1934), pp.223–34. © 1906 Trustees under the Will of Mary Baker Eddy. All rights reserved. The quotation from the Christian Science textbook by Mary Baker Eddy is used by permission of the Trustees under her Will.

than the Roman scourge, but it is equally as cutting. Cold disdain, stubborn resistance, opposition from church, state laws, and the press, are still the harbingers of truth's full-orbed appearing.

A higher and more practical Christianity, demonstrating justice and meeting the needs of mortals in sickness and in health, stands at the door of this age, knocking for admission. Will you open or close the door upon this angel visitant, who cometh in the quiet of meekness, as he came of old to the patriarch at noonday?

Truth brings the elements of liberty. On its banner is the Soul-inspired motto, "Slavery is abolished." The power of God brings deliverance to the captive. No power can withstand divine Love. What is this supposed power, which opposes itself to God? Whence cometh it? What is it that binds man with iron shackles to sin, sickness, and death? Whatever enslaves man is opposed to the divine government. Truth makes man free. *Mental emancipation*

You may know when first Truth leads by the fewness and faithfulness of its followers. Thus it is that the march of time bears onward freedom's banner. The powers of this world will fight, and will command their sentinels not to let truth pass the guard until it subscribes to their systems; but Science, heeding not the pointed bayonet, marches on. There is always some tumult, but there is a rallying to truth's standard. *Truth's ordeal*

The history of our country, like all history, illustrates the might of Mind, and shows human power to be proportionate to its embodiment of right thinking. A few immortal sentences, breathing the omnipotence of divine justice, have been potent to break despotic fetters and abolish the whipping-post and slave market; but oppression neither went down in blood, nor did the breath of freedom come from the cannon's mouth. Love is the liberator. *Immortal sentences*

Legally to abolish unpaid servitude in the United States was hard; but the abolition of mental slavery is a more difficult task. The despotic tendencies, inherent in mortal mind and always germinating in new forms of tyranny, must be rooted out through the action of the divine Mind. *Slavery abolished*

Men and women of all climes and races are still in bondage to material sense, ignorant how to obtain their freedom. The rights of man were vindicated in a single section and on the lowest plane of human life, when African slavery was abolished in our land. That was only

449

prophetic of further steps towards the banishment of a world-wide slavery, found on higher planes of existence and under more subtle and depraving forms.

The voice of God in behalf of the African slave was still echoing in our land, when the voice of the herald of this new crusade sounded the

Liberty's crusade

keynote of universal freedom, asking a fuller acknowledgment of the rights of man as a Son of God, demanding that the fetters of sin, sickness, and death be stricken from the human mind and that its freedom be won, not through human warfare, not with bayonet and blood, but through Christ's divine Science.

God has built a higher platform of human rights, and He has built it on diviner claims. These claims are not made through code or creed, but

Cramping systems

in demonstration of "on earth peace, good-will toward men." Human codes, scholastic theology, material medicine and hygiene, fetter faith and spiritual understanding. Divine Science rends asunder these fetters, and man's birthright of sole allegiance to his Maker asserts itself.

I saw before me the sick, wearing out years of servitude to an unreal master in the belief that the body governed them, rather than Mind.

The lame, the deaf, the dumb, the blind, the sick, the sensual, the sinner, I wished to save from the slavery of their own beliefs and from

House of bondage

the educational systems of the Pharaohs, who to-day, as of yore, hold the children of Israel in bondage. I saw before me the awful conflict, the Red Sea and the wilderness; but I pressed on through faith in God, trusting Truth, the strong deliverer, to guide me into the land of Christian Science, where fetters fall and the rights of man are fully known and acknowledged.

I saw that the law of mortal belief included all error, and that, even as oppressive laws are disputed and mortals are taught their right to

Higher law ends bondage

freedom, so the claims of the enslaving senses must be denied and superseded. The law of the divine Mind must end human bondage, or mortals will continue unaware of man's inalienable rights and in subjection to hopeless slavery, because some public teachers permit an ignorance of divine power,—an ignorance that is the foundation of continued bondage and of human suffering.

Discerning the rights of man, we cannot fail to foresee the doom of all oppression. Slavery is not the legitimate state of man. God made man

Native freedom

free. Paul said, "I was free born." All men should be free. "Where the Spirit of the Lord is, there is liberty." Love and Truth make free, but evil and error lead into captivity.

450

Christian Science raises the standard of liberty and cries: "Follow me! Escape from the bondage of sickness, sin, and death!" Jesus marked out the way. Citizens of the world, accept the "glorious liberty of the children of God," and be free! This is your divine right. The illusion of material sense, not divine law, has bound you, entangled your free limbs, crippled your capacities, enfeebled your body, and defaced the tablet of your being. Standard of liberty

If God had instituted material laws to govern man, disobedience to which would have made man ill, Jesus would not have disregarded those laws by healing in direct opposition to them and in defiance of all material conditions.

The transmission of disease or of certain idiosyncrasies of mortal mind would be impossible if this great fact of being were learned,—namely, that nothing inharmonious can enter being, for Life *is* God. Heredity is a prolific subject for mortal belief to pin theories upon; but if we learn that nothing is real but the right, we shall have no dangerous inheritances, and fleshly ills will disappear. No fleshly heredity

The enslavement of man is not legitimate. It will cease when man enters into his heritage of freedom, his God-given dominion over the material senses. Mortals will some day assert their freedom in the name of Almighty God. Then they will control their own bodies through the understanding of divine Science. Dropping their present beliefs, they will recognize harmony as the spiritual reality and discord as the material unreality. God-given dominion

If we follow the command of our Master, "Take no thought for your life," we shall never depend on bodily conditions, structure, or economy, but we shall be masters of the body, dictate its terms, and form and control it with Truth.

There is no power apart from God. Omnipotence has all-power, and to acknowledge any other power is to dishonor God. The humble Nazarene overthrew the supposition that sin, sickness, and death have power. He proved them powerless. It should have humbled the pride of the priests, when they saw the demonstration of Christianity excel the influence of their dead faith and ceremonies. Priestly pride humbled

If Mind is not the master of sin, sickness, and death, they are immortal, for it is already proved that matter has not destroyed them, but is their basis and support.

We should hesitate to say that Jehovah sins or suffers; but if sin and suffering are realities of being, whence did they emanate? God made all

No union of
opposites

that was made, and Mind signifies God,—infinity, not finity. Not far removed from infidelity is the belief which unites such opposites as sickness and health, holiness and unholiness, calls both the offspring of spirit, and at the same time admits that Spirit is God,—virtually declaring Him good in one instance and evil in another.

Self-constituted
law

By universal consent, mortal belief has constituted itself a law to bind mortals to sickness, sin, and death. This customary belief is misnamed material law, and the individual who upholds it is mistaken in theory and in practice. The so-called law of mortal mind, conjectural and speculative, is made void by the law of immortal Mind, and false law should be trampled under foot.

Sickness from
mortal mind

If God causes man to be sick, sickness must be good, and its opposite, health, must be evil, for all that He makes is good and will stand forever. If the transgression of God's law produces sickness, it is right to be sick; and we cannot if we would, and should not if we could, annul the decrees of wisdom. It is the transgression of belief of mortal mind, not of a law of matter nor of divine Mind, which causes the belief of sickness. The remedy is Truth, not matter,—the truth that disease is *unreal*.

If sickness is real, it belongs to immortality; if true, it is a part of Truth. Would you attempt with drugs, or without, to destroy a quality or condition of Truth? But if sickness and sin are illusions, the awakening from this mortal dream, or illusion, will bring us into health, holiness, and immortality. This awakening is the forever coming of Christ, the advanced appearing of Truth, which casts out error and heals the sick. This is the salvation which comes through God, the divine Principle, Love, as demonstrated by Jesus.

God never
inconsistent

It would be contrary to our highest ideas of God to suppose Him capable of first arranging law and causation so as to bring about certain evil results, and then punishing the helpless victims of His volition for doing what they could not avoid doing. Good is not, cannot be, the author of experimental sins. God, good, can no more produce sickness than goodness can cause evil and health occasion disease.

Mental
narcotics

Does wisdom make blunders which must afterwards be rectified by man? Does a law of God produce sickness, and can man put that law under his feet by healing sickness? According to Holy Writ, the sick are never really healed by drugs, hygiene, or any material method. These merely evade the question. They are soothing syrups to put children to sleep, satisfy mortal belief, and quiet fear.

We think that we are healed when a disease disappears, though it is

452

liable to reappear; but we are never thoroughly healed until the liability to be ill is removed. So-called mortal mind or the mind of mortals being the remote, predisposing, and the exciting cause of all suffering, the cause of disease must be obliterated through Christ in divine Science, or the so-called physical senses will get the victory. The true healing

Unless an ill is rightly met and fairly overcome by Truth, the ill is never conquered. If God destroys not sin, sickness, and death, they are not destroyed in the mind of mortals, but seem to this so-called mind to be immortal. What God cannot do, man need not attempt. If God heals not the sick, they are not healed, for no lesser power equals the infinite All-power; but God, Truth, Life, Love, does heal the sick through the prayer of the righteous. Destruction of all evil

If God makes sin, if good produces evil, if truth results in error, then Science and Christianity are helpless; but there are no antagonistic powers nor laws, spiritual or material, creating and governing man through perpetual warfare. God is not the author of mortal discords. Therefore we accept the conclusion that discords have only a fabulous existence, are mortal beliefs which divine Truth and Love destroy.

To hold yourself superior to sin, because God made you superior to it and governs man, is true wisdom. To fear sin is to misunderstand the power of Love and the divine Science of being in man's relation to God, —to doubt His government and distrust His omnipotent care. To hold yourself superior to sickness and death is equally wise, and is in accordance with divine Science. To fear them is impossible, when you fully apprehend God and know that they are no part of His creation. Superiority to sickness and sin

Man, governed by his Maker, having no other Mind,—planted on the Evangelist's statement that "all things were made by Him [the Word of God]; and without Him was not anything made that was made,"—can triumph over sin, sickness, and death.

Many theories relative to God and man neither make man harmonious nor God lovable. The beliefs we commonly entertain about happiness and life afford no scatheless and permanent evidence of either. Security for the claims of harmonious and eternal being is found only in divine Science. Denials of divine power

Scripture informs us that "with God all things are possible,"—all good is possible to Spirit; but our prevalent theories practically deny this, and make healing possible only through matter. These theories must be untrue, for the Scripture is true. Christianity is not false, but religions which contradict its Principle are false.

In our age Christianity is again demonstrating the power of divine

Principle, as it did over nineteen hundred years ago, by healing the sick and triumphing over death. Jesus never taught that drugs, food, air, and exercise could make a man healthy, or that they could destroy human life; nor did he illustrate these errors by his practice. He referred man's harmony to Mind, not to matter, and never tried to make of none effect the sentence of God, which sealed God's condemnation of sin, sickness, and death.

In the sacred sanctuary of Truth are voices of solemn import, but we heed them not. It is only when the so-called pleasures and pains of sense

Signs following
pass away in our lives, that we find unquestionable signs of the burial of error and the resurrection to spiritual life.

There is neither place nor opportunity in Science for error of any sort. Every day makes its demands upon us for higher proofs rather than

Profession and proof
professions of Christian power. These proofs consist solely in the destruction of sin, sickness, and death by the power of Spirit, as Jesus destroyed them. This is an element of progress, and progress is the law of God, whose law demands of us only what we can certainly fulfil.

In the midst of imperfection, perfection is seen and acknowledged only by degrees. The ages must slowly work up to perfection. How long

Perfection gained slowly
it must be before we arrive at the demonstration of scientific being, no man knoweth,—not even "the Son but the Father;" but the false claim of error continues its delusions until the goal of goodness is assiduously earned and won.

Already the shadow of His right hand rests upon the hour. Ye who can discern the face of the sky,—the sign material,—how much more

Christ's mission
should ye discern the sign mental, and compass the destruction of sin and sickness by overcoming the thoughts which produce them, and by understanding the spiritual idea which corrects and destroys them. To reveal this truth was our Master's mission to all mankind, including the hearts which rejected him.

When numbers have been divided according to a fixed rule, the quotient is not more unquestionable than the scientific tests I have

Efficacy of truth
made of the effects of truth upon the sick. The counter fact relative to any disease is required to cure it. The utterance of truth is designed to rebuke and destroy error. Why should truth not be efficient in sickness, which is solely the result of inharmony?

Spiritual draughts heal, while material lotions interfere with truth, even as ritualism and creed hamper spirituality. If we trust matter, we distrust Spirit.

454

Whatever inspires with wisdom, Truth, or Love—be it song, sermon, or Science—blesses the human family with crumbs of comfort from Christ's table, feeding the hungry and giving living waters to the thirsty.

Crumbs of comfort

Mary Baker Eddy's own book and the Bible are the two authoritative texts of the Church of Christ, Scientist. This organization was chartered under Massachusetts law in 1879 and reorganized under a permanent, self-perpetuating board of directors in 1892. The denomination has grown to major size and influence and is efficiently organized, even though Mrs. Eddy at first seemed to be hesitant about forming a separate religious group at all.

The Mother Church, as the central organization in Boston is called (all local congregations are called branches), does not release statistics of membership. In order to qualify for eligibility as a religious group providing chaplaincies in World War II, Christian Scientists were forced to reveal their membership. They used the figures of a 1936 census which listed 268,915 people as affiliated with the denomination. At the founder's death in 1910 there had been 1,114 American branches; in 1965 there were approximately 3,300. The strength of the movement can be judged in part by the fact that millions of copies of Science and Health with Key to the Scriptures have been sold—most of them in the United States, where perhaps 80 per cent of the world's Christian Scientists reside.

To sociologists, Christian Science represents a typical "cult which became a church." Originally only a small following gathered around Mrs. Eddy. One of the first of the followers was Asa Gilbert Eddy, who became her third husband as well as the first "practitioner," as a professional healer within the denomination is called. After a period of slow growth the small band of admirers increased, gradually becoming the large, organized body just described. To the public, Christian Science is best known as a faith-healing movement because of its well-advertised belief that diseases of the body can be cured by a scientific application of the divine Principle which is the heart of the religion.

From a legal standpoint, Christian Scientists have frequently provided interesting test cases. From 1918 through 1921 in "The Great Litigation"

455

in the Massachusetts courts, the Mother Church successfully fought off schisms and dissensions which would have broken the tight national organization. At other times Christian Scientists have opposed in the courts efforts to fluoridate public water supplies, or to enact or enforce compulsory measures for vaccination. Frequently Christian Science has come under legal attack and into public attention when it has been sued by those who were attracted from conventional medicine to religious healing which, they feel, failed them.

To church historians the Church of Christ, Scientist, and the book on which it is based represent "egocentricity" in religion. That is, it is not first of all preoccupied with social questions or the amelioration of society as such. It is directed to the felt needs of individuals, particularly to those who have experienced ill health. This is not to say that Christian Scientists have not been responsible as citizens or that the church body has never taken an interest in social problems. It distinguished itself after World War II with its record of war relief. But, characteristically it declines to involve itself and its members directly in social causes or, for that matter, in an understanding of religious faith as having its base and immediate consequence in men's social relations.

To literary experts Science and Health has provided a text for continuing controversy. Most savage was Mark Twain's early satire: "When you read it you seem to be listening to lively and aggressive and oracular speech delivered in an unknown tongue." More moderate, but still repugnant to Christian Scientists, have been the numerous critical biographies and literary analyses. And there are balanced appraisals, sometimes written by members of the church, which find acceptance among both members and nonmembers.

In the general consensus, Mrs. Eddy is seen to have captured in her writing and her movement the optimistic spirit of much of the nineteenth-century American experience. The promises of better health, of a serene outlook on life, of a meaningful religious experience, of the chance to escape poverty and enslaving habits have attracted many. Christian Scientists, whose attitudes and actions are presumably influenced strongly by this book, are known to be peace-loving, studious, and generally law-abiding.

In highly literate circles the denomination is best known for the Christian Science Monitor. This daily newspaper was founded in 1908 by Mrs. Eddy, not only to perpetuate the ideas of Science and Health but also to combat the "yellow journalism" of the period. One of the most often quoted, most influential of the nation's newspapers, it fuses the emphases of Christian Science with calm and fair appraisals of world news. In particular, many of the attitudes toward freedom enunciated in Science and Health are reflected on the Monitor's pages.

Except for its reintroduction of concern over faith healing into orthodox Christian circles and its influence on a number of imitative "new thought" religions, Christian Science has had little direct impact on the broad stream of national intellectual life. What Science and Health and its author produced is a large, often-noticed, well-defined, and highly disciplined religious body. If any religion deserves to be represented by the documentary tradition associated with its founder, Christian Science is the one. The Board of Directors permits no adaptation of the text and no unofficial exegesis of it by members. It provides lectures which are read in all churches of the denomination and prepares lesson material for those under the age of twenty. There are no ordained ministers, and no missionaries, in the usual sense of those terms. Christian Scientists are uninterested in recreational and social activities in their churches. Instead, they propagate their beliefs "documentarily" through lectures, classes, reading rooms, and literary materials placed on public display. Every such literary evidence or teaching device is based on the Bible and, even more directly, on Science and Health with Key to the Scriptures.

Emma Lazarus
The New Colossus
1883

EDITED BY JOHN HIGHAM

For nine frustrating years, from 1877 to 1886, a committee of New York business and society leaders collected funds to pay for a pedestal on which a gigantic Statue of Liberty might stand in New York Harbor. The statue itself, the inspiration and creation of a French sculptor, Frédéric Auguste Bartholdi, was under construction in Paris. It was to be a gift to America from the French people, a symbol and pledge of friendship between the two republics. Americans needed only to erect it properly; yet the task almost exceeded the limits of the sluggish public spirit of the day.

At one point, in 1883, when the statue was almost ready to ship and the pedestal only half-finished, the Pedestal Fund Committee organized a temporary art exhibition as a fund-raising device. Prominent New Yorkers lent some of their treasures, and a number of artists and writers contributed original drawings and letters to a portfolio which was put up for auction. After some urging, Emma Lazarus produced a sonnet for the occasion. The entire portfolio, including the sonnet, sold for $1,500, a disappointing sum.

A finely bred, bookish young lady, Miss Lazarus rarely wrote in a patriotic vein. But this occasion touched obliquely a new and vital concern of hers. Until 1881 she had produced derivative, self-consciously literary verse, the tinkling melodies then fashionable in the world of genteel culture. Belonging to one of the oldest and most secure of New

York Jewish families, she had abandoned the synagogue in her youth and had largely lost a sense of Jewish identity. Then the horrifying outbreak of anti-Jewish pogroms in Russia, and the sight of the first bedraggled refugees arriving in New York, gave her a theme and a mission. With a new passion, she wrote henceforth mainly as a champion of the Jews. She became the first modern American laureate of their history and culture. To her the Statue of Liberty, facing seaward, would hold out to all uprooted folk the same message of succor that she, Emma Lazarus, was expressing to and for her fellow Jews.

Not like the brazen giant of Greek fame,
With conquering limbs astride from land to land;
Here at our sea-washed, sunset gates shall stand
A mighty woman with a torch, whose flame
Is the imprisoned lightning, and her name
Mother of Exiles. From her beacon-hand
Glows world-wide welcome; her mild eyes command
The air-bridged harbor that twin cities frame.

"Keep, ancient lands, your storied pomp!" cries she
With silent lips. "Give me your tired, your poor,
Your huddled masses yearning to breathe free,
The wretched refuse of your teeming shore.
Send these, the homeless, tempest-tost to me,
I lift my lamp beside the golden door!"

Absorbed in the cause of the Jews, Miss Lazarus seems to have taken no further interest in the Statue of Liberty once her poem was written. Nor did her contemporaries pay much heed to "The New Colossus." When she died in 1887, four years after its composition, the obituaries failed to

---

The original manuscript of the poem, which is followed here, is in the possession of the American Jewish Historical Society in New York City. (The "brazen giant" referred to in the first line is the Colossus of Rhodes, a statue of the sun god Helius which once stood at the harbor of Rhodes; it was known in ancient and medieval times as one of the Seven Wonders of the World.)

mention it. The reviewers of her collected works, which appeared in 1889, concentrated on her specifically Jewish poems. One critic conceded that "her noble sonnet" on the Bartholdi statue had given many their "first apprehension of the glory in even the more sordid elements in our American life." Others ignored the poem completely. After the turn of the century Miss Lazarus herself was largely forgotten outside a small Anglo-Jewish literary circle.

In 1903, on the twentieth anniversary of the writing of "The New Colossus," another shy, poetry-loving spinster who belonged to the old New York aristocracy, Georgina Schuyler, secured permission to put a bronze tablet containing the entire poem on an interior wall of the statue's pedestal. This she did primarily as a memorial to Miss Lazarus, whom she evidently had known and admired. The event passed without ceremony or public notice. In fact, the poem rested there for another thirty years without attracting any publicity at all.

This long neglect is remarkable; for the ideas that the poem expressed were deeply ingrained in American tradition. The concept of America as a refuge from European oppression supplied one of the original, fertilizing elements of our national consciousness. Jefferson, Emerson, Lowell, and many a lesser patriot had voiced its continuing appeal. In the late nineteenth century, however, pride in America's receptive mission dimmed. A gradual liberalization of political institutions throughout most of Europe blurred the once-sharp image of the immigrant as one who had been unfree in his native country. Meanwhile, the new problems of an urban, industrial age inspired a strong movement in America to restrict immigration. By 1886, when the New Colossus was finally unveiled upon her completed pedestal, there was already considerable alarm about the huddled masses streaming through the golden door. The lavish dedication ceremonies took place without a single reference to Miss Lazarus' sonnet and without serious attention to its theme.

Not only the uneasy mood of the time but also the statue itself resisted the generous construction Miss Lazarus placed upon it. The creators of the monument did not intend a symbol of welcome. Bartholdi and the French liberals who supported his work prized America not as an asylum but as an example of republican stability. They constructed a passive figure, austere and unresponsive, a model of frozen perfection, holding a torch high to illuminate the darker world beyond the sea. Its official name was "Liberty Enlightening the World." The meaning of the physical object would have to change before the sonnet could become a living document.

The immigrants themselves wrought that transformation, as they arrived in this country in the years after the statue was erected. The vast majority debarked at New York, and to every exultant heart and straining eye this first American presence was a profoundly moving sight. The immigrants perceived the statue as waiting for them, big with promise. They saw it not as a beacon to other lands but as a redemptive salutation to themselves. The memory of that awesome moment and the unspoken greeting it contained was a thing to cherish, a thing to tell one's children about. In 1906 Edward A. Steiner, an immigrant intellectual who was unaware of Emma Lazarus' poem, predicted that a great poet would someday put into words the inspiring emotions that millions of immigrants felt on encountering "this new divinity into whose keeping they now entrust themselves."

Miss Lazarus' words were rediscovered only after the immigrants' response to the statue penetrated our fund of national myths, revitalizing the old eighteenth-century idea of America as an asylum. While a bitter controversy over immigration pitted older against newer American groups, the Statue of Liberty remained—in the dominant native culture —an aloof, impersonal symbol, conveying a warning rather than a welcome to the outside world. After the restrictive Immigration Act of 1924 was passed, however, fear and rancor subsided; the great influx from overseas was ended. Immigration as a mass movement receded into history. Meanwhile, the children of immigrants from southern and eastern Europe grew up into full participation in American life. To ease their Americanization, public school curricula devoted increasing attention to the immigrants' love for and contributions to America. By 1926 fourth-grade children in St. Louis, Missouri, were studying the Statue of Liberty with the object of understanding what it meant to immigrants. By then some of the school textbooks on American history included pictures of immigrant families gazing joyfully at Bartholdi's Colossus. That immobile figure gradually joined the covered wagon as a symbol of the migrations that had made America.

In the late 1930's, more than fifty years after its composition, Emma Lazarus' poem finally attracted public interest. The event that called it forth from obscurity was a recurrence of the very problem that had moved Miss Lazarus in the first place: the plight of Jewish refugees. Their efforts to escape Nazi barbarism coincided with a growing revulsion of American opinion against racism and with a steady movement of the United States toward war with Germany. In contrast to the situation in the 1880's, when Americans were turning away from a cosmopolitan, humane outlook, the circumstances of the late 1930's united a particular concern for the Jews with a broader movement to strengthen ethnic democracy. Immigration policy did not change significantly. But a nation striving to overcome its own ethnic hatreds, to dignify influential minority groups, and to gird for war against Hitler needed to define itself anew as a bastion against persecution.

Louis Adamic, a Yugoslav-American journalist, did more than anyone else to popularize "The New Colossus." About 1934 he launched a one-man crusade to elevate the status of immigrant groups and to propagate an eclectic sense of American nationality. After 1938 he adopted the Lazarus sonnet as the keynote of practically everything he wrote or said. He quoted it endlessly in books, pamphlets, and public lectures. During the 1940's the words of the poem became a familiar litany in mass-circulation magazines, children's stories, and high-school history texts. In 1945 Georgina Schuyler's commemorative tablet was moved from the second-story landing to the main entrance of the statue. Beginning in 1947, the World Almanac included the poem as a regular feature. Curiosity about its forgotten author awakened. Now she seemed less a Jewish than an American poet, a human statue of liberty. According to the title of one rapturous biography, she was Emma Lazarus, Woman with a Torch.

Although the Statue of Liberty was not intended to beckon the tired and the poor, they had come to it. Because it received them no longer in significant numbers, it could enshrine their experience as a transcendental national memory. Because few Americans now were immigrants, all Americans could think of themselves as having been immigrants. Like the myth of the frontier, the myth of the asylum acquired a re-membered glory in an age that wished to preserve the spirit of a reality that was largely gone.

Yet the reality of refuge in America has never wholly disappeared, and the myth has not been merely compensatory. Its revival encouraged efforts to live up to the dictates of "The New Colossus." In 1965 Congress repealed the discriminatory features of the Immigration Law of 1924. President Lyndon B. Johnson, signing the new law at the base of the Statue of Liberty, alluded to the Lazarus poem and declared that the nation was returning "to the finest of its traditions." In the same spirit the President used the occasion to announce a large-scale program for reception of refugees from Cuba.

462

Henry W. Grady
The New South
1886

EDITED BY THOMAS D. CLARK

The South of 1886 was a section struggling to forget the immediate past of Civil War and Reconstruction. It was trying to reckon with current economic and social realities, and to project itself into the future. Newspaper editors from Richmond to Dallas had published stories of centennial celebrations of the Declaration of Independence and the surrender at Yorktown, and they anticipated the centennial of the framing of the Constitution. Already Union veterans and even whole regiments were returning South to visit the scenes of their actions in battle, to cultivate friendship with former foes, and to engage in extravagant expressions of national unity.

On every hand there were challenges for a young and vigorous editor in the New South, such as Henry W. Grady of the Atlanta Constitution. The region was falling woefully behind in the development of industry. The earth contained minerals, but native sons often lacked the managerial experience and imagination to take advantage of this resource. The substance of the land was being drawn away by wasteful and primitive agricultural practices. And capital to finance progress in all these areas was scarce. Travelers from the North wrote and published impressions of the land below the Potomac. Promotional departments of the various state governments published and distributed hundreds of pamphlets and reports at home and abroad. They sought to attract to the South capitalists and immigrants with ready purses and willing hands.

There was, despite its surface stagnation, a distinguishable stirring in the South. At the same time there existed an uncertainty born of the confusion and excesses of Reconstruction, a reluctance to break ties with the traditions of the Old South, and a timidity and doubt as to the attitudes of the rest of the nation toward the region. This was the South of which Henry W. Grady wrote in the Constitution.

A native of Athens, Georgia, a graduate of the University of Georgia, and a former law student at the University of Virginia, Grady had come to maturity with the rise of the postwar South. In reporting the Florida election dispute in 1876, the young journalist gained national attention. He scooped his fellow reporters and wired reports of the election board's decisions to the Constitution and the New York Herald well ahead of his competitors. The Charleston earthquake and tidal wave of 1886 gave Grady a second opportunity to attract widespread attention.

In repeated editorials and stories, Henry W. Grady emphasized the South's promise, even though he was critical of its many failures. Frequently also he described the South's iron, marble, and coal deposits, its water and timber resources, and its reservoir of cheap labor. To him a New South was a-borning. The term "New South" was not original with Grady. No one knows when it was first used. Maybe southern soldiers turning back from Appomattox saw in their heartbreak and frustration some kind of new beginning for their section.

Grady's views were confirmed by John Hamilton Inman, who had gone north in 1865 from Dandridge, Tennessee, to make his fortune. Inman had helped organize the New York Cotton Exchange and the Tennessee Coal, Iron and Railroad Company. He had also played a part in expanding the Louisville and Nashville Railroad Company, and had organized several local railroads into the Southern Railway system. He, like Grady, sensed the new impluse in the Old Confederacy, and he was in a position to translate this optimism to men with capital in the North. He helped direct at least $100 million of northern investment capital to the South.

John H. Inman was a member of the New England Society in New York City. He suggested to his associates in that society that they invite a young southerner to speak at their annual banquet. In 1886 he believed, from his knowledge of the progressive editorials appearing in the Atlanta Constitution, that Henry W. Grady could convey a sense of the rising South to a New York audience, and at the same time cultivate good will for the section. On November 6, 1886, an invitation arrived in Atlanta asking the young editor to address the New England Society at its meeting on December 22. Grady's editorial staff prevailed upon him to accept the challenge, and he chose the subject "The New South." Actually Grady made his speech in New York in response to a toast to "The New South."

In accepting an invitation to speak on such a subject, Grady was highly conscious of the fact that he risked uttering in New York some sentiment which would irritate members of his northern audience, or which would involve him in bitter controversy with sensitive and critical southerners. Though he gave most careful thought to the content of his speech, he did not prepare a text copy. Grady waited to judge first-hand the nature of his audience, and to allow the stimulus of the moment to buoy him up in his address. In this kind of speaking he was a genius. Crowd psychology and excitement played an enormous part in his success as an orator.

Before the Georgia editor in the banquet hall of Delmonico's Restaurant in New York sat an illustrious audience of eastern business and professional men. At the head table Grady was flanked by Horace Russell, Dr. DeWitt Talmadge, General William T. Sherman, J. Pierpont Morgan, Lyman Abbott, Russell Sage, Seth Thomas, Elihu Root, George W. Lincoln, H. M. Flagler, F. Hopkinson Smith, and John H. Inman. Many of these men were actively interested in the economic development of the South. Grady's address followed a speech by Dr. Talmadge and remarks by General Sherman. When he arose to speak the band played "Marching through Georgia." The young Georgian said later, of this moment, "Every nerve in my body was strung as tight as a fiddle string, and all tingling. I knew then that I had a message for that assemblage, and as soon as I opened my mouth it came rushing out."

"T HERE was a South of slavery and secession—that South is dead. There is a South of union and freedom—that South, thank God, is living, breathing, growing every hour." These words, delivered from the immortal lips of Benjamin H. Hill, at Tammany

The speech is reprinted as it originally appeared in the *Anniversary Celebration of the New England Society in the City of New York* (December 22, 1886); it has been compared with the text published in *Joel Chandler Harris' Life of Henry W. Grady Including His Writings and Speeches* (New York, 1890), pp. 83–93.

Hall in 1866, true then, and truer now, I shall make my text to-night.

Mr. President and Gentlemen: Let me express to you my appreciation of the kindness by which I am permitted to address you. I make this abrupt acknowledgment advisedly, for I feel that if, when I raise my provincial voice in this ancient and august presence, I could find courage for no more than the opening sentence, it would be well if, in that sentence, I had met in a rough sense my obligation as a guest, and had perished, so to speak, with courtesy on my lips and grace in my heart. (Laughter.) Permitted through your kindness to catch my second wind, let me say that I appreciate the significance of being the first Southerner to speak at this board, which bears the substance, if it surpasses the semblance, of original New England hospitality (applause), and honors a sentiment that in turn honors you, but in which my personality is lost, and the compliment to my people made plain. (Laughter.)

I bespeak the utmost stretch of your courtesy to-night. I am not troubled about those from whom I come. You remember the man whose wife sent him to a neighbor with a pitcher of milk, and who, tripping on the top step, fell, with such casual interruptions as the landings afforded, into the basement; and while picking himself up had the pleasure of hearing his wife call out: "John, did you break the pitcher?"

"No, I didn't" said John, "but I be dinged if I don't." (Loud laughter.)

So, while those who call to me from behind may inspire me with energy if not with courage, I ask an indulgent hearing from you. I beg that you will bring your full faith in American fairness and frankness to judgment upon what I shall say. There was an old preacher once who told some boys of the Bible lesson he was going to read in the morning. The boys, finding the place, glued together the connecting pages. (Laughter.) The next morning he read on the bottom of one page: "When Noah was one hundred and twenty years old he took unto himself a wife, who was"—then turning the page—"140 cubits long (laughter), 40 cubits wide, built of gopher wood (laughter), and covered with pitch inside and out." (Loud and continued laughter.) He was naturally puzzled at this. He read it again, verified it, and then said: "My friends, this is the first time I ever met this in the Bible, but I accept it as an evidence of the assertion that we are fearfully and wonderfully made." (Immense laughter.) If I could get you to hold such faith to-night I could proceed cheerfully to the task I otherwise approach with a sense of consecration.

466

Pardon me one word, Mr. President, spoken for the sole purpose of getting into the volumes that go out annually freighted with the rich eloquence of your speakers—the fact that the Cavalier as well as the Puritan was on the Continent in its early days, and that he was "up and able to be about." (Laughter.) I have read your books carefully and I find no mention of that fact, which seems to me an important one for preserving a sort of historical equilibrium if for nothing else.

Let me remind you that the Virginia Cavalier first challenged France on this continent—that Cavalier John Smith gave New England its very name, and was so pleased with the job that he has been handing his own name around ever since—and that while Miles Standish was cutting off men's ears for courting a girl without her parents' consent, and forbade men to kiss their wives on Sunday, the Cavalier was courting everything in sight, and that the Almighty had vouchsafed great increase to the Cavalier colonies, the huts in the wilderness being as full as the nests in the woods.

But having incorporated the Cavalier as a fact in your charming little books I shall let him work out his own salvation, as he has always done with engaging gallantry, and we will hold no controversy as to his merits. Why should we? Neither Puritan nor Cavalier long survived as such. The virtues and traditions of both happily still live for the inspiration of their sons and the saving of the old fashion. (Applause.) But both Puritan and Cavalier were lost in the storm of the first Revolution; and the American citizen, supplanting both and stronger than either, took possession of the Republic bought by their common blood and fashioned to wisdom, and charged himself with teaching men government and establishing the voice of the people as the voice of God. (Applause.)

My friends, Dr. Talmage has told you that the typical American has yet to come. Let me tell you that he has already come. (Applause.) Great types like valuable plants are slow to flower and fruit. But from the union of these colonist Puritans and Cavaliers, from the straightening of their purposes and the crossing of their blood, slow perfecting through a century, came he who stands as the first typical American, the first who comprehended within himself all the strength and gentleness, all the majesty and grace of this republic—Abraham Lincoln. (Loud and long continued applause.) He was the sum of Puritan and Cavalier, for in his ardent nature were fused the virtues of both, and in the depths of his great soul the faults of both were lost. (Renewed applause.) He was greater than Puritan, greater than Cavalier, in that he was American (renewed applause), and that in his homely form were first gathered the vast and thrilling forces of his ideal government—charging it with such tremendous meaning and so elevating it above human suffering that martyrdom, though infamously aimed, came as a fitting crown to a life consecrated from the cradle to human liberty. (Loud and prolonged cheering.) Let us, each cherishing the traditions and honoring his fathers, build with reverent hands to the type of this simple but sublime life, in which all types are honored; and in our common glory as Americans there will be plenty and to spare for your forefathers and for mine. (Renewed cheering.)

In speaking to the toast with which you have honored me, I accept the term, "The New South," as in no sense disparaging to the old. Dear to me, sir, is the home of my childhood and the traditions of my people. I would not, if I could, dim the glory they won in peace and war, or by word or deed take aught from the splendor and grace of their civilization —never equalled and, perhaps, never to be equalled in its chivalric strength and grace. There is a New South, not through protest against the old, but because of new conditions, new adjustments and, if you please, new ideas and aspirations. It is to this that I address myself, and to the consideration of which I hasten lest it become the Old South before I get to it. Age does not endow all things with strength and virtue, nor are all new things to be despised. The shoemaker who put over his door "John Smith's shop. Founded in 1760," was more than matched by his young rival across the street who hung out this sign: "Bill Jones. Established 1886. No old stock kept in this shop."

Dr. Talmage has drawn for you, with a master's hand, the picture of your returning armies. He has told you how, in the pomp and circumstance of war, they came back to you, marching with proud and victorious tread, reading their glory in a nation's eyes! Will you bear with me while I tell you of another army that sought its home at the close of the late war—an army that marched home in defeat and not in victory—in pathos and not in splendor, but in glory that equalled yours, and to hearts as loving as ever welcomed heroes home. Let me picture to you the footsore Confederate soldier, as, buttoning up in his faded gray jacket the parole which was to bear testimony to his children of his fidelity and faith, he turned his face southward from Appomattox in April, 1865. Think of him as ragged, half-starved, heavy hearted, enfeebled by want and wounds; having fought to exhaustion, he surrenders his gun, wrings the hands of his comrades in silence, and lifting his tear-stained and pallid face for the last time to the graves that dot the old Virginia hills, pulls his gray cap over his brow and begins the slow and painful journey. What does he find—let me ask you, who went to your homes eager to find in the welcome you had justly earned, full payment for four years' sacrifice—what does he find when, having followed the battlestained cross against overwhelming odds, dreading death not half so much as surrender, he reaches the home he left so prosperous and beautiful? He finds his house in ruins, his farm devastated, his slaves free, his stock killed, his barns empty, his trade destroyed, his money worthless; his social system, feudal in its magnificence, swept away; his people without law or legal status, his comrades slain, and the burdens of others heavy on his shoulders. Crushed by defeat, his very traditions are gone: without money, credit, employment, material or training; and beside all this, confronted with the gravest problem that ever met human intelligence—the establishing of a status for the vast body of his liberated slaves.

What does he do—this hero in gray with a heart of gold? Does he sit down in sullenness and despair? Not for a day. Surely God, who had stripped him of his prosperity, inspired him in his adversity. As ruin was never before so overwhelming, never was restoration swifter. The soldier stepped from the trenches into the furrow; horses that had charged Federal guns marched before the plow, and fields that ran red with human blood in April were green with the harvest in June; women reared in luxury cut up their dresses and made breeches for their husbands, and, with a patience and heroism that fit women always as a garment, gave their hands to work. There was little bitterness in all this. Cheerfulness and frankness prevailed. "Bill Arp" struck the keynote when he said: "Well, I killed as many of them as they did of me, and now I am going to work." (Laughter and applause.) Or the soldier returning home after defeat and roasting some corn on the roadside, who made the remark to his comrades: "You may leave the South if you want to, but I am going to Sandersville, kiss my wife and raise a crop, and if the Yankees fool with me any more I will whip em again." (Renewed applause.) I want to say to General Sherman—who is considered an able man in our parts, though some people think he is a kind of careless man about fire—that from the ashes he left us in 1864 we have raised a brave and beautiful city; that somehow or other we have caught the sunshine in the bricks and mortar of our homes, and have builded therein not one ignoble prejudice or memory. (Applause.)

But in all this what have we accomplished? What is the sum of our work? We have found out that in the general summary the free negro counts more than he did as a slave. We have planted the schoolhouse on the hilltop and made it free to white and black. We have sowed towns and cities in the place of theories and put business above politics. (Applause.) We have challenged your spinners in Massachusetts and your ironmakers in Pennsylvania. We have learned that the $400,000,000 annually received from our cotton crop will make us rich, when the supplies that make it are home-raised. We have reduced the commercial rate of interest from 24 to 6 per cent., and are floating 4 per cent. bonds. We have learned that one northern immigrant is worth fifty foreigners, and have smoothed the path to southward, wiped out the place where Mason and Dixon's line used to be, and hung our latch-string to you and yours. (Prolonged cheers.) We have reached the point that marks perfect harmony in every household, when the husband confesses that the pies which his wife cooks are as good as those his mother used to bake; and we admit that the sun shines as brightly and the moon as softly as it did "before the war." (Laughter.) We have established thrift in city and country. We have fallen in love with work. We have restored comfort to homes from which culture and elegance never departed. We have let economy take root and spread among us as rank as the crab grass which sprung from Sherman's cavalry camps, until we are ready to lay odds on the Georgia Yankee, as he manufactures relics of the battlefield in a one-story shanty and squeezes pure olive oil out of his cotton seed, against any Down-easter that ever swapped wooden nutmegs for flannel sausages in the valleys of Vermont. (Loud and continuous laughter.) Above all, we know that we have achieved in these "piping times of peace" a fuller independence for the South than that which our fathers sought to win in the forum by their eloquence or compel on the field by their swords. (Loud applause.)

It is a rare privilege, sir, to have had part, however humble, in this work. Never was nobler duty confided to human hands than the uplifting and upbuilding of the prostrate and bleeding South, mis-guided, perhaps, but beautiful in her suffering, and honest, brave and generous always. (Applause.) In the record of her social, industrial, and political illustration we await with confidence the verdict of the world.

But what of the negro? Have we solved the problem he presents or progressed in honor and equity towards the solution? Let the record speak to the point. No section shows a more prosperous laboring population than the negroes of the South; none in fuller sympathy with the employing and land-owning class. He shares our school fund, has the fullest protection of our laws and the friendship of our people. Self-interest, as well as honor, demand that he should have this. Our future, our very existence depend upon our working out this problem in full and exact justice. We understand that when Lincoln signed the Emancipation Proclamation, your victory was assured; for he then committed you to the cause of human liberty, against which the arms of man cannot prevail (applause); while those of our statesmen who trusted to make slavery the corner-stone of the Confederacy doomed us to defeat as far as they could, committing us to a cause that reason could not defend or the sword maintain in the light of advancing civilization. (Renewed applause.) Had Mr. Toombs said, which he did not say, that he would call the roll of his slaves at the foot of Bunker Hill, he would have been foolish, for he might have known that whenever slavery became entangled in war it must perish, and that the chattel in human flesh ended forever in New England when your fathers—not to be blamed for parting with what didn't pay—sold their slaves to our fathers—not to be praised for knowing a paying thing when they saw it. (Laughter.) The relations of the southern people with the negro are close and cordial. We remember with what fidelity for four years he guarded our defenseless women and children, whose husbands and fathers were fighting against his freedom. To his eternal credit be it said that whenever he struck a blow for his own liberty he fought in open battle, and when at last he raised his black and humble hands that the shackles might be struck off, those hands were innocent of wrong against his helpless charges, and worthy to be taken in loving grasp by every man who honors loyalty and devotion. (Applause.) Ruffians have maltreated him, rascals have misled him, philanthropists established a bank for him, but the South, with the North, protests against injustice to this simple and sincere people. To liberty and enfranchisement is as far as law can carry the negro. The rest must be left to conscience and common sense. It should be left to those among whom his lot is cast, with whom he is indissolubly connected and whose prosperity depends upon their possessing his intelligent sympathy and confidence. Faith has been kept with him in spite of calumnious assertions to the contrary by those who

471

assume to speak for us or by frank opponents. Faith will be kept with him in the future, if the South holds her reason and integrity. (Applause.)

But have we kept faith with you? In the fullest sense, yes. When Lee surrendered—I don't say when Johnston surrendered, because I understand he still alludes to the time when he met General Sherman last as the time when he "determined to abandon any further prosecution of the struggle"—when Lee surrendered, I say, and Johnston quit, the South became, and has since been, loyal to this union. We fought hard enough to know that we were whipped, and in perfect frankness accepted as final the arbitrament of the sword to which we had appealed. The South found her jewel in the toad's head of defeat. The shackles that had held her in narrow limitations fell forever when the shackles of the negro slave were broken. (Applause.) Under the old regime the negroes were slaves to the South, the South was a slave to the system. The old plantation, with its simple police regulation and its feudal habit, was the only type possible under slavery. Thus was gathered in the hands of a splendid and chivalric oligarchy the substance that should have been diffused among the people, as the rich blood, under certain artificial conditions, is gathered at the heart, filling that with affluent rapture, but leaving the body chill and colorless. (Applause.)

The old South rested everything on slavery and agriculture, unconscious that these could neither give nor maintain healthy growth. The new South presents a perfect Democracy, the oligarchs leading in the popular movement—a social system compact and closely knitted, less splendid on the surface but stronger at the core—a hundred farms for every plantation, fifty homes for every palace, and a diversified industry that meets the complex needs of this complex age.

The new South is enamored of her new work. Her soul is stirred with the breath of a new life. The light of a grander day is falling fair on her face. She is thrilling with the consciousness of growing power and prosperity. As she stands upright, full-statured and equal among the people of the earth, breathing the keen air and looking out upon the expanding horizon, she understands that her emancipation came because in the inscrutable wisdom of God her honest purpose was crossed and her brave armies were beaten. (Applause.)

This is said in no spirit of time-serving or apology. The South has nothing for which to apologize. She believes that the late struggle between the States was war and not rebellion, revolution, and not conspiracy, and that her convictions were as honest as yours. I should be unjust to the dauntless spirit of the South and to my own convictions if I did not make this plain in this presence. The South has nothing to take back. In my native town of Athens is a monument that crowns its central hill—a plain, white shaft. Deep cut into its shining side is a name dear to me above the names of men, that of a brave and simple man who died in brave and simple faith. Not for all the glories of New England— from Plymouth Rock all the way—would I exchange the heritage he left me in his soldier's death. To the foot of that shaft I shall send my children's children to reverence him who ennobled their name with his heroic blood. But, sir, speaking from the shadow of that memory, which I honor as I do nothing else on earth, I say that the cause in which he suffered and for which he gave his life was adjudged by higher and fuller wisdom than his or mine, and I am glad that the omniscient God held the balance of battle in His Almighty hand, and that human slavery was swept forever from American soil—the American Union saved from the wreck of war. (Loud applause.)

This message, Mr. President, comes to you from consecrated ground. Every foot of the soil about the city in which I live is as sacred as a battle-ground of the republic. Every hill that invests it is hallowed to you by the blood of your brothers, who died for your victory, and doubly hallowed to us by the blow of those who died hopeless, but undaunted, in defeat—sacred soil to all of us, rich with memories that make us purer and stronger and better, silent but staunch witnesses in its red desolation of the matchless valor of American hearts and the deathless glory of American arms—speaking an eloquent witness in its white peace and prosperity to the indissoluble union of American States and the imperishable brotherhood of the American people. (Immense cheering.)

Now, what answer has New England to this message? Will she permit the prejudice of war to remain in the hearts of the conquerors, when it has died in the hearts of the conquered? (Cries of "No! No!") Will she transmit this prejudice to the next generation, that in their hearts, which never felt the generous ardor of conflict, it may perpetuate itself? ("No! No!") Will she withhold, save in strained courtesy, the hand which straight from his soldier's heart Grant offered to Lee at Appomattox? Will she make the vision of a restored and happy people, which gathered above the couch of your dying captain, filling his heart with

473

grace, touching his lips with praise and glorifying his path to the grave; will she make this vision on which the last sigh of his expiring soul breathed a benediction, a cheat and a delusion? (Tumultuous cheering and shouts of "No! No!") If she does, the South, never abject in asking for comradeship, must accept with dignity its refusal; but if she does not; if she accepts in frankness and sincerity this message of good-will and friendship, then will the prophecy of Webster, delivered in this very Society forty years ago amid tremendous applause, be verified in its fullest and final sense, when he said: "Standing hand to hand and clasping hands, we should remain united as we have been for sixty years, citizens of the same country, members of the same government, united, all united now and united forever. There have been difficulties, contentions, and controversies, but I tell you that in my judgment

> Those opposed eyes,
> Which like the meteors of a troubled heaven,
> All of one nature, of one substance bred,
> Did lately meet in th'intestine shock,
> Shall now, in mutual well beseeming ranks,
> March all one way.

(Prolonged applause.)

Although Grady was intoxicated by his visible audience at Delmonico's, he was even more eager to appeal to his vast unseen audience. He was conscious that his speech would have wide coverage in the national press. His words would be examined with the utmost editorial scrutiny. Friend and foe alike would respond to it. Sectional accord within the Union would be affected.

The oration was not really profound, nor did it have a meaty content. There were oratorical flourishes and conscious digressions into light after-dinner humor. In describing the Confederate soldier and his cause Grady resorted to pure southern melodrama. None of these things is important. The real importance of the speech lay in three areas: first, it fixed the term "New South" in the American mind; second, it assured men of capital of the stability of the South; and, finally, it made Henry W. Grady into an articulate leader of a New South which in his address he had had to define much more clearly. He now had to think more specifically of the South's potentialities in terms of both human beings and natural resources. This he did a year later in speaking before a state-fair audience in Dallas, Texas. In the latter speech he enlarged upon many points which he had only hinted at in the New York speech. In more precise detail he discussed the position of the Negro in the New South. He felt it would be wisest for southern whites not to separate the races politically. The white vote should be of such size and depth of integrity that it would automatically ensure white supremacy. Grady viewed a racially factionalized state as being worse than Reconstruction itself. Nevertheless he expressed a philosophy of race relations which was to fix in the southern mind the principle of "separate but equal" a decade before the Supreme Court handed down its decision of Plessy v. Ferguson.

Grady's utterances in New York and Dallas helped to change men's thinking both North and South. For the northern businessman, the South suddenly stood in a new perspective, social and economic. For the southerner, Grady spoke a new promise. The region after all was not irretrievably wedded to the traditions of the Old South, to a ruinous system of one-crop agriculture, or to technological or professional hopelessness. A fellow southerner had laid down the challenge of accepting change. Grady proposed replacing the old defeatism of war and Reconstruction with optimistic effort toward industrial and commercial progress. The South had struggled hard for a catch phrase, something that would help give it a sense of direction and an impetus to reunite itself spiritually and economically with the rest of the nation. The term "New South" as cast in Henry Grady's speech was just such a catch phrase.

Whether or not southern newspapers quoted the New South speech directly, its influence upon the region's editorial mind was evident. Scores of editorials discussed reunification of the nation, the need for industry in the South, threats of danger from staple-crop agriculture, and the Negro in southern society. Grady's speech also caught the imagination of northern editors. It appealed to them as an excellent piece of free-hand southern oratory which offered the North just enough gracious compliments to give assurance of the South's conciliatory attitude. Many believed that Grady revealed more clearly than anyone else the innermost emotions of the young postwar generation of southerners. He displayed his personal reactions without a trace of bitterness. He proved that northerner and southerner could communicate with each other in a spirit of good will.

On the other hand, the nation's press also carried adverse criticism of the Georgia orator. Some southern editors felt he had been too ready to admit failures of the old southern system. For some Grady had been too extravagant in praise of Lincoln, and not harsh enough with General Sherman. In the North, the Chicago Tribune felt the southern spokesman was insincere, and accused him of being a trimmer. Such criticism apparently had little influence. Grady overnight had become the spiritual embodiment of the New South. Seldom again would the term "New South" be used without invoking Grady's interpretation of it. The speech had the further effect, on the popular level, of stimulating interest in eloquent expression. It was widely praised as having set a new mark for American oratory; and in classrooms and on stages across the land, boy orators revived the excitement of Grady's message.

Historians in the main have accepted Grady's thesis that in 1886 the Old South was a thing of memory, and the new was a current reality. Clearly the region would attract industry, revise its farming procedures, recognize the Negro as an important productive force, and heal the wounds of war and Reconstruction. The South's future lay in its unity with the rest of the nation, and in a more effective use of capital and resources. Sherman may have been a careless man with fire, but the sun of hope shone anew on the rising towers of the new urban and industrial South.

James Cardinal Gibbons
The Question of the "Knights of Labor"
1887

EDITED BY JOHN TRACY ELLIS

The most famous document in the history of the relationship of the Catholic Church in the United States to the American labor movement is known as "the memorial on the Knights of Labor." It was composed in February, 1887, at Rome and signed on February 20 by James Cardinal Gibbons, Archbishop of Baltimore, although in its composition the cardinal had the assistance of John Ireland, Bishop of St. Paul, John J. Keane, Bishop of Richmond, and Denis J. O'Connell, Rector of the American College at Rome. It was addressed to Giovanni Cardinal Simeoni, Prefect of the Congregation de Propaganda Fide, the department of ecclesiastical government which had jurisdiction over the Church in missionary lands, the category in which the United States was at the time placed by the Holy See.

The Knights of Labor, in which a very large number, if not a majority, of the members were Catholics, had recently passed through a series of severe trials. Among these were the railroad strikes of the late winter and early spring of 1886 and the Haymarket Massacre in Chicago in May of that year. For these disturbances of the public peace many Americans held the Knights responsible. It was an attitude that was illustrated in Puck (March 23, 1887) in a cartoon drawn by Joseph Keppler concerning Gibbons' memorial. This showed a large group of union men attacking a single "scab," while a procession of Catholic bishops advanced to the scene. The latter were described as labor's "new ally," and

477

the question was asked: "Does the Catholic Church sanction mob law?"

Although Cardinal Gibbons and his associates deplored the use of violence in any form in labor's attempts to gain its ends, they were convinced that the laboring men—in this case the Knights of Labor—had been the victims of grave abuses by their employers. To these prelates, labor's cause was worthy of support. And beyond the goal of support to a worthy cause, they were intent that the Catholic Church in the United States should not align itself with the enemies of labor when the overwhelming majority of the Church's members were working men and their families. Conscious as they were of the irreparable losses suffered by the Church in Europe because of alignments of the wrong kind, these churchmen were determined that the American people should not receive an image of the Catholic Church as the upholder of the rich and the powerful. They felt it imperative, therefore, to speak out. And a circumstance that gave a special urgency to their efforts related to their coreligionists in Canada. The American churchmen were aware that, four years previously, Elzear-Alesandre Taschereau, Archbishop of Quebec, had sought a ruling on the Knights of Labor from Rome and that after a long delay the Holy Office had condemned them in September, 1884, as a forbidden society. They were further aware that the Archbishop of Quebec was then (1887) in Rome, like Gibbons, to get his red hat as a cardinal and that he was seeking confirmation from the Holy See of the decree of 1884 regarding the Knights. The American prelates also knew that there were some conservative bishops of their own country who would welcome a similar condemnation of the labor organization which would apply to the United States. To men of the mind of Gibbons, Ireland, Keane, and O'Connell, an action of that kind would have been an unmitigated calamity, and they determined, therefore, that the strongest possible protest should be lodged by the dean of the American hierarchy with the official of the Roman Curia who was most responsible for framing ecclesiastical policy relating to the Church in the United States.

*TO HIS EMINENCE CARDINAL SIMEONI, PREFECT OF THE SACRED
CONGREGATION OF THE PROPAGANDA:*

YOUR EMINENCE:

IN SUBMITTING to the Holy See the conclusions which after several
months of attentive observation and reflection, seem to me to sum
up the truth concerning the association of the Knights of Labor, I
feel profoundly convinced of the vast importance of the consequences
attaching to this question, which forms but a link in the great chain of
the social problems of our day, and especially of our country.

In weighing this question I have been very careful to follow as my
constant guide the spirit of the Encyclicals, in which our Holy Father,
Leo XIII, has so admirably set forth the dangers of our time and their
remedies, as well as the principles by which we are to recognize
associations condemned by the Holy See. Such was also the guide of the
Third Plenary Council of Baltimore in its teaching concerning the
principles to be followed and the dangers to be shunned by the faithful
either in the choice or in the establishment of those associations toward
which the spirit of our popular institutions so strongly impels them. And
considering the dire consequences that might result from a mistake in
the treatment of organizations which often count their members by the
thousands and hundreds of thousands, the council wisely ordained that
when an association is spread over several dioceses, not even the bishop
of one of these dioceses shall condemn it, but shall refer the case to a
standing committee of all the archbishops of the United States; and
even these are not authorized to condemn unless their sentence be
unanimous; and in case they fail to agree unanimously, then only the
supreme tribunal of the Holy See can impose a condemnation; all this in
order to avoid error and confusion of discipline.

This committee of archbishops held a meeting, in fact, toward the
end of last October, especially to consider the association of the Knights
of Labor. We were not persuaded to hold this meeting because of any
request on the part of our bishops, for none of them had asked for it;
and it should also be said that, among all the bishops we know, only two
or three desire the condemnation. But the importance of the question in
itself, and in the estimation of the Holy See led us to examine it with
greatest attention. After our discussion, the results of which have already

---

The document is taken from Henry J. Browne, *The Catholic Church and the
Knights of Labor* (Washington, D.C.: The Catholic University of America Press,
1949), Appendix III, pp. 365–78.

been communicated to the Sacred Congregation of the Propaganda, only two out of the twelve archbishops voted for condemnation, and their reasons were powerless to convince the others of either the justice or the prudence of such a condemnation.

In the following considerations I wish to state in detail the reasons which determined the vote of the great majority of the committee —reasons whose truth and force seem to me all the more evident today; I shall try at the same time to do justice to the arguments advanced by the opposition.

1. In the first place, in the constitution, laws and official declarations of the Knights of Labor, there can clearly be found assertions and rules which we would not approve; but we have not found in them those elements so clearly pointed out by the Holy See, which places them among condemned associations.

(a) In their form of initiation there is no oath.

(b) The obligation to secrecy by which they keep the knowledge of their business from strangers or enemies, in no wise prevents Catholics from manifesting everything to competent ecclesiastical authority, even outside of confession. This has been positively declared to us by their president.

(c) They make no promise of blind obedience. The object and laws of the association are distinctly declared, and the obligation of obedience does not go beyond these limits.

(d) They not only profess no hostility against religion or the Church, but their declarations are quite to the contrary. The Third Plenary Council commands that we should not condemn an association without giving a hearing to its officers or representatives; "auditis ducibus, corypheis vel sociis praecipuis." Now, their president in sending me a copy of their constitution, says that he is a Catholic from the bottom of his heart; that he practices his religion faithfully and receives the sacraments regularly; that he belongs to no Masonic or other society condemned by the Church; that he knows of nothing in the association of the Knights of Labor contrary to the laws of the Church; that, with filial submission he begs the Pastors of the Church to examine all the details of their organization, and, if they find anything worthy of condemnation, they should indicate it, and he promises its correction. Assuredly one does not perceive in all this any hostility to the authority of the Church, but on the contrary a spirit in every way praiseworthy. After their convention last year at Richmond, he and several of the officers and members, devout Catholics, made similar declarations concerning their feelings and the action of that convention, the documents of which we are expecting to receive.

(e) Nor do we find in this organization any hostility to the authority and laws of our country. Not only does nothing of the kind appear in their constitution and laws, but the heads of our civil government treat with the greatest respect the cause which they represent. The President of the United States told me personally, a month ago that he was then examining a law for the amelioration of certain social grievances and that he had just had a long conference on the subject with Mr. Powderly, president of the Knights of Labor. The Congress of the United States, following the advice of President Cleveland is busying itself at the present time with the amelioration of the working classes, in whose complaints they acknowledge openly there is a great deal of truth. And our political parties, far from regarding them as enemies of the country, vie with each other in championing the evident rights of the poor workmen, who seek not to resist the laws, but only to obtain just legislation by constitutional and legitimate means.

These considerations, which show that in this association those elements are not to be found which the Holy See condemns, lead us to study, in the second place, the evils which the associations contend against, and the nature of the conflict.

2. That there exists among us, as in the other countries of the world, grave and threatening social evils, public injustices, which call for strong resistance and legal remedy, is a fact which no one dares to deny, and the truth of which has been already acknowledged by the Congress and the President of the United States. Without entering into the sad details of these wrongs,—which does not seem necessary here,—it may suffice to mention only that monopolies on the part of both individuals and of corporations, have already called forth not only the complaints of our working classes but also the opposition of our public men and legislators; that the efforts of these monopolists, not always without success, to control legislation to their own profit, cause serious apprehension among the disinterested friends of liberty; that the heartless avarice which, through greed of gain, pitilessly grinds not only the men, but particularly the women and children in various employments, make it clear to all who love humanity and justice that it is not only the right of the laboring classes to protect themselves, but the duty of the whole people to aid them in finding a remedy against the dangers with which both

civilization and the social order are menaced by avarice, oppression and corruption.

It would be vain to deny either the existence of the evils, the right of legitimate resistance, or the necessity of a remedy. At most doubt might be raised about the legitimacy of the form of resistance and the remedy employed by the Knights of Labor. This then ought to be the next point of our examination.

3. It can hardly be doubted that for the attainment of any public end, association—the organization of all interested persons—is the most efficacious means, a means altogether natural and just. This is so evident, and besides so conformable to the genius of our country, of our essentially popular social conditions, that it is unnecessary to insist upon it. It is almost the only means to invite public attention, to give force to the most legitimate resistance, to add weight to the most just demands.

Now there already exists an organization which presents a thousand attractions and advantages, but which our Catholic workingmen, with filial obedience to the Holy See, refuse to join; this is the *Masonic* organization, which exists everywhere in our country, and which, as Mr. Powderly has expressly pointed out to us, unites employer and worker in a brotherhood very advantageous for the latter, but which numbers in its ranks hardly a single Catholic. Freely renouncing the advantages which the Church and their consciences forbid, workingmen form associations, having nothing in common with the deadly designs of the enemies of religion and seeking only mutual protection and help, and the legitimate assertion of their rights. But here they also find themselves threatened with condemnation, and so deprived of their only means of defense. Is it surprising that they should be astonished at this and that they ask *Why?*

4. Let us now consider the objections made against this sort of organization.

(a) It is objected that in these organizations Catholics are mixed with Protestants, to the peril of their faith. Naturally, yes, they are mixed with Protestants in the workers' associations, precisely as they are at their work; for in a mixed people like ours, the separation of religions in social affairs is not possible. But to suppose that the faith of our Catholics suffers thereby is not to know the Catholic workers of America who are not like the workingmen of so many European countries— misguided and perverted children, looking on their Mother the Church as a hostile stepmother—but they are intelligent, well instructed and devoted children ready to give their blood, as they continually give their means (although small and hard-earned) for her support and protection. And in fact it is not in the present case that Catholics are mixed with Protestants, but rather that Protestants are admitted to the advantages of an association, two-thirds of whose members and the principal officers are Catholics; and in a country like ours their exclusion would be simply impossible.

(b) But it is said, could there not be substituted for such an organization confraternities which would unite the workingmen under the direction of the priests and the direct influence of religion? I answer frankly that I do not believe that either possible or necessary in our country. I sincerely admire the efforts of this sort which are made in countries where the workers are led astray by the enemies of religion; but thanks be to God, that is not our condition. We find that in our country the presence and explicit influence of the clergy would not be advisable where our citizens, without distinction of religious belief, come together in regard to their industrial interests alone. Without going so far, we have abundant means for making our working people faithful Catholics, and simple good sense advises us not to go to extremes.

(c) Again, it is objected that the liberty of such an organization exposes Catholics to the evil influences of the most dangerous associates, even of atheists, communists and anarchists. That is true; but it is one of the trials of faith which our brave American Catholics are accustomed to meet almost daily, and which they know how to disregard with good sense and firmness. The press of our country tells us and the president of the Knights of Labor has related to us, how these violent and aggressive elements have endeavored to seize authority in their councils, or to inject their poison into the principles of the association; but they also verify with what determination these evil spirits have been repulsed and defeated. The presence among our citizens of this destructive element, which has come for the most part from certain nations of Europe, is assuredly for us an occasion of lively regrets and careful precautions; it is an inevitable fact, however, but one which the union between the Church and her children in our country renders comparatively free from danger. In truth, the only grave danger would come from an alienation between the Church and her children, which nothing would more certainly occasion than imprudent condemnations.

(d) An especially weighty charge is drawn from the outbursts of violence, even to bloodshed, which have characterized several of the strikes inaugurated by labor organizations. Concerning this, three things are to be remarked: first, strikes are not an invention of the Knights of Labor, but a means almost everywhere and always resorted to by employees in our land and elsewhere to protest against what they consider unjust and to demand their rights; secondly in such a struggle of the poor and indignant multitudes against hard and obstinate monopoly, anger and violence are often as inevitable as they are regrettable; thirdly, the laws and chief authorities of the Knights of Labor, far from encouraging violence or the occasions of it, exercise a powerful influence to hinder it, and to keep strikes within the limits of good order and legitimate action. A careful examination of the acts of violence which have marked the struggle between capital and labor during the past year, leaves us convinced that it would be unjust to attribute them to the association of the Knights of Labor. This was but one of several associations of workers that took part in the strikes, and their chief officers, according to disinterested witnesses, used every possible effort to appease the anger of the crowds and to prevent the excesses which, in my judgment, could not justly be attributed to them. Doubtless among the Knights of Labor as among thousands of other workingmen, there are violent, or even wicked and criminal men, who have committed inexcusable deeds of violence, and have urged their associates to do the same; but to attribute this to the organization, it seems to me, would be as unreasonable as to attribute to the Church the follies and crimes of her children against which she protests. I repeat that in such a struggle of the great masses of the people against the mail-clad power, which, as it is acknowledged, often refuses them the simple rights of humanity and justice, it is vain to expect that every error and every act of violence can be avoided; and to dream that this struggle can be prevented, or that we can deter the multitudes from organizing, which is their only practical means of success, would be to ignore the nature and forces of human society in times like ours. The part of Christian prudence evidently is to try to hold the hearts of the multitude by the bonds of love, in order to control their actions by the principles of faith, justice and charity, to acknowledge frankly the truth and justice in their cause, in order to deter them from what would be false and criminal, and thus to turn into a legitimate, peaceable and beneficent contest what could easily become for the masses of our people a volcanic abyss, like that which society fears and the Church deplores in Europe.

Upon this point I insist strongly, because, from an intimate acquaintance with the social conditions of our country I am profoundly convinced that here we are touching upon a subject which not only concerns the rights of the working classes, who ought to be especially dear to the Church which our Divine Lord sent to evangelize the poor, but with which are bound up the fundamental interests of the Church and of human society for the future. This is a point which I desire, in a few additional words to develop more clearly.

5. Whoever meditates upon the ways in which divine Providence is guiding contemporary history cannot fail to remark how important is the part which the power of the people takes therein at present and must take in the future. We behold, with profound sadness, the efforts of the prince of darkness to make this power dangerous to the social weal by withdrawing the masses of the people from the influence of religion, and impelling them towards the ruinous paths of license and anarchy. Until now our country presents a picture of altogether different character— that of a popular power regulated by love of good order, by respect for religion, by obedience to the authority of the laws, not a democracy of license and violence, but that true democracy which aims at the general prosperity through the means of sound principles and good social order.

In order to preserve so desirable a state of things it is absolutely necessary that religion should continue to hold the affections, and thus rule the conduct of the multitudes. As Cardinal Manning has so well written, "In the future era the Church has no longer to deal with princes and parliaments, but with the masses, with the people. Whether we will or no this is our work; we need a new spirit, a new direction of our life and activity." To lose influence over the people would be to lose the future altogether; and it is by the heart, far more than by the understanding, that we must hold and guide this immense power, so mighty either for good or for evil. Among all the glorious titles of the Church which her history has merited for her, there is not one which at present gives her so great influence as that of *Friend of the People*. Assuredly, in our democratic country, it is this title which wins for the Catholic Church not only the enthusiastic devotedness of the millions of her children, but also the respect and admiration of all our citizens, whatever be their religious belief. It is the power of precisely this title which renders persecution almost an impossibility, and which draws toward our holy Church the great heart of the American people.

485

And since it is acknowledged by all that the great questions of the future are not those of war, of commerce or finance, but the social questions, the questions which concern the improvement of the condition of the great masses of the people, and especially of the working people, it is evidently of supreme importance that the Church should always be found on the side of humanity, of justice toward the multitudes who compose the body of the human family. As the same Cardinal Manning very wisely wrote, "We must admit and accept calmly and with good will that industries and profits must be considered in second place; the moral state and domestic condition of the whole working population must be considered first. I will not venture to formulate the acts of parliament, but here is precisely their fundamental principle for the future. The conditions of the lower classes as are found at present among our people, can not and must not continue. On such a basis no social edifice can stand." In our country, especially, this is the inevitable program of the future, and the position which the Church must hold toward the solution is sufficiently obvious. She must certainly not favor the extremes to which the poor multitudes are naturally inclined, but, I repeat, she must withold them from these extremes by the bonds of affection, by the maternal desire which she will manifest for the concession of all that is just and reasonable in their demands, and by the maternal blessing which she will bestow upon every legitimate means for improving the condition of the people.

6. Now let us consider for a moment the consequences which would inevitably follow from a contrary course, from a lack of sympathy for the working class, from a suspicion of their aims, from a hasty condemnation of their methods.

(a) First, there is the evident danger of the Church's losing in popular estimation her right to be considered the friend of the people. The logic of men's hearts goes swiftly to its conclusions, and this conclusion would be a pernicious one for the people and for the Church. To lose the heart of the people would be a misfortune for which the friendship of the few rich and powerful would be no compensation.

(b) There is a great danger of rendering hostile to the Church the political power of our country, which openly takes sides with the millions who are demanding justice and the improvement of their condition. The accusation of being, *"un-American,"* that is to say, alien to our national spirit, is the most powerful weapon which the enemies of the Church know how to employ against her. It was this cry which aroused the Know-Nothing persecution thirty years ago, and the same would be quickly used again if the opportunity offered itself. To appreciate the gravity of this danger it is well to remark that not only are the rights of the working classes loudly proclaimed by each of our two great political parties, but it is very probable that, in our approaching national elections there will be a candidate for the office of President of the United States as the special representative of these complaints and demands of the masses. Now, to seek to crush by an ecclesiastical condemnation an organization which represents nearly 500,000 votes, and which has already so respectable and so universally recognized a place in the political arena, would to speak frankly, be considered by the American people as not less ridiculous as it is rash. To alienate from ourselves the friendship of the people would be to run great risk of losing the respect which the Church has won in the estimation of the American nation, and of destroying the state of peace and prosperity which form so admirable a contrast with her condition in some so-called Catholic countries. Already in these months past, a murmur of popular anger and of threats against the Church has made itself heard, and it is necessary that we should move with much precaution.

(c) A third danger, and the one which touches our hearts the most, is the risk of losing the love of the children of the Church, and of pushing them into an attitude of resistance against their Mother. The whole world presents no more beautiful spectacle than that of their filial devotion and obedience. But it is necessary to recognize that, in our age and in our country, obedience cannot be blind. We would greatly deceive ourselves if we expected it. Our Catholic working men sincerely believe that they are only seeking justice, and seeking it by legitimate means. A condemnation would be considered both false and unjust, and would not be accepted. We might indeed preach to them submission and confidence in the Church, but these good dispositions could hardly go so far. They love the Church, and they wish to save their souls, but they must also earn their living, and labor is now so organized that without belonging to the organization there is little chance to earn one's living.

Behold, then, the consequences to be feared. Thousands of the most devoted children of the Church would believe themselves repulsed by their Mother and would live without practicing their religion. The revenues of the Church, which with us come entirely from the free offerings of the people, would suffer immensely, and it would be the same with Peter's pence. The ranks of the secret societies would be filled with Catholics, who had been up to now faithful. The Holy See, which has constantly received from the Catholics of America proofs of almost unparalleled devotedness, would be considered not as a paternal authority, but as a harsh and unjust power. Here are assuredly effects, the occasion of which wisdom and prudence must avoid.

In a word, we have seen quite recently the sad and threatening confusion caused by the condemnation inflicted by an Archbishop upon a single priest in vindication of discipline—a condemnation which the Archbishop believed to be just and necessary, but which fell upon a priest who was regarded as the friend of the people. Now, if the consequences have been so deplorable for the peace of the Church from the condemnation of only one priest, because he was considered to be the friend of the people, what will not be the consequences to be feared from a condemnation which would fall directly upon the people themselves in the exercise of what they consider their legitimate right?

7. But besides the danger which would result from such a condemnation and the impossibility of having it respected and observed one should note that the form of this organization is so little permanent, as the press indicates nearly every day, that in the estimation of practical men in our country, it cannot last very many years. Whence it follows that it is not necessary, even if it were just and prudent, to level the solemn condemnations of the Church against something which will vanish of itself. The social agitation will, indeed, last as long as there are social evils to be remedied; but the forms of organization and procedure meant for the attainment of this end are necessarily provisional and transient. They are also very numerous, for I have already remarked that the Knights of Labor is only one among several forms of labor organizations. To strike, then, at one of these forms would be to commence a war without system and without end; it would be to exhaust the forces of the Church in chasing a crowd of changing and uncertain phantasms. The American people behold with perfect composure and confidence the progress of our social contest, and have not the least fear of not being able to protect themselves against any excesses or dangers that may occasionally arise. And, to speak with the most profound respect, but also with the frankness which duty requires of me, it seems to me that prudence suggests, and that even the dignity of the Church demands that we should not offer to America an ecclesiastical protection for which she does not ask, and of which she believes she has no need.

8. In all this discussion I have not at all spoken of Canada, nor of the condemnation concerning the Knights of Labor in Canada. For we

would consider it an impertinence to involve ourselves in the ecclesiastical affairs of another country which has a hierarchy of its own, and with whose needs and social conditions we do not pretend to be acquainted. We believe, however, that the circumstances of a people almost entirely Catholic, as in lower Canada, must be very different from those of a mixed population like ours; moreover, that the documents submitted to the Holy Office are not the present constitution of the organization in our country, and that we, therefore, ask nothing involving an inconsistency on the part of the Holy See, which passed sentence *juxta exposita*. It is of the condition of things in the United States that we speak, and we trust that in these matters we are not presumptuous in believing that we are competent to judge. Now, as I have already indicated, out of the seventy-five archbishops and bishops of the United States, there are about five who would desire a condemnation of the Knights of Labor, such as we know them in our country; so that our hierarchy are almost unanimous in protesting against such a condemnation. Surely, such a fact ought to have great weight in deciding the question. If there are difficulties in the case, it seems to me that the prudence and experience of our bishops and the wise rules of the Third Plenary Council ought to suffice for their solution.

9. Finally, to sum it all up, it seems clear to me that the Holy See should not entertain the idea of condemning an association:

1. When the condemnation does not seem to be *justified* either by the letter or the spirit of its constitution, its law and the declaration of its leaders.

2. When the condemnation does not seem *necessary*, in view of the transient form of the organization and the social condition of the United States.

3. When it does not seem to be *prudent*, because of the reality of the grievances of the workers, and the admission of them made by the American people.

4. When it would be *dangerous* for the reputation of the Church in our democratic country, and possibly even arouse persecution.

5. When it would be *ineffectual* in compelling the obedience of our Catholic workers, who would regard it as false and unjust.

6. When it would be *destructive* instead of beneficial in its effects, impelling the children of the Church to disobey their Mother, and even to join condemned societies, which they have thus far shunned.

7. When it would be almost *ruinous* for the financial maintenance of the Church in our country, and for the Peter's pence.

489

8. When it would turn into suspicion and hostility the outstanding devotedness of our Catholic people toward the Holy See.

9. When it would be regarded as a cruel blow to the authority of the bishops of the United States, who, it is well known, protest against such a condemnation.

Now, I hope the considerations here presented have shown with sufficient clearness that such would be the condemnation of the Knights of Labor in the United States.

Therefore, with complete confidence, I leave the case to the wisdom and prudence of your Eminence and the Holy See.

Rome, February 20, 1887.

J. Cardinal Gibbons,
Archbishop of Baltimore.

In March, 1925, Pope Pius XI told Monsignor Joseph Cardijn, Belgian crusader for social justice, that the principal scandal of the Catholic Church in Europe in the nineteenth century was its loss of the working classes. That a similar calamity did not overtake the Church in the United States was due largely to the energetic action of Cardinal Gibbons and his associates at Rome in February, 1887, in warning the Holy See of the dangers to the Church that would follow a condemnation of the Knights of Labor as a society forbidden to Catholic men. As Gibbons correctly foretold to Cardinal Simeoni, the Knights were even then entering a decline that would end in their extinction, and the American Federation of Labor, organized on another basis, was rapidly advancing to supplant them. Yet a blow dealt the Knights would have also been felt by the A.F.L., since so large a percentage of the latter's early membership was drawn from Catholic ranks.

It would be an exaggeration to say that the memorial on the Knights of Labor was responsible for winning over all Catholics of the United States, especially the well-to-do and highly placed, to a friendly attitude toward organized labor. But what was more important, it helped keep the vast majority of the Church's members, the workingmen and their families, loyal to their religious inheritance. In other words, the laboring classes here were given no excuse as they had been in Europe, to sever their affiliation with the Church because of its close alliance with the captains of industry. Strain and stress there certainly were from time to time between individual bishops and priests and their working-class flocks in the years after 1887. But the heightened tempo of industrialization in this country was never accompanied by any wholesale defection from the Catholic workmen's religious loyalties, as was true of so many of their European coreligionists. Less than half of the working classes of nominally Catholic countries in Western Europe—in France not more than 10 per cent of the males—attend Sunday Mass regularly, as compared to the 70 per cent or more of American Catholics who fulfill this weekly obligation.

It is frequently impossible for the historian to say precisely what factors account for the enduring importance and significance of a given event. The historian of American Catholicism is no exception in this regard, and yet he knows that the general influences flowing from an action taken by the leaders of an institution usually shape the behavior of those affiliated with that institution. Gibbons' memorial on the Knights of Labor served to fix the pattern of official Catholic policy toward labor, a pattern that in general has remained one of friendly interest and sympathy, even when many individual Catholics have declined to be guided by the reasoning underlying the statement of Gibbons and his coworkers. Without the strong stand taken in 1887 by these men, it is difficult to envision the advanced social consciousness displayed by their successors in signing the so-called Bishops' Program of Social Reconstruction of February, 1919. The latter document was, in fact, found so radical by some that Stephen C. Mason, president of the National Association of Manufacturers, predicted that it would lead to "a covert effort to disseminate partisan, pro-labor union, socialistic propaganda under the official insignia of the Roman Catholic Church in America." And John A. Ryan, the man who had written the offending document, as late as 1941 cited Cardinal Gibbons' action in the Knights of Labor case as one that had given him "great satisfaction, not only on account of my interest in organized labor but because it vindicated the vigilance and social vision of Cardinal Gibbons and the American Hierarchy." Here was proof of the enduring influence of the memorial of 1887 on the development and elaboration of Catholic thought in the field of labor relations.

Up to about 1820 the membership of the Catholic Church in the United States had been composed largely of native-born Americans. But a large-scale Catholic immigration began in that decade and grew until it was checked by the immigration-restriction acts of the 1920's. The most significant fact in the Church's history in this country was that during the century from 1820 to 1920 an estimated total of over 9,300,000 immigrants were added to its fold, the overwhelming majority of whom were simple people of the farming and laboring classes. If, then, the minority of conservative prelates in the American Church led by Michael A. Corrigan, at the time Coadjutor Archbishop of New York, had prevailed in their desire to have the Knights of Labor condemned, there could not have been the remarkable progress that the Church has made in the free American society during the last three-quarters of a century, a progress that is reflected in its present membership of nearly 45,000,000 souls. The bond forged between the clergy and laity in the days of the immigrant's loneliness and bewilderment in a new environment has endured in spite of the enemies who have sought to break it down.